space tessellations

experimenting with
parquet deformations

space tessellations

experimenting with parquet deformations

Edited by
Werner Van Hoeydonck
Christian Kern
Eva Sommeregger

Birkhäuser
Basel

Table of Contents

Research Perspectives

Teaching Perspectives

In Memoriam: William S. Huff (1927–2021)

From HfG Ulm to Louis Kahn's Design Office From Symmetry to Parquet Deformations with Temporality and Flow

Dénes Nagy

William S. Huff lecturing at the Hochschule für Gestaltung, Ulm. First published in William S. Huff, *An Argument for Basic Design*, Ulm 12/13, March 1965, pp. 25–36. © Photography Roland Fürst, HfG-Archiv/Museum Ulm.

On 21 January 2021, William S. Huff passed away at the age of 93. We hoped very much that we could discuss with him the progress of this book's preparation, but we now have a different and very sad duty: We should remember his life and work and pay tribute to him with the latest developments in connection with parquet deformation, a topic that was very special for him.

William was born in Pittsburgh in 1927. He served in the navy during World War II and was awarded the Victory Medal and the Asiatic Pacific Area Medal in 1945–1946. He completed his studies in architecture at Yale University, from which he graduated in 1952. William, who also had Swiss roots, was eager to spend some time in Europe, and a Fulbright Fellowship made it possible. He went to the German city Ulm and studied at the Hochschule für Gestaltung, or HfG (Ulm School of Design), in 1956–1957. After returning to the United States, he joined the office of Louis Kahn in Philadelphia in 1958. He started his teaching career at the Department of Architecture, Carnegie Mellon University in Pittsburgh in 1960, but he also worked in Kahn's office in the summers of 1961 and 1962. He returned to HfG Ulm several times to teach courses throughout the 1960s. In 1974 he joined the State University of New York at Buffalo and taught there as an associate, and later as a full professor, until 1998, when he became a professor emeritus.

Since my background is in mathematics and the history of science, it was not obvious that we would begin a collaboration from the late 1980s onward. Teaching at the College of Engineering and Applied Science, Arizona State University in 1986–1988, I organized two local conferences, titled "Symmetry in a Cultural Context", with the hope that artists and scholars would come together and share some ideas that could also be fruitful in different fields. Following the success of these two events, I decided to organize a larger international congress and exhibition in 1989, for which I choose a site in Hungary, my home country, in order to also benefit East–West cooperation.

Referring to C. P. Snow's famous essay titled "Two Cultures", I suggested a different terminology as well as a related approach: We have just one culture, but it is, using an analogy from brain research, a "split culture", and similar to the function of the *corpus callosum* that links the two hemispheres of the human brain, we need some "bridges" between the two sides. Here symmetry, which is used in various fields of art and science, could be one of the possible bridges that helps the interactions between the two hemispheres of culture.

Looking for international partners, I wrote to William S. Huff because his series of booklets titled *Symmetry, An Appreciation of Its Presence in Man's Consciousness*, published between 1967 and 1977, excited me. The booklets were designed by the graphic artist Tomás Gonda (1926–1988). This series was privately printed with support from the US Office of Education and distributed in Northern America for those universities with design programs. William immediately became a strong supporter of the planned event and later became a founding member of the International Society for the Interdisciplinary Study of Symmetry (SIS-Symmetry), which maintains a duty to organize triennial congresses and exhibitions. These events, which have the overarching title "Symmetry: Art and Science", reached many parts of the world: Budapest, 1989; Hiroshima, 1992; Washington, DC, 1995; Haifa, 1998; Sydney, 2001; Tihany at Lake Balaton, 2004; Buenos Aires, 2007; Artists' City Gmünd, 2010; Crete, 2013; Adelaide, 2016; Kanazawa, 2019. Another event is currently planned in Porto, 2022. William did not miss an SIS-Symmetry event until the last two, but he did participate in those via Skype. In 2007, we elected him to the position of Honorary President, and he remained one of the most active members of the Society.

During our events in Haifa and Tihany, William connected with Claudio Guerri, a leading personality in semiotics and professor of architecture at the University of Buenos Aires. They became collaborators, and William became a regular visitor of the conferences of SEMA (Sociedad de Estudios Morfológicos de Argentina), which is our partner organization in South America. Incidentally, for our Buenos Aires congress in 2007, two books were published: the bilingual English and Spanish edition of parts 2–3 of William's series of booklets on symmetry and the reprint of the Spanish translation of the German book by K. L. Wolf and D. Kuhn with the title *Forma y simetría*. In 2011, Claudio Guerri also published the introductory part of William's series of booklets on symmetry; the complete work has six parts.

Of course, we do not claim that our interdisciplinary approach to symmetry was new. Many fine scholarly works were published in the past; moreover, there were two "holly years" of symmetry when important books were published. The Dutch chemist F. M. Jaeger's *Lectures on the Principle of Symmetry and Its Applications in All Natural Sciences* and the Scottish mathematical biologist D'Arcy W. Thompson's *On Growth and Form* were released in 1917. Then, in 1952, five books were published in five languages, specifically the Italian architect C. Bairati's *La simmetria dinamica, Scienza ed arte nell'architettura classica,* [*Dynamic Symmetry, Science and Art in Classical Architecture*], the Polish logician and mathematician S. Jaśkowski's *O symetrii w zdobnictwie i przyrodzie* [*On Symmetry in Decorative Art and Nature*], the German-American mathematician and theoretical physicist H. Weyl's *Symmetry*, the German chemist K. L. Wolf and historian of science D. Kuhn's *Gestalt und Symmetrie*, and the Russian crystallographer G. Wulff's (Yu. Vul'f) *Simmetriya i ee proyavlenie v prirode* [*Symmetry and Its Manifestation in Nature*].

This publishing coincidence in 1952 is quite amazing. Among these titles, Weyl's is the best known due to the author's great reputation in mathematics, physics, and even in philosophy. The book is available in ten languages, including three different Spanish and three different Chinese translations. Wulff's book was actually in its third revised edition in 1952, and its original publication in 1908 marked the start of the Russian tradition in this field, which was initiated by E. S. Fedorov's discovery of the 17 wallpaper groups and the 230 space groups in mathematical crystallography in 1890–1891. It was continued by, among others, A. V. Shubnikov's monograph in 1940 and its new edition by Shubnikov and Koptsik in 1972, which was later translated into English and given the title *Symmetry in Science and Art* (New York, 1974).

Thus, the novelty of SIS-Symmetry was not the interdisciplinary interest in symmetry, but the fact that society had started to organize regular events and provided a forum for international and interdisciplinary cooperation. William was always a great supporter of our activities, and he invited some very good artists and scholars to join us, including the Swiss geometric artist Caspar Schwabe; the Australian linguist Lynn Arnold, who is the former prime minister (premier) of South Australia; and more recently, the Belgian, Vienna based artist and architect Werner Van Hoeydonck, the editor of this book.

From 1989 onward, we had a lot of opportunities for personal discussions with William. He often spoke to me about his years at HfG Ulm and Kahn's office. The Hochschule für Gestaltung in Ulm, which was named by the secondary name of the Bauhaus at Dessau (Hochschule für Gestaltung in Dessau), was established in 1953 with initial support by the American High Command for Germany, and it existed until 1968, when

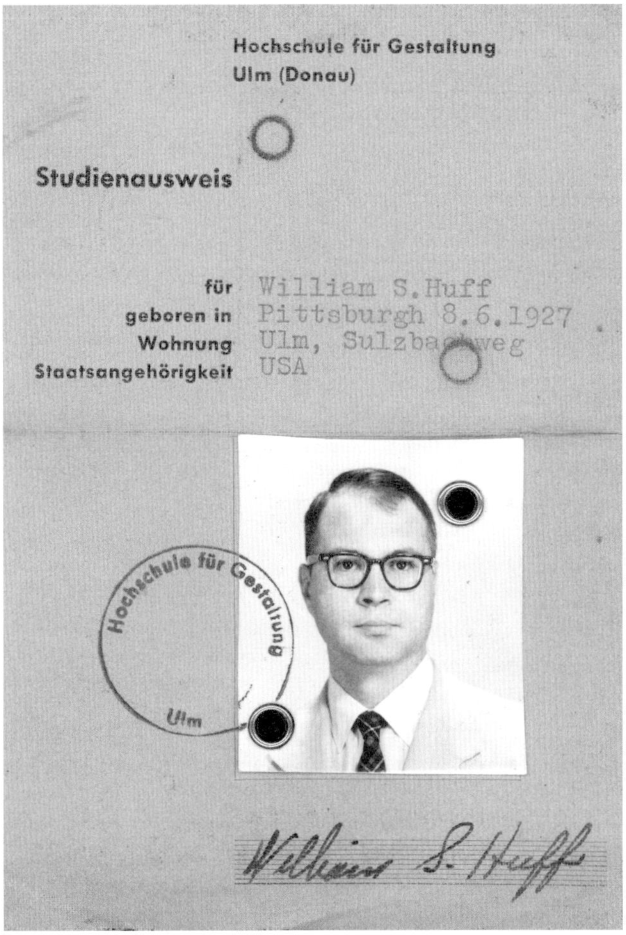

William S. Huff's Student Card, Academic Year 1956/1957. © HfG-Archiv/Museum Ulm, HfG-Ar, BDSA Hu.

the Regional Parliament withdrew the funding. William arrived at HfG Ulm, the first American student there, in 1956, during a time of important transition in the institution. The first rector, Bauhaus-trained Swiss artist and designer Max Bill, resigned in 1956, and Argentine concrete artist, designer, educator, and philosopher Tomás Maldonado took over the leadership. This move also meant that Bill's arts and crafts focus in design was replaced by an interdisciplinary art-science approach with social and economic considerations, as well as by direct connections with industry.

In this way, HfG Ulm pioneered the field of design science. Maldonado invited some leading scholars to teach courses or to give lectures. The long list included, among others, American designer-inventor Buckminster Fuller, the French pioneer of information science A. Abraham Moles, the American father of cybernetics Norbert Wiener, and German chemist Karl Lothar Wolf. William told me that Maldonado himself gave lectures on symmetry, but he also invited K. L. Wolf to present further details. I was pleased with this piece of information because I knew two books by Wolf and realized his special interest in linking science with art.

We have already mentioned the first book by K. L. Wolf and D. Kuhn, titled *Gestalt und Symmetrie*, which was published in 1952 and presented a systematic survey of symmetric figures. It is the same work that was later translated into Spanish, known as *Forma y simetría*, in Buenos Aires. The second book was written jointly by K. L. Wolf and R. Wolff in 1956 (not related, see different name spellings). Their book has a very long title: *Symmetrie: Versuch einer Anweisung zu gestalthaftem Sehen und sinnvollem Gestalten, systematisch dargestellt und an zahlreichen Beispielen erläutert* [Symmetry: Attempt towards an Instruction in Creative Seeing and Meaningful Forms, Systematically Presented and Explained with Numerous Examples]. This book has a text-volume and a figure-volume with hundreds of well-selected illustrations, from symmetric polyhedra to tracks of animal footprints, from works of art to musical scores.

Wolf's lectures on symmetry had a great impact on William. He also shared with me a story about when H. Weyl came to give a lecture on symmetry at HfG, but I believe the guest was not actually Weyl, but perhaps someone else. Of course, Weyl could have also given a lecture on symmetry in Ulm, since he had retired from the Princeton Institute for Advanced Study in 1951 and moved back to Zürich, which is not far from Ulm, but he passed away in December 1955, shortly before William's arrival. When I checked the catalogue of the HfG Library, which is kept at the Ulm Museum, I realized they had a fine selection of books in both art and science, including a German translation of Weyl's book on symmetry.

William also had a great time in Louis Kahn's office. I learned from him that many design offices, including Kahn's, had a copy of D'Arcy Thompson's book *On Growth and Form*. The original 1917 edition was already a massive book, but the second edition, published in 1942, became a two-volume set with more than 1,100 pages. Artists and architects were impressed by Thompson's presentation of organic shapes and his view on morphogenesis. He also presented interesting problems for mathematicians, but biologists were less happy because Thompson suggested that the development of living organisms was determined by physical and mathematical laws, while Darwin's natural selection is just secondary. Indeed, biologists made a drastically abbreviated edition of Thompson's book, in which those chapters that contradicted their view were deleted, but they appreciated some parts of the book. It is interesting to add that Thompson was awarded the Darwin medal in 1946.

I guess that William's strong interest in Thompson's work was due to his time in Kahn's office. It is possible that when he returned to teach courses in the early 1960s, William suggested that the HfG buy a copy, as the HfG Library has only the 1959 reprint edition. Incidentally, Kahn was often invited to give lectures at universities, but he was usually very busy and, in some cases, asked William to make a presentation. When Kahn was offered a university position, he declined it but nominated William. This led to William's teaching career, first in Pittsburgh at Carnegie Mellon University, and later in Buffalo at the State University of New York. Until the closure of HfG Ulm in 1968, he was regularly invited to Ulm and gave courses there. Thus, William's method of teaching *basic design* in the US was a continuation of the tradition started in Ulm.

Incidentally, some of the former members of HfG were also invited to teach at leading universities. For example, Maldonado went to Princeton and then to Bologna and Milan, Moles became a professor in Strasbourg, Ritter in Berkeley, and Roericht in Berlin, though his tableware was taken into the collection of the Museum of Modern Art in New York. Aicher designed the pictograms for the 1972 Summer Olympics in Munich; the logo of Lufthansa, in collaboration with Tomás Gonda; and worked for various companies.

William, while teaching basic design courses, united his interest in symmetric patterns and the theory of continuous transformations, which were related to his earlier study of the works by K. L. Wolf and by D'Arcy Thompson, respectively. It is interesting to see the scientific background of this topic. Periodic patterns and their symmetries were studied intensively in crystallography in order to describe the structure of solid-state materials in which equivalent atoms (ions or molecules) are arranged. On the two-dimensional plane, there are exactly 17 repetition types (wallpaper groups). In contrast, there are infinite possibilities to represent each of those with an arbitrary repeated element. An interesting case is the study of periodic parquets (monohedral tilings, tessellations, or mosaics) where equal copies of a given figure fill the plane without gaps and overlaps.

It is not surprising that such parquets were studied at HfG Ulm. Their library had books by Heesch, Speiser, Wolf, and even an early paper by Buerger and Lukesh that linked atomic structures and wallpapers. Crystallographers and mathematicians were interested in extending the topic of periodic patterns in various ways—for example coloring these systematically, which may represent different physical properties (magnetism, spin, etc.) or dealing with the three-dimensional cases, but it was usually required that the same unit be repeated. Wolf also presented patterns where the basic unit may grow with a similar transformation and combined this process with a rotation that led to spiral structures. It is also interesting to consider the rearrangement of atoms in a given crystalline material due to heating or other physical effects, a process that leads to a different structure. Artists and designers may study similar events by drawing a periodic parquet to feel its rhythm, which is too monotonous, then using a continuous deformation in order to gradually change the structure and the related rhythm, and finally reach a new periodic parquet. D'Arcy Thompson's book devoted an entire chapter to the theory of transformations, which he used for the comparison of related forms in biology. In connection with the history of this idea, he referred to Vitruvius's and especially to Dürer's study of human proportions, where, for example, the facial expressions are transformed and modified by slight variations.

William gave credit to Maldonado for the development of the initial concept of parquet deformation at HfG in the mid-1950s, and he was also inspired by some of M. C. Escher's drawings, but then William went on to elevate parquet deformation into a form of art. Since temporality plays a role here, it has an interesting Oriental analogy. William compared Chinese and Japanese handscrolls and parquet deformations. In both cases, a temporal element exists when they are created and usually also during the process of observation by the viewer. The direction is, however, different: in the Far East as well as in the case of Arabic illuminated manuscripts, the process goes from right to left, while in Western culture it goes from left to right. In 1994 we organized a conference in Tsukuba Science City, Japan, and invited William to present his East–West comparison; his paper appeared in the proceedings *Katachi U Symmetry* (edited by T. Ogawa, K. Miura, T. Masunari, and D. Nagy, Tokyo, 1996). William worked with a large number of students to present parquet deformations. Many of them became distinguished architects and designers, and they remember William's course.

Some people may ask the following question: Is hand drawing important in the digital age? Our answer is definitely yes. For the development of the human brain and for keeping some parts active, it is essential to do sophisticated manual tasks. If someone would like to draw a parquet deformation with a computer, the first task would be making a detailed study of the possible transformation, and the best way to do so is to sketch some parts by hand. Last, but not least, the person who draws a parquet deformation would feel the flow of the composition in order to create a new parquet. Moreover, using the terminology of positive psychology, some people may even achieve "flow"—a mental state in which a person is energized and has positive feelings. (M. Csíkszentmihályi's book on flow became widely known in 1993, when coach Jimmy Johnson showed it to the camera during the Super Bowl halftime show and claimed that he used it in preparing his team, which then won; see *Flow: The Psychology of Optimal Experience*, New York, 1990.) Incidentally, in 2012, William participated, together with Claudio Guerri, in the Yale School of Architecture symposium and exhibition asking *Is drawing dead?* During this event, many distinguished architects emphasized the importance of hand drawing.

William's description of the discussions at HfG Ulm was often so expressive that I felt as though I were there, having a chat with Tomás Maldonado, walking to Nick Roericht's house on campus, and discussing semiotic questions with Martin Krempen. Then, suddenly this fantasy became reality in 2003: William invited Claudio Guerri and me to the celebration of the 50th anniversary of the HfG's founding in Ulm. We spent some days together with the "heroes" of Ulm and witnessed the survival of the spirit of the school. We should thank William for "transforming" parquet deformation into an important field in basic design education and for the inspiration to see and feel the "flow".

Post Scriptum

It was great publicity for parquet deformation when Douglas Hofstadter, who wrote the "Metamagical Themas" column in *Scientific American* from January 1981 to July 1983, devoted the very last column, except for a later half-column, on William's parquet deformations. In the subtitle he described parquet deformation as "a subtle, intricate art form". Later, Hofstadter collected his columns into a book with additional notes (New York, 1985), and this column became the tenth chapter, just after his column on "Pattern, Poetry, and Power in the Music of Frédéric Chopin". Symbolically, Hofstadter and Huff met again for the cover design of our periodical *Symmetry: Culture and Science* in 1990. The layout was designed by Gunter Schmitz, a colleague of William at both the HfG in Ulm and then the university in Buffalo; the image on the front cover was designed by William; and on the back cover we used Hofstadter's ambigrams "Symmetry", "Hungary", and "Budapest", which he kindly made for us. Moreover, I signed the introduction, titled "Manifesto on (Dis)symmetry", with his ambigram expressing my name. Thereafter, I often used this "signature" in our publications, giving credit to Douglas Hofstadter and in recognition of the foundation of SIS-Symmetry in 1989–1990. I will do the same thing here.

But let us first jump to the proceedings of our last congress in Kanazawa, Japan, 2019. William, as our honorary president, authored an introductory essay titled "Thanks, Dénes/In Gratitude: A Home for a Life's Driven Diversions". It is shocking to see that it became his last paper. SIS-Symmetry and SEMA are very much honored by these words, and we are glad he felt that we could provide a "home" for his ideas. It is our duty to help these ideas to flourish.

This "signature", where "Dénes" (five letters) flows into "Nagy" (four letters) and vice-versa with twofold rotation, was a gift by Douglas Hofstadter for the first SIS-Symmetry congress in 1989.

Biography of the Author

Dénes Nagy is a Hungarian-Australian mathematician, historian of science, and theoretician of architecture. He started his teaching career at the Eötvös Loránd University in Budapest. His later appointments: Arizona State University (Tempe, 1986–1988), University of the South Pacific (Suva, 1989–1993), University of Tsukuba (Tsukuba Science City, 1993–2000). In 2001, he was appointed as an Honorary Research Professor of the Institute for the Advancement of Research, ACU, Melbourne, Australia. He is the Founding President of SIS-Symmetry (International Society for the Interdisciplinary Study of Symmetry), which organizes triennial art-science congresses and exhibitions: (1) Budapest, 1989; (2) Hiroshima, 1992; (3) Washington, DC, 1995; (4) Haifa, 1998; (5) Sydney, 2001; (6) Tihany at Lake Balaton, 2004; (7) Buenos Aires, 2007; (8) Artists' City Gmünd, Austria, 2010; (9) Crete, Greece, 2013; (10) Adelaide, South Australia, 2016, (11) Kanazawa, Japan. In the framework of SIS-Symmetry, he worked together with the architect William S. Huff for a longer period. He is also the Chair of the Committee for Folk Architecture of the Hungarian Academy of Sciences, Veszprém. He was given many honorary titles and awards, including Doctor honoris causa, Honorary Membership of the SEMA in Buenos Aires, Award of *Pro Scientia absoluta vera*, and the *Katachi*-prize in Japan. In 2012, the President of Hungary awarded him the Knight's Cross. He gave invited lectures in more than 20 countries in six languages. His list of publications includes 26 volumes and around 200 papers in English, Hungarian, German, French, Russian, Ukrainian, Slovenian, Japanese, Chinese, and Persian. He was the co-editor of the *Encyclopedia of Hungarian Scientists*. The list of his co-authors and co-editors include, among others, Nobel Prize winners Eugene P. Wigner and Danny Shechtman, physicist Kodi Husimi, and historian László Makkai.

Introduction

Werner Van Hoeydonck and
Eva Sommeregger

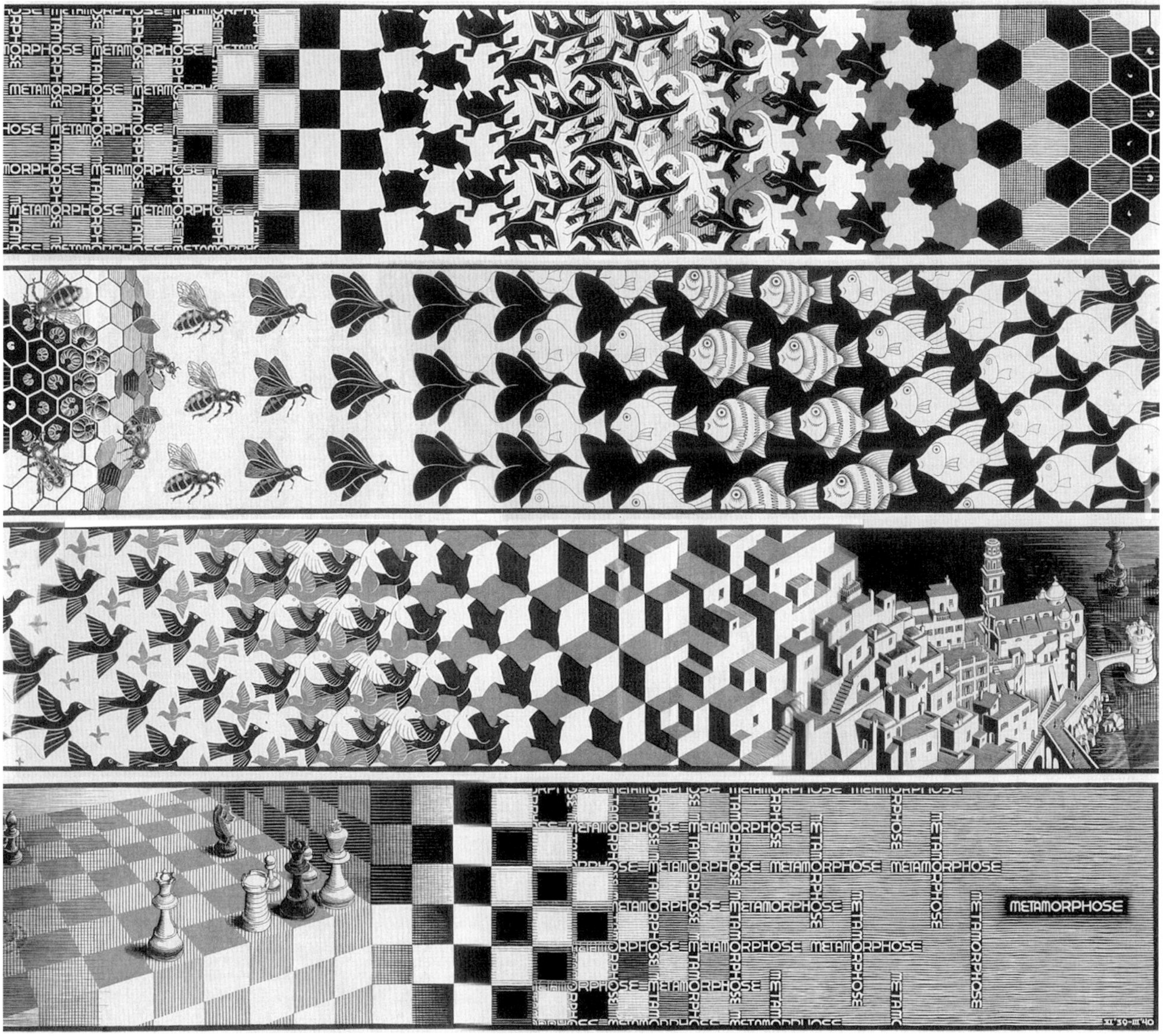

Fig.: M.C. Escher's *Metamorphosis II*. © 2021 The M.C. Escher Company–The Netherlands. All rights reserved by mcescher.com.

Experiments

The Way Things Go is the title of an experimental work by artists Peter Fischli and David Weiss in 1987. In this piece, a chain reaction of a series of physical and chemical experiments takes place that is then captured by an approximately 30-minute-long film. In an inventive and playful manner, the piece involves self-made structures using water, fire, foam, fog, a tire, a candle, a balloon, a banana, a chair, and a table, among others. These contribute to an ongoing course of events that creates suspense over whether one of the experiments might, at some point, abruptly end and thus interrupt the continuous connection of mutually dependent settings. Shown at the Documenta 8 exhibition, as well as in the permanent collections of the Centre Georges Pompidou and MoMA New York, the work gives the experiment a firm position within the field of the arts.

Scientifically speaking, an experiment is an empirical form of investigation to gain knowledge. Coined by the early modern philosopher Francis Bacon, the Latin expressions of *experientia quaesita* and *experimentum* describe a sought-after experience.[1] Experimentation involves observing and actively intervening in a process by making intentional changes in its defining conditions. In order to represent a valid form of knowledge, it is essential that the series of steps involved in the experiment are repeatable so that its results can be witnessed as often as desired.

Within that context, the artistic experiment presents a special case: Unlike an experiment understood in the strict scientific sense—that is, the attempt to attain measurable results—an artistic experiment is an open research activity designed by those who conduct it.[2] Equally, an artistic experiment may not necessarily be reproducible; in some cases, a process may even be deliberately set up in order not to comply with this requirement. In its urge to investigate and express, the making of art is experimental in itself—be that in its thorough examination of a medium or in its ways of seeing and doing things.[3]

Genesis of the Experiments Conducted for this Book

This book explores experiments from an artistic perspective, using as its example the design and geometry exercises conducted by students at the Center for Three-Dimensional Design and Model Making, a subunit of the Institute of Art and Design at Vienna's University of Technology. The university was founded in 1815 under the name of Imperial-Royal Polytechnic Institute, and the Center for Three-Dimensional Design and Model Making has been involved in the education of architects since as early as 1866, providing studies of three-dimensional form ranging from ornamental plastic in the nineteenth century to sculpture in the twentieth century and art and design in the expanded field in the twenty-first century. Most lecturers affiliated with the center have or had a firm background in the arts[4]—a fact that signals the university's willingness to embrace artistic exploration within the curriculum of architecture. The center has, thus, always enjoyed a particular status within the faculty, offering space for investigations and design from an artistic perspective.

In addition to a number of free electives and optional modules, the center runs a mandatory second-year course in the Bachelor of Architecture program that is rarely found within the obligatory subjects of architectural curricula: a basic design course titled "Three-Dimensional Design". Freed from the usual demands regarding the ways in which a future architectural design might be used or practiced, students in this class deal with three-dimensional objects as they are by exploring an object's actual sculptural traits. During the course of a four-month semester and guided by a brief, students design and build a physical three-dimensional object, sometimes using digital techniques, and explore its possibilities and limitations via sensory perception and while considering its materiality and the tools and production methods involved.

The student works realized in the three-dimensional design classes of the fall/winter semesters of 2017/18 and 2018/19 form the backbone of this book. The topics of these two courses were the result of fruitful conversations and collaborations. In summer 2017, independent researcher Werner Van Hoeydonck—architect, specialist in geometry and ornamentation, and co-editor of this book—contacted a long-time affiliate with the center—architect, researcher, and educator Anita Aigner—regarding the notion of ornaments. Aigner had dealt with the topic in a series of free electives and in 2006 had organized a symposium, titled "Surface Control", that linked contemporary debates with the ornaments' lesser-known historical, cultural scientific, and design-related practical dimensions.

Van Hoeydonck's expertise is the field of geometry, and his particular interest lies in so-called parquet deformations, which are best known through the works of M. C. Escher. Parquets, also known as tiling or tessellation, refer to regular, interlocking geometric patterns covering a surface, without gaps or overlaps. Parquet deformation, accordingly, includes a transformation of the tiles, and parquet deformation drawings necessarily need to be viewed by observers from one side to the other, as the involved shapes slightly change from one tile to the next, with the form introduced on one end differing completely from the form at the other. As a term, "parquet deformations" was coined by William S. Huff, professor of architecture at the State University of New York and at the Ulm School of Design. Huff started to systematically investigate parquet deformations in the assignments given to basic design students in the 1960s. Unlike Escher, who used manifold shapes in his artworks, such as animals, chess pieces, and landscapes, Huff concentrated on geometrical forms only. In other exercises, such as the "trisections of the cube", students built skillful physical models from wood, which are still hosted in the archive of the Ulm School of Design, and according to Huff, were an attempt to take parquet deformations into three dimensions.[5]

The question of parquets in three dimensions inspired Aigner and Van Hoeydonck, and they developed an idea for an experiment: As with Huff, the teaching of a basic design course could be used as a productive realm for experimentation—that is, as a springboard for designing novel geometries. This time, however, something should be examined that Huff was no longer able to investigate himself: The intended experiment would consist of taking parquet deformations from two to three dimensions. In other words, could the planar, gradually changing drawings of parquet deformations be translated into spatial objects using the very same transformational logic? This would result in a special case of a three-dimensional parquet, also called a tessellation of space (a gap-free "space filling", "close packing" of polyhedra or "honeycomb"). After further discussions with the center's head, Christian Kern, the idea to experiment with parquet deformation in three dimensions was then used as the design brief for the three-dimensional design course of fall 2017/18.

In the following year, Peter G. Auer, architect, educator, researcher and also a long-term affiliate of the center, followed in the footsteps of the parquet deformation brief and developed the so-called "Cellular Space Sequences" exercise that would once again make use of an experiment translating two-dimensional geometric patterns into three-dimensional objects. This time, however, students designed cellular arrangements made from solid volumes into which connective void spaces were placed.

Presenting the Experiments' Outcomes

Approximately 450 students completed the experiment in each of the two years—a selection of their works form the core of this book and are displayed in the chapters carrying the names of the respective experiments: "3D Parquet Deformation" and "Cellular Space Sequences". Both chapters progress chronologically so that readers can follow the logic of the assignments given to students. In both cases, initial two-dimensional exercises are shown, leading to a selection of three-dimensional models built at the end of the semester. Christian Kern, also head of teaching at the center, provides a thorough introduction into the teaching assignment and its backgrounds and methodologies at the beginning of the "3D Parquet Deformation" chapter.

Following the notion of the artistic experiment, this book focuses on presenting investigations rather than judging the results obtained by students as right or wrong. The topics investigated by the students' works overlap in many instances, and they have been grouped accordingly during the editing process of the book. The "3D Parquet Deformation" chapter features works that explore "Composition", "Dissolving", "Gradual Changes", "in Motion", "Materiality Matters", "Multiplication", and "On Stage". The "Cellular Space Sequences" chapter collects works examining "Balance", "Crystalline", "Gradual Changes", "Materiality Matters", "Multiply", and "Opening Up the Inside". Themes do not follow any (scientific) criteria chosen beforehand; instead, they have arisen from carefully studying the students' works and distilling ideas from them—ideas that reoccur, that blur into one another, and that do not present a systematic evaluation regarding a particular direction, be it materiality or geometric rule sets. Rather, the topics extracted from the works do not follow any given order; they stand next to one another to build relationships. Readers might be reminded of Jorge Luis Borges's fictional "Chinese encyclopedia", which excels in absurdity and breaking the limitations of ordering systems. It is cited by Michel Foucault in the foreword to the *Order of Things* publication. Animals are ordered after categories such as "suckling pigs", "sirens", "belonging to the Emperor", "drawn with a very fine camelhair brush", or "from a long way off look like flies".[6] The present book might not be able to reproduce the absurdity of Borges' Chinese encyclopedia, nor Foucault's "shattering laugh" when reading it for the first time[7]—rather the book takes Borges's encyclopedia as a point of departure not to classify, but to present a deliberate choice.

Within the linear scope of this book, the student works can be found in the second part of the book, preceded by a chapter titled "Research Perspectives" at the beginning. This chapter does pioneering work in making the concept of parquet deformations more accessible. It showcases important historical texts that offer profound insight, as well as selected perspectives written by specialists in contemporary geometric discourse: Their articles explain methodological approaches and provide outlooks into possible future developments, proving that there exists continuous and renewed interest in parquet deformations. The chapter also includes reprints of historic articles, as well as contemporary contributions conceived by international scholars, carefully selected by Werner Van Hoeydonck for this publication.

Douglas Hofstadter, theoretical physician and writer, wrote a monthly column titled "Metamagical Themas" for the renowned *Scientific American* magazine and made parquet deformations known to a wider audience through a piece on parquet deformations in July 1983. Hofstadter gave his kind permission for the inclusion of a reprint of the extended version from his 1985 book *Metamagical Themas*, titled "Parquet Deformations: A Subtle, Intricate Art Form", supplemented with original images gathered from the Ulm archive for this publication.

Providing new material gathered from the Ulm archive, Werner Van Hoeydonck historically contextualizes the invention of the first parquet deformation in his chapter "Past and Future of William Huff's Parquet Deformations". Having been in conversation with historic witnesses, he expands on Huff's own research and examines possible future developments and the role of geometric exercises in basic design courses.

In "*Grundlehre* at the HfG—A Focus on 'Visuelle Grammatik'", William S. Huff, the inventor of parquet deformations, provides an extensive overview of how he experienced basic design education at the Ulm School of Design, both as a student and later as a teacher.[8] In this essay, a reprint from 2003 and beautifully illustrated by outstanding student works newly selected by Van Hoeydonck for the present book, Huff describes the pedagogic work of Tomás Maldonado and elaborates on historical and formal developments in the concepts of basic design courses—from the preliminary courses at the Bauhaus directed by Josef Albers to modern-day practices in basic design education—as witnessed by him.

In "Geometry of Structures and Its Philosophical Aesthetic Background", Cornelie Leopold, mathematician, philosopher, and professor affiliated with the University of Kaiserslautern, examines the relationships between mathematical, philosophical, and design approaches in teaching at the Ulm School of Design, illustrated by examples of foundation courses. The strong connection between a theoretical background in structural thinking and hands-on practical realizations in composition and design was one characteristic of the Ulm School of Design, where Huff studied and taught. Leopold paints a picture of the fertile climate that ultimately made it possible to devise the parquet deformation assignment.

Craig S. Kaplan, from the University of Waterloo in Canada, writes from the perspective of a mathematician and computer scientist, albeit using code as a creative medium. He has designed parquet deformations himself and published papers on Escher's geometrical metamorphoses and parquet deformations in Islamic design. His essay "The Tiles, They Are a-Changin'" compiles his latest research on parquet deformations.

Architect and professor Tuğrul Yazar from the Istanbul Bilgi University describes parquet deformations from a computational perspective. Having used a parquet deformation assignment in teaching computer aided design software, he explores novel methods to analyze and design parquet deformations using state-of-the-art programs *Rhino* and *Grasshopper*.

Jay Bonner, independent scholar and author of the book *Islamic Geometric Patterns: Their Historical Development and Traditional Methods of Construction*, speculates on the combination of parquet deformation with Islamic design in "Pattern Manipulation through Hinged Tessellations".

Finally, in "*Parakeet3D*: Algorithmic Re-Envisioning of Geometrical Pattern Morphogenesis", Esmaeil Mottaghi and Arman Khalil Beigi Khameneh, lecturers at the University of Tehran and inventors of the *Parakeet* software, open the field of systematically scripting parquet deformations.

In the book's first article, positioned at the very beginning of the publication, Dénes Nagy, mathematician, science historian, and architecture theoretician, provides an epitaph on William S. Huff, who sadly passed away on january 21, 2021. We dedicate this book to his memory.

References

[1] Siegfried Gehrmann, Natur, Erfahrung, Experiment – Francis Bacon und die Anfänge der modernen Naturwissenschaft. "Erfahrung" – Über den wissenschaftlichen Umgang mit einem Begriff. Essener Unikate, 16/2001, pp. 53–63.

[2] Nicole Vennemann, Das Experiment in der zeitgenössischen Kunst. Initiierte Ereignisse als Form der künstlerischen Forschung, transcript, Bielefeld, 2018.

[3] Bernd Löbach-Hinweiser. Kunst und Wissenschaft. Band 4: Experimentelle Kunst, Designbuch, 2016.

[4] Helmut Kuhn, Walter Ritzer, 150 Jahre Technische Hochschule Wien, self-published, 1965, pp. 321–323.

[5] Email from William S. Huff to Werner Van Hoeydonck, 31.08.2019.

[6] Michel Foucault, The Order of Things. An Archeology of the Human Sciences, Pantheon, New York, 1970, p. xv.

[7] ibid.

[8] This text first appeared in 2003. See [Ed.] Ulmer Museum and the archive of the Ulm School of Design, Ulmer Modelle – Modelle nach Ulm: Hochschule für Gestaltung Ulm 1953–1968, Ostfildern-Ruit, Hatje Cantz, 2003.

Biography of the Authors

Werner Van Hoeydonck
See p. 63

Eva Sommeregger has a degree in architecture from the Vienna University of Technology, a master's degree in architectural design from the Bartlett School of Architecture in London, and a doctorate from the Academy of Fine Arts Vienna. At universities in Vienna and London, she gained teaching experience at the bachelor, master, and dissertation levels and generated third-party funding. In 2010 she received the Margarete Schütte-Lihotzky grant, in 2011 she received a Schindler grant at the MAK Center Los Angeles, and in 2018 she co-founded the MAGAZIN exhibition space for contemporary architecture in Vienna. Her architectural practice includes writing, curating, and developing experimental (post)digital spaces. Her work has been exhibited at MOMA New York and the Venice Architecture Biennale, among others.

Research Perspectives

Parquet Deformations: A Subtle, Intricate Art Form

Douglas R. Hofstadter

What is the difference between music and visual art? If someone asked me this question, I would have no hesitation in responding. To me the major difference is temporality. Works of music intrinsically involve time; works of visual art do not. More precisely, pieces of music consist of sounds intended to be played and heard in a specific order and at a specific speed. Music is therefore fundamentally one-dimensional; it is tied to the rhythms of our existence. Works of visual art, in contrast, are generally two- or three-dimensional. Paintings and sculpture seldom have any intrinsic "scanning order" built into them that the eye must follow. Mobiles and other pieces of kinetic art may change over time, but often without any specific initial state or final state or intermediate states. You are free to come and go as you please.

There are, of course, exceptions to this generalization. European art has grand friezes and historic cycloramas, and Oriental art has intricate pastoral scrolls up to hundreds of feet long. These types of visual art impose a temporal order and speed on the scanning eye. There is a starting point and an end point. Usually, as in stories, these points represent states of relative calm, particularly at the end. In between, various types of tension are built up and resolved in an idiosyncratic but pleasing visual rhythm. The calmer end states are usually orderly and visually simple, whereas the tenser intermediate states are usually more chaotic and visually confusing. If one replaces "visual" by "aural", virtually the same can be said of music.

I have been fascinated for many years by the idea of trying to capture the essence of the musical experience in visual form. I have my own ideas about how this can be done; in fact, I spent several years working out a form of visual music. By no means, however, do I think there is a unique or best way to carry out this task of "translation", and indeed I have often wondered how others might attempt to do it. I have seen a few such attempts, but most of them struck me as being unsuccessful. One striking counterexample is the set of "parquet deformations" meta-composed by William S. Huff, professor of architectural design at the State University of New York at Buffalo.

I say "meta-composed" with good reason. Huff himself has never executed a single parquet deformation. He has elicited hundreds of them, however, from his students, and in so doing he has brought a high degree of refinement to this form of art. He might be likened to the conductor of a fine orchestra. Although the conductor makes no sound in the course of a performance, we credit the person doing the job, to a great degree, for the quality of the sound. We can only guess at how much preparation and coaching went into the performance.

So it is with William S. Huff. For 23 years, his students in Buffalo and at Carnegie Mellon University have been prodded into flights of artistic inspiration, and it is thanks to Huff's vision of what constitutes quality that some beautiful results have emerged. Not only has he elicited outstanding work from students, but he has also carefully selected what he thinks are the best pieces, and these he is keeping in archives. For these reasons, I will at times refer to "Huff's creations", but it is always in this more indirect sense of "meta-creations" that I will mean it.

I don't wish to take credit from the students who executed the individual pieces, but there is a larger sense of the term "credit" that goes exclusively to Huff, the person who has shaped this entire art form himself. Let me use an analogy. Gazelles are marvelous beasts, yet it is not they themselves but the selective pressures of evolution that are responsible for their species' unique and wondrous qualities. Huff's judgments and comments have here played the role of those impersonal, selective evolutionary pressures, and out of them has been molded a living and dynamic tradition, a "species" of art exemplified and extended by each new instance.

Fig. 1: "Fylfot Flipflop", by Fred Watts. Basic Design Studio of William S. Huff, Spring 1963, Carnegie Mellon University (CIT). © HfG-Archiv/Museum Ulm, HfG-Ar, BDSA, Hu P 01. 018.

All that remains to be addressed by way of introduction is the meaning of "parquet deformation." Actually, it is nearly self-explanatory. Traditionally, a parquet is a regular mosaic made of inlaid wood on the floor of an elegant room, and a deformation—well, it's somewhere in between a distortion and a transformation. Huff's parquets are more abstract: They are regular tessellations (or tilings) of the plane, ideally drawn with zero-thickness line segments and curves. The deformations are not arbitrary but must satisfy two basic requirements:

1. There must be change only in one dimension, so that it is possible to see a temporal progression in which one tessellation gradually becomes another;
2. At each stage, the pattern must constitute a regular tessellation of the plane—that is, there must be a unit cell that could combine with itself so that it could cover an infinite plane exactly.

(Actually, the second requirement is not usually adhered to strictly. It would be more accurate to say that the unit cell at any stage of a parquet deformation can be easily modified so as to allow it to tile the plane perfectly.)

From this very simple idea emerge some stunningly beautiful creations. Huff explains that he was originally inspired, back in 1960, by the M. C. Escher woodcut "Day and Night." In that work, forms of birds tiling the plane are gradually distorted (as the eye scans downward) until they become diamond shaped, looking like the checkerboard pattern of cultivated fields seen from the air. Escher, of course, became famous for his tessellations, both pure and distorted, as well as for the other haunting games he played with art and reality.

Whereas Escher's tessellations are almost always based on animal forms, Huff decided to limit his scope to purely geometric forms. In a way, that is like a decision by a composer to follow austere musical patterns, totally eschewing anything that might conjure up a "program" (that is, some kind of image or story behind the sounds). An effect of this decision is that the beauty and visual interest must come entirely from the complexity and subtlety of the interplay of abstract forms. There is nothing to "charm" the eye, as there is with pictures of animals. There is only the unembellished perceptual experience. Because of the linearity of this form of art, Huff has likened it to visual music. He writes:

> Although I am spectacularly ignorant of music, tone-deaf and hated those piano lessons (yet can be enthralled by Bach, Vivaldi or Debussy), I have the students "read" their designs as I suppose a musician might scan a work: the themes, the events, the intervals, the number of steps from one event to another, the rhythms, the repetitions (which can be destructive, if not totally controlled, as well as reinforcing). These are principally temporal, not spatial, compositions (although all predominantly temporal compositions have, of necessity, an element of the spatial and vice versa—e.g., the single-frame picture is the basic element of the moving picture).

What are the basic elements of a parquet deformation? First there is the class of allowed parquets. On this Huff writes: "We play a different (or rather, tighter) game from Escher's. We work with only A tiles (i.e., congruent tiles of the same handedness). We do not use, as he does, A and A' tiles (i.e., congruent tiles of both handedness), although an exception to this rule is the example called Dual. Finally, we don't use A and B tiles (i.e., two different interlocking tiles), since two such tiles can always be seen as subdivisions of a single larger tile."

The other basic element is the repertory of standard deforming devices. Typical devices include lengthening or shortening a line; rotating a line; introducing a "hinge" somewhere inside a line segment so that it can "flex"; introducing a "bump" or "pimple" or "tooth" (a small intrusion or extrusion having a simple shape) in the middle of a line or at a vertex; shifting, rotating, expanding, or contracting a group of lines that form a natural subunit; and variations on these themes.

To understand these descriptions, you must realize that a reference to "a line" or "a vertex" is actually a reference to a line or a vertex inside a unit cell, and therefore, when *one* such line or vertex is altered, *all* the corresponding lines or vertices that play the same role in the copies of that cell undergo the same change. Since some of those copies may be at 90 degrees (or other angles) with respect to the master cell, one locally innocent-looking change may induce changes at corresponding spots, resulting in unexpected interactions whose visual consequences can be quite exciting. Without further ado, let us proceed to examine some specific pieces.

Look at the piece titled "Fylfot Flipflop". It is an early one, executed by Fred Watts at Carnegie Mellon in 1963. If you simply let your eye skim across the top line, you will get the distinct sensation of scanning a tiny mountain range. At each edge, you begin with a perfectly flat plain and then move into gently rolling hills, which become taller and steeper, eventually turning into jagged peaks; past the center point these start to soften into lower foothills, which gradually tail off into the plain again. This much is obvious even at a casual glance. Subtler to see is the line just below, whose zigging and zagging is 180 degrees out of phase with the top line. Notice that in the very center that line is completely at rest: a perfectly horizontal stretch flanked on each side by increasingly toothy regions. Below it there are seven more horizontal lines. Thus, if one completely filtered out the vertical lines, one would see nine horizontal lines stacked above one another, the odd-numbered ones jagged in the center, the even-numbered ones smooth in the center.

Now what about the vertical lines? Both the left-hand and the right-hand borderlines are perfectly straight vertical lines. Their immediate neighbors, however, are as jagged as possible, consisting of repeated 90-degree bends, back and forth. The next vertical line nearer the center is practically straight up and down again. Then there is a wavy line again, and so on. As you move across the picture you see that the jagged lines gradually get less jagged and the straight ones get increasingly jagged, until in the middle the roles are completely reversed. The process then continues, so that by the time you have reached the other side the lines are back to normal. If you could filter out the horizontal lines, you would see a simple pattern of quite jagged lines alternating with less jagged ones.

When these two extremely simple, independent patterns—the horizontal and the vertical—are superposed, what emerges is an unexpectedly rich perceptual feast. At the far left and right the eye picks out fylfots—that is, swastikas—of either handedness contained inside perfect squares. In the center the eye immediately sees that the central fylfots are all gone, replaced by perfect crosses inside pinwheels.

And then a queer perceptual reversal takes place. If you just shift your focus of attention diagonally by half a pinwheel, you will notice that there is a fylfot right there before your eyes! In fact, suddenly fylfots appear all over the central section, where before you had been seeing only crosses inside pinwheels. And conversely, of course, now when you look at either end, you will see pinwheels everywhere with crosses inside them. No fylfots! It is an astonishingly simple design, yet the effect catches nearly everyone off guard.

This is a simple example of the ubiquitous visual phenomenon called "regrouping", in which the boundary line of the unit cell shifts so that structures jump out at the eye that before were completely submerged and invisible, whereas conversely, of course, structures that a moment ago were completely obvious are now invisible, having been split into separate conceptual pieces by the act of regrouping, or shift of perceptual boundaries. It is both a perceptual and a conceptual phenomenon, a delight to the subtle combination of eye and mind that is most sensitive to pattern.

For another example of regrouping take a look at "Crossover", executed by Richard Lane, also at Carnegie Mellon in 1963. Something really amazing happens in the middle, but I won't tell you what. Just find it yourself by careful looking.

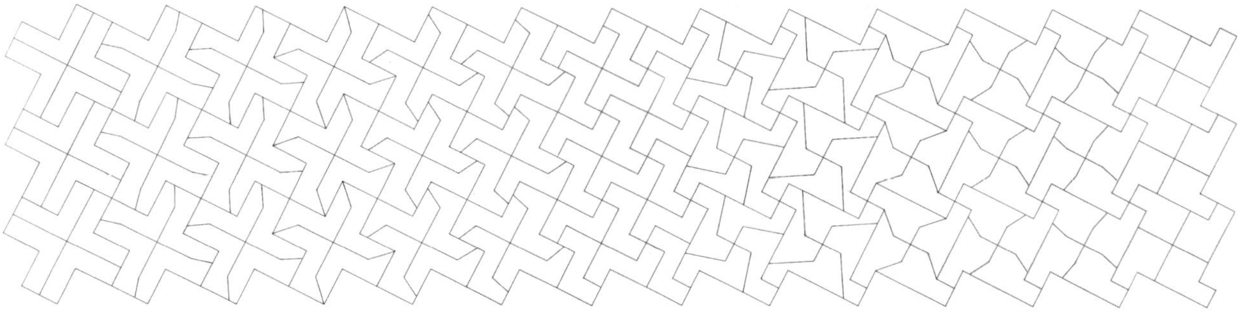

Fig. 2: "Crossover", by Richard Lane. Basic Design Studio of William S. Huff, Spring 1963, Carnegie Mellon University (CIT). © HfG-Archiv/Museum Ulm, HfG-Ar, BDSA, Hu P 01. 015.

By the way, there are still features left to be explained in "Fylfot Flipflop". At first it appears to be mirror-symmetric. For instance, all the fylfots at the left end are spinning counterclockwise, while all the ones at the right end are spinning clockwise. So far, so symmetrical. In the middle, however, all the fylfots go counterclockwise. This surely violates the symmetry. Furthermore, the one-quarter-way and three-quarter-way stages of the deformation, which ought to be mirror images of each other, bear no resemblance at all to each other. Can you figure out the logic behind this subtle asymmetry between the left and right sides? This piece also illustrates yet another way parquet deformations resemble music. A unit cell—or rather, a vertical cross-section consisting of a stack of unit cells—is analogous to a measure in music. The regular pulse of a piece of music is given by the repetition of unit cells across the page. And the flow of a melodic line across measured boundaries is modeled by the flow of a visual line—such as the mountain-range lines—across many unit cells.

Bach's music is always called up in discussions of the relation between mathematical patterns and music, and this occasion is no exception. I am reminded particularly of some of Bach's texturally more uniform pieces, such as certain preludes from "The Well-Tempered Clavier", where in each measure there is a certain pattern executed once or twice and possibly more times. From measure to measure this pattern undergoes a slow metamorphosis, meandering in the course of many measures from one region of harmonic space to far-distant regions and then slowly returning by some circuitous route. For specific examples you might listen to (or look at the scores of) Book I, No. 1 and No. 2, and Book II, No. 3 and No. 15. Many of the other preludes have this feature in places, although not for their entirety.

Bach seldom deliberately set out to play with the perceptual systems of his listeners. Artists of his century, although they occasionally played perceptual games, were considerably less sophisticated about, and less fascinated by, issues we now deem part of perceptual psychology. Such phenomena as regrouping would have intrigued Bach, and I sometimes wish he had known of certain effects and had been able to try them out, but then I remind myself that whatever time Bach might have spent playing with newfangled ideas would have had to be subtracted from his time for producing the masterpieces we know and love, and so why tamper with something so precious?

On the other hand, I do not find this argument 100 percent compelling. Who says that if you are going to imagine playing with the past, you have to hold the lifetimes of famous people constant in length? If we can imagine telling Bach about perceptual psychology, why can't we also imagine adding a few extra years to his lifetime to let him explore it? After all, the only divinely imposed (that is, absolutely unslippable) constraint on Bach's years is that they and Mozart's years add up to 100, no? Hence, if we give Bach five extra years, then we merely take five away from Mozart. It is painful, to be sure, but not all that bad. We could even let Bach live to 100! (Mozart would never have existed.)

Although it is difficult to imagine and impossible to know what Bach's music would have been like if he had lived in the twentieth century, it is certainly not impossible to know what Steve Reich's music would have been like if he had lived in this century. In fact, I am listening to a record of it right now. Now, Reich's music really is conscious of perceptual psychology. All the way through he plays with perceptual shifts and ambiguities, pivoting from one rhythm to another, from one harmonic origin to another, constantly keeping the listener on edge and tingling with nervous energy. Imagine a piece resembling Ravel's *Bolero*, only with a much finer grain size, so that instead of its having roughly a one-minute unit cell it has a three-second unit cell. Its changes are so tiny that sometimes you can barely tell it is changing at all, whereas at other times the changes jump out at you. What Reich piece am I listening to? Well, it hardly matters, since most of his music satisfies this characterization, but for the sake of specificity you might try *Music for a Large Ensemble, Octet, or Violin Phase*. Let us now return to parquet deformations.

"Dizzy Bee", executed by Richard Mesnik at Carnegie Mellon in 1964, involves perceptual tricks of another kind. The left side looks like a perfect honeycomb or, somewhat less poetically, a perfect bathroom floor. When we move to the right, its perfection seems in doubt as the rigidity of the lattice gives way to shapes that seem rounder. Then we notice that three of them have combined to form one larger shape: a superhexagon made up of three rather squashed pentagons. The curious thing is that if we now sweep our eyes from right to left back to the beginning, we can no longer see the left side in quite the way we saw it before. The small hexagons now are constantly grouping themselves into threes, although the grouping changes quickly. In our mind we experience "flickering clusters" where groups form for an instant and then disband, their components immediately regrouping in new combinations. The poetic term "flickering clusters" comes from a famous theory of how water molecules behave, in which the bonds are hydrogen bonds rather than mental ones.

Even more dizzying, perhaps, is "Consternation", executed by Scott Grady at SUNY at Buffalo in 1977. This is another parquet deformation in which hexagons and cubes vie for perceptual supremacy. It is so complex and agitated in appearance that I scarcely dare to

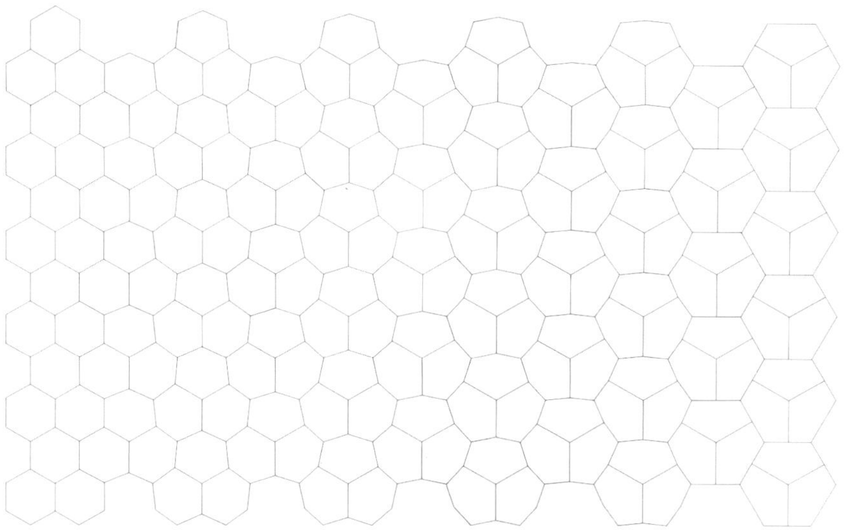

Fig. 3: "Dizzy Bee", by Richard Mesnik. Basic Design Studio of William S. Huff, Spring 1965, Carnegie Mellon University (CIT). © HfG-Archiv/Museum Ulm, HfG-Ar, BDSA, Hu P01. 023.

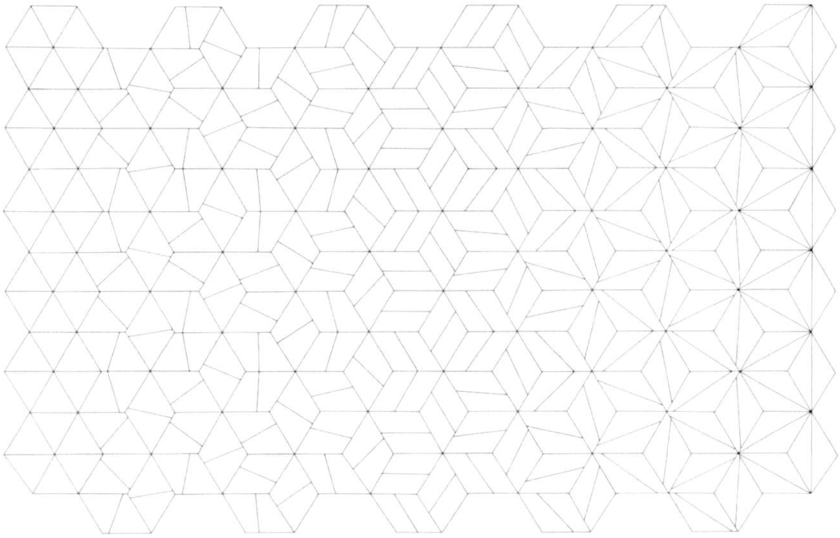

Fig. 4: "Consternation", by Scott Grady. Basic Design Studio of William S. Huff, Spring 1965, Carnegie Mellon University (CIT). © HfG-Archiv/Museum Ulm, HfG-Ar, BDSA, Hu P05. 014.

attempt an analysis of it. In its intermediate regions I find the same exciting kind of visual pseudochaos as exists in Escher's best deformations.

Perhaps irrelevantly, but I suspect not, the names of many of these studies remind me of pieces by Zez Confrey, a composer best known in the 1920s for his novelty piano pieces such as "Dizzy Fingers" and "Kitten on the Keys" and my favorite, "Flutter By, Butterfly". Confrey specialized in pushing rag music to its limits without losing musical charm, and some of the results seem to me to have a saucy, dazzling appeal not unlike the jazzy appearance of this parquet deformation.

The next parquet deformation, "Oddity out of Old Oriental Ornament", executed by Francis O'Donnell at Carnegie Mellon in 1966, is based on an extremely simple principle: the insertion of a "hinge" in one single line segment and the subsequent flexing of the segment at that hinge. The reason for the stunningly rich results is that the unit cell giving rise to the tessellation occurs both vertically and horizontally, so that flexing it one way induces a crosswise flexing as well, and the two flexings combine to yield this curious and unexpected pattern.

Another deformation that shows the amazing results of an extremely simple but carefully chosen transformation principle is "Y Knot", executed by Leland Chen at SUNY at Buffalo in 1977. If you look at it with full attention, you will see that its unit cell is in the "Cucaracha" shape of a three-bladed propeller and that the unit cell never changes in shape. All that does change is the Y lodged tightly inside the unit cell. And the only way the Y changes is by very slowly rotating clockwise. Admittedly, in the final stages of rotation this forces some previously constant line segments to extend themselves a bit, but that does not change the outline of the unit cell in any way. It is remarkable what well-chosen simplicity can do.

Fig. 5: “Oddity out of Old Oriental Ornament”, originally by Francis D. O’Donnell, Spring 1966, reworked by Kathleen Harrigan, Spring 1987. Note by Huff: “Variant: keeping a constant module.” Basic Design Studio of William S. Huff, Carnegie Mellon University (CIT). © HfG-Archiv/Museum Ulm, HfG-Ar, BDSA, Hu 01. 027.

Three of my favorites are “Quirky Cogs” (Arne Larson, Carnegie Mellon, 1963), “Trifoliolate” (Glenn Paris, Carnegie Mellon, 1966) and “Arabesque” (Joel Napach, SUNY at Buffalo, 1979). They all share the feature of getting increasingly intricate as you move to the right. Most of the preceding deformations do not have this extreme quality of irreversibility—that is, the ratcheted quality signaling that an evolutionary process is taking place. I can’t help wondering if the designers did not think they had painted themselves into a corner, particularly in the case of “Arabesque”. Is there any way you can back out of that supertangle except by retrograde motion, namely by retracing your steps? I suspect there is, but I wouldn’t care to try to find it.

As a contrast, consider “Razor Blades”, an extended study in relative calmness. It was executed at Carnegie Mellon in 1966, but unfortunately is unsigned. Like “Fylfot Flipflop”, the first piece I described, this one can be broken up into long, wavy horizontal lines and vertical structures crossing them. It is a little easier to see them if you start at the right side. For instance, you can see that just below the top there is a long snaky line with numerous little nicks in it, undulating its way to the left and in so doing shedding some of those nicks, so that at the very edge it has degenerated into a perfect square wave, as such a periodic waveform is called in Fourier analysis. Complementing this horizontal structure is a similar vertical structure that is harder to describe. The thought that comes to my mind is that of two ornate, rather rectangular hourglasses with ringed necks, one on top of the other. You can see for yourself.

As with “Fylfot Flipflop”, each of these patterns by itself is intriguing, but of course the real excitement comes from the daring act of superposing them. Incidentally, I know of no piece of visual art that better

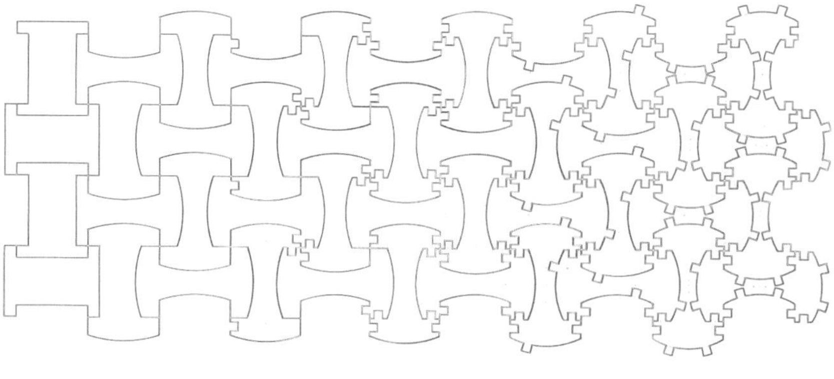

Fig. 7: “Quirky Cogs”, by Arne Larson. Basic Design Studio of William S. Huff, Spring 1963, Carnegie Mellon University (CIT). © HfG-Archiv/Museum Ulm, HfG-Ar, BDSA, Hu P 01. 005.

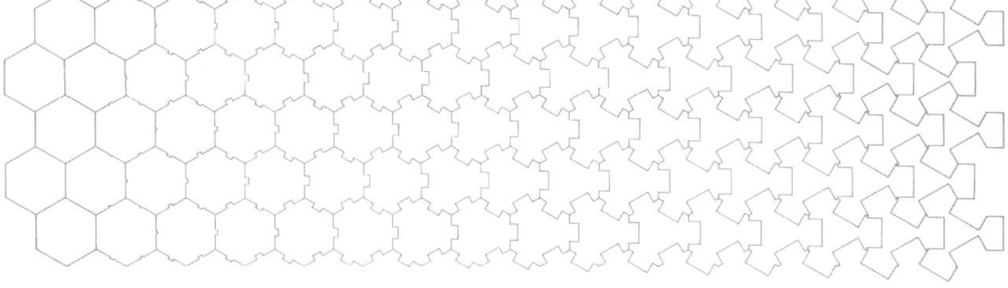

Fig. 8: “Trifoliolate”, by Glenn Paris. Basic Design Studio of William S. Huff, Spring 1966, Carnegie Mellon University (CIT). © HfG-Archiv/Museum Ulm, HfG-Ar, BDSA, Hu P 01. 029.

Fig. 6: “Y Knot”, by Leland Chen. Basic Design Studio of William S. Huff, Spring 1977, SUNY at Buffalo. © HfG-Archiv/Museum Ulm, HfG-Ar, BDSA, Hu P 01. 030. Editorial note: for the right orientation you have to turn the book 90° clockwise.

Fig. 9: “Arabesque” — II, by Joel Napach. Basic Design Studio of William S. Huff, Spring 1979, redone Fall 1980, SUNY at Buffalo. © HfG-Archiv/Museum Ulm, HfG-Ar, BDSA, Hu P 05. 017. Editorial note: for the right orientation you have to turn the book 90° clockwise.

Fig. 10: “Razor Blades”, anonymous. Basic Design Studio of William S. Huff, 1966, Carnegie Mellon University (CIT). © HfG-Archiv/Museum Ulm, HfG-Ar, BDSA, Hu P 08. 019.
Editorial note: for the right orientation you have to turn the book 90° clockwise.

Fig. 11: “Cucaracha”, by Jorge Gutierrez. Basic Design Studio of William S. Huff, May 1977, SUNY at Buffalo. © HfG-Archiv/Museum Ulm, HfG-Ar, BDSA, Hu P 01. 031.
Editorial note: for the right orientation you have to turn the book 90° clockwise.

captures the feeling of beauty and intricacy of a Steve Reich piece, created by slow "adiabatic" changes floating on top of the chaos and dynamism of the lower-level frenzy. Looking back, I see I began by describing this parquet deformation as "calm". Well, what do you know? Perhaps I would be a good candidate for one of *The New Yorker*'s occasional notes titled "Our Forgetful Authors".

More seriously, there is a reason for this inconsistency. One's emotional response to a given work of art, whether the work is visual or musical, is not static and unchanging. There is no way of knowing how you will respond the next time you hear or see one of your favorite pieces. It may leave you unmoved or it may thrill you to the bone. It depends on your mood, on what has recently happened, on what happens to strike you, and on many other subtle intangibles. One's reaction can even change in the course of a few minutes. And so I won't apologize for this seeming lapse.

Let us now look at "Cucaracha", executed by Jorge Gutiérrez at SUNY at Buffalo in 1977. It moves from the utmost geometricity—a lattice of perfect diamonds—through a sequence of gradually more arbitrary modifications until it reaches some kind of near-freedom—a dance of strange, angular, quasi-organic forms. This fascinates me. Is entropy increasing or decreasing in this rightward flow toward freedom?

A gracefully spiky deformation is the one wittily titled "Beecombing Blossoms", executed by Laird Pylkas at SUNY at Buffalo in 1983. Huff told me Pylkas struggled for weeks with it and at the end, when she had resolved her difficulties, she mused: "Why is it that the obvious ideas always take so long to discover?"

As our last study, let us take "Clearing the Thicket", executed by Vincent Marlowe at SUNY at Buffalo in 1979, which mixes straight lines and curves, right angles and cusps, explicit squarish swastikoids and implicit circular holes. Rather than demonstrating my inability to analyze the ferocious complexity of the design, I should like to use it as the jumping-off point for a brief discussion of computers and creativity.

Some totally new things are going on in this particular parquet deformation, things that have not appeared in any previous one. Notice the hollow circles at the left that shrink as you move to the right; notice also that at the right there are hollow "anticircles" (concave shapes made from four circular arcs turned inside out) that shrink as you move to the left. Now, according to Huff, such an idea had not appeared in any previously created deformations. This means that something unusual happened here: something genuinely creative, something unexpected, unpredictable, surprising, intriguing, and, not least, inspiring to future creators.

So the question naturally arises: Would a computer have been able to invent this parquet deformation? Well, put it this way: It is a naïve and ill-posed question, but we can try to make some sense of it. The first thing to remind ourselves of is that the term "computer" refers to nothing more than an inert hunk of metal and semiconductors. To go along with this bare computer, this hardware, we need software and energy. The former is a specific pattern inserted into the hardware, binding it with constraints and yet imbuing it with goals; the latter is what breathes "life" into it, making it act according to those constraints and goals.

The next point is that the software is what really controls what the machine does; the hardware simply obeys the software's dictates, step by step. And yet the software could exist in a number of different "instantiations": realizations in different computer languages. What really counts about the software is not

Fig. 12: "Beecombing Blossoms", by Laird B. Pylkas. Basic Design Studio of William S. Huff, Spring 1983, SUNY at Buffalo. © HfG-Archiv/Museum Ulm, HfG-Ar, BDSA, Hu P 07. 026.

Fig. 13: "Clearing the Thicket", by Vincent Marlowe. Basic Design Studio of William S. Huff, Spring 1979, SUNY at Buffalo. © HfG-Archiv/Museum Ulm, HfG-Ar, BDSA, Hu P 05. 016.

its literal aspect but a more abstract, general, overall "architecture", which is best described in a nonformal language such as English. We might say that the plan, the sketch, the central idea of a program is what we are talking about here, not its final realization in some specific formal language or dialect. That is something we can leave to apprentices to carry out after we have presented them with our informal sketch.

So the question actually becomes less mundane-sounding and more theoretical and philosophical: *Is there an architecture to creativity?* Is there a plan, a scheme, a set of principles that, if it were elucidated clearly, could account for all the creativity embodied in the collection of all parquet deformations, past, present, and future?

Note that we are asking about the collection of parquet deformations, not about some specific work. It is a truism that any specific work of art can be re-created, even re-created in various slightly novel ways, by a programmed computer.

For example, the Dutch artist Piet Mondrian evolved a highly idiosyncratic, somewhat cryptic style of painting over a period of many years. You can see, if you trace his development over time, exactly where he came from and where he was headed. If you focus on a single Mondrian work, however, you cannot sense this stylistic momentum, this quality of dynamic, evolving style that any great artist has. Looking at one work in isolation is like taking a snapshot of something in motion: You capture its instantaneous position but not its momentum. Of course, the snapshot might be blurred somehow, in which case you would get a sense of the momentum but would lose information about the position. When you are looking at just a single work of art, however, there is no mental blurring of its style with that of recent works or soon-to-come works; you have exact position information ("What is the style now?") but no momentum information ("Where was the style and where is it going?").

Some years ago, A. Michael Noll, a mathematician and computer artist, took a single Mondrian painting —an abstract, geometric study with seeminly random elements—and from it extracted some statistics on the patterns. Given these statistics, he programmed a computer to generate numerous pseudo-Mondrian paintings having the same or different values of these randomness-governing parameters. Then he showed the results to viewers who had no foreknowledge of what he was up to. The reactions were interesting: More people preferred one of the pseudo-Mondrians than preferred the genuine Mondrian!

This is quite amusing, even provocative, but it also is a warning. It proves that a computer can certainly be programmed, after the fact, to imitate—and imitate well—mathematically capturable stylistic aspects of a given work. But it also warns us: Beware of cheap imitations!

Consider parquet deformations. Undoubtedly a computer could be programmed to do any specific parquet deformation or minor variations on it without too much trouble. There simply are not that many parameters to any given deformation. But the essence of any artistic act lies not in selecting particular values for certain parameters but far deeper: in the balancing of myriad intangible and mostly unconscious mental forces, a judgmental act that results in many conceptual choices eventually adding up to a tangible, perceptible, measurable work of art.

Once the finished work exists, scholars looking at it may seize on certain of its qualities that lend themselves to being easily parametrized. Anyone can do statistics on a work of art once the work is there to be scrutinized, but the ease of doing so can obscure the fact that no one could have said a priori what kinds of mathematical observables would turn out to be relevant to the capturing of stylistic aspects of the as-yet-unseen work of art.

Huff's own view on this question of mechanizing the art of parquet deformations closely parallels mine. He believes some basic principles could be formulated at the present time that would enable a computer to generate relatively stereotyped yet novel creations of its own. He stresses, however, that his students occasionally come up with rule-breaking ideas that enchant the eye for reasons deeper than any he has been able to verbalize. In this way the set of explicit rules gets gradually enlarged. Comparing the creativity that goes into parquet deformations with the creativity of a great musician, Huff writes:

> I don't know about the consistency of the genius of Bach, but I did work with the great American architect Louis Kahn (1901–1974) and suppose it must have been somewhat the same with Bach. That is, Kahn, out of moral, spiritual and philosophical considerations, formulated ways he would and ways he would not do a thing in architecture. Students came to know many of his ways, and some of the best could imitate him rather well (although not perfectly). But as Kahn himself developed he constantly brought in new principles that brought new transformations to his work, and he even occasionally discarded an old rule. Consequently he was always several steps ahead of his imitators who knew what was but couldn't imagine what will be. And so it is that computer-generated "original" Bach is an interesting exercise. But it isn't Bach—that unwritten work that Bach never got to, the day after he died.

The real question is: What kind of architecture is responsible for all these ideas? Or is there any one architecture that could come up with them all? I would say that the ability to design good parquet deformations is probably deceptive in the same way as the ability to play good chess is: It seems more mathematical than it actually is.

A brilliant chess move, once the game is over and can be viewed in retrospect, can be seen as logical, as "the correct thing to do in that situation". But brilliant moves do not originate from the kind of logical analysis that occurs after the game; there is no time during the game to check out all the logical consequences of a move. Good chess moves spring from the organization of a good chess mind: a set of perceptions arranged in such a way that certain kinds of ideas leap to mind when subtle patterns or cues are present. The way perceptions have of triggering old and buried memories underlies skill in any type of human activity, not only chess. It is just that in chess the skill is particularly deceptive, because after the fact it can all be justified by a logical analysis, a fact that seems to hint the original idea came from logic.

Writing lovely melodies is another one of those deceptive arts. To the mathematically inclined, notes seem like numbers and melodies like number patterns. Therefore all the beauty of a melody seems as if it ought to be describable in some simple mathematical way. So far, however, no formula has produced even a single good melody. Of course, you can look back at any melody and write a formula that will produce it and variations on it. But this is retrospective, not prospective. Lovely chess moves and lovely melodies (and lovely theorems in mathematics) have this in common: Every one has idiosyncratic nuances that seem logical a posteriori but are not easy to anticipate. To the mathematical mind, chess-playing skill and melody-writing skill and theorem-writing skill seem obviously formalizable, but the truth turns out to be more tantalizingly complex than that. Too many subtle balances are involved.

So it is with parquet deformation, I reckon. Each one taken alone is in some sense mathematical. Taken as a class, however, they are not mathematical. This is what is tricky about them. Don't let the apparently mathematical nature of an individual deformation fool you; the architecture of a program that could create all these parquet deformations and more good ones would have to incorporate computerized versions of concepts and judgments, and those are much more elusive and complex than mere numbers.

At this point, many critics of computers and artificial intelligence, eager to find something "computers can't do" (and never will be able to do), often go too far: They jump to the conclusion that art and, more generally, creativity are fundamentally uncomputerizable. This is hardly the implied conclusion! The implied conclusion is that if computers are to be enabled to act human, we shall have to wait until we have good computer models of such human properties as perception, memory, mental categories, learning, and so on. We are a long way from that. There is no reason to assume, however, that those goals are in principle unattainable, even if they remain far off for a long time.

In this article, I have been playing with the double meaning of the term "architecture": It means both the design of a habitat and the abstract essence of a grand structure of any kind. The former has to do with hardware and the latter with software. In a certain sense, William Huff is a professor of both brands of architecture. Obviously his professional training is in the design of "hardware", namely genuine habitats for human beings, and he works in a school where that is what they do. He is also, however, in the business of forming in the minds of his students a softer kind of architecture: the mental architecture that underlies the skill to create beauty. Fortunately for him he can take for granted the complexity of a human brain as the starting point on which to build this architecture. But even so, there is a great art to instilling a sense for beauty and novelty.

When I first met Huff and saw how abstract and seemingly impractical were the marvelous works produced in his design studio—ranging from parquet deformations to strange ways of slicing a cube to gestalt studies using thousands of dots to eye-boggling color patterns—at first I wondered why this man was a professor of architecture. But after I had conversed with him and his colleagues, my horizons were extended about the nature of their discipline.

The architect Louis Kahn had great respect for the work of William S. Huff, and it is with his words that I would like to conclude:

> What Huff teaches is not merely what he has learned from someone else but what is drawn from his natural gifts and belief in their truth and value. In my belief what he teaches is the introduction to discipline underlying shapes and rhythms, which touches the arts of sight, the arts of sound and the arts of structure. It teaches students of drawing to search for the abstract and not the representational. This is good as a reminder of order for the instructors/architectural sketchers (like me), and good especially for the student sketchers without background. It is the introduction to exactitudes of the kind that instill the religion of the ordered path.

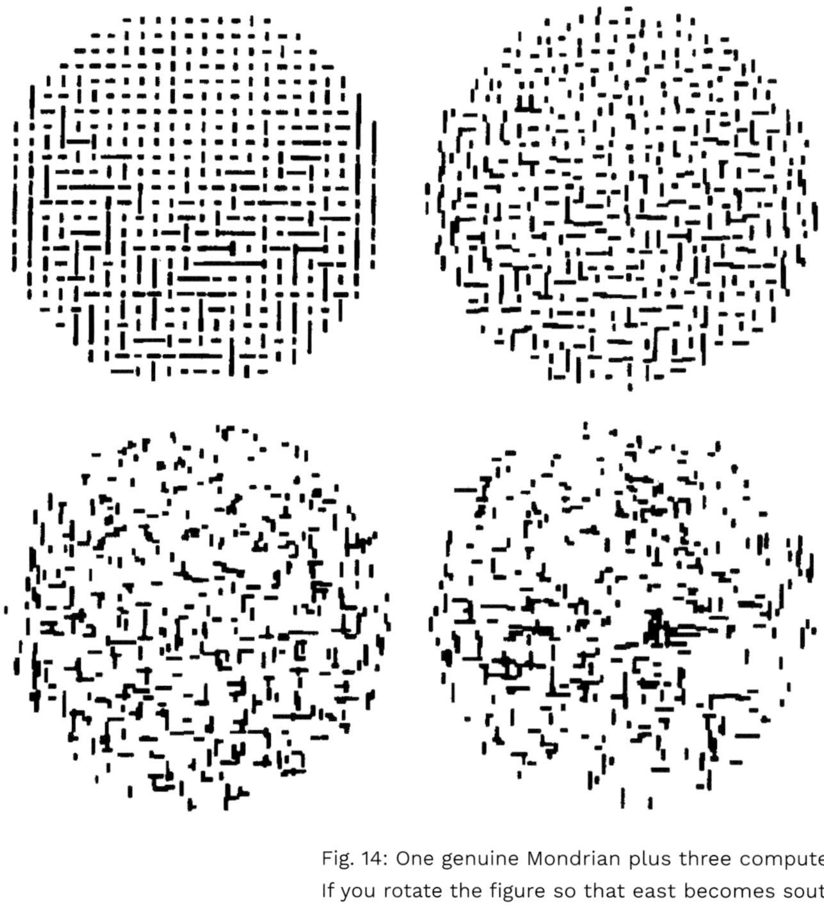

Fig. 14: One genuine Mondrian plus three computer imitations. Can you spot the Mondrian? If you rotate the figure so that east becomes south, it will be the one in the northwest corner. The Mondrian, done in 1917, is titled "Composition with Lines"; the three others, done in 1965, comprise a work called "Computer Composition with Lines", and were created by a computer at Bell Telephone Laboratories at the behest of computer tamer A. Michael Noll. The subjectively "best" picture was found through surveys; it is the one diagonally opposite the genuine Mondrian!

Post Scriptum

"The religion of the ordered path"—a lovely phrase. Though it is ambiguous, it captures the spirit of the dedicated quest after patterned beauty, and particularly after the reasons that certain particular patterns are beautiful.

In this article, I repeatedly claimed that it is relatively easy to make a computer program that creates attractive art within a formula, but not at all easy to make a computer program that constantly comes up with novelty. Some people familiar with the computer art produced in the last couple of decades might pick a fight with me over this. They might point to complex patterns produced by simple algorithms, and then add that there are certain simple algorithms which, when you change merely a few parameters, come up with astonishingly different patterns that no human would be likely to recognize as being each other's near kin. An example is a very simple program I know, which fills a screen with rapidly changing sixfold-symmetric dot patterns that look like magnified snowflakes; in just a few seconds, any given pattern will dissolve and be replaced by an unbelievably different sixfold-symmetric pattern. I have stood transfixed at a screen watching these patterns unfold one after another, unable to anticipate in the slightest what will happen next—and yet knowing that the program itself is only a few lines long! I have seen small changes in mathematical formulas produce enormous visual changes in what those formulas represent graphically.

The trouble is, these parameter-based changes—knob-twiddlings, as I like to call them—are of a different nature than the kinds of novel ideas people come up with when they vary a given idea. For a machine to make simple variants of a given design, it must possess an algorithm for making that design which has explicit parameters; those parameters are then modifiable, as with the pseudo-Mondrian paintings.

But the way people make variations is quite different. They look at some creation by an artist (or computer), and then they abstract from it some quality that they observe in the creation itself (not in some algorithm behind it). This newly abstracted quality may never have been thought of explicitly by the artist (or programmer or computer), yet it is there for the seeing by an acute observer. This perceptual act gets you more than half the way to genuine creativity; the remainder involves treating this new quality *as if it were an explicit knob*: "twiddling" it as if it were a parameter that had all along been in the program that made the creation.

That way, the perceptual process is intimately linked up with the generative process: A loop is closed in which perceptions spark new potentials and experimentation with new potentials opens up the way for new perceptions. The element lacking in current computer art is the ion of perception with generation. Computers do not watch what they do; they simply do it. When programs are able to look at what they've done and perceive it in ways that they never anticipated, then you'll start to get close to the kinds of insight-giving disciplined exercises that Louis Kahn was speaking of when he wrote of the "religion of the ordered path".

One of my favorite parquet deformations is called "I at the Center", by David Oleson at Carnegie Mellon in 1964. This one violates the premise with which I began my article: one-dimensionality. It develops its central theme—the uppercase letter "I"—along two perpendicular dimensions at once. The result is one of the most lyrical and graceful compositions that I have seen in this form.

I am also pleased by the metaphorical quality it has. At the very center of a mesh is an I—an ego; touching it are other things—other I's—very much like the central I, but not quite the same and not quite as simple; then, as one goes further and further out, the variety of I's multiplies. To me this symbolizes a web of human interconnections. Each of us is at the very center of our own personal web, and each one of us thinks: "I am the most normal, sensible, comprehensible individual." And our identity—our "shape" in personality space—springs largely from the way we are embedded in that network—which is to say, from the identities (shapes) of the people we are closest to. This means that we help to define others' identities even as they help to define our own. And very simply but effectively, this parquet deformation conveys all that, and more, to me.

Fig. 15: “I at the Center”, by David Oleson. Note by Huff: “Original.” Basic Design Studio of William S. Huff, Spring 1964, Carnegie Mellon University (CIT). © HfG-Archiv/Museum Ulm, HfG-Ar, BDSA, Hu P 06. 011.

Biography of the Author

Douglas Hofstadter has taught for four decades at Indiana University in Bloomington, where he holds the title of Distinguished Professor in the College of Arts and Sciences. His undergraduate degree (Stanford, 1965) was in mathematics, and his doctorate (Oregon, 1975) in theoretical physics. At IU, he teaches cognitive science and comparative literature. Hofstadter is best known for his books on minds, thinking, and consciousness. They include *Gödel, Escher, Bach: an Eternal Golden Braid* (1980 Pulitzer Prize for General Nonfiction); *The Mind's I* (coauthored in 1981 with philosopher Daniel Dennett); *Fluid Concepts and Creative Analogies* (written in 1995 with members of his cognitive-science research group); *I Am a Strange Loop* (a personal view of the human condition, published in 2007); and *Surfaces and Essences: Analogy as the Fuel and Fire of Thinking* (coauthored in 2013 with French cognitive psychologist Emmanuel Sander). In 1981–1983 he wrote the monthly column "Metamagical Themas" for *Scientific American*, and his collected columns were published as a book with that title in 1985. Starting in his early teens, Hofstadter plunged into the study of languages other than English, and this led to a long-term interest in literary translation. He has translated books and poems from many languages into English, including, in 1999, a verse translation of Alexander Pushkin's novel-in-verse *Eugene Onegin*, and he has written two books about translation: *Le Ton beau de Marot: In Praise of the Music of Language* (published in 1997), and *Translator, Trader,* 2009. Currently he is working on a memoir titled *My Wild Grace Chase*.

Past and Future of William S. Huff's Parquet Deformations

Werner Van Hoeydonck

Fig. 1: "Circlewaves", 2016, design by Luisa Paumann and Werner Van Hoeydonck.

William S. Huff, American architect and inventor of parquet deformations, offered the following comment on our design, "Circlewaves":

> NNNNOOOOOOOOOOOO, this is not a parquet deformation. Can we call it a "parquet deformation interrupted by deforming circles"? You can design anything you want. Just don't call it a parquet deformation. A parquet is a repeating figure that fills space. A parquet deformation takes these repeating (space-filling) figures and slowly deforms them, according to a limited set of rules. Your design has introduced into one set of repeating, but deforming figures, a new figure, a circle—that itself is repeating but deforming (though deforming, in this case, only in size, but not shape). Incidentally, the beginning of your design is NOT even a "parquet deformation" either, because you have two different sets of pieces: a set of right-handed pieces and a set of left-handed pieces. And, incidentally, the end of your design has three different pieces, because the original piece becomes two different pieces at the end. William[1]

Craig Kaplan, the computer scientist from Canada who has studied parquet deformations and Escher's "Metamorphoses" for over 20 years, had already warned me about Huff's "strict" rules:

> Your "Circlewave" design is lovely. For the record, Huff would not consider it a genuine parquet deformation. Look at what Hofstadter labels "Rule 2": At each stage, the pattern must constitute a regular tessellation of the plane. I think we're meant to interpret that as saying that the pattern must be decomposed into copies of a single shape, whereas you have two different shapes—a distorted "I" and a circle. On the other hand, I have never adhered too strictly to those rules myself. I think there's a wide range of aesthetic opportunities in patterns that evolve in space, and see no need to limit myself if a new opportunity arises. So, I encourage you to continue with your experiments.[2]

My fascination with parquet deformations started in 2016. While I was showing my geometrical patterns at an international fair for visual communication, Farhad Kay, an entrepreneur from Berlin, told me about his carpentry company, Ligas, and his plans. He had ordered a five-axis CNC milling machine to produce wall and ceiling panels with patterns. These would not be just any patterns, however; he wanted to produce patterns that do not repeat. This was an interesting challenge that made me search the internet using keywords such as "transforming patterns" and "metamorphoses". Previously, I had been designing classical, symmetrical, repeating geometrical patterns. Within a short period of time I came across David Bailey's website, which is focused on Escher patterns, but has an interesting section about parquet deformations and an extensive bibliography, as well as references.[3]

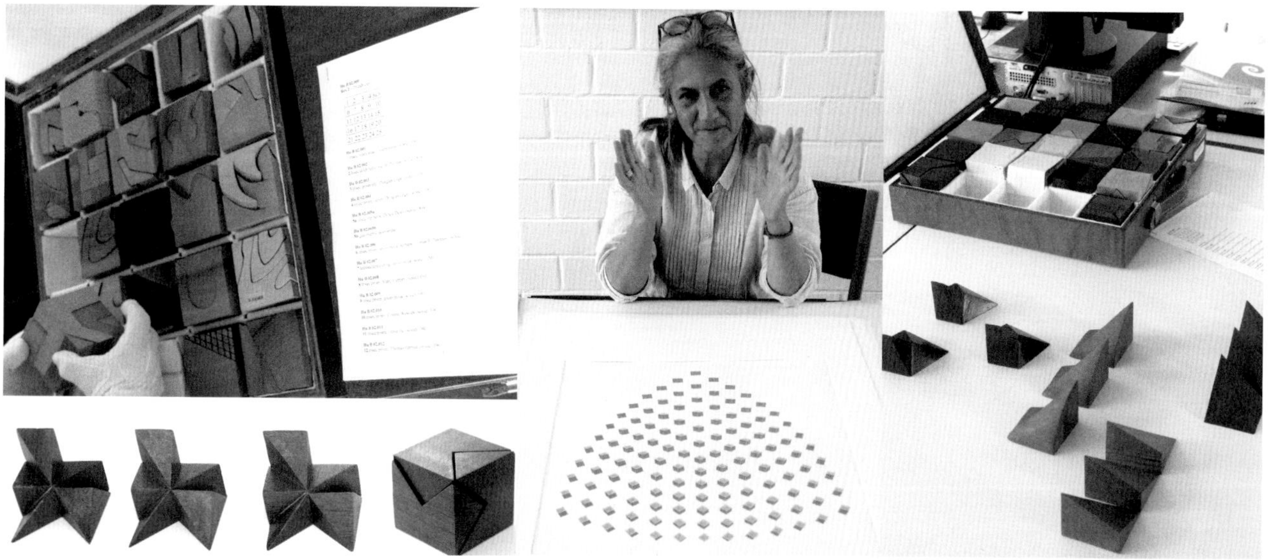

Fig. 2: Marcela Quijano, curator at the HfG archive in Ulm, August 2017; in front of her, "Axonometry Cubed" by Thomas Breen. SUNY at Buffalo. Top left and right: the boxes with the trisections of the cube. Bottom left: three congruent pieces of a cube's trisection. Photos: Werner Van Hoeydonck.

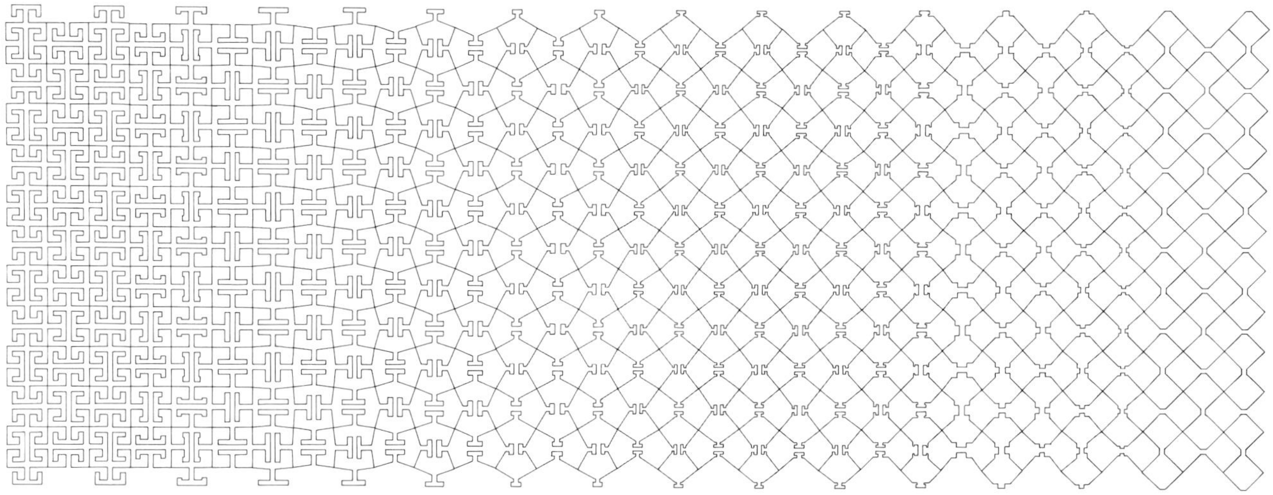

Fig. 3: Maurizio Sabini, Venetian Net, 19 × 27.88 in, India ink. Basic Design Studio of William S. Huff, Spring 1982, State University of New York at Buffalo (SUNY). © HfG-Archiv/Museum Ulm, HfG-Ar, BDSA, Hu P 01. 033.

Trip to Ulm

The Ulm archive, as I soon learned, was the key archive to visit. William S. Huff arrived at the Ulm School of Design in October 1956 on a Fulbright scholarship and completed basic teaching under Tomás Maldonado. Beginning in 1960, he developed a basic design course at the Carnegie Institute of Technology in Pittsburgh, based on Tomás Maldonado's teaching model. He developed basic design courses at numerous universities, including the HfG, to which he returned repeatedly as a guest lecturer from 1963 to 1968. Huff donated the best results of his student's works to the HfG archive and thus made them available for research.[4]

Marcela Quijano, who in 2017 was still curator at the HfG archive and was responsible for the Huff donation, showed me the collection of drawings and models made by Huff's students between 1961 and 1998. The collection contains the best results from all his student assignments, resulting in nine portfolios (each of which includes approximately 50 drawings) and 20 wooden boxes containing models of different sizes and materials.[5] Boxes 1 and 2 contain the "trisections of the cube". As I discovered later, the "trisections of the cube" were Huff's attempt to experiment with parquet deformations in three dimensions.[6]

The portfolios consist of large sheets of archival, best-quality drawing paper or fine-line illustration cardboard with semitransparent sheets between them to protect them. The precise, intricate final drawings are traced with ruler, pen, and Indian ink or composed of black and white only, some of them with only shades of water-colored gray tones. Many works are brightly colored with acrylics, inks, airbrush, or watercolors. Sometimes, one can see the underlying grids in sharp pencil. The parquet deformations are rather impressive in size; some are even up to 100 cm in length. They are composed of short line segments, and no sequence in at least one direction is the same, which implies that total concentration was required to draw them. Regarding the graphical work, Huff preferred the classical ink pen, as, in his opinion, no fineliner, rapidograph, or other kind of technical pen could start and end a line in the same sharp way or compete with it in precision.[7] Maurizio Sabini, a former student of Huff's, shared with me the following anecdote regarding Huff's method of encouraging his students to reach such levels of perfection: "Huff sat down at the drafting board, the students all around him, adjusted the ruler, took the pen, filled it carefully with ink, adjusted the line thickness. Then he drew a long line from the left to the middle, abruptly stopped the line, then a second line from the right to the middle and stood up; the connection in the middle was perfect. We were baffled ..."[8]

Certainly, drawing by hand in a precise way was necessary for all architects in pre-computer times. In hand drawing, there are different levels of perfection; if the first draft in pencil is executed well, one can fully concentrate on the final draft in ink. Regardless, the level of perfection achieved by Huff's students is amazing and impressive. Although these drawings are not so "perfect" as those that can be plotted now, the personal touch—the small "errors"—make one aware that these are hand drawings in which every single line had to be drawn. No "copy and paste" perfectionism was possible here. William Huff must have "drilled" his students to get this right, as one can see in the Ulm portfolios. It is likely that not all students were able to achieve Huff's high standards, and, obviously, only the results judged to be the best were archived by Huff. Many of these student works are worthy of being displayed permanently in a museum. The Museum of Modern Art in New York acquired 45 works by Huff's students in the early 1970s; unfortunately, they seem to have been lost. While this is unusual for such a prestigious institution, apparently the MOMA is no longer able to locate them.[9] One hopes that these works will resurface at some point. Fortunately, these missing works, which include three parquet deformations, are well documented in the HfG archive. For the present book, Dr. Martin Mäntele, the current director of the Ulm archive, sent me all nine of the portfolios digitally. Seen in its totality, this collection is a treasure trove—for future research and publications as well. Each drawing is documented by two high-resolution images. The front shows the actual student work, along with a 10-centimeter scale; on the back, the lower right corner presents Huff's meticulous documentation of the work.

To get a sense of the atmosphere and knowledge offered to the students of the Ulm School of Design, I visited the school—which was designed by Max Bill—and studied the library. Among books related to all fields of design, art, and architecture, a broad range of sciences are present, along with seminal works of the time, which is typical of the school's interdisciplinary approach to design. The books on patterns, symmetry, topology, and geometry by the specialists in the field at that time are important to understanding the roots of Huff's parquet deformation assignment and his lifelong study of symmetry in all its varieties.[10]

A Search for Sources

William Huff, having studied architecture at Yale and specialized in basic design at Ulm, was well equipped with practical and theoretical knowledge from famous scholars, architects, and artists. His students recall that he could talk for hours about art, but he also liked to use images and poetic metaphors to instruct and inspire the students. This was certainly also the case for the parquet deformation assignment. Although this assignment spanned 40 years, documentation of his more elaborate writings on parquet deformations is rather rare, and most of these sources were written toward the end of his teaching career. I will now present and discuss all the relevant sources and quote Huff extensively to allow the reader to hear his voice.

In 2017, when we assigned our students parquets and parquet deformations, we had only one written source by Huff: a document called "Best Problems", dated 1979, in which Huff defines the assignment in a very concise way.[11] Divided into three parts—the task, the principle, and the pedagogic goal—the A4 document offers some clues and keywords regarding the way that Huff wanted students to be introduced to this assignment. The task is "to fashion a continuous series of parquet events into a temporal composition of flowing (rather than static) rhythms; to execute the design with ruling pen and ink." The analogy to music in the chosen terminology—"temporal composition of flowing rhythms"—is not a coincidence:

> When I was young, my mother made me take piano lessons. I wanted to make sculpture out of soap and to make colored things. This experience made me hate music—any music at all. It took me a long time to appreciate it, but it still was something that I did not understand. Working with these parquet deformations had me learning (or thinking that I was learning) more about the composition of music that I had ever dreamed that I could do.[12]

In the principle, Huff defines a "pure" parquet as an endless configuration of congruent (same) pieces (tiles) that pack the plane without overlapping or leaving holes. The underlying structure of a parquet is a lattice. Huff refers here to the five planar lattices, named for the famous French physicist and crystallographer August Bravais. He also points out that three of these lattices—the oblique (parallelogram, rhombic) lattice and the two rectangular lattices—have certain limitations concerning subdivision into equal parts and are limited in their rotational possibilities: A parallelogram allows only a twofold rotational subdivision. An examination of the approximately 100 parquet deformations archived in Ulm leads one to conclude that Huff preferred the square and the special rhombic lattice (60°, 120°), allowing both equilateral triangular and regular hexagonal tessellations. In his 2003 lecture to the Sociedad de Estudios Morfológicos de Argentina (SEMA), Huff explains that the five planar lattices are related to the three regular grids (triangular, square, hexagonal) but should not be confused with a grid, since a grid defines the lines, while a lattice is a set of points:

> In the case of the parquet deformations, the grid becomes the lattice; and, therefore, by definition, it is invariant. Thus, the deformations take place on the contours of the tile that are nailed to two lattice points (or to one rotor), between which they can be elaborated to extreme lengths, kinks, or turns or in multi-fold contours that are anchored on centers or axes of rotation.[13]

Huff does not offer any strategies or methods in "Best Problems"; he merely states that variant shapes of any one lattice system can be subtly deformed to another lattice system and that these continuous deformations can be deformed along “syngenometric” lines. Syngenometry is a type of lower symmetry, to put it simply, in which there is similarity in form but also gradual change. These different levels and types of symmetry were an important research topic throughout Huff’s career.[14]

If one follows the defining syngenometric lines on the border of a parquet deformation step by step and from tile to tile—if it is not framed—one will better understand the different “parquet events”. In other words, one understands how the lines deform and at which speed (tempo), which connects to the topic of temporality.

In “The Landscape Handscroll and the Parquet Deformation”, written for an important intercultural and interdisciplinary conference in Japan[15], Huff explains his fascination with the factor of time in art:

> The different arts are frequently classified as either spatial or temporal. The spatial arts (painting, sculpture, architecture) occupy two-dimensional or three-dimensional real space. The temporal arts (music, dance, poetry, theater) occupy the dimensional space of the instantaneous present, continuously advancing through a dimension that unfurls in time—regularly regarded as “the fourth dimension of the space-time continuum”. This classification is, to be sure, an oversimplification; for there is, of necessity, temporality in all spatial art and spatiality in all temporal art. A two-dimensional easel-painting or wall-hanging reveals its full composition at once; yet it is not fully comprehended in a glance. The eye flits, involuntarily, over the plane—from detail to detail, from figure to ground, from homogeneity to heterogeneity—in a never ending, randomized sequence that is experienced through time. Absolute comprehension is, perhaps, never attained; but the aggregate of the viewer’s fitful perceptual impulses contributes to an ever fuller comprehension. The third dimension of sculpture extends the viewer’s interaction with this art form. The many aspects of a piece of sculpture are experienced only by the viewer’s moving around it. Mobiles, of course, themselves move, while the viewer remains stationary. Architecture is experienced not only by the viewer’s moving around it, but through it. The moving viewer (or moving mobile) and the viewer’s moving eye involve an ingredient of time.[16]

Huff found in the Sino-Japanese handscroll an art form that must be experienced in a different way, section by section, to fully grasp what is happening; this is a temporal visual composition. A parquet deformation—in Huff’s analogy to the oriental scroll—is not intended to be viewed spatially, but temporally, as a sort of visual music. Viewing them is akin to the manner in which film is seen, poetry read, and music heard:

> Music, linearly regulated in respect to time, does have spatial elements (notes and chords). Even as entities with evident periods, these spatial elements, separated by intervals of time, occupy no more than the zero-dimensional moment of the present. The handscroll does have a real, two-dimensional presence; one of its planar dimensions is, however, so extremely elongated that it induces the palpable temporal component that explicitly channels one’s experiencing of it. The young medium of film constructed from a flow of captured spatial moments (discrete photographs), whose transience tricks the mind into perceiving continuous movement—may be broadly viewed as illustrative of the special nature of temporal visual arts. In a manner arguably comparable to film, the handscroll is unrolled and rerolled, frame by frame—though at the full discretion of a solitary viewer. I bolster this contention with the statement of an expert on Chinese art, Wen C. Fong: Working in the handscroll format, which unfolds one section at a time from right to left, the painter employs serial images, his focus moving in cinematic fashion in the development of his narrative.[17]

Seeking comparable examples of temporal plastic compositions in Western art, Huff suggests some examples: the Parthenon’s frieze, the Column of Trajan, the Bayeux tapestry, Mantegna’s Camera picta, Monet’s *Water Lilies* series, and Jackson Pollock’s paintings. Since both Western and Eastern art have made art in which temporality plays an important role, Huff concludes “that the early landscape handscrolls have an aesthetic structure—within the specific culture and age—that accords to the individual artist’s own sense of drama and that any canons, West or East, are destined to be contested and even renounced by succeeding generations, if that art form is to remain vital.”[18] Furthermore, Huff found the same aesthetic modalities in Eastern and Western Art and quotes art historian Nelson Wu:

> The student will quickly recognize that all pictorial expressions have the same building blocks: line, area, color, space, movement, and all the other privileges and limitations that are, part and parcel, the birthright of a two-dimensional art. These components in their analyzed form, simple and pure, are universalities, behaving like musical tones, favoring no particular culture or tradition and belonging to all.[19]

The same universalities are to be found in Huff’s parquet deformation assignment. The lattices, the grids, the lines, and the possible symmetric operations are universal, but the organization depends “on the dynamics of the student's chosen motifs—and the magic that can be extracted [...] many parquet deformations follow the general classical structure of beginning with simplicity and building to complexity. Yet some begin with complexity and build down. Some have extensive lulls at their centers. Some have their points of departure at their centers. Some have multiple climaxes."[20]

The pedagogic goal of the parquet deformation, as stated in Huff's 1979 "Best Problems", was to "have the student become totally familiar not only with the families of congruent figures (tiles, parquets) that fill a plane and their topological relationships, but with the fundamental principle of continuous deformations (after Dürer and D'Arcy Thompson) and to have him design an aesthetically coherent composition that is essentially temporal in contrast to the spatial compositions more familiar of the history of our western visual culture."[21]

Temporality is achieved through subtlety. Subtle, geometrically interrelated shape changes are achieved through continuous deformation of one spatially evolving geometrical basic idea, respecting the topological relationships in a certain chosen structural field (lattices and grids). In "An Argument for Basic Design", written in 1965—while Huff was already teaching at the Ulm School of Design—he writes: "By structure I strictly mean: the relationship or arrangement of parts or elements. To design, then, is first of all, to structure; and for me the study of structure (in the abstract) is the equal of that which has been known as basic design or foundation studies."[22]

Huff also points out that structure is the one term that still has value, "whereas terms like unity, harmony and proportion, rhythm, scale, composition, form, even truth and virtue are words that once held great meaning, evoking an air of cultured sensibility, are not so easily used anymore. Lacking firmness if such 'eternal' terms are used, their meanings have also lost their usefulness for contemporary design problems, or at least are inadequate to describe them."[23]

The parquet deformation assignment, though, was not a real-world design assignment, but an abstract exercise to improve the students' aesthetic acuities and to familiarize them with the topological relationships among parquets, with the transformational possibilities of their symmetries and restrictions of their defining structures. Huff considered two distinct areas in the study of structure—the physical and the perceptual:

> The physical refers to how a structure, as far as we can humanly determine, actually is (from the microcosmic atom to the macrocosmic universe). In the physical manipulation of structure, we are interested in those things that are invariant and those that are variant, with the study of deformations and transformations constituting perhaps the most crucial underlying motif. The perceptual refers to the normal behavior patterns of our sensory receptors, i.e. our everyday touching of the world and the meanings we construct out of these encounters. Analogous to the variant and invariant factors of the physical situation, those things that possess identities (or grouping properties) and those that create contrasts are the basic concerns of perceptual phenomena.[24]

Identity versus contrast, symmetry versus asymmetry, order versus disorder—such general terms were not subtle enough for Huff to describe all possible levels of symmetry in structures. A more precise vocabulary was needed for the subtler levels of symmetrical structure. In his paper "Ordering Disorder after K. L. Wolf", Huff urges the universal adoption of the classification of these subtler symmetries and, in fact, the whole range of structure, as formulated by the German chemist K. L. Wolf (1901–1969), an authority on molecular structure:

> In many of these recently organized interdisciplinary associations, the memberships have moved from a focus on rigid regularities—passionate preoccupations with crystals and their models, the regular and semi-regular polyhedral—to lesser regularities. However, I have noticed that, while many scientists and artists do now speak in shared terms about highly regular symmetries, neither employs a comprehensive, much less unambiguous, terminology about entities that seem to be less than symmetrical. We use and hear such words as "disorder", "broken symmetry", "irregularity", "randomness", and even "chaos". Many things that are called "broken symmetry" and the like are, in fact, not. Rather they are often lesser symmetries—that is, orders or degrees (in other words, different levels) of symmetry that are lower than isometry.[25]

Huff completed Wolf's classification—which deals with a logical sequence of degrees of regulation—with two extra levels: autometry and hypometry. The adapted list (see also Cornelie Leopold's chapter) starts with autometry (maximum symmetry) and moves to isometry, homoeometry, syngenometry, katametry, hypometry, heterometry, and finally katametry (the lowest level of symmetry). Every level is defined by invariants and variants in relation to position, size, angle, shape, certainty, and rule. The parquet deformation assignment was viewed by Huff as a project related to the symmetric level of syngenometry, one that was developed along syngenometric lines.[26] These lines outline the basic geometrical idea, as can be seen in Figure 4.

Huff frequently quotes Louis Kahn in his paper "Ordering Disorder after K. L. Wolf", in another context, but Kahn's words can also be interpreted, in my opinion, to explain syngenometry:

Fig. 4: Paul Randazzese, "Brocade". Basic Design Studio of William S. Huff, Spring 1989, State University of New York at Buffalo (SUNY). © HfG-Archiv/Museum Ulm, HfG-Ar, BDSA, Hu P 05. 023. Note the syngenometric lines.

> Order is equivalent to natural law. Not only is the consummately symmetrical crystal an integral part of Order, but the cataclysmically exploding star is no less so. Kahn refers to Order as “the possibility to be”, vis-à-vis his word Desire, “the will to be”: From the macro- to the microcosmic scale, the dual components of Order and Desire—when, and only when, concordant—beget Existence.[27]

Order, the possibility to be, can be considered the invariant grid, whereas Desire, the will to be, stands for the line in its desire to shift its shape, to become a different—yet still recognizably similar—line. A successful parquet deformation then comes into existence; when the invariant grid guides a syngenometric line which gradually takes over control, the grid is always there but loses its dominance and can, in fact, disappear.

To describe aesthetic coherence in a general sense, Huff refers to the Renaissance architect Alberti in his paper “On Regulation and Hidden Harmony”, offering a perfect quote to describe a balanced parquet deformation:

> Compartition will be seemly when it is neither jumpy, nor confused, nor disorganized, nor disconnected, nor composed of incongruous elements; it should be made up of members neither too numerous, nor too small, nor too large, nor too dissonant or ungraceful, nor too disjointed or distant from the rest of the body. Alberti leaves it to aesthetic judgment to sort this out.[28]

Huff was a subtle man, yet harmony alone was not subtle enough. He assigned his students to explore the lowest level of symmetry, katametry, in his *programmed design* assignments, in which harmony does not fully disappear, but becomes indiscernible. Huff uses another quote from Kahn, an analogy to music, as a tool to eliminate perfect harmony and support the acceptance of dissonance: “When a dish fell in Mozart’s kitchen, it broke—made a terrible noise. The maid screeched ...; but Mozart said, ‘Ah, dissonance!’ And dissonance belonged immediately to music.”[29]

> Dissonances can jolt us from a too gentle lull that harmony might produce. But how much dissonance can be tolerated? Richard Strauss’s tone poems (to my taste) strike a stimulatory balance. On the other hand, Bach and Händel, masters of harmony, make glorious art with structural intricacy. Works of some moderns become tedious (to me) because of too much dissonance or too much intricacy. Tedium can be created by bewilderment; one’s temper can dismiss

sensory onslaughts. Alberti's instruction, anticipatory of Gestalt, did not say "no discord", but "not too much discord". Thus, dissonance enters, and we exercise our aesthetic judgment—as we do regarding any piece of art; for harmony in itself does not a work of art make. Gestalt does not formulate aesthetic judgment; it does expedite the articulation of situations (of mind and of utterance) on which aesthetic judgment is based. Gestalt appreciates harmony; Gestalt appreciates dissonance.[30]

The parquet deformations that were selected by Huff and conserved in Ulm are all aesthetically coherent designs, according to Huff's subtle sense for aesthetics. Huff obviously liked Hofstadter's description of his way of teaching as "a kind of performance", since he used a quote by Hofstadter on his work in the "Handscroll Paper" in 1996:

> "Huff himself has never executed a single parquet deformation. He has elicited hundreds of them, however, from his students, and in so doing he has brought this form of art to a high degree of refinement. He might be likened to the conductor of a fine orchestra. Although the conductor makes no sound in the course of a performance, we give much credit to the person doing the job for the quality of the sound. We can only guess at how much preparation and coaching went into the performance. And what about the selection of the pieces and tempos and styles—not to mention the many-year process of culling the performances themselves?"[31]

In the same "Handscroll" paper, Huff reveals how he became acquainted with parquets, discusses the underlying issues and mathematical backgrounds in full detail, and explains the main methods used to design a parquet deformation. Since his paper is highly instructive, accurate, and unique, I will quote Huff extensively without interruption:

> Among the variety of teaching assignments developed in my design studio, the parquet deformation offers, as I have suggested, an uncommon experience in the realm of aesthetics—the challenge to deal with a visual art that derives its essential vigor from the factor of time, but that is fitted, nonetheless, with a full complement of planar tangibles. Underlying the students' task are rigorous two-dimensional mathematical determinants that involve particulars of symmetry and topology and that must be obeyed in devising operable design strategies. In the mid-1950s, the topic of the parquet pattern was introduced by Tomás Maldonado into the design curriculum of the Foundation Course at Germany's Hochschule für Gestaltung. Finding little guidance in a search of contemporaneous texts for an English equivalent, I anglicized the term *Parkettierung*, which appeared in German texts. If Martin Gardner's column, "Mathematical Games" for Scientific American, is a reliable indicator of the evolution of the nomenclature of this inglenook of geometry, it was not until the mid-1970s that the words tile and tiling took dominance over other expressions. Regular tessellation was the preferred term of the 1960s; and articles of the time routinely cited "floor and wall tiles" as

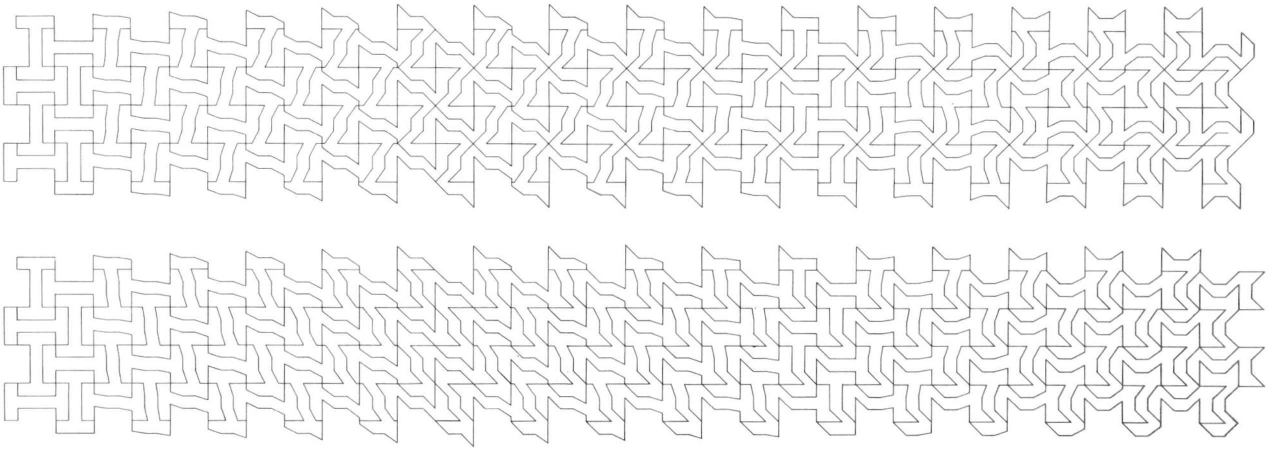

Fig. 5: Moritz Kreitz, "One-handed Two-handed Dual". Basic Design Studio of William S. Huff, May 1966, Carnegie Mellon University. © HfG-Archiv/Museum Ulm, HfG-Ar, BDSA, Hu P 01. 024. The version below is one of the few examples with A and A' tiles, also called enantiomorphic tiles (tiles of both-handedness).

merely some among a number of examples of this sort of planar configuration. A parquet pattern (or monohedral tiling—Grünbaum) is defined as a space-filling array of congruent pieces—precluding, on that account, any gaps between pieces or any overlapping of them. A puristic approach is to admit only pieces that are superposable. Congruence does not, however, stipulate handedness; and there are, indeed, patterns whose pieces conform to the three strictures of congruence, no gaps, and no overlaps—but are also enantiomorphic (or nonsuperposably left- and right-handed). Might these be called improper parquet patterns or tilings?[32]
The age-old one-by-two brick can be arranged relatively randomly (i.e., nonperiodically) to cover the plane. Other parquet pieces can fill the plane in various irregular or semiregular ways. The remarkable "rep-tiles" build into expanding replicas of themselves, and some pieces can be set into circular or spiral arrangements. However, the parquet patterns most encountered, owing to their frequent application throughout the history of ornament, are periodic; and periodic patterns come under the regime of the 17 wallpaper groups, which, in turn, submit to the five planar Bravais lattices. It is well-known that there are only three regular parquet patterns: regular arrays of equilateral triangles, of squares, and of regular hexagons. It is not as well-known that there is an infinity of other-shaped pieces that can fill the plane monohedrally. The shapes of such pieces and their periodic arrangements conform to the same geometric constraints that govern crystals; and understanding those constraints expedites the designing of odd and intricate pieces, which, precisely, determine a pattern's reticular interplay. Two general mechanisms prevail: (1) the deformation of the pieces' boundaries between lattice points, involving an equal give-and-take of areas that have been dislocated by those altered boundaries; (2) the subdivision of pieces into yet smaller congruent pieces by the corresponding multiple (according to 2-, 3-, 4-, or 6-fold rotational symmetry) of alike, but otherwise capriciously shaped contours, anchored only at the original pieces' axes of rotation. By virtue of their repetitive, even spread over the plane, the periodic parquet patterns are of a sort that most readily accommodates continuous deformation, the incremental molding of one piece into a differently shaped piece; and the two stipulated design mechanisms that play a crucial part in the fashioning of novel parquet pieces are the selfsame mechanisms that facilitate the fashioning of a parquet deformation. It is worth noticing that the wallpaper group of the pattern can change as a deformation is evolved. For example, square pieces with fourfold rotors and four mirror axes can be continuously deformed into pieces with only twofold rotors and two mirror axes (e.g., double headed axes) and deformed again into pieces with only twofold rotors (e.g., S- or Z-shapes).[33]

Huff concludes his paper by referring to Thompson and makes interesting comparisons with the artist M. C. Escher:

The intriguing possibility of the incremental deformability of one parquet pattern into another came to our attention

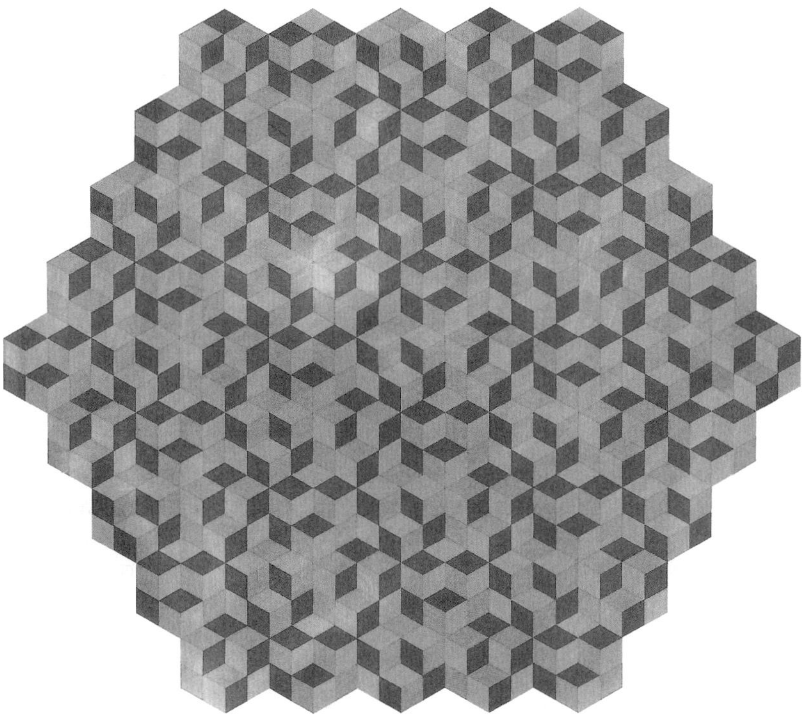

Fig. 6: *Parkettierungsaufgabe 1956/57*, Hochschule für Gestaltung Ulm; taught by Tomás Maldonado, student: William S. Huff. Three colors proceed successively toward neutralization: a secondary of the first order (orange); a tertiary of the first order (yellow–gray); a tertiary of the second order (green–gray). To see this work in color: *Ulmer Modelle–Modelle nach Ulm*, Ostfildern-Ruit, Hatje Cantz, 2003, p. 179.

in 1960 when it was recognized in one student's designs of several very different looking patterns that there were underlying, but far from obvious morphological relationships between them. The instigation of our first continuous deformation between such patterns was buttressed by a writing of a morphologist and two designs of a driven graphic illustrator: D'Arcy Wentworth Thompson's seminal chapter "On the Theory of Transformations, or the Comparison of Related Forms" in *On Growth and Form*; M. C. Escher's two beguiling woodcuts "Day and Night" and "Metamorphosis". In the latter, Escher, taking an artist's license with geometry, cunningly shifted his lengthy ribbon of a design from a square grid to a regular hexagonal grid and back—two times in violation, of course, of the principle of the invariance of the Bravais lattice type, once one has been established in a design with periodicity. Resemblances between Escher's designs and the parquet deformations oblige that attention be given to their substantial dissimilarities. Both Escher's and our bodies of work, involving periodic patterns, conform, of course, to the same geometry. Our design studio deals all but exclusively with superposable pieces (A pieces only)—though occasionally with enantiomorphic ones (A and A' pieces). Patterns of both sorts are found in Escher's designs. On the other hand, Escher is quite apt to employ two different interlocking pieces (A and B pieces—fishes and birds). These designs are clever, but not as difficult to achieve as might be assumed: the two different pieces, taken together, merge into one proper parquet piece; the dividing contours between the two sub pieces are under no mathematical constraints and are, therefore, completely pliant to the command of the artist. In this way, designs that have the geometry of the simpler wallpaper groups can appear to be far more complex than they actually are. While an Escher design and a parquet deformation both exploit the trickery of interlocking congruent pieces, a significant difference between the two concoctions is evident in the aesthetics of their pieces' respective modes of rendition. The lure of Escher's designs lies within the contours of his pieces—that is, how they are graphically treated, be that as fishes, birds, lizards, or horsemen. Erase the rendered surfaces of his pieces—the leftover contours emerge insipid. Corollarily, Escher's figurative imaging of his pieces inhibits the entrancing potential of unconstrained contours to create their own rhythmic sensations. In the case of our deformations, the contours are the object; they make the music. Fill between these contours with colors, textures, or figurative subjects—the music crashes.

Pure Parquets, Indian Baskets, and Mathematical Pastimes

Tomás Maldonado's *Parkettierungsaufgabe* in the basic design course of 1956 in Ulm fascinated Huff as a student. Huff mentions that he was probably the only one in his class who actually executed this assignment.[34]

In 1960, when William Huff started teaching basic design at Carnegie Mellon University, he assigned his students the task of developing three variations (see Figure 7) of a pure parquet. The pure parquet studies were important to Huff. They were archived just as carefully and in the same way as the parquet deformations and are the forerunners that ultimately led to them. That is why he included dozens of them in his gift to the HfG-archive in Ulm:

> When I set up a basic design curriculum for the Carnegie Institute of Technology, first implemented in 1960, parquetry or tiling was among my curriculum's various topics. Before I assigned this topic to my class, however, I made a study of how a variety of different parquet shapes could be fashioned. In fact, my resolve to continue an

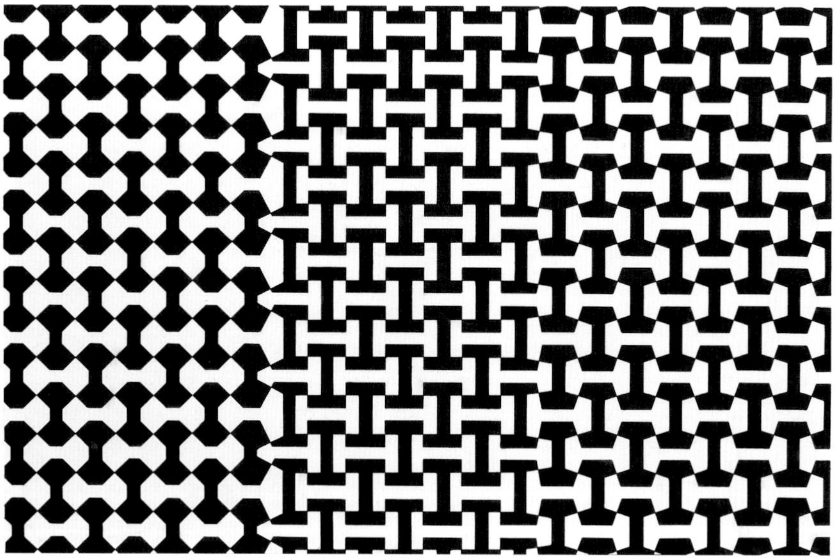

Fig. 7: "Parquetry Study in Three Variants" by James D. Richardson, Spring 1961, Carnegie Mellon University. © HfG-Archiv/Museum Ulm, HfG-Ar, BDSA, Hu P 09. 030. Note the borders between the parquets: The connection is already in the spirit of a parquet deformation.

Fig. 8: Museum of Indian Baskets, designed by William S. Huff (1966–1972). Collage by Werner Van Hoeydonck. Ground floor plan by William S. Huff; front view photo by Harvey Kaplan; interior photos by Clyde Hare. Source: Maurice L. Zigmond, Gotlieb Adam Steiner and the G. A. Steiner Museum, Journal of California and Great Basin Anthropology, 1979, Vol. 1, No. 2, pp. 322–330. Courtesy of Malki Museum. Top right, upper basket: "Beacon Lights" by Datsolalee, 1904–1905. The basket collection now resides in the New York State Historical Association's collections at Fenimore Art Museum in Cooperstown, New York. The private museum building was demolished.

> exploration of parquetry had been stimulated/solidified by a fascinating small book, which I had picked up for pennies in Philadelphia a year or two earlier, Major MacMahon's *New Mathematical Pastimes*.[35]

Before looking deeper into MacMahon's book, one must ask if there could have been any other early influences that made Huff more suited to Maldonado's parquet assignment than the other students in Ulm. When I was studying Huff's inventory of his archive, the William S. Huff Papers, at the University at Buffalo, State University of New York, a particular architectural project fascinated me: Huff's Museum of Indian Baskets.[36]

William S. Huff's grandfather Gottlieb Adam Steiner (1844–1916) was a collector of Indian woven baskets and patterned ceramics. One of Huff's first commissions as an architect was to design a private museum for his mother, Elsa Steiner Huff—who continued her father's hobby of collecting Indian baskets—where this collection could be displayed. The floor plan of the museum is very structured, has a twofold rotation, and looks like a pattern in itself. The museum displayed 555 baskets from at least 62 Native American tribes. William Steiner Huff later became responsible for this collection and made inventories of each piece, including all the details known to him from the records, with the same perfectionism with which he made inventories of his students' works. A masterpiece in the Steiner Huff Collection is a work from Dat So La Lee, the Washo name of Mrs. Louisa Keyser of the Washo tribe, located around Lake Tahoe in Nevada. She was said to be one of the most famous basket weavers of Native American art. Her Washo tribe's roots may be traced back 9,000 years. Dat So La Lee made this particular basket in 1904–1905; she worked on it for 14 months, making 29 stitches per inch, or 80,000 stitches in all, and named it *Beacon Lights*. Its flame design is said to commemorate the large signal fires built on hills and mountains whenever it was necessary to call her tribe, the Washo people, together.[37] The titling of a work with a memorable name reminds me of the poetic names that Huff gave to every parquet deformation. I assume there is a connection between Huff's having been reared with an awareness of this basket collection and his interest in patterns. The Carnegie Museum in Pittsburgh displayed a portion of Steiner's basket collection between 1913 and 1937. Young William was ten years old in 1937 when the collection was placed in storage in his mother's house.

In his final email to me, written shortly before he passed away, William Huff forwarded a link with information on his grandfather, this special collection, and the building he designed, writing that this building and the collection were a source of pride to him. This is important, as it links the pure parquets and the parquet deformations in relation to the long history of patterns. Similar basket patterns, derived from the structures of weaving techniques, adorned with motifs and geometrical shapes, can be seen in other ancient cultures on every continent. These basic forms—zig-zag lines, squares, triangles, rhombic forms (two triangles), and hexagons—are indeed universal; they are the elemental building blocks in Huff's parquet deformation assignment. "Leather of the Lesser Gator" is an excellent example of this unique and subtle shapeshifting between the fundamental shapes of the square, the triangle, and the rhombus. Never before in the long history of geometrical patterns had there been a comparable attempt to subtly deform one elemental geometrical form into another, thereby showing fundamental relationships between basic forms. The history of geometrical patterns is based mainly on repetitions of the same forms or motifs. Huff and his students opened a completely new chapter of design possibilities based on the structural interrelationships and shapeshifting between basic forms.

The possibility of shapeshifting, in the sense of a "give-and-take process" on the borders of tiles, is clearly present in the aforementioned book *New Mathematical Pastimes* by Major Percy Alexander MacMahon.[38] This book inspired Huff to further explore the topic of patterns in his Basic Design Studio. In Part I, MacMahon introduces geometrical edge-matching puzzles, which are similar to the

Fig. 9: Thomas C. Davies, "Leather of the Lesser Gator". Basic Design Studio of William S. Huff; 19 × 19 in, India ink. Spring 1969, Carnegie Mellon University. © HfG-Archiv/Museum Ulm, HfG-Ar, BDSA, Hu P 01. 007.

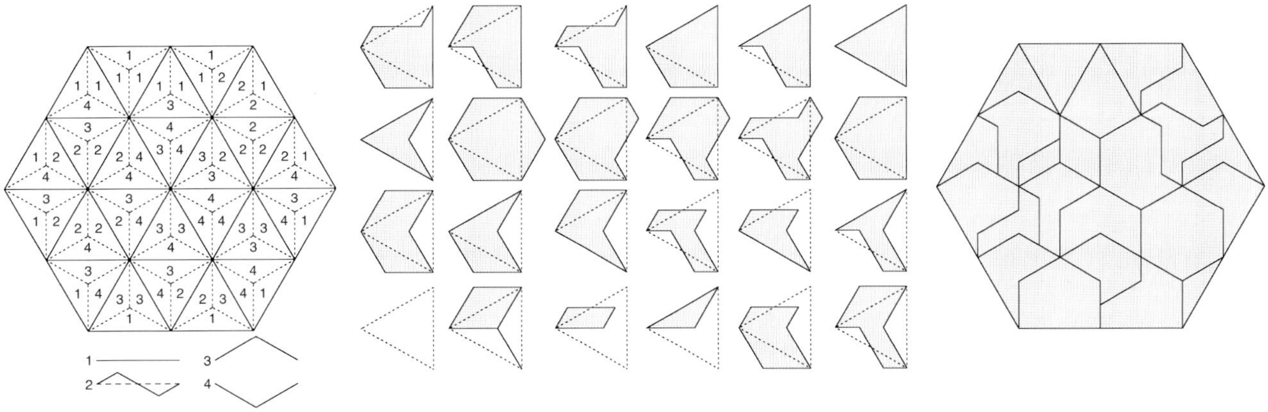

Fig. 10: "New Mathematical Pastimes" by Percy Alexander Mac Mahon; copyright Paul Garcia and Tarquin Reprints, 2004; reprint of the original 1930 edition, pp. 56–58. On the left, the transformation diagram with numbers for the System C1, 1, 2, or 1 to 1, 2 to 3, and 3 to 4. Bottom left: the four chosen new boundaries. The piece each of whose compartments is colored 4 vanishes, giving the 23 pieces (middle). On the right: the assemblage of the new pieces according to the original diagram on the left. Redrawn by the author with kind permission of Andrew Griffin, publisher of the Tarquingroup.

Fig. 11. Peter Hotz, The Original (with frame). Basic Design Studio of William S. Huff, Spring 1961, Carnegie Institute of Technology. © HfG Archiv/ Museum Ulm, HfG-Ar, BDSA, Hu P 01. 011. There are two other unframed versions in Ulm.

well-known domino games, but he explores them in an original way. Depending on how many numbers or colors are involved, he sets up different square and hexagonal diagrams, challenging the pastime seeker to arrange the pieces according to pre-established connecting rules, such as "one has to connect to one and two to two", or, in the colored variation, "red has to connect with red, etc." In the second part of the book, "The Transformation of Part I", he uses the same square, triangular, and hexagonal diagrams, but this time the connections must be made according to a give-and-take formfitting, without numbers or colors. The borderlines are deformed according to a limited set of symmetrical straight, V-, or Z-lines, but duos of asymmetrical lines also occur, so that a completely new set of tiles appears, in which none of the pieces is the same. The pastime seeker then has to puzzle the pieces together until the original diagram has been restored.

In Part III of the book, MacMahon examines what can be done with pieces that are similar in shape and size to make designs of repeating patterns for decorative work, based on triangular, square, pentagonal, and hexagonal pieces. Examining the drawings of Parts II and III, one can easily see correspondences to Huff's students' works. Even the so-called Cairo tiling is displayed, a tiling which is also present in the very first parquet deformation by Peter Hotz.

In his 2003 SEMA lecture notes, Huff recalls how this happened:

> Peter Hotz, a gifted student, made the observation, when I visited his drafting board (then, I did some board-to-board criticism in the studio during the development phase), that incremental changes could be affected from one parquet variation to another. In fact, he had sketched not three variants of the original parquet, but five or six [...] At the time that Peter put together his design, the first parquet deformation, I considered it to be a one-time variant of my assignment. But after reading D'Arcy Thompson's chapter/article [on] "continuous deformation," I had second thoughts and assigned to my whole class, in the third year of my teaching, the assignment to produce parquet deformations. The second part of the term under discussion, deformation, came as already mentioned from D'Arcy Thompson—the parquet deformation being, of course, a continuous deformation. [...] The recognized potential of innumerable variants of any given parquet (an array of congruent tiling) led to connecting variant tilings to one another serially through continuous deformation.[39]

Huff's fair acknowledgment that it was a student who invented the first parquet deformation—he always credited his students for their creations—is a good example of his and Maldonado's pedagogical method, creating an assignment as a challenge for the students to experiment with, often leading to surprising outcomes. Huff mentions this: "The good pedagogue is on constant alert, knows when he sees it, and is ready to promulgate something extraordinary that occurs under his instruction."[40]

In *On Growth and Form*, D'Arcy Thompson uses the terms *transformation* and *deformation* interchangeably. Both terms are used about 20 times each in Chapter 7, "The Theory of Transformations, or the Comparison of Related Forms".[41] *Trans*formation definitely has a more positive connotation than *de*formation, which also means distortion or misshaping. Huff probably preferred the term deformation because it better describes the active process of shapeshifting, with different steps in a continuous permutation, as opposed to transformation, describing more the end result of the process.

The distortion of grid systems was not D'Arcy Thompson's invention, but an artist's:

> D'Arcy Thompson credited his use of continuous deformation as an analytical tool for classifying species according to a design tool devised by Dürer. Albrecht Dürer gridded the face, usually in profile, of the "ideal" man. Then, he distorted the grid: the grid was elongated along its vertical, elongated horizontally, turned into a trapezoid in which the shorter cord was at the top, and into a trapezoid in which the shorter cord was at the bottom. Each resulting profile was a recognizable facial type. His deformations allowed the painter facial varieties. Dürer also drew his versions of the Vitruvian man and Vitruvian woman—both "ideal" Teutonic body types. He then measured off critical measurements of the body along the vertical axis: chin, shoulders, breast, navel, crotch, knee, ankle. Then he elongated the vertical measurements

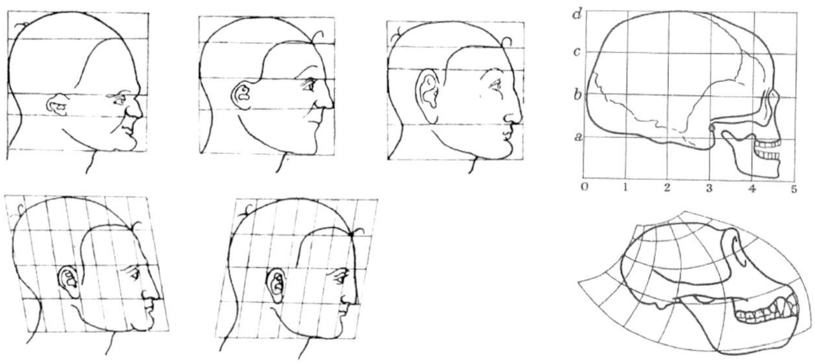

Fig. 12: D'Arcy Wentworth Thompson, *On Growth and Form*, Chapter 7 "The Theory of Transformations, or the Comparison of Related Forms", 2nd ed., Vol. 2, 1959, Cambridge University Press, figures newly arranged from pp. 1026–1095. Three faces top left: Thompson was inspired by Dürer's grid-stretching technique; changes between the parts of the face result in totally different characters. Two faces bottom left: Dürer changes the angle of the coordinate system, another technique resulting in different characters. Two drawings right: Thompson, inspired by Dürer, uses different transformations of coordinate systems to compare related species, in this case a human skull in a regular Cartesian coordinate system transformed into a chimpanzee skull. Collage by the author. Courtesy of Cambridge University Press.

> proportionally, while preserving the horizontal measures. Presto! A Watussi's body type. He compressed the vertical proportionally. Presto, an Eskimo body type. D'Arcy Thompson adopted Dürer's device to explain morphological differences among related species. He laid a grid on the profile of a human skull; then, he marked off similar features found in the chimpanzee skull and showed how the grid had gracefully/continuously deformed.[42]

In Huff's parquet deformations, the grid itself was not to be deformed or stretched. In 2017, grid deformations were an extra experiment proposed to our students at the Technical University Vienna. Thompson and Dürer's grid-stretching technique was integrated into the assignment as an opportunity to make parquet deformations more spatial and served as an important step toward our experiments with parquet deformations in 3D. The students were allowed to deform spatial grids in the 3D assignment as well. In some cases, this resulted in gracefully contracting or expanding structures, as the reader will see in the second part of this book.

Huff's "Classroom Tutorial"

Nicholas Bruscia, assistant professor in the Department of Architecture at the University of Buffalo, the same university where William Huff taught, works very much in the spirit of Huff, experimenting in 2D and 3D, and makes original and contemporary assignments challenging his students in a similar way to Huff's. He

Fig. 13: M.C. Escher's *Liberation*, April 1955, Lithograph, 434 × 199 mm.

sent me a 77-page document that is not dated but must have been compiled in this form around 1983. The document looks like a portfolio or a classroom tutorial and is titled "The Parquet Deformations from the Basic Design Studio of William S. Huff at Carnegie Mellon University, Hochschule für Gestaltung and State University of New-York at Buffalo from 1960 to 1983".[43]

The tutorial contains eleven examples of pure parquets—seven of them in black and white—followed by 39 parquet deformations, which are all currently archived in Ulm. This "sample map, manual, tutorial, syllabus or presentation map" is the first collection of parquet deformations and served as the basis for Hofstadter's *Scientific American* article in 1983, bringing parquet deformations a broad scope of attention in America's most popular science magazine. Douglas Hofstadter explained to me how he got to know Huff:

> What happened was that Bill Huff wrote me a letter on February 14th, 1982, telling me all about parquet deformations and sending me a few of them as samples. I replied with considerable interest, and Bill and I started corresponding, and I became fascinated with parquet deformations. Eventually, in February of 1983, I visited Bill in Buffalo for a couple of days, and during that visit I met some of his colleagues and his students (and I think I gave a talk there, but that's a bit blurry in my memory) —and then, of course, as a result of my visit, I had tons of new material, and my column in *Scientific American* was published in July of 1983. I hope this helps clarify how the connection was established. Yours, Doug.[44]

The parquets and parquet deformations are classified in groups according to their lattice structures. In parentheses I added the names of the works displayed and described in Hofstadter's article:

Twelve examples developed lineally on the square lattice ("Fylfot Flipflop", "Crossover", "Crazy Cogs", "Razor Blades", "Oddity Out of Old Oriental Ornament", and "Clearing the Thicket"); five examples developed lineally across the diagonal of the square lattice ("Cucaracha"); 13 examples developed lineally upon the special (60°–120°) rhombic lattice ("Dizzy Bee", "Consternation", "Trifoliolate", "Arabesque", "Y Knot", and "Beecombing Blossoms"); seven examples developed planarly (in more than one direction) upon the square lattice ("I at the Center"); two examples developed planarly upon the special (60°–120°) rhombic lattice. Furthermore, the tutorial contains "two clumsy examples (by good students) demonstrating that not all deformation attempts work out aesthetically; an attempt to deform 'rep-tile' groupings (two examples); dual developments: (a) all same-handed congruent parquets (b) interlocking handed and other handed parquets." See also Figure 5. At the end of the syllabus Huff shows a "parquet deformation developed lineally in conventional versus boustrophedon modes of transcription", followed by "a temporal scroll of Escher (probably to become included in text portion)".[45] See Figure 13.

In Huff's tutorial, there are only four pages with short explanations. The first parquet deformation by student Hotz is described in the following way:

> The first parquet deformation, executed in 1961, consists of a virtual catalog of familiar repeating tiles linked continuously together: There is (a) the basic grid of squares, (b) the semi-regular, equal sided, overlapping hexagons, (c) the cross, (d) the brick, basket weave, (e) the pinwheel, (f) the modified pinwheel with the accentuated swastika crossing, and (g) return to the square grid. The transitions of this original development are not always meted as harmoniously as are effected in its progeny of the studies that followed. [See Figure 14.][46]

The syllabus leading to Hofstadter's article mainly shows examples, text is scarce, and he describes only "Crossover", "From Five to Four and Two Halves", "Dizzy Bee", and "Consternation", in only a few sentences with diagrams, as shown in Figure 14. The SEMA lecture of 2003[47] is a better source for additional information on *Strategies*. Huff does not cover every possible situation, merely the basic ones:

> Strategies on the square lattice:
> 1. opposite sides: paired with mirror concave and with mirror convex.
> 2. adjacent sides: paired with mirror concave and with mirror convex.
> 3. all four sides; twofold S or Z-shape.

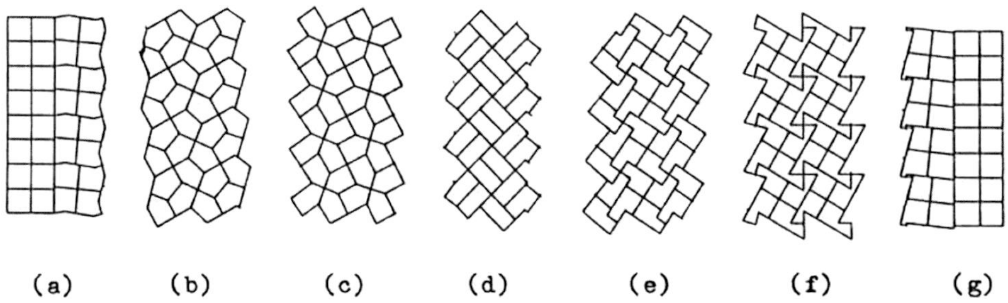

Fig. 14: Huff's analysis of the first parquet deformation by Peter Hotz, 1961.

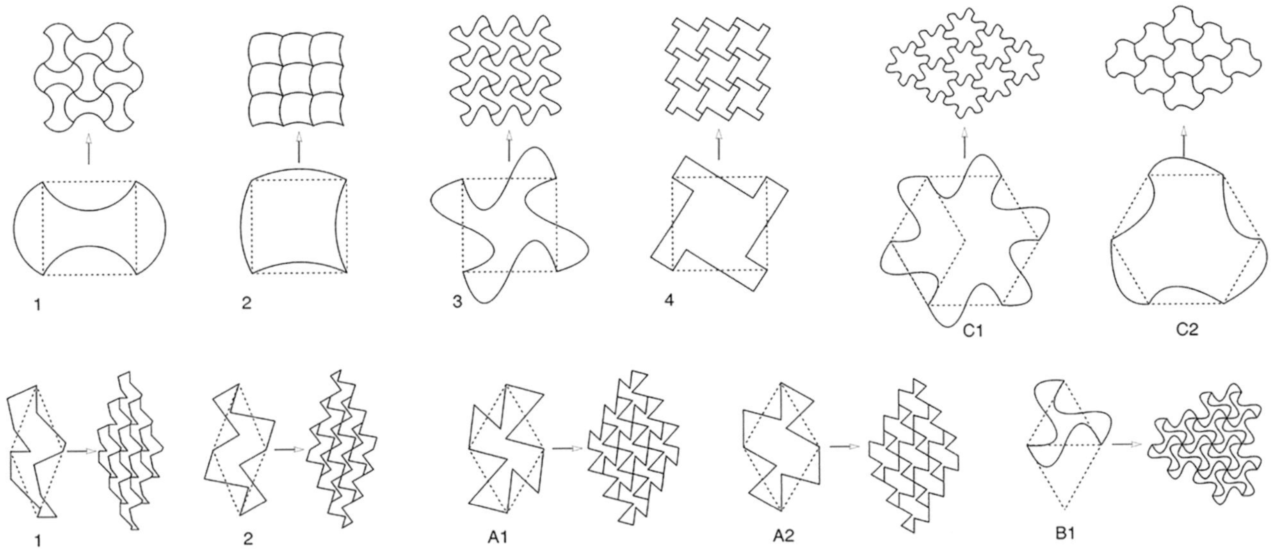

Fig. 15: Basic strategies on the square (1, 2, 3, 4 top left), parallelogram (1 and 2 bottom left), special rhombic (60°–120°) lattice (A1, A2), triangle (B1) and hexagon (C1, C2). Note that the arrangement of elements serves only to illustrate the tiling. To turn them into a parquet deformation, all lines must evolve in space. Drawing by the author.

4. What happens when the convex and concave lines of Points 1 and 2 do not have mirror property? In some cases, congruent, but opposite-handed tiles are created. (Occasionally, I allowed these situations.)

Strategies on the parallelogram lattice:

1. opposite sides: any line repeated along the x-axis; any line repeated along the y-axis. This reproduces the most basic of the 17 wallpaper groups (two-dimensional crystallographic groups).
2. opposite sides: twofold S or Z-shape. In this case, tiles can be oriented in two directions, where in Case 1 they are oriented in only one direction.

Strategies on the special rhombic lattice:

A. On the lattice itself

1. opposite sides: paired with two different kinds of 2-fold S or Z curves
2. all sides: same 2-fold S or Z curves

B. Trace regular triangular grid over the special rhombic lattice

1. all sides: same 2-fold S or Z curves

C. Trace regular hexagonal grid over the special rhombic lattice

1. all sides: same 2-fold S or Z curve
2. Alternating sides: mirror concave and mirror convex lines.

> This brings us to the second major strategy of parquetry—one that subdivides certain parquetry designs. Those tiles that have 2-fold, 3-fold, 4-fold, or 6-fold properties can be subdivided by 2-fold S or Z curved lines or lines that pass or passes through the center of the tile. These lines can be rotated incrementally or continuously within the cells as part of the whole strategy of deformation.[48]

Huff describes basic strategies, processes that can also be understood by looking, examining, or retracing the parquet deformations themselves, since there is much more happening in the more complex ones. To cover all the strategies in the approximately 100 parquet deformations archived in Ulm, a catalogue of strategies must be made ranging from conventional, basic strategies to the more intricate "hybrids", in which different operations are combined. Such a catalogue should also give information regarding the syngenometric lines, the rhythm (temporality/subtleness), vertical and horizontal axes, symmetry groups, subgrids, and lattices involved. This is future work, and cooperation with mathematicians is needed to help categorize them, always keeping in mind that the descriptions and vocabulary should be accurate in a mathematical sense but, at the same time, understandable to the designer.

After this extensive overview of all relevant texts by Huff available to me at this moment concerning parquet deformations, I want to share my thoughts on

Fig. 16: Robert Skolnik, “Opus Optimum”, India ink, 28 × 39.81 in. Basic Design Studio of William S. Huff, Spring 1966, Carnegie Mellon University. © HfG-Archiv/Museum Ulm, HfG-Ar, BDSA, Hu P 08. 020. (Editor's note: Original orientation is 90° clockwise)

Fig. 17: Loosening Huff's rules. In this design two forms start to interact, a rectangle and a square. Design by the author. (Editor's note: Original orientation is 90° clockwise)

some possible futures for parquet deformations as an exercise for designers, or "a subtle, intricate art form", as Douglas Hofstadter describes it so well, but also on applications in design and architecture, the use of CAD and the possibilities that arise when we loosen some of the strict rules that Huff set up.

Possible Futures of Parquet Deformations

In the long tradition of "small forms" in architecture and design, otherwise called ornaments, a multifaceted series of factors can be discerned in the course of the twentieth century. These include the widespread reception of Adolf Loos's notion of ornament, the advent of the International Style and the standardization of building components, ultimately leading to the slow disappearance of the visible use of these small forms in architecture and in the curriculum of architectural education. The small forms became, at best, underlying, invisible grids that helped to control standardization, or they served in the background as proportion systems. Over the course of the twentieth century, mathematicians continued the work started by crystallographers to systematically analyze and define spatial structures in 2D and 3D. Huff knew *Tilings and Patterns*, which appeared in 1987, 26 years after the first parquet deformation had been made. He also knew *Flachenschlüß*, which appeared in 1963.[49] Apart from his mentioning both books, they do not seem to have significantly influenced the parquet deformation assignment. This becomes clear through an arbitrary comparison of a parquet deformation from 1998 with one from 1961. During almost 40 years, Huff's strict rules remained unchanged, although exceptions were allowed occasionally (see Figure 5 as an example). This resulted in a very consistent body of work of some 100 parquet deformations, now archived in Ulm. In this book, one will find some of the finest examples. It would be of significant benefit to bring them all online as study material to inspire future designers. The parquet deformation assignment makes students more aware of the geometrical patterns that surround them, they learn that these patterns have all been classified (into 17 wallpaper groups) and they grasp the underlying structural grids and lattices that define them, as well as how these are all related and how they can be transformed. The notions of gradual change, geometrical coherence and subtle transformations inherent in this assignment increase the students' visual acuities and spatial thinking. The world of polygons and polyhedra, along with their geometrical constraints and subtle transformational possibilities, offer exactly that benefit. They are the perfect playground for young students' experiments. The grids, lattices and space-filling structures offer them the necessary scaffolding to explore space, preventing them from getting lost in space. The accomplishments of the mathematicians and geometers who specialized in this field are an open invitation for designers and architects to use this knowledge in their designs.

In thinking of possible futures for the parquet deformation assignment, one can indeed find new inspiration in books such as *Tilings and Patterns*, as they are filled with ideas waiting to be explored. At least seven of the 28 methods in *Flächenschluß* can be used to develop parquet deformations. Teachers need not be afraid: The topic is visual, and no formulas are needed to experiment with patterns and polyhedra. It is here that universities and art schools play a crucial role, although the reluctance to teach about patterns and ornaments is still present, which is understandable, because the topic was neglected—if not condemned—(see Adolf Loos's "Ornament and Crime") for such a long time. It is exactly through Huff's renewed look at the "small" forms, available now through the ongoing research of mathematicians and geometers, that this reluctance to small forms or ornaments can be overcome. Our students were completely open to and interested in the subject and immediately fascinated by trying to find new solutions or new combinations of operations. The motifs in the history of patterns must be studied in a prospective way instead of a perspective way, seeing them as a starting point for possible deformations and not as an endpoint or a result. Otto Antonia Graf, my personal mentor and professor at the Academy of Fine Arts Vienna, taught me this and always emphasized seeing the "transformational potential" in forms, which is one of the great benefits of the parquet deformation assignment. Another advantage is that students learn to think parametrically without the use of a computer. Every deformation of one basic form is guided by a "transformational idea" which can be depicted in one single drawing in which all the steps of the deformation are seen at once. This is a very fruitful in-between step if one wants to use CAD or parametric modeling tools such as *Grasshopper*, since a computer will always need an "idea" in order to help in experimenting with variations, improving subtleness and accuracy, and so on.

Another way to reinvent parquet deformations would be to loosen some of their strict rules, but then one must find a new name for such an assignment, out of respect for Huff's legacy. This recalls Huff's email at the beginning of this article: "You can design anything you want. Just don't call it a Parquet deformation." David Bailey's phrase "geometrical tessellating metamorphosis", Craig Kaplan's "evolving patterns", and Jay Bonner's "pattern manipulation" are good suggestions.

Which strict rules could or should be loosened? I have a few proposals: If one allows more than one tile, any vertex can transform into a slowly popping-up polyhedron, circle, or any other form under the same rule of temporality and subtleness. One could allow lattices other than the five Bravais lattices used by Huff. Many of the diagrams in *Tilings and Patterns* could then serve as a starting point, such as tilings based on star polyhedra, as seen in the pioneering work of Craig Kaplan.[50] At my invitation for this book, Craig Kaplan again made new and pioneering research focusing on the possibilities of shapeshifting between Laves tiles, and he concentrates on the isohedral tilings described in *Tilings and Patterns*. If one allows more than one polyhedron from scratch—a feature which is already integrated into the *Parakeet* software by Esmaeil Mottaghi and Arman Khalil Beigi—a new world of possibilities again opens. Jay Bonner, a specialist in Islamic design, shows the possibilities of pattern manipulation through hinged tessellations, in which a device from a 3D operation is used in a sequential way in 2D. We should also consider allowing A and A‘ tiles, if the opportunity arises.

Finally, to bring new life to the assignment, one may explore possible applications in the real world of architecture and design to share this art form with the public. Applications in fields such as fabric and fashion design, graphic design, car design, and home decoration are obvious, and we have access to powerful laser cutters, CNC machines, milling, molding, and casting techniques, as well as large-format printers, that may be used to integrate such designs into architectural projects.

Richard Lane's parquet deformation "Crossover" was used on a large scale by the famous architect Emilio Ambasz in *Pro Memoria Garden*, a project for a labyrinth in Lüdenhausen, Germany, in 1978. Although Ambasz won the competition, the garden was for some reason not created, but Ambasz's design is now in the Museum of Modern Art (MoMA) collection.[51] Huff was not unhappy about the fact that a colleague of his had used one of his student's works, but what he could not tolerate was that neither Richard Lane nor Huff's Basic Design Studio were credited or referenced, although the design was an exact copy of "Crossover". Several letters to the MOMA and to the publisher, Rizzoli, are proof of this.[52] I mention Ambasz's project, not only to show that Huff had nothing against applications if referenced properly, but also because of its scale: It was a parquet deformation designed as a labyrinth made of hedges and at least as long as a football field. It was also a social project involving children in taking care of the garden.

Craig Kaplan shows in his chapter a very nice application of a parquet deformation in low-relief casted bronze for the Museum of Mathematics in New York. Parquet deformations are also perfectly suited for wall paneling (with acoustic properties) for spaces such as restaurants, hotels, and offices. Recently, Azmi Merican, from Kuala Lumpur, founded Azmas Rugs, an initiative that allows farmers and their families in India to gain an additional income on the loom in their backyard and started producing rugs with parquet deformations designed by Craig Kaplan and myself. Azmas Rugs will also produce a carpet based on a work by one of Huff's students, and—this is important—Azmi Merican contacted the author, now a successful American architect, to ask for permission. Studio Nov24's chief designer, Hamideh Jafari, is currently developing a beautiful collection of woven, high-quality carpets under my guidance. They are manufactured in India and Iran and are based on parquet deformations. The young mathematician Edmund Harris decorated four walls around elevator entrances with very sophisticated 2D parquet deformations printed as wallpaper.

In architecture, there is a need and demand for new, more sophisticated patterns that go beyond mere decoration. The potential of patterned screens to provide shade for a façade, lend privacy to a balcony, or act as a divider in an office space is also obvious. Kinetic façades and screens are another possible but tricky challenge. The diagrams and the vocabulary used in kinetic design are, in any case, similar to the parquet deformation vocabulary: flux, flow, movement, temporality, sequences, framework, events, spatial transformation techniques, subtlety, and morphology, among other terms.[53] There are many more examples and many more applications to imagine, which I leave to the reader's imagination.

The main reason that I see for a revival of morphologically transformed patterns, whether as a design challenge for students or as real-life applications, is that the concept behind them suits today's challenging times very well. Society must rethink and transform many systems and structures. Experimenting with parquet deformations is an excellent illustration of the transformation processes needed in the world. Space tessellations is a general term selected as the main title for this book, because it is about connecting the unconnected through a new kind of spatial and structural reasoning, exploring relationships and connections that have not been made before.

Space tessellations in architecture is ongoing research open to anyone. With the help of this book, we hope to reach architects, artists, and universities worldwide and invite them to the world of parquet deformations and their inherent transformational ideas. Three-dimensional corollaries of two-dimensional geometric principles relating to the science of tiling are both fascinating and of high value to geometric artists and architects alike. In particular, the relationship between 2D parquet deformations and 3D space-filling polyhedral networks is original research that has great potential for expanding the design understanding and repertoire for architectural expression; this includes the architectonics of spatial layout, vaulting design, and, especially, space-frame structures. It facilitates and expands current understanding of the use of these 2D and 3D structures as scaffolding for geometric patterns and architectural expression. Within the two-dimensional realm, this has already been well documented, but, when extrapolated to three-dimensional geometry, this research is still in its infancy, apart from some important exceptions.[54] Space tessellations as a field has the potential to introduce new realms of geometric inspiration and beauty to contemporary artists and architects. In addition to architects, geometric artists, and designers, both mathematicians and computer programmers are welcome to become key members of this research. I truly hope that the research and experiments presented in this book will inspire you.

Acknowledgment

I would like to thank William S. Huff, his students, and his family for keeping Huff's legacy alive. The HfG Archive in Ulm, especially Marcela Quijano and Martin Mäntele for their support. The staff at the Institute of Art and Design, TU Wien, especially Anita Aigner and Peter Auer for setting up the assignments, the external lecturers, and all the students and student assistants who participated in our experiments. I also want to thank Marie Reichel, the graphic designer of this book, Eva Sommeregger and Christian Kern, co-editors and sparring partners in realizing this project. For their support and feedback, I want to thank Claudio Guerri from the University of Buenos Aires, Nicholas Bruscia and Rose Orcutt from the University of Buffalo, Martin Aurand of the Carnegie Mellon University Architecture Archives and Leslie Lubbers, director of the Memphis Museum. My gratitude goes to all the international contributors: Dénes Nagy, Douglas Hofstadter, William. S. Huff, Cornelie Leopold, Tuğrul Yazar, Jay Bonner, Craig Kaplan, Esmaeil Mottaghi, and Arman Khalil Beigi. Special thanks to David Bailey, who always keeps me updated on parquet deformations. I am extremely grateful to Christian Kern for his support and to the sponsors and private donors that made my work on this book possible: Azmi Merican, Paul Mercelis, Kristof Morel, Irene Jochems, Greet Van Hoeydonck, Geert L M Pauwels. Very special thanks to Sunnive Van Hoeydonck and Luisa Paumann for their ongoing support. Finally, Birkhäuser's team for this book: David Marold, Bettina. R. Algieri and Ada St. Laurent, for making this book reality in a highly professional manner. A very special thank you to Anita Aigner, who believed in my Space Tessellations project from the first second, and to my mentors in the past, Gilbert Decouvreur and Otto Antonia Graf.

References

[1] Email from William S. Huff to Werner Van Hoeydonck, 31 August 2019.

[2] Email from Craig Kaplan to Werner Van Hoeydonck, 12 May 2017.

[3] David Bailey's webpage: http://www.tess-elation.co.uk/.

[4] https://hfg-archiv.museumulm.de/en/hfg-collection/collection-hfg-stiftung/.

[5] The nine major assignments that William S. Huff regularly gave to his students in his basic design classes were 1. Symmetry or Programmed Design; 2. Two-Fold Mirror-Rotation (or Inversion) Symmetry; 3. Mirror-Rotation-Dilatation; 4. Parquet Deformations; 5. Trisection of the Cube; 6. One-Sided Surfaces: Variations on the Möbius Band; 7. Depth Cue; 8. Figurative–Ground; 9. Raster.

[6] In 2015, William Huff in an email to Marcela Quijano, curator at the HfG Ulm archive in an email to me in August 2018.

[7] Online talk with Professor Maurizio Sabini, former student of William Huff, April 2021.

[8] Ibid.

[9] William S. Huff Papers, University Archives, State University of New York at Buffalo, MS 139.2. Item descriptions provided by William S. Huff, pp. 12–17. On page 17 Huff writes, "I only now realized that the collection was considered to be lost." https://library.buffalo.edu/archives/pdf/ms-139-2-public-partial-inventory.pdf.

[10] A full catalogue of the HfG library is available online as a downloadable 1,005-page pdf; the "small" library contains around 6,000 books. https://hfg-archiv.museumulm.de/wp-content/uploads/2019/01/f_05_bibliothek.pdf.

[11] "Best Problems", 1979. Tim McGinty, professor in the architecture department of the University of Wisconsin, collected 24 assignments in a "Best Beginning Design Projects Collection" and shared this compilation among his 23 colleagues working at different universities across the US. In the introduction Mr. McGinty writes, "If you use any of these projects, remember that they are the creative fruit of your peers and they deserve credit. If you print or republish them, you should ask their permission." For this compilation Huff selected the parquet deformation and one of his other assignments, the mirror-rotation symmetry assignment.

[12] Lecture notes for SEMA, 2013; SEMA stands for Sociedad de Estudios Morfológicos de Argentina. These lecture notes were sent to me by Claudio Guerri, honorary president of SEMA.

[13] Ibid.

[14] In handling symmetry, I have moved my students from isometry (e.g., wallpapers), through homoemetry (e.g., spirals) and syngenometry (e.g., deformations), to katametry (e.g., programmed design). Katametry involves the lessening of regulation; nonetheless, regulation remains. In William S. Huff, "On Regulation and Hidden Harmony", *Harmony of Forms and Processes*, Lviv, 2008, p. 3.

[15] Selected papers from the international interdisciplinary symposium entitled Katachi U Symmetry, held at the University of Tsukuba in Japan, 21–25 November 1994. Two interdisciplinary concepts, *katachi* and symmetry, born in the East and West, respectively, came together to further advance intercultural cooperation. The scope of topics covered included: 1. Science on Form; 2. Geometrical Arts and Morphology; 3. Invisible - Visible I Viewing Invisible Images by Comparing them to Visible Forms; 4. Sensing Order; 5. Symmetry, Dissymmetry, and Broken Symmetry in Art and Science. Huff's paper is titled "The Landscape Handscroll and the Parquet Deformation", in *Katachi U Symmetry*, T. Ogawa, K. Miura, T. Masunari, D. Nagy (eds.), Springer-Verlag, Tokyo, 1996, pp. 307–314.

[16] Huff, William S. "The Landscape Handscroll and the Parquet Deformation", In *Katachi U Symmetry*, T. Ogawa, K. Miura, T. Masunari, D. Nagy (eds.), Springer-Verlag, Tokyo, 1996, pp. 307–314. For some good examples of handscrolls, see Willmann, Anna, "Japanese Illustrated Handscrolls", *Heilbrunn Timeline of Art History*, The Metropolitan Museum of Art, 2000. http://www.metmuseum.org/toah/hd/jilh/hd_jilh.htm, November 2012. Huff also references Wen C. Fong, *Beyond Representation: Chinese Painting and Calligraphy, 8th–14th Century,* Yale University Press, 1992, pp. 87–88.

[17] Ibid.

[18] Ibid.

[19] Ibid.

[20] Ibid.

[21] "Best Problems", 1979.

[22] William S. Huff, "An Argument for Basic Design", *Ulm* 12/13, *Journal of the Ulm School of Design*, 1965.

[23] Ibid.

[24] Ibid.

[25] William S. Huff, "Ordering Disorder after K. L. Wolf", *Forma*, 15, Proceedings of the 2nd Katachi U Symmetry Symposium, Tsukuba, 1999, Part 2, 2000, pp. 41–47.

[26] See Note 12.

[27] Huff, "Ordering Disorder", pp. 41–47.

[28] William S. Huff, "On Regulation and Hidden Harmony", *Harmony of Forms and Processes*, Lviv, 2008. References to Alberti: Leon Battista, "On the Art of Building in Ten Books", trans. from Latin by Joseph Rykwert, Neil Leach, and Robert Tavernor, MIT Press, Cambridge, 1485/1988, p. 183. References to Kahn: *What Will Be Has Always Been*, R. S. Wurman (ed.), New York, 1986, p. 77.

[29] William S. Huff, "*Grundlehre* at the HfG—With a Focus on 'Visuelle Grammatik'", *Ulmer Modelle – Modelle nach Ulm*, Ostfildern-Ruit, Hatje Cantz, 2003, p. 196.

[30] Huff, "On Regulation", p. 77.

[31] Huff, "The Landscape Handscroll", pp. 87–88; Douglas R. Hofstadter, "Metamagical Themas. Parquet Deformations: Patterns of tiles that shift gradually in one direction", *Scientific American* 249, July 1983, pp. 14–20. See also: Douglas R. Hofstadter, "Parquet Deformations: A Subtle, Intricate Art Form", *Metamagical Themas—Questing for the Essence of Mind and Pattern*, Basic Books Inc., 1985, pp. 191–212. The integral version of 1983 with 14 examples of parquet deformations is reprinted in this book with Douglas Hofstadter's kind permission.

[32] Huff, "The Landscape Handscroll", pp. 87–88.

[33] Ibid.

[34] Huff, "*Grundlehre*".

[35] Huff, "The Landscape Handscroll", pp. 87–88.

[36] William S. Huff Papers, State University of New York at Buffalo; Maurice L. Zigmond, Gotlieb Adam Steiner and the G. A. Steiner Museum, *Journal of California and Great Basin Anthropology*, 1979, Vol. 1, No. 2: pp. 322–330. Zigmond quotes Huff's offering an analysis of the architectural concept which prompted his design of the building. Huff points out that the individual cells of the floor plan "are interlocked in what is known as the 'basket weave' pattern, but that this arrangement has nothing to do with the contents of the

interior. It was in the '50s at the Alhambra (in Spain), that I reflected on the applicability of such a tile pattern in structuring a building; it was not a nod to the Indian basket—though not an unhappy coincidence! Also many suppose the building's silhouettes reflect Pueblo Indian dwellings. Again, I had no such thought; rather, the design is a result of my own particular grasp of principles of architecture—proportion, composition, outline, etc. The plan possesses 2-fold, rotational symmetry—to be distinguished from bilateral, or mirror, symmetry. The front, though asymmetrical of itself is consequently the same as the back. It is made up of 10 interlocking, repeating cells (and two towers) so laid out that they provide a variety of spatial experiences: the cluster, the vista, the dead end."

[37] Ibid.

[38] Major P. A. MacMahon, *New Mathematical Pastimes*, Cambridge University Press, 1921.

[39] Lecture notes for SEMA, 2013.

[40] Huff, "*Grundlehre*", p. 187.

[41] "The Theory of Transformations, or the Comparison of Related Forms", D'Arcy Wentworth Thompson, *On Growth and Form*, 2nd ed., Vol. 2, Cambridge University Press, 1959, pp. 1026–1095.

[42] Lecture notes for SEMA, 2013.

[43] A classroom tutorial from 1983, University of Buffalo, sent to me as a PDF by Nick Bruscia, Assistant Professor at the Department of Architecture, University of Buffalo.

[44] Email from Douglas Hofstadter to Werner Van Hoeydonck, 29 April 2021. (Bill was the nickname of William Huff)

[45] A classroom tutorial from 1983, University of Buffalo.

[46] A classroom tutorial from 1983, University of Buffalo.

[47] Lecture notes for SEMA, 2013.

[48] Ibid.

[49] Branko Grünbaum and G. C. Shephard, *Tilings and Patterns*, Dover, 2016; Heinrich Heesch and Otto Kienzle, *Flächenschluss: System der Formen lückenlos aneinanderschliessender Flachteile*, Springer, 1963; Robert Williams, *The Geometrical Foundation of Natural Structure: A Source Book of Design*, Dover Editions, 1979.

[50] C. Kaplan, "Islamic Patterns", ACM SIGGRAPH Art Exhibition, 2008; C. Kaplan, "Curve Evolution Schemes for Parquet Deformations", Bridges Proceedings 2010, *Mathematics, Music, Art and Culture*.

[51] Emilio Ambasz's *Pro Memoria Garden* was the winning entry in a competition for a memorial that would remind future generations of the horrors of war. The unrealized project consists of a series of small, irregularly shaped gardens divided by seven-foot hedgerows and narrow paths. Children of the town of Lüdenhausen would be assigned one of the plots at birth and assume responsibility for taking care of it at age five. This, it was hoped, would teach them a respect for life. Over time, the hedges would be removed to make a single large communal garden. Ambasz usually addresses the mystical and poetic side of architecture in his work, but here he has used what he considers to be architecture's ability

to produce myth-making acts to suggest a collective commitment to the performative dimension of public space. His practice of giving "poetic form to the pragmatic", as he has described it, is in this case imbued with a specific political project. https://www.moma.org/collection/works/648?artist_id=141&page=1&sov_referrer=artist.

[52] William S. Huff Papers, University Archives, State University of New York at Buffalo, MS 139.2. Item descriptions provided by William S. Huff, pp. 10–11. On p. 11 Huff writes: "Aside from thickening Lane's ink lines into hedges and using the reverse orientation, the significant addition is two lollypop trees at entrance and end of the garden. See Ambasz's acknowledgments at the end of the catalog, which gives no acknowledgment to Lane or the Huff basic design studio." https://library.buffalo.edu/archives/pdf/ms-139-2-public-partial-inventory.pdf.

[53] Jules Moloney, *Designing Kinetics for Architectural Facades—State Change*, Routledge, 2011.

[54] Robert Williams, *The Geometrical Foundation of Natural Structure: A Source Book of Design*, Dover Editions, 1979.

Biography of the Author

Werner Van Hoeydonck received a master's degree in Architecture in Ghent, Belgium in 1992. His final design project (Concert Hall Ghent) was graded with the highest distinction and received the Van Hove Prize. His thesis on the work of Andrea Palladio and his Flemish translation of Palladio's *Quattro Libri dell' Archittetura* was awarded with a scholarship at the Academy of Fine Arts Vienna (1993–1996), where Van Hoeydonck studied under Prof. Dr. Otto Antonia Graf and became acquainted with Graf's analytical method of "drawing-thinking, thinking-drawing". Graf's research on both Otto Wagner and Frank Lloyd Wright deeply influenced Van Hoeydonck. In 1996 he organized a Graf lecture on Frank Lloyd Wright at the Henry Van Velde Institute in Antwerp. In 1998 he wrote the main catalogue text for the Otto Wagner exhibition in Ghent (Witte Zaal). After several working experiences in architectural offices in Vienna and Belgium, in 2000 Van Hoeydonck founded his own practice, Tek7-architects in Antwerp, Belgium, realizing around 100 projects, mainly private houses and renovations. In 2012 Van Hoeydonck returned to Vienna and founded Ornamental Art and Design, a research, design, and art studio focused on geometrical patterns and ornaments. He regularly organizes drawing workshops in his studio and at several art schools in Vienna. Since 2013 he is a member of DESIGN AUSTRIA and exhibited at the Vienna Design Week and in Palais Neupauer Breuner. In 2016 he started the research project "Space Tessellations", which brought him to lecture at the Technical University Vienna (Institute for Art and Design, WS 2017, 2018, 2021) and at the Academy of Fine Arts (Descriptive Geometry, since 2018). The primary focus of his research and teaching activities is to make young students aware of the potential of two and three-dimensional geometry in architecture and design. In 2019 he took part in the SIS congress and exhibition (The International Society for the Interdisciplinary Study of Symmetry) in Kanazawa, Japan and published his first paper, "William Huff's Parquet Deformations, Three Viennese Experiments". An adapted short paper with the same title was published for the Bridges conference in Helsinki in 2020. *Space Tessellations: Experimenting with Parquet Deformations* is his first book.

https://wernervanhoeydonck.blog/

Grundlehre at the HfG
— A Focus on "Visuelle Grammatik"

William S. Huff

I. An "Opinion"

We must complain about the over-schematic and insufficient presentation of the achievements of Josef Albers. As a clarification of the again and again debated question of to whom the importance of the Bauhaus didactics of that time and of today must be ascribed —we are speaking here mainly of the preparatory course (practical and formal education)—the book of Wingler[1] is of little help. Itten, as initiator of the Bauhaus didactics, is overestimated by Wingler; Moholy-Nagy, as indefatigable stimulator, is evaluated correctly; but Albers is completely underestimated. [...] Wingler seems to have overlooked the fact that Albers took upon himself perhaps the most difficult task in the development of the Bauhaus didactics, a task, which he solved brilliantly, i.e., he transformed the different and partly contradictory components (pedagogical activism, mystical expressionism and exaggerated constructivism) into a systematic, coherent and operable subject of teaching.

—Tomás Maldonado[2]

Hermann von Baravalle in the *Grundlehre* classroom, 1959.

Helene Nonné-Schmidt lecturing, 1956/57, on the Theory of Color according to Philipp Otto Runge, whose color sphere shows above her head on the blackboard.

Tomás Maldonado, 1958.

Editorial Note: All three images copyright HfG Archiv/Ulmer Museum, Ulm.

Josef Albers was 35 in 1923, when he began teaching a section of the *Vorlehre* at the Bauhaus in Weimar; Tomás Maldonado was 33 in 1955, when he began teaching the *Grundlehre* (Foundation Course) at the Hochschule fur Gestaltung (HfG) in Ulm. These were essentially both of these men's first teaching roles; each had come generally from similar backgrounds, committed to art. In Albers's case, he had to cast off his earlier training in Germany's prevailing Expressionism, a vein of art that ran contrary to developments in Paris and Moscow. In Maldonado's case, the wiser from having the advantage of coming along three decades later, he had taken a leading role in an avant-garde movement, which referred anew to the same Paris and Moscow that had reoriented Albers.

[1] Hans Maria Wingler, *Das Bauhaus 1919–1933, Weimar, Dessau, Berlin und die Nachfolge in Chicago seit 1937*, Cologne, 1962.

[2] Tomás Maldonado, "Opinions: Is the Bauhaus Relevant Today?", ulm 8/9, September 1963, p. 12. Liberties have been taken in amending punctuation.

II. An Authentic Restoration of a Bauhaus *Vorlehre* in the HfG *Grundlehre*

One former *Bauhäusler* praises the most legendary of the successes of the Bauhaus: "None of us, probably not even Gropius and Itten, nor even Moholy-Nagy and Albers, who later directed the *Vorkurs*, could imagine at the time that it would be this very *Vorkurs* that would conquer the schools of arts and crafts throughout the world." [3]

Unfortunately, the conquest was more impression than substance. After the abrupt closing of the Bauhaus in 1933, the school's ideas were diluted and dispersed worldwide—the spread was broad, but shallow. This was the special fate of the *Vorlehre*. Whose *Vorlehre*, however, was being submitted for emulation? The problem is that there were innumerable versions of it and versions upon versions—the psyched-up expressionistic version of Itten, the overly simplistic experimental version of Moholy-Nagy, the rationalistic "open-eyed"[4] version of Albers. Furthermore, the instruction of both Kandinsky and Klee, scheduled as part of the required *Formlehre*,[5] considerably enlarged the host of permutations.

Since at least the mid-twentieth century, most schools of architecture and design have claimed a foundation course that followed the precepts of the Bauhaus—though some have gone out of their way to declare virtually the impossible, an unwavering resistance to that sort of persuasion. An old issue of the *Yale Alumni Magazine*—from around the time that I took an introductory design course, required for entering Yale's Department of Architecture—offers an example from my personal experience. Under "Commencement Activities: Art", the following was reported:

> Other exhibits illustrate the work in some of the newer experimental courses conducted by Professors Gute and Switzer. These are developments from the famous Bauhaus courses and demonstrate a philosophic approach to the basic problems of form and materials which serve as a common denominator for later specializations in one of the arts.[6]

These teachers of mine do deserve my due respect; their effort at reform was a resolute departure from the Beaux Arts training for which Yale had been routinely acclaimed some few years before. That what was being presented had much of an affinity to the Bauhaus, however, was sadly delusional—well, perhaps it did correspond to it in a very limited way.[7] Ironically, only a few years later, Yale engaged not only an authentic representative of the Bauhaus, but the one who most epitomized the concept of *basic design*—Josef Albers.

When the design school opened at Ulm in 1953, Max Bill dominated the curriculum, at least on paper. He was the director of the school, head of Architecture, head of Product Form, and the head of the *Grundlehre*; only Otl Aicher headed Visual Communication, and Max Bense headed Information. The pity was that Bill took on the air of the traditional European professor who sometimes went to the lecture room, but more often delegated instruction to assistants and surrogates.[8] Bill was, in the main, a truant of his newly assumed responsibilities.[9] Of course, in the first academic year, there was only the Foundation Course instruction to deliver; and Bill had the Hochschule buildings to design.

Yet, there was one redeeming glimmer: Bill's assistants and surrogates were an extraordinary lot. Through the prestige that he had established in Zurich, Europe's second art capital, along with his own overpowering, if not overbearing, personality, he was able to attract a remarkable group of person ages: *Bauhäusler* who were still around—only 20 years having intervened between the closing of the Bauhaus and the opening of the HfG. He was able to assemble a majority of the surviving Bauhaus faculty for the inauguration of the new HfG buildings in 1955; but even before that, Bill, a former Bauhaus student himself, brought back two Bauhaus masters from his student days to resurrect, in effect, the Bauhaus *Vorkurs*: Josef Albers and Walter Peterhans. In addition, he brought from earlier Bauhaus days the former master Johannes Itten[10] and a fourth Bauhaus person, the former student Helene Nonné-Schmidt. Even Bill himself participated in the *Grundlehre* instruction. The Bauhaus *Vorkurs* finally had a new home that was genuine—and one where the *Vorkurs* could be reevaluated. It was up to Maldonado to do just that.

The two most consequential of these former *Bauhäusler* were Albers and Nonné-Schmidt—both giving instruction in color, but to different ends. Albers presented his renowned, two-decade, post-Bauhaus treatment of the perception of color. Solidly based on the teachings of Paul Klee and studies of her husband, Joost Schmidt,[11] Nonné-Schmidt's hands-on instruction thoroughly covered the theory of color (a topic whose primacy, in the consideration of practicing design, was vehemently disputed by Albers).[12]

Max Bill, the original director of the *Grundkurs*, essentially adopted the Albers model of basic design. Bill, arguably the leading exponent of *Art Concret*, pursued principles in his art that were, if not coincidental to those of Albers, at least in rapport with them. Aside from the building complex designed by Bill for the HfG, a most agreeable masterpiece in facility and in temper, one of Bill's most important acts was the luring of Albers to teach during the school's first two academic years—December 1953–January 1954 and May–August 1955[13]—if for no other reason than that the second visit afforded Maldonado an opportunity to

[3] Heinrich König, "The Bauhaus—Yesterday and Today", in *Bauhaus and Bauhaus People*, Eckhard Neumann (ed.), New York, 1970: p. 120.

[4] "When I arrived at Black Mountain College one of the boys asked me what I planned to teach. 'To open eyes' was my answer—and my first educational sentence in English." Josef Albers, *Search Versus Re-Search*, Hartford, CT, 1969: p. 11.

[5] "Instruction in form", courses in formal studies that complemented the *Vorkurs*.

[6] "Art", *Yale Alumni Magazine* 12, July 1949, p. 23.

[7] I took the course during academic 1947/48. In a letter home, dated 28 September 1947, I wrote: "My art class is a little puzzling though. In that class we aren't painting, aren't drawing, aren't etching, no—we're 'filling space': Filling space with planes, lines, and solids. Our media are cardboard, wire, and clay. But it isn't quite as crazy as it may seem, for it fits in perfectly with architecture (which in itself is filling space). It gives us some theories of composition." In fact, our training gave us little or no frame of reference. One assignment was stated this way: "Express *Connecticut*—in watercolors." Such an assignment didn't do anything but stir confoundment in me. Was there a future for me in design? It was because of this preliminary training at Yale that I quested half-mindfully, so to say, and stumbled eventually into the Maldonado *Grundlehre*.

[8] I found the instruction at the HfG School to be more North American than European in style.

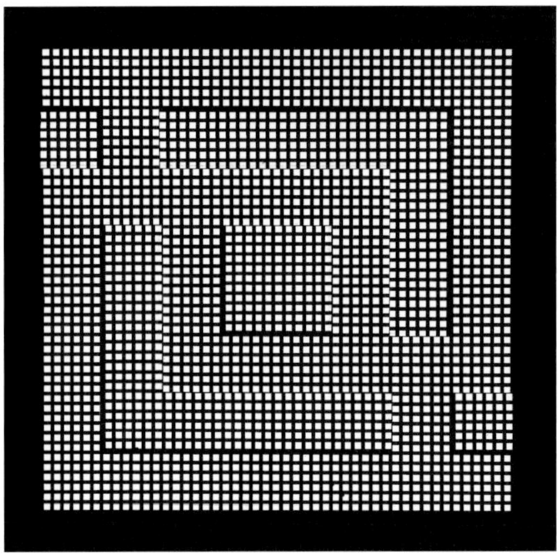

Jeffrew Orling. Basic Design Studio of William S. Huff, Fall 1966, Carnegie Mellon University (CIT). © HfG-Archiv/Museum Ulm, HfG-Ar, BDSA, Hu P 05. 037. Assignment: Raster—Single element.

Daniel Deboy, "Clocking the Day". Basic Design Studio of William S. Huff Spring 1990, SUNY at Buffalo. © HfG-Archiv/Museum Ulm, HfG-Ar, BDSA, Hu P 02. 050. Assignment: Programmed Design.

[9] *bauhäusler in ulm: Grundlehre an der HfG 1953–55*, Ulm, 1993, p. 23.

[10] It was widely rumored that, when Albers learned that Itten had been brought from Zurich (for but a mere week) in April 1955, Albers declared that, after his second stint, which had followed Itten's visit, he would not return to the HfG as a visiting teacher-and he did not. Albers feigned that Bill's gesture to Itten indicated a capricious regard for the integrity of the *Grundlehre*.

[11] Though Joost Schmidt, according to H. Nonné-Schmidt, had been a close friend of Albers, Albers objected to Bill's having hired Schmidt's wife to teach color—that component of design that he thought was being thoroughly covered by himself.

[12] "Originally, we began our color course with a presentation of various color systems, of color theories./With the discovery that color is the most relative medium in art, and that its greatest excitement lies beyond rules and canons, a more sensitive discrimination was needed./The more a creative use of color developed, the less desirable became a merely trustful and obedient application./The seeing of color became our first concern./As a result, we came to present color systems not at the beginning but at the end of our course." Josef Albers, *Interaction of Color*, New Haven, 1963: p. 66. And that presentation of color theory at the end of his course was given short shrift.

[13] *bauhäusler in ulm*, p. 17.

[14] In Maldonado's original Kuhberg house, aside from one large painting of his own, he displayed no other paintings, with the exception of one by student Mavignier and an Albers *Homage to the Square*.

interact with Albers.[14] At the same time, Bill's persuasion of Maldonado to join the faculty must be listed as his third major contribution to the vital being of the new school—ironic as that turned out to be.

III. Basic Design Becomes Interdisciplinary

Events that were no less imprudent in quirky human ways, than those that shaped the original Bauhaus *Vorlehre*, shaped the *Grundlehre* at the Hochschule fur Gestaltung. Max Bill had an incomparable model in his former teacher Josef Albers, who wired up the classroom with the Gestalt reviews of his students' work—characterized by Hannes Beckmann, another of Albers's Bauhaus students, as "a kind of group therapy".[15] Bill was inexplicably indifferent to this—putting his professional commitments and artistic preoccupations in Zurich above his performances in the classroom at the HfG. It was a grievous miscalculation on his part. Tensions over teaching practices, personality clashes, even private indiscretions, caused a political upheaval that split the HfG student body: two to one (pro-Bill vs. anti-Bill). Virtually by default, yet by and large ready, Maldonado was thrust into the looming void. Maldonado rendered the all-but-indispensable Bill dispensable.

Maldonado's 1963 "opinion" about Albers's contribution to "the preparatory course" has to be indicative of what he had in mind when he took on the *Grundlehre* in 1955—after having assisted Bill's *Grundlehre* during the preceding academic year. Maldonado reaffirmed the Albers basic design model, as it was eventually articulated,[16] by avoiding so-called *semantic* issues, the materialization that takes place in the applied design process, as well as pragmatic issues, the appraisal of the usefulness of the product of design,[17] while effectively dealing with only *syntactic* issues of design—form, color, and texture. However, he made a significant contribution to that model by supplementing the visual training component of the *Grundlehre* with interdisciplinary content: that is, with abstract bodies of knowledge that augmented the universally recognized formal (form, color, texture) issues of design. In line with this, Maldonado has stated the following:

> [The Bauhaus didactic, particularly its *Vorkurs*] was a question of argumentative exaltation of expression, intuition, and action, above all of "learning by doing". But this educational philosophy is in crisis. It is incapable of assimilating the new types of relations between theory and practice, engendered by the most recent scientific developments. We know now that theory must be impregnated with practice, practices with theory. It is impossible today to act without knowledge, or to know without doing.[18]

Maldonado, having joined his artistic inclinations with a cadre of Argentinean *Art Concretists* in Buenos Aires, came to have high regard for the work of both Max Bill and Georges Vantongerloo. He went to Zurich in 1948[19] to get to know Bill (as well as to Paris to meet Vantongerloo) and undertook to write a monograph[20] on Bill. Eventually urged by Bill to take a post at the HfG, Maldonado accepted with the stipulation that he would go for one probationary year. Unsure in his German, he functioned largely as an aid to Bill in the school's second academic year; this included both administrative troubleshooting and assisting in the *Grundlehre*. That in time the two had the fateful falling-out is a story for a different setting from this,[21] but Maldonado's involvement with writing on Bill's conceptualization of art and, later, his observation of Albers's teaching, very likely helped to temper his reaffirmation of a purely formal approach to the visual training part of the *Grundlehre* course.[22]

That being the case, Maldonado gave basic design a vigorous infusion of *Art Concret* with his insightful inclusion of two branches of geometry, namely *symmetry theory and visual topology*.[23] Elements of *Art Concret* had already been introduced by Bill himself in the few assignments that he had presented—and by Peterhans, too. Maldonado can be said, then, to have expanded that base with the lectures on symmetry[24] and topology—and by the design studio assignments that addressed each of these disciplines.[25]

The other interdisciplinary body of knowledge that Maldonado brought into play was *perception*, particularly *Gestalt psychology*. Subjecting the geometric artifact to the perceptual experience gave a validating nod to Albers's aphoristic formulation: "The origin of art: The discrepancy between physical fact and psychic effect."[26]

But Albers had not initially come to this. Since he had, while at the Bauhaus, rejected the neurotic expressionism of Itten and, yes, the over-formalization of van Doesburg, that which was left at his disposal in the Bauhaus's store of "new ideas"[27] was the study of materials at a basic level.[28] He quarried this vein imaginatively with his students in workshop probes that focused on the potentials of the "physical-mechanical qualities"[29] of various, intentionally chosen, common materials: paper,[30] metal wire, metal sheets, wire screening, glass, and even sand. This "idea" was embedded in the very fabric of the Bauhaus (if the Bauhaus had even one thread of consistency throughout most of its history)[31] for the students' options in design studies were discharged in the so-called workshops (*Werkstätte*), where each student was expected to master one particular material of choice:[32] stone (sculpture), wood, metal, textiles (weaving), color (mural painting), glass (stained glass), clay (pottery).

[15] Hannes Beckmann, "Formative years", in Neumann, *Bauhaus and Bauhaus People*, pp. 197–198. See also: "The group discussions of the results of the exercises induce accurate observation and new way of 'seeing'", Josef Albers, "Creative Education", in Wingler, *Bauhaus*, p. 143.

[16] As noted in a later passage of this section, there was one notable exception to the exclusivity of formal content in Albers's compass of basic design: his compelling workshop directive to students to poke around the physical properties of materials. With this sort of study, a foray into concrete substance, Albers's course technically ventured over the boundary line of the strictly syntactic realm of formal abstractions and into the semantic realm of materiality.

[17] Initiated in academic year 1955/56, Maldonado's lectures on *semiotics* (covered later in this paper) were primarily based on Charles Morris, though C. S. Peirce was appropriately cited as Morris's forerunner. Even though there is a general disagreement today among semioticists over some interpretations that Morris attached to Peirce, Morris's three terms *syntactic, semantic, and pragmatics* have been considered to be very effective—useful even in conceptual fields beyond linguistics, such as design. See Charles Morris, *Foundation of the Theory of Signs*, Chicago, 1938.

[18] Tomás Maldonado, "New Developments in Industry and the Training of the Designer", in *Architecture Culture 1943–1968: A Documentary Anthology*, Joan Ockman (ed.), New York, 1993, p. 299.

[19] Mario H. Gradowczyk and Nelly Perazzo, *Abstract Art from the Rio de la Plata: Buenos Aires and Montevideo*, 1933–1953, New York, 2001, p. 48.

[20] Tomas Maldonado, *Max Bill*, Buenos Aires, 1955.

[21] See Tomás Maldonado, "From Buenos Aires to Ulm", *form + zweck* 20, 2003, pp. 15–21.

[22] A point will be made here and kept in mind elsewhere in this chronicle: *Grundlehre* is not neatly synonymous with *basic design*. In a recent email (5 June 2003), Maldonado cautioned: "One must not confuse the Grundlehre AT ULM that consisted of a set of many disciplines, with the 'Visuelle Einführung' (or Visuelle Grammatik) that was only one of them." To be sure, I am focusing here, though not exclusively, on the history of that *Visuelle Grammatik*, as it was incubated by Itten, formulated by Albers, filtered through Bill, and construed by Maldonado. Maldonado's point about basic *studies* has been a part of my comprehension about basic design from the earliest occasion of Maldonado's having made clear to me the distinction between the two. (This point is visited later in this paper.)

[23] Though both symmetry and topology were already well developed by the nineteenth century (through Kepler, Euler, Klein, Möbius, Peano, Schönflies, Federov, etc.), both are quite recent branches of geometry, relative to Pythagorean and Euclidean geometry; and neither had yet been specifically applied to design. One intriguing coincidence (yet there are no known connections) is the parallel set of topics that have shown up in the world of graphic artist M. C. Escher.

[24] Hermann Weyl and K. L. Wolf both lectured on symmetry at the HfG; Helmut Emde, an anthroposophist, presented geometry and mathematics in a thorough supplemental course in which all students engaged.

[25] The inclusion of these geometries might have origins in Maldonado's work on the Bill monograph. In an article in the monograph, "The Mathematical Approach in Contemporary Art", Max Bill stated, "I am convinced of the possibility of developing art wherein the mathematical approach is fundamental", and he further stated, "The mainspring of allvisual art is Geometry, the correlation of elements on a surface or in space. Thus, even as mathematics is one of the essential forms of primary thought and consequently one of the principal means by which we take cognizance of the world that surrounds us, it is also intrinsically a science of the relationship of object to object, group to group, and movement to movement. And since this science encompasses all these phenomena and gives them a meaningful arrangement, it is natural that these relationships themselves should also be captured and given form." Maldonado, *Max Bill*, p. 37.

[26] Albers, *Search*, p. 10.

[27] Eugen Gomringer, *Josef Albers*, New York, ca. 1968, p. 27.

[28] "We begin at the beginning, which is (and has been in all essential production) the material itself." Albers, *Search*, p. 33.

[29] Ibid.

[30] Albers reprised his famous Bauhaus paper-folding assignment during his first HfG visit, 1953/54.

[31] The HfG held students to a high standard in regard to craft; and it backed up those expectations with well-equipped workshops (plaster, wood, metal, and eventually plastics), where all students were trained by first-rate masters in all of the school's selection of shops, including photography. Craft at the HfG was, perhaps, a virtuous compulsion—it stopped short of being a fetish.

[32] This was part of a delusory retrieval of medieval practices, symbolized by Lyonel Feininger's woodcut of the Cathedral of Socialism and by the signature name of the *Bauhaus* itself—a belated attempt to turn the clock back on the 500-year run of the Renaissance.

Yuqing (Karen) Li, "Checkering of Grid over Grid: 16 in 15". Basic Design Studio of William S. Huff, Spring 1998, SUNY at Buffalo. © HfG-Archiv/Museum Ulm, HfG-Ar, BDSA, Hu P 02. 026. Assignment: Programmed Design. (Editor's note: Original in color)

It cannot, in truth, be claimed that the Bauhaus defined basic design—since not even Albers's activities, while there, could have constituted that. Its definition had to come out of Albers's subsequent achievements—those that were fashioned at Black Mountain and clinched at Yale.[33]

Thus, Maldonado's earlier statement on Albers's achievement at the Bauhaus (the sounding board of this paper) has to be reconsidered in respect to a later statement: "It must be said that the best qualified historians of the Bauhaus doubt the existence of a unified didactic principle in the preparatory course—as much at Weimar as at Dessau."[34]

Probably tentatively, at first, Albers came to infuse basic design with Gestalt. Beginnings of this can very likely be accredited to Karlfried Graf von Durckheim-Montmartin's lectures on *Gestalt psychology* at the Bauhaus, which had been arranged by Hannes Meyer.[35] The equivocal *figure-ground* phenomenon struck Albers immensely; and aside from Gestalt proper, Albers became intrigued with the contradictory read that could be achieved through the manipulation of depth cues in linear perspectives.[36] Maldonado picked up on Gestalt and depth perception, as well, and presented both in a comprehensive manner—far more thoroughly than Albers did. Furthermore, Maldonado's directives for exercises that involved perception (as can be seen in descriptions, given below) were far more elaborate than his directives that addressed symmetry and topology. The case can be made that Gestalt was dealt with unevenly and almost furtively by Albers (which did include his Gestalt teaching), but comprehensively and directly by Maldonado. In 1955/56, lecturers Hans Joachim Firngau and Herbert Schober were brought to the HfG to bolster the psychology of perception.[37]

Maldonado, who had been pondering the problem of the background, otherwise *ground*, as a problem of *Art Concret*,[38] was introduced to Gestalt theory in 1946 by Aldo Pellegrini, a medical doctor and Surrealist poet—a major figure in the Argentine art scene of the day. Pellegrini had suggested to Maldonado that an approach to his question might be gained through Gestalt and gave him two texts: Köhler's *Gestalt Psychology* and Koffka's *Principles of Gestalt Psychology*.[39] Maldonado's involvement with Gestalt was, however, not an immediate embrace; rather, it was an evolving affair.[40]

The radical organization of the *Bauhaus* around one's mastery of one material was, in the long run, unsustainable. It was essentially replicated at the New Bauhaus (later, School of Industrial Design) in Chicago. In this case, however, certain materials were already being bundled into six workshops as, for instance, wood and metal; glass, stone, clay, and plastics; etc., Wingler, Bauhaus, p. 194. Following the Bauhaus imperative in regard to material, *Bauhäusler* Hin Briedendieck was responsible for Chicago's preliminary workshop, which could put on exhibit "strikingly new and strange" (Moholy-Nagy: below) arrays of "wood carvings, mechanically produced" under the brief, "Problem: To determine the specific possibilities of machine-working of wood", Wingler, *Bauhaus*, p. 598. Briedendieck eventually acknowledged shortcomings of this Bauhaus "idea". In his article "The Legacy of the Bauhaus", *Art Journal* 12, 1, 1962, pp. 16, 18, 20, he shared some of his misgivings:

[The Basic Workshop] was intended to "release the creative power of the student", Moholy, *The New Vision*, p. 20. [...] The student is not required or encouraged to produce "premature practical results" (Moholy). Instead, he is offered an opportunity to experiment freely with various materials and tools. There is a strong emphasis on initiative within a "do-it-yourself" set-up, using conventional and unconventional means, often achieving strikingly new and strange configurations. [...]

A meeting arose from a general concern expressed [...] by other faculty members. "Although the purpose of the Foundation Course is to allow the student to develop his creative abilities freely and without restriction—in the following semesters, where the students are channeled in the direction of practical problems, the smallest limitation becomes a new obstacle and his creativeness has shown a tendency to 'freeze'. In most cases they completely ignored all their previous training and fell back on the conventional."

The following remarks by Briedendieck addressing this concern have been rearranged:

[The student] may well be merely the extension of his tools or even an unwitting victim of the numerous incidental events in the process. [...] Learning by doing dominates. The emphasis has been on the manipulative aspects, on training rather than knowledge. [...] But it is precisely the aim of design education to impart to the student the means of achieving authority and command in order to gain ascendancy over the accidental.

These "accidents" of the Chicago students were apparently not difficult to come by—and the students must have been duly praised for them. When an even newer Bauhaus was founded in Ulm in 1953, the divisions of design were arranged and named along practical professional lines: Architecture (later Building); Product Form (Industrial Design), Visual Communication (Graphics), and Information (Verbal Text).

[33] Though I am referring here to the conceptualization of what basic design is, the term itself has its murky history. Albers claimed, with justification I am sure, that he settled on the term "basic design" (undoubtedly while at Black Mountain) as the least unsatisfactory term in a long list of unsatisfactory terms.

[34] Ockman, *Architecture Culture*, p. 298.

[35] Individual psychology vis-à-vis social psychology. Wingler, *Bauhaus*, pp. 10, 159.

[36] Albers's *Constellations* came out of this.

[37] "Firngau was the last surviving Gestalt psychologist from the famous Berlin School. His teaching of the psychology of perception was exemplary. Schober [...] related the latest in the physiology of vision—a field in which he was 'the' German authority." Email from Dolf Zillmann, Dean Emeritus for Graduate Studies, University of Alabama, 18 June 2003. Schober went on to lecture in later years at the HfG.

[38] Tomás Maldonado, "Concrete Art and the Problem of the Unlimited", in *Tomás Maldonado*, Mario H. Gradowczyk and William S. Huff (eds.), Buenos Aires, March 2003. This paper comes two years after his introduction to Gestalt.

[39] Wolfgang Köhler, *Gestalt Psychology*, 1929; Kurt Koffka, *Principles of Gestalt Psychology*, New York, 1935. "Two years later Pellegrini published in 'Argonauta,' the publishing house he owned, the Spanish translation of Köhler's book (Psicologia de la Forma)." Email from Tomás Maldonado, 27 May 2003.

[40] "In my paper of 1946 I mentioned 'psicologia della struttura' (*Gestaltpsychologie*). However, I believe [...] that there was not an explicit and continual influence of Gestalttheorie in my way of thinking. Originally the dichotomy of 'figura-fondo' doesn't come from *Gestalttheorie*, but rather from the traditional art-historian terminology. Only later, between 1946 and 1948, I began to be convinced of the importance of Gestalttheorie for Concrete Art." Maldonado, 27 May 2003.

Maldonado's subsequent, comprehensive coverage of Gestalt at the HfG corresponded to his own remonstrance to "impregnate" knowledge. Albers, on the other hand, would exhort his students not to read books: There were no solutions for their design assignments in any of them, he would warn. Then, suddenly in a group critique, he would talk all around the Gestalt principle of *figure-ground* in such a manner that an innocent observer might be led to believe that Albers was discovering that principle in a student's work—at that very moment. Aside from probably hearing von Durckheim-Montmartin lecture, Albers must have read some "forbidden" books. (He himself wrote some significant ones.) To be sure, Albers was a bit of a *Schwindler*—one of his favorite interlingual words whose Germanic form he preserved in his excellently articulated English.

In his *Grundkurs* at the HfG, Maldonado did introduce in lecture form other bodies of knowledge, foremost among which were ergonomics and semiotics. It is important to emphasize, however, that Maldonado never tainted his *Grundlehre* assignments, in which visual training was involved, with a mandate to apply material of either an ergonomic or a semiotic nature—while both symmetry and topology were specified in certain assignments; for mandating either ergonomic or semiotic material, as a part of a visual task, would have been to insert semantic and pragmatic issues into it. Thus, the basic design component of the *Grundlehre* under Maldonado, though expanded interdisciplinarily in respect to Albers's version of it, remained wholly abstract, wholly nonobjective—dealing purely and solely with formal, syntactic, issues.

Maldonado's justification for the inclusion of ergonomics and semiotics in lecture form in the *Grundlehre* was that these were issues that should be covered by basic *studies* (to be distinguished from basic *design*)—practical basic issues that students would encounter when they advanced to the specific design departments of their choice.

It is to be noted that Albers also used the term *basic studies* as distinguished from basic design—essentially in the same manner that Maldonado did. The only difference was that, while Maldonado's basic studies referred to the advanced practical years in a school of design, Albers's basic studies referred to the advanced practical years in a school of fine arts. In the latter part of a succinct statement on basic design for the *Yale Alumni Magazine* Albers wrote this:

> Our department of design/therefore promotes particularly/basic studies:/
> Basic Design and Basic Drawing/Basic Color and Basic Sculpture,/also Lettering and Drafting/as required training/for specialized studies:/
> in drawing and painting/in graphic design and photography/in typography and printmaking/elemental and structural sculpture.[41]

It is important, then, in making the argument that basic design *is a discipline* unto itself, that the clear distinction between basic *design* and basic *studies* be kept in mind.

There were essentially two important years of the Maldonado *Grundkurs*: Academic year 1955/56 was its formative year; academic year 1956/57, in which I took part, was its consolidating year. In the years that immediately followed, Maldonado's participation in the *Grundkurs* tapered off, as he shifted his focus of interest, first, to the Visual Communication Department, where he worked out practical studies in *visual semiotics*,[42] and, later, to Product Form, where he stressed *ergonomics*. This shift coincided with his subsequent roles in the administration of the school and the buildup of its curriculum along methodological lines. In fact, in the two unique years of the *Grundlehre*,[43] during which Maldonado essentially developed his *Visuelle Einführung* (introductory visual training), he was trying and testing many ideas that would later shape the curriculum of the school as a whole. By 1962, he had revived the HfG journal, *ulm*,[44] in which HfG ideas

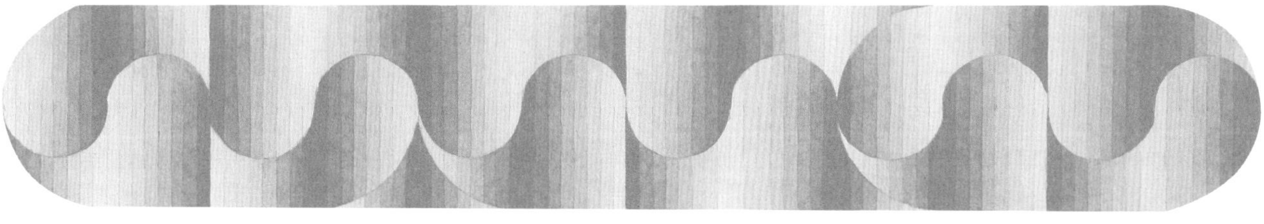

Ota Ulc, "The Out and In of Yang and Yin". Basic Design Studio of William S. Huff, Fall 1992, SUNY at Buffalo. © HfG-Archiv/Museum Ulm, HfG-Ar, BDSA, Hu P 05. 031.
Assignment: Conflicting Depth Cues.

[41] Josef Albers, "To design is", *Yale Alumni Magazine* 21, April 1958, p. 6.

[42] Reportage and corporate identity were two other feathers of Visual Communication that had been pursued from the department's inception.

[43] Maldonado was not the only instructor of what the *Grundlehre* was as a whole: other instructors were Hermann von Baravalle, Helene Nonné-Schmidt, Otl Aicher, and Herbert Ohl (the last in 1956/57 only). Maldonado continued to teach the visual introduction component of the *Grundlehre* in the years of 1957/58, 1958/59, and 1959/60.

[44] Its squarish format, which made shelving difficult, was scrapped for a more conventional vertical format. The first issue in this form was *ulm* 6, October 1962, designed by Tomás Gonda.

Marsha Berger, "In-tri-cut". Basic Design Studio of William S. Huff, Fall 1970, Carnegie Mellon University (CIT). © HfG-Archiv/Museum Ulm, HfG-Ar, BDSA, Hu P 08. 021.
Assignment: Parquet Deformations.

could be disseminated to a larger design community of academics and professionals—a goodly number of whom had already shown considerable curiosity in the Hochschule by their pilgrimages to the Kuhberg.

IV. The Maldonado *Grundlehre* Assignments

A list of the *Aufgaben* (assignments) from the Maldonado section of the *Grundlehre* of 1955/56 is as follows:[45]

Visuelle Einführung
(visual introduction) Kurs Maldonado

- Sierpinskifläche (Sierpinski curve)
- Peanofläche (Peano surface)
- Weierstrass-Kurve (Weierstrass curve)
- Schwarz als Farbe (black as color)
- Symmetrien (symmetries)
- Genau–Ungenau (exact through inexact)
- Ungenau–Genau (inexact through exact)[46]
- Räumliche Wirkung (spatial effect)
- Gleichgewicht dreier Flächen (balancing of three planes)
- Störung (interruption)[47]

A list of *Aufgaben* from the *Grundlehre* of 1956/57: [48]

- Symmetrie (symmetry)
- Parkettierung (parquetry—now termed “tiling”)
- Näherung, Zweideutigkeit, Gleichheit–Gestalt Übung (proximity wins; neither wins; similarity wins—Gestalt exercise)
- Vordergrund–Hintergrund, Zweideutigkeit, Hinter-grund–Vordergrund–Tiefenwahrnehmung Übung (foreground, central square of format advances▯ambiguity, central square neither advances nor recedes▯background, central square recedes—depth perception exercise)
- Modifizierte Peano Kurve mit verschiedenen Farben und Schwarz als noch eine Farbe–Schwarz muß nicht ein Loch sein (modified Peano curve with several colors and black as one of the colors—black must not become a hole)
- Ungenau durch Genau oder Ungenauigkeit durch Genauigkeit (inexactness through exactness)
- Genau durch Ungenau oder Genauigkeit durch Ungenauigkeit (exactness through inexactness) assigned, but none were executed
- Wahrnehmung Übung (perception exercise)—in two rows, a six- or seven-step deformation of a square ring into a succession of round-cornered rings: upper row of rings deformed mechanically in order to actualize optical problems; lower row of rings altered visually so that all optical pro blems appear to be corrected, especially that all rings appear to belong to the same family[49]

In looking back at the 1956/57 *Grundkurs* in which I participated, there was a question in my mind about the Raster: No assignment mandated a raster, yet somehow the potential of rasters was discussed (halftone and three-color printing with black—and even TV rasters).[50] Furthermore, our class was aware that handsome rasters had been executed in the preceding class. The vexing question of the raster was only recently clarified by Dolf Zillmann, who had participated in the *Grundlehre* of 1955/56:

> To the best of my knowledge, it all [the first appearance of the Raster] came about spontaneously in dealing with “ungenau durch genau”. In addressing this Aufgabe, Peter Seitz [...] and I used Rasters in different ways.[51] It was not part of the assignment. In fact, nobody thought it was a big deal —like greatly innovative. Only after Tomás, upon completion of the *Aufgabe*, singled out the Rasters as something special and as a wonderful solution to his problem did the Raster become the focus of attention. The Raster became popular overnight. And as you know, Almir Mavignier helped to make it a bit of a centerpiece of concrete art. Be this as it may, it was Tomás who saw something special in the Raster. To us, it was merely a tool to solve an assignment, and our eyes had to be opened to it.[52]

The raster, which, as texture rather than artifact, had already struck the bent of the young *Art Concretist*, suddenly showed its “didactic importance”;[53] it became something that was wanting of further exploration.

Some of Maldonado’s assignments were, very likely, exploratory for himself as well as for his student. Zillmann is dead right: The good pedagogue is on constant alert, knows when he sees it, and is ready to promulgate something extraordinary that occurs under his instruction. It is not unreasonable to conclude that this was a part of Maldonado’s pedagogic strategy.

Maldonado presented a group of assignments (listed below in the order in which they were given) to my first-year architectural class in Pittsburgh in 1963.[54] Many were variations of those that had been given at the HfG in the *Grundlehre* of either 1955/56 or 1956/57. In sum, they comprised a characteristic cross-section of the Maldonado repertoire of exercises—though due to the short duration of his visit, he did not present any of his more mentally challenging assignments, such as *inexactness through exactness*.

A. “Two Rows of 7 to 9 Transformations of a Rectangle”: from a central elongated rectangle, transformations to the left, to be the inverse of those to the right. Upper row to be done with straight lines, lower row with curved lines.[55]

B. “Series of 6 to 7 Steps of the Transformation of a Square Ring into Successive Round- Cornered Rings—But not into complete Os”: upper row, in black, to be altered optically in order to counteract

Thomas Davies. Basic Design Studio of William S. Huff, Spring 1964, Carnegie Mellon University (CIT). © HfG-Archiv/Museum Ulm, HfG-Ar, BDSA, Hu P 02. 036. Assignment: Symmetry. Note by Huff: "Four errors in execution of program."

[45] This list came from Hans (Nick) Roericht. Reviewed by myself in the HfG-Archiv collection, the identification plates, documented by different students on their submissions, show a certain fancifulness in the range of names that were individually given to the different *Aufgaben*.

[46] Roericht does not list this Aufgabe, but Dolf Zillmann responded to it in an exemplary way.

[47] Roericht's index of *Aufgaben* lists one title as "Strömungen". It may be in error for "Störung", since the HfG-Archiv has student work from 1955/56 with this description. In the 1954/55 *Grundlehre*, Albers had presented his classic assignment, titled "Gestörte Ordnung". See Hochschule für Gestaltung Ulm: *Die Moral der Gegenstände*, Herbert Lindinger (ed.), Berlin, 1987: p. 34.

[48] From the memory and files of W. S. Huff.

[49] This classic exercise *in this form* was found among undated notes of mine. I have still not found a classmate who can verify its having been assigned to the 1956/57 *Grundlehre*, yet that is most likely the time of its first appearance. A variation of this was given at Carnegie Institute of Technology in 1963. Maldonado connected this assignment to the subtlety of typefaces, which are adjusted to overcome optical problems.

[50] Maldonado, who had contacts with Telefunken at the time of my *Grundlehre*, had noted that the TV image was transmitted as a raster of dots that streamed across the TV tube, line by line. He speculated that perhaps the Peano curve could be a better path for the raster. I am advised that some computer chip circuitry has since been designed in that manner.

[51] See Lindinger, *Hochschule für Gestaltung Ulm*, p. 45.

[52] Email from Dolf Zillmann, 4 February 2003.

[54] Email from Tomás Maldonado, 3 July 2003.

[55] Nine exercises assigned by Tomás Maldonado to first-year architectural students (Basic Design Studio of William S. Huff) at Carnegie Institute of Technology, 25 March to 19 April 1963. These descriptions were carefully recorded in 1963. Exercise B was critiqued on 3 April; A, on 9 April; D, E, F, G, and H, on 19 April. No solutions were executed for Exercises C (the faculty member in charge of the shop would not allow plaster to come into it) or I (not enough time was left for it).

Prior to this time, this exercise was unknown to me. The HfG-Archiv has a variant of this exercise, executed at the HfG.

[56] In a purer version, which may have been assigned in the 1956/57 HfG *Grundlehre*, only black was applied to the rings (see above).

[57] This exercise was unknown to me before 1963. The assignment's directive matches a sculpture by Max Bill: *Column with Triangular and Hexagonal Section*, 1966. See Max Bill (Buffalo Fine Arts Academy and Albright-Knox Art Gallery, 1974), p.

various perceived flaws. Lower row, the same in two colors—one color for the ring, one color inside the ring.[56]

C. "Transformation of a Shaft with One Regular Polygonal Face at One End and with a Different Regular Polygonal Face at the Other End": to be executed in plaster.[57]
D. "Black as a Color, Not a Hole": on an 8 by 8 grid, use colors; from 6 to 10 squares are to be black.[58]
E. "Elementary Raster Problem":[59] using only one element (in size and shape), located at the intersections of a grid, have the field of elements produce a Gestalt through the rotation (orientation) of the element only. Repeat the square formatted field twice on the same plate: the element of the first field to be rendered in black, differentiated colors to be added to the element of the second field.
F. "Peano Curve": create a Gestalt with subtractive color.[60]
G. "Modified Peano Curve": apply two colors of the same value.[61]
H. "No Prima Donna": within a horizontal rectangular format, arrange ten vertical stripes: three in different textures, four in different colors, three in black. No stripe is to dominate.
I. "Sierpinski Triangle": the smaller (upright) triangles are to be colored in R, Y, and B, according to a given diagram. Apply grays to all (inverted) triangles between the colored triangles; the grays must be optically adjusted for balance in both hue and intensity, according to their surrounding colors.[62]

Not surprisingly, Maldonado altered his assignments from class to class, and frequently shuffled a directive for one format to a different format. In most of his exercises, many of which were tests (études) in perceptual skills, the layouts were strictly prescribed; and the optical irritations that were identified (often subconscious and subtle, yet with the power to distract from the harmony of the whole) were to be altered to suit the eye. The outcomes, either more or less successful, were subject to an intense saturation of critical aesthetic absorption. The collective group opinion of the trained and in-training (instructor and students) yielded (after interactive deliberation) the verdict on the degree of success of such exercises in respect to its aesthetic evaluation. This transpired by calling upon a faculty that every able designer must attempt to master—thus the utter necessity that students develop a sharpened aesthetic response able to judge every phase of the assignment along its development—which is to say, to carry through any act of design.

Maldonado's more open assignments were posed as challenges, which could lead to surprising outcomes. Some of the themes of his assignments, can, very likely, be traced to Buenos Aires, where, as the articulate exponent of *Art Concret*, he began to build his immense library of information. Certainly, however, two of his most challenging assignments had to have come out of his period in Zurich with Max Bill: "Ungenau durch Genau" and "Genau durch Ungenau". In his monograph on Bill, the initial draft of which accounted for a large part of the time that he spent in Zurich in 1948, he wrote about such conundrums:

> The new theme trend is also manifest in the pictorial production of Bill. Certain notions as continuous - discontinuous, precise–imprecise, limited–unlimited, which constitute his favourite thematic repertoire, are, undoubtedly, filtrations coming from the most up-to-date scientific expression. [...] The lines, dots and sfumatos help invalidate the traditional concept of precision as it was understood until Mondrian—to give way to a new concept: the imprecision–precision. Imprecise–precise because in works of art of this type the purpose is constructive, even when certain external resources be diffuse and not very strict.[63]

An unpublished paper (until 2003), which he wrote in 1948, takes up what Maldonado considered at the time (as mentioned above) to be the main problem of *Art Concret*:

> Figure versus ground is the fundamental issue of Concrete Art. Any figure on a ground determines a space. If this occurs within a plane, on its surface that space is illusory. [...] Concrete Art is a continuous effort to destroy this illusory space. [...] That is why recently two great

Andrew Liu "Limbo". Basic Design Studio of William S. Huff, Fall 1996, SUNY at Buffalo. © HfG-Archiv/Museum Ulm, HfG-Ar, BDSA, Hu P 04. 022. Assignment: Conflicting Depth Cues.

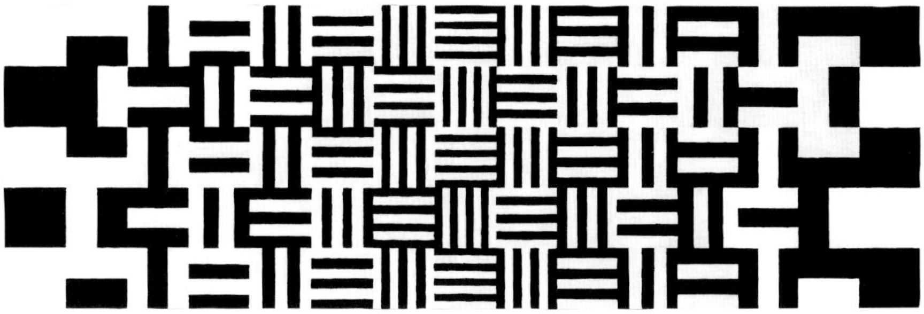

Robert Hand, “Figure–Texture–Ground Study–Variant 2, Five by Fifteen Checkers”. Basic Design Studio of William S. Huff, Spring 1964, Carnegie Mellon University (CIT). © HfG-Archiv/Museum Ulm, HfG-Ar, BDSA, Hu P 09. 025. Assignment: Symmetry. Note by Huff: “Fails symmetry test.”

[58] This directive was linked to a modified Peano curve format in the 1956/57 *Grundlehre*.

[59] I have called this type of assignment the “Single Element Raster”.

[60] A Peano curve assignment was given a different directive in the 1955/56 *Grundlehre*, with handsome results. See Lindinger, *Hochschule fur Gestaltung Ulm*, pp. 46–47.

[61] The directive of Exercise D “Black as a Color” and the modified Peano curve format of Exercise G had been combined in the same assignment in the 1956/57 *Grundlehre*. Maldonado’s directive at Carnegie to use two colors of the same value enters the province of one of Albers’s most subtle interaction of color exercises (vanishing boundaries).

[62] Examples from the 1955/56 *Grundlehre* are in the HfG-Archiv. See *Ulm Design: The Morality of Objects*, Herbert Lindinger (ed.), Cambridge, MA, 1991, p. 47.

[63] Maldonado, *Max Bill*, p. 18.

[64] Maldonado, “Concrete Art”, pp. 11, 13; see also Maldonado, Max Bill, p. 18.

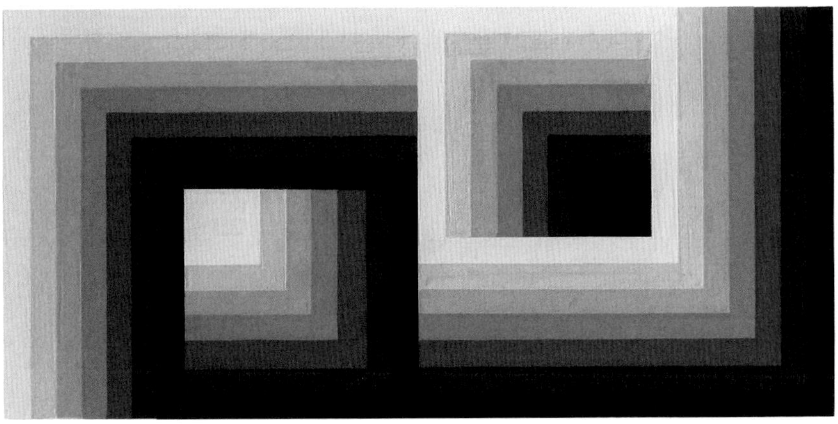

Jorge E Calle, “Copan”. Basic Design Studio of William S. Huff, Fall 1989, SUNY at Buffalo. © HfG-Archiv/Museum Ulm, HfG-Ar, BDSA, Hu P 04. 027. Assignment: Conflicting Depth Cues.

> Concrete artists, Vantongerloo and Bill, have suggested that the route might be to overcome the limited figures. To liquidate the figures, in a word, and to make the ground vibrate to a maximum (by using subtle, non-figurative elements) would be one of the ways.[64]

Undoubtedly, this ruminant can explain Maldonado's enthusiasm for Zillmann and Seitz stumbling upon rasters as their solutions to "Ungenau durch Genau". In effect, Zillmann and Seitz had come up with a marvelous way to "vibrate the ground".

The companion assignment, "Genau durch Ungenau", baffled our *Grundlehre* class of 1956/57. As I remember, no solutions were produced—at least, no adequate ones. It was deemed a conceptually impossible directive. Yet I learned in my recent contacts with Dolf Zillmann that in the 1955/56 *Grundlehre*, which preceded ours, Maldonado had judged Zillmann to have had come up with "a perfect solution": "One of [his assignments] was to generate something precise with patently imprecise means. I remember taking a piece of firewood, the end of which was shaped like a slice from a round pie, and using it as a stamp, rotating it around an imagined point to create a precise circle. Whatever the value of the result, Tomás thought it to be a perfect solution to his assignment, and the piece received a disproportional amount of attention."[65]

Gwen Herr, "Here's Herr's Herringbone". Basic Design Studio of William S. Huff, Fall 1969, Carnegie Mellon University (CIT). © HfG-Archiv/Museum Ulm, HfG-Ar, BDSA, Hu P 04. 026.
Assignment: Conflicting Depth Cues.

Jeffrey D. Roos. Basic Design Studio of William S. Huff, Fall 1981, SUNY at Buffalo. © HfG-Archiv/Museum Ulm, HfG-Ar, BDSA, Hu P 09. 014.
Assignment: Programmed Design.
(Editor's note: Original in color)

The principle calculation of the Maldonado pedagogy seems to have operated along two tracks: a student acquiring mastery of their visual acuity—through Gestalt, in specific, and perception, in general; the student's exploration of and experimentation with formal syntax—augmented by symmetry theory, visual topology, and other mathematical curiosities, such as the Peano and Weierstrass curves. Many of the sources of knowledge that Maldonado introduced were very current in respect, at least, to the publication dates of the texts at his disposal.

In 1949, while still in Argentina, he came across the Peano and Weierstrass curves and the Sierpinski triangle in a Spanish version of Hans Hahn's "The Crisis in Intuition",[66] later to be published in James R. Newman's *World of Mathematics*.[67] He seriously entertained such paradoxes of *curve theory* as potential features for his *Art Concret* productions. In 1950, he was impressed by a French pamphlet by M. A. Sainte-Laguë on topology.[68] Then, during his initial involvement with the HfG *Grundlehre*, he acquired three key writings, Walther Lietzmann's *Anschauliche Topologie*, K. L. Wolf and D. Kuhn's *Gestalt und Symmetrie*, and A. S. Parchomenko's *Was ist eine Kurve?*[69] Furthermore, aside from expanding his bookshelf with these topics, he kept current on most of these interests with the latest issues of *Scientific American*. By introducing these things in the context of visual training, Maldonado resolutely deviated from Albers's injunction not to read books; rather, Maldonado suffused the *Grundlehre* with "operational, manipulable, real knowledge".[70]

[65] Letter from Dolf Zillmann, 19 September 2002.

[66] Hans Hahn, "La crisis de la intuición", in *Crisis y reconstrucción de las ciencias exacas*, La Plata, 1936.

[67] Hans Hahn, "The Crisis in Intuition", in *The World of Mathematics*, James R. Newman (ed.), vol. 3, New York, 1956, 1956–1976. An article in the same volumes, exemplary in the eyes of Maldonado for its remarkable scientific lucidity, was singled out as a rare reading assignment: Leonhard Euler, "The Seven Bridges of Königsberg", in *World of Mathematics*, Vol. 1, Newman, pp. 573–580.

[68] M. A. Sainte-Laguë, *La topologie*, Paris, 1949.

[69] Walther Lietzmann, *Anschauliche Topologie*, Munich, 1955; K. L. Wolf and D. Kuhn, *Gestalt und Symmetrie: Eine Systematik der symmetrischen Körper*, Tübingen, 1952; A. S. Parchomenko, *Was ist eine Kurve?*, Berlin, 1957. A series of lectures in Buenos Aires 1957 and 1958 on symmetry, topology, perception theory, and semiotics prompted Wolf and Kuhn's text on symmetry to be translated into Spanish: *Forma y simetria: Una sistemática de los cuerpos simétricos*, translated by Renate Leisse de Mertig and Mario H. Gradowczyk, Buenos Aires, 1959.

[70] Ockman, *Architecture Culture*, p. 299.

James T. Mountain, Inversion with Dilatative Motif. Basic Design Studio of William S. Huff, Spring 1989, SUNY at Buffalo. © HfG-Archiv/Museum Ulm, HfG-Ar, BDSA, Hu P 06. 028. Assignment: Programmed Design. Note by Huff: "Marginal craft".

Richard E. Stehlik, "four checkered homeometric grids". Basic Design Studio of William S. Huff, Fall 1964, Carnegie Mellon University (CIT). © HfG-Archiv/Museum Ulm, HfG-Ar, BDSA, 08. 009. Assignment: Symmetry. (Editor's note: Original in color)

It was implied, rather than stated, that an aesthetic could emerge from either track; the critical response to matters of perception and the visual concretization (programming, so to say) of mathematical and geometric abstractions.[71] Indeed, that did seem to occur, more than not—especially when the two tracks were conducted in tandem.

V. A New Model, Partly Executed, Partly Not

Maldonado was responsible for bringing a critical mass of methodologists (in mathematics and in the soft sciences) into the HfG faculty, who eventually returned the favor by taking over the administration of the school for a two-and-a-half-academic-year period—June 1960 to December 1962. While the design-oriented faculty did finally regain the reins of the school from the methodologists,[72] it must be concluded that this surreal interlude did not have only negative consequences (one of the negatives having been that the students analyzed design problems with exquisite thoroughness, but did not design any longer).[73] In hindsight, the interruption advanced the development of the school, not only by challenging the original Bill model (as Maldonado was already doing), but by provoking Maldonado's reevaluation of his own emphasis on the role of methodology in design—that is, that methodology was running the risk of becoming "methodolatry".[74]

While Maldonado's teaching in the *Grundlehre* was curtailed for a brief period, his interest in the basic design problem did not abate; there were new ideas to try. After academic year 1960/61, when Friedrich Vordemberge-Gildewart had taken on the responsibility of most of the visual training in the *Grundkurs*,[75] the unified *Grundkurs* was abolished.[76] There had already been experimentation in the latter years of the unified *Grundkurs* to assign some tasks of an applied nature—ones differentiated according to a student's elected discipline.[77] That was the beginning of putting into practice one element of Maldonado's straightforward, idealized curricular model, which mapped basic design vis à vis *applied design (the Design–non-applied/ Design–applied model*).

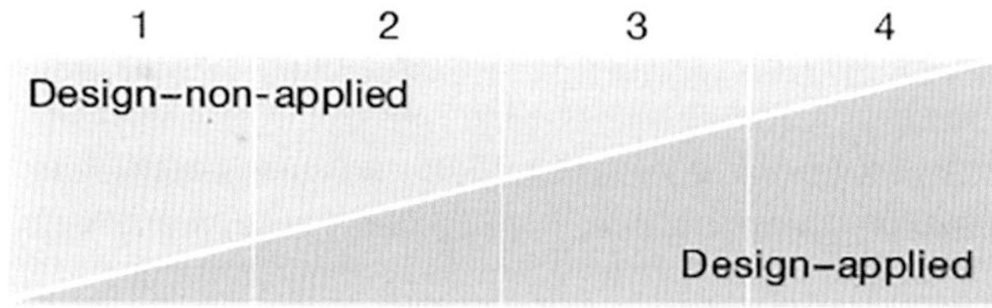

Art historian Kenneth Frampton, an early HfG observer, made the following report:

> It should be noted that the foundation course, or *Grundlehre*,[78] had been discontinued, after Maldonado had been appointed as head of the industrial design department with the reorganization of 1962. After this year, students were channeled into one of the three departments from the very beginning; that is, from the first year they entered directly into their chosen specialty, be it *building, product design or visual communication.*[79]

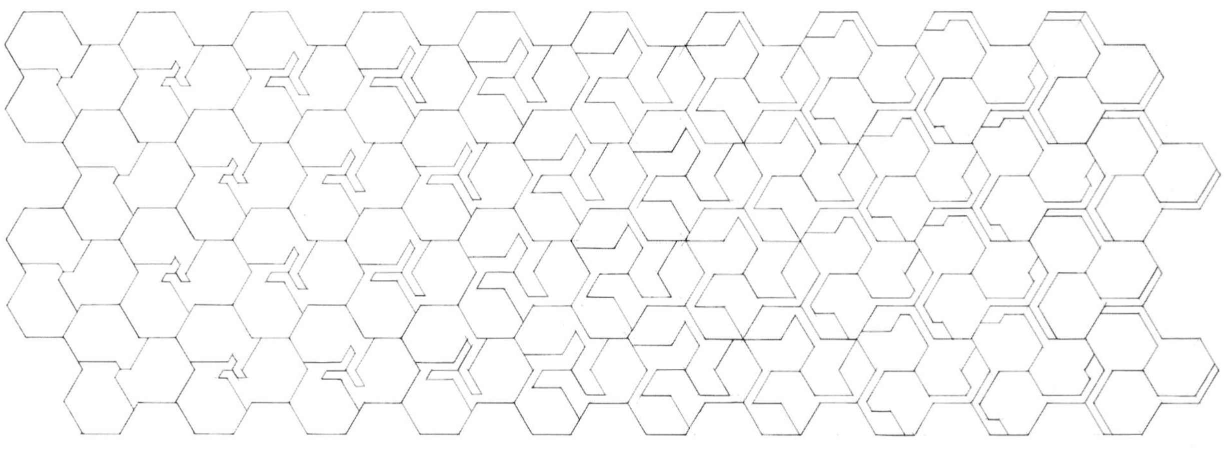

William Mc Adams, "Tri-Cellular Trade". Basic Design Studio of William S. Huff Spring 1989, SUNY at Buffalo. © HfG-Archiv/ Museum Ulm, HfG-Ar, BDSA, Hu P 06. 018. Assignment: Parquet Deformations

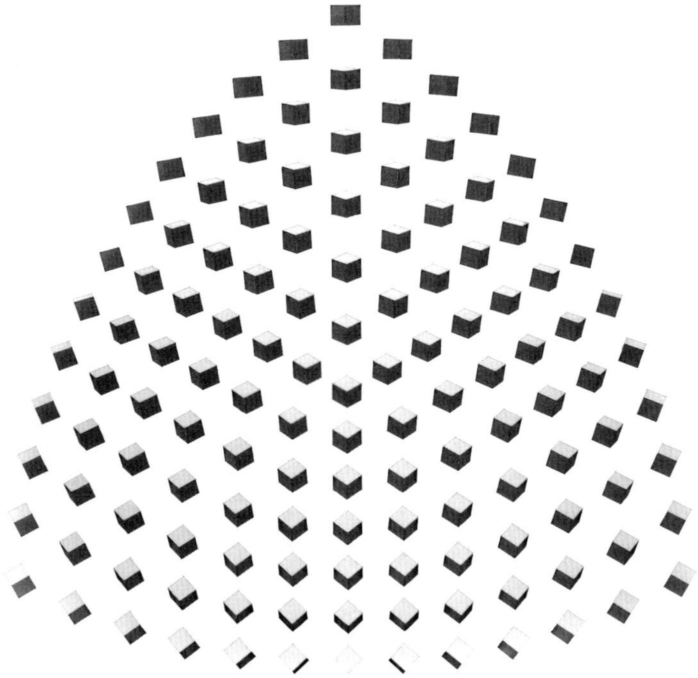

Thomas Breen, "Axonometry Cubed". Basic Design Studio of William S. Huff, Fall 1993, SUNY at Buffalo. © HfG-Archiv/Museum Ulm, HfG-Ar, BDSA, Hu P 02. 019. Assignment: Programmed Design: Syngenometry, Note by William Huff: "Axonometry Cubed—one isometric view of a cube at the center, three axes of dimetric views, three fields of trimetric views, and three borders of orthogonal views." (Editor's note: Original in color)

71 Many geometers (H. von Baravalle was not one of them, K. L. Wolf was) are often unaware of many of the visual ramifications of the equations with which they work. At the same time, these geometers make aesthetic judgments in respect to the equations themselves.

72 "On December 15, 1962, a new constitution for the HfG came into effect. On December 20, 1962, Otl Aicher was elected Director for the academic years 1962/63 and 1963/64. Tomás Maldonado was elected Vice-Director." *ulm* 7, January 1963, p. 2.

73 Maldonado, *form + zweck*, p. 20.

74 See Tomás Maldonado and Gui Bonsiepe, "Science and Design", *ulm* 10/11, May 1964, p. 10. Also see an earlier expression of these realizations: "There are those who believe that all design problems can only be solved by mathematical formalization. [...] The designers of [this] category seem to have a much more intransigent opinion on methods than the scientist themselves. The scientists sometimes have doubts about scientific methods, but the designer of the kind referred to—never", Tomás Maldonado, "Opinions: Preliminary Note", *ulm* 6, October 1962, p. 3.

75 With Vordemberge-Gildewart as his instrument, Horst Rittel, leader of the insurgent group, made known to me (during my visit in June 1960) that "now the HfG students will learn to use color!"—meaning a shattering of the obsessively insistent use of only black, white, and gray (plus the little red dot) by the students in Product Form and in Building, since Visual Communication, by its nature, could not have done very well without the use of color. It did not work. It took an event in 1963 to do that: a lecture by the GK Industrial Design Association of Tokyo, led by Yoshio Nishimoto.

76 Some confusion is found in various articles about the year in which this took place. Citing 1961/62 are: Karl-Achim Czemper "Die pädagogischen Ziele der Grundlehre", *output* 6/7, 1961, pp. 1–10; Hans Roericht, *HfG-Synopsis*, Ulm, 1982. Tomás (Milan, [2002]); citing 1962/63 are: Kenneth Frampton, "Apropos Ulm: Curriculum and Critical Thinking", *Oppositions 3*, May 1974, p. 27; Lindinger, *Hochschule fur Gestaltung Ulm*, p. 33.

77 Maldonado, *form + zweck*, p. 19.

78 *Vorkurs*, *Grundlehre*, and *basic design* have often been used synonymously in articles by numerous writers (including, I admit, myself). In Frampton's article, there is a distinct clash of these terms that allows misinterpretation to gain hold.

79 This was based on "tables that Gunter Schmitz made available to [a] Montreal seminar" in February 1968. Frampton, *Oppositions*, pp. 27–28. Actually, there were still four departments at that time; it is not known (at the time of this article) how beginning students were handled in the Information Department in 1961/62.

Though Frampton wrote in this same passage (but well removed from the above) that "for a student of industrialized building [...] some 45 percent of his time would have been spent in *basic design*", this falls short of Frampton's making clear that only the *Grundkurs* as a *unified* entity had been abolished, not basic design studies as such.[80]

To reiterate, what this curricular reform did, under Maldonado's guidance, was to mandate that each department take charge of its own *Grundlehre* curriculum,[81] and each could tailor its own first-year tasks (both its specific formal tasks and its specific applied tasks). In an oversimplification of this, it could be said that the three-dimensional assignment types of the originally unified introductory courses were carried over into Product Form[82] and the two-dimensional assignment types into Visual Communication.[83] Under "3D Non-Functional Projects",[84] among a number of formal projects, one extensive study of nonorientable surfaces (square, circular, or triangular sheets, some with round holes, were given simple cuts, twisted, reattached) was conducted during one first-year session in Product Form. At the same time, in accord with Maldonado's *basic design/applied design* model, rather elementary applied design tasks (e.g., simple tools or everyday utensils, rudimentary graphic pieces, or clever building components) were assigned in the first-year courses of the respective departments. In Product, for instance, a lamp and an assortment of office implements were assigned.[85]

In Building, among the formal exercises that served this department's purposes,[86] one of Josef Albers's Bauhaus assignments was given new life —paper-folding, which Albers had reprised for the first *Grundkurs* of 1953/54. Albers had permitted cuts to be made in the paper in earlier days of his assignment,[87] but later forbade them. One instructor in Building, perhaps Herbert Ohl, reintroduced the slitting of the paper (usually one- or two-ply Bristol board) with small repetitive cuts in the process of paper-folding.

I myself had a part in continuing the Maldonado model of visual training in the Visual Communication Department from 1963 until the school's closing in 1968.[88] I shared these tasks with Maldonado himself, Herbert Lindinger, and Tomás Gonda. (After one year of protest and noncompliance, Film—a subdepartment of Visual Communication, and a new one at that—opted out of Visual Communication's compartmentalized *Grundkurs*.) Maldonado, Zeischegg, and Bonsiepe, and possibly others, developed the compartmentalized *Grundkurs* material for Product Form.

Though the breakup of the unified *Grundlehre* was carried out in 1961, Maldonado's idealized curricular diagram was only partly implemented. That is to say, a systematic continuance of basic design in the advanced years was never implemented despite his argument that upper-level students liked to return to purely formal assignments from time to time: "They have nostalgie for it."

Albers had championed this idea, as well. On the one hand, he welcomed former students who returned to his basic design classes for a rejuvenescent fix;[89] and in a variation of this position, "it was most rewarding" to him "that many graduate students from various fields of study [...] enrolled in basic art courses officially assigned to beginners."[90] But this was catch-as-catch-can. In fact, one should look back to the Bauhaus as the design school where an intermingling of the formal (basic design) and the practical (applied design) was actually carried on throughout the whole curriculum. Shortcomings of the workshop system have been noted. But the continuance of formal issues in advanced training was assured by the workshop system as laid out:

> The Bauhaus [...] ruled (1) that every [workshop student][91] is taught by two masters, a craftsman and an artist, who work in close cooperation; (2) that instruction in crafts and in the theory of form are fundamental: no [workshop student] can be excused from either.[92]

The lines that separate the strictly formal from the practical might, at times, have been blurred; but the possibility to revisit formal issues on a continuing basis was built into these two rules.[93]

In the 1990s at the University at Buffalo, I pressed for my withdrawal from our department's required pre-architectural design program[94] and, in turn, requested that I be permitted to offer my basic design course *on an elective basis* to students in the graduate program.[95] This type of design instruction was entirely new to a great number of our graduate students, many of whom came from abroad. I was not supported by much of my faculty (though certain eminent, but not "in-charge" colleagues gave my mission their morale-boosting backing); and the department's administration, though allowing it, nonetheless constantly thwarted it. At any rate, I can claim success in the trial: evidenced in small part by the splendid results of the students and in large part by how the students approached the opportunity with a maturity that undergraduate students seldom brought to the classroom.

VI. An Elaboration of the Maldonado Model

I was 29 in 1956, when I found what I had been seeking in design—perhaps, from the very start of my entry into that arena. I was 33 when I dared to meet the challenge of teaching my long-sought chimera—and to make it into a worthy adult occupation. Upon returning

[80] Had the HfG abandoned basic design under the reorganization of 1961/62, my article, “An Argument for Basic Design”, would scarcely have been given space in the HfG journal, *ulm* 12/13, March 1965, pp. 25–38, nor would there have been reason for the HfG to invite me to conduct five annual guest courses in my modified-Maldonado version of basic design from 1963 to the closing of the school. Furthermore, the *ulm* journals, from 1963 on, made a special point to publish teaching results of each department’s first year.

[81] Maldonado considers this to be an important accomplishment: “We took this approach one step further and the basic curriculum was structured differently for each department. That was the end of the idea that there was one curriculum that could serve as the basis, a basic curriculum that was the foundation for all designing activities.” Maldonado, *form + zweck*, p. 19. My one concern is for the immature students who approach design with very little formal grounding from their previous education. Under the unified *Grundlehre*, these students had the advantage of an eye-opening year before committing their futures to a particular design specialty.

[82] “In connection with the preparation of an introductory course in three-dimensional design for the first study-year of the Industrial Design Department, Walter Zeischegg made a series of studies in the field of experimental geometry.” See “Experiments with Regular Solids”, *ulm* 7, January 1963, pp. 11–12.

[83] “Visual Communication Department: 1. Study-year”, taught by Herbert Lindinger and William S. Huff, *ulm* 17/18, June 1966, pp. 40–45.

[84] “3D Non-Functional Projects”, Industrial Design Department, first year 1965/66, taught by Gui Bonsiepe, *ulm* 17/18, June 1966, pp. 21–34.

[85] “Warning and Repair Lamp for Cars”, Industrial Design Department, first year 1963/64, taught by Herbert Lindinger; “Office Implements”, Industrial Design Department, first year 1963/64, taught by Tomás Maldonado; “Microphone”, Industrial Design Department, first year 1962/63, taught by Tomás Maldonado, *ulm* 12/13, March 1965, pp. 48–53.

[86] “The department described the instruction for the incoming students as ‘Einführung in die besondere Teilproblematik des industrialisierten Bauens. Aufgaben aus begrenzten wichtigen Teilbereichen werden analytisch erfasst, verglichen und konstruktiv neu gestaltet.’” Gunter Schmitz, email from 9 September 2002. See also “Basic Design for Architects”, Building Department, first year 1966/67, taught by Gunter Schmitz, *ulm* 19/20, August 1967), pp. 41–46.

[87] Wingler, *Bauhaus*, pp. 431, 433, 435.

[88] In 1963, I also taught the first year of Building.

[89] Beckmann, in Neumann, *Bauhaus*, pp. 196–197.

[90] Albers, *Search*, p. 25.

[91] The text here reads “apprentice and journeyman”. For an explanation of this ranking system, see Herbert Bayer, Walter Gropius, and Ise Gropius (eds.), *Bauhaus* 1919–1928, New York, 1938, p. 26.

[92] Bayer, Gropius, and Gropius, *Bauhaus*, p. 25.

[93] That most of the “artist” masters at the Bauhaus had been an integral part of the Modern Movement undoubtedly put the handling of formal issues in the workshops on the highest of planes.

[94] My basic design course in this program was autonomous, so it was not an issue of any need of independence that spurred my request to shift gears—rather, it was my desire to put the Maldonado *basic/applied design* model to the test.

[95] I can personally recommend this route; for, after all, this is the one that I took: I attended the visual course at the HfG after obtaining a degree in Architecture from Yale. I was well

to the States from Ulm in 1957, I had no intention to teach anything at all, much less to teach basic design. After a year's immersion in the fundamentals of design at the Hochschule, I returned to the pursuit of an architectural career and had the good fortune to be taken into the office of Louis Kahn in Philadelphia. I also lobbied for the adoption of the HfG model of *basic design*—with an emphasis, of course, on the Maldonado curriculum—by at least one leading American school of architecture. I considered Yale's Department of Architecture to be, perhaps, the most likely of loci for this to come off—in part, because now I could point to an authentic *and tested* alternative to the poor shadow of a Bauhaus-style introductory course that I had been obliged to take eight years earlier; in part, because the Bauhaus's Albers, who had arrived at Yale after my experience with that most wanting of introductory courses, was still heading the Department of Art and had a skilled staff under him.[96] My cause was politely heard, but went nowhere.

At one point, Kahn suggested that I serve as his assistant for a new Urban Design studio at the University of Pennsylvania. I told him that I feared that I would be more the student than the assistant in a studio of this unfamiliar territory. I did propose, however, that I could confidently assist the faculty member who was in charge of Penn's introductory course. Kahn responded: "No, you should not assist anyone in an introductory course. You are the one to set up a new introductory course." I took this remark seriously and immediately began to outline a course along the lines of my HfG *Grundlehre* experience. As it turned out, Penn's dean was not prepared for this proposal, even with Kahn's weight behind it; but upon learning of my outline of a basic design course, Carnegie Institute of Technology's head of Architecture, Paul Schweikher,[97] a friend of both the Alberses and Mies van der Rohe, lost no time in latching onto what he considered a most timely opportunity to further the reinvigoration of his department's program.

Short of any formal sanction, I deemed that I had Tomás Maldonado's and other HfG faculty members' tacit consent to carry on an HfG-type *Grundlehre* instruction in Pittsburgh—for suddenly, sheer chance had veered me far off the course of my original intent, merely to spread the word in the States about a consequent course of a progressive school of design. I had stuck out my neck; my head was on the platter.

As it turned out, in the course of time, two of my former HfG classmates from 1956/57 have also conducted their versions of the Maldonado *Grundlehre*: Shutaro Mukai, as founder and head of the Department of Science of Design at the Musashino Art University in Tokyo for 35 years, and Thomas Dawo at Krefeld. Giovanni Anceschi, whom I did not know in his HfG days, has also worked in this arena at Milan's Politecnico under the aegis of Maldonado. Sudhakar Nadkarni helped to found and then headed the Industrial Design Centre, IIT, in Mumbai, where he set up much of the introductory course, as well as other parts of the design program, along HfG lines.[98]

In my teaching of basic design for most of 38 years (1960–1998), I did, then, unapologetically adopt the HfG *Grundlehre* model, as it had struck me: mainly the Maldonado portion, potent in its approach to visual training, but also key segments from Helene Nonné-Schmidt and Hermann von Baravalle[99]—all eye-opening experiences; a dash of Albers's *interaction of color* was included in it too. My students were assiduously primed about the various origins of this course of study.

From my experience at Ulm, I took note of a differentiation between two types of assignments—exercises, tightly prescribed in order to develop skills and to reinforce particulars of information, and projects, loosely stipulated along thematic lines, but formulated as challenges to ingenuity and creativity.[100] Over time, I edited and modified various HfG exercises in minor ways to suit my goals for my students. At the same time, though the projects that I developed inescapably had HfG genes, I elaborated from where Maldonado had left off—much of which was responding to significant breakthroughs of the students, who themselves were not always cognizant of what they had unwittingly wrought.

Aside from three of Maldonado's classic exercises that address perception, there was only one project that I have expressly adapted from Maldonado: *Symmetry*. His assignment statement to our class was rather loose and went something to this effect: "Make a design from the combination of two or more of Wolf's[101] 13 isometric and/or homeometric operations of symmetry."[102] In time, upon my review of the ramifications of Wolf's *lower levels* of symmetry (syngenometry and katametry), this project was retitled *The Programmed Design*. Simple programs that produced complex structures were abetted: structures, whose invariant properties (akin to the secrets of *natural law*) were not obviously discernible—even though the design, from beginning to end, had been wholly determined, once the student had (free of choice) selected the motif element(s) and rule(s) of operation. An aesthetic (of no particular preconception) was always the goal—but that precluded the indulgence of any *arbitrary* intervention whatsoever, in order to bring about a more desirable outcome. Only an across-the-board alteration of the program would do: that is, the uniform alteration of the element(s) or of the rule(s) or of both.

The Parquet Deformation[103] grew out of Maldonado's *Parkettierung Aufgabe*[104]—which few, if any, other than

Luis Perelman, “Étude 3 of 3”. Basic Design Studio of William S. Huff, May 1961, Carnegie Mellon University (CIT). © HfG-Archiv/Museum Ulm, HfG-Ar, BDSA, Hu P 04. 042. Assignment: Raster—Lineal Halftone.

prepared to receive this fundamental training.

96 Robert Engman, Erwin Hauer (who designed a whole series of modular screens, based admittedly on the 1947/48 “lattice-oriented shell surface” by the HfG’s Walter Zeischegg, whom Hauer had known at the Vienna Academy of Fine Arts. See ulm 14/15/16 [December 1965], p. 41), Norman Ives, Neil Welliver, and Sewell Sillman. I was too naïve at that time to realize how threatening such a proposal might have been considered among the Albers group. In respect to the faculty of Architecture, many probably thought that Albers was entirely enough of a Bauhaus force for any American school to handle.

97 Both Schweikher and Kahn were the design instructors of my “thesis” year at Yale. Prior to Schweikher’s heading the Department of Architecture at Carnegie, he headed Architecture at Yale; and it was at his request that Albers set up the course “Structural Organization” for the Architectural Department which was in name only any different from what he taught in the Art Department’s basic design course.

98 Nadkarni is now head of the Department of Design at the Indian Institute of Technology (IIT) in Guwahati, India.

99 Both Nonné-Schmidt and von Baravalle were “a heritage of Max Bill’s *Grundkurs*”, Maldonado, 3 July 2003.

100 “Discovery and Invention, the Criteria of Creativeness”, Albers, *Search*, p. 32.

101 Wolf and Kuhn, *Gestalt*.

102 In 1965, I received a grant from the US government for a proposal to present Wolf’s 13 symmetry operations and other matters of symmetry in a visual format. A series of booklets, designed by Tomás Gonda, were put out under the title: *Symmetry: An Appreciation of Its Presence in Man’s Consciousness*.

103 Douglas R. Hofstadter, “Parquet Deformations: Patterns of Tiles That Shift Gradually in One Direction”, in “Metamagical Themas”, *Scientific American* 249, July 1983, pp. 14–20. Also see Douglas R. Hofstadter, “Parquet Deformations: A Subtle, Intricate Art Form”, chapter in *Metamagical Themas: Questing for the Essence of Mind and Pattern*, New York, 1985, pp. 191–212.

104 See Lietzmann, *Topologie*.

myself, executed in our class of 1956/57. The recognized potential of innumerable variants of any given *parquet* (an array of congruent tiling) led to connecting variant tilings to one another serially through *continuous deformation*[105]—a device that the morphologist D'Arcy Thompson appropriated from Dürer, the artist, and developed for his analysis of evolutionarily related species. As a design device, the operation of continuous deformation permeates the spatiality of a planar image, unraveling it through temporality[106]—superbly establishing that the dimension of time is not the exclusive prerogative of music and drama.

The *Color-Raster* came out of Maldonado's latent interest in rasters, which was stimulated by solutions to an assignment in the 1955/56 *Grundlehre*. At first, my students worked with halftones and three-color rasters along the lines of black-and-white and color clichés; but in succeeding years, the assignment eventually culminated in repeated demonstrations that pigments, on a dark ground (or with no ground showing between the raster elements), work the way that spectral light works: RGB *pigments* in particular will produce a whole spectrum of colors through "mixing in the eye".[107] (Splatters of a limited range of reds, mingled with splatters of a limited range of greens in the favorable context, will produce a rich yellow.) The brief for *Conflicting Depth Cues* calls for pitting one cue against another to create contradictory perceptions. Since Albers[108] and Escher had already saturated both the art market of the elite and the bazaar of pop with their subtle and not-so-subtle tricks of the eye (and brain) created, on the whole, through linear perspective, I had my students concentrate on the potentials of the other depth cues to elicit captivating visual contradictions. *The Figurative Ground*[109] project engaged not only the Gestalt principle of *figure-ground*, but the manipulation of texture[110] and sfumato,[111] and the topology of the maze. By juxtaposing gradients of texture or sfumato, figuration can be made to appear abruptly and to disappear just as abruptly. When carefully traced, all figurative figments will prove to be integral parts of their very own, singular ground.

Regarding assignments of the third dimension, which I presented on an intermittent basis, I continued Maldonado's examination of *Nonorientable Surfaces*, treated by Bill for many years as a major sculptural foil. I posed one question: "Can symmetry be introduced into any topological variant of the Möbius band?" Yes, the answer promptly turned up from my students' first tests; *the potential of twofold rotational symmetry is lodged in such a configuration*.[112] The elusive principle of *Twofold Mirror-Rotation Symmetry*, whose clarification I had failed to grasp from Maldonado and which was poorly depicted by Wolf,[113] had me looking into crystallography, where I learned that a theory of symmetry was not possible before *Fourfold Mirror-Rotation Symmetry*,[114] a most uncommon structure in nature,[115] had been grasped. Remarkable objects, based on the properties of twofold, fourfold, and sixfold mirror-rotation, have been given shape by many hands and heads of my students; these abstract objects often exhibit a monumental quality. *The Trisection of the Cube* (into congruent solids) emerged analogously from parquetry (or congruent tiling of the plane). While three-dimensional congruent sectioning of any complexity was simmering in my mind, I encountered a trove of fine plaster models of congruently sectioned solids in the basic design studio of Andrzei Pawlowski, Departmental Dean of Industrial Design,[116] whom I had visited at Krakow's Akademie Sztuk Pieknych in 1970. At first, my students continued to investigate the congruent sectioning of any regular or feasible semi-regular solid; but the assignment settled into the *trisectioning of the cube*, when our attention was drawn to an error of omission in Martin Gardner's regular column for *Scientific American* in 1980[117]—suggesting a topic that was wide open to exploration.

In my visual training courses,[118] mostly for architectural design students, I rigorously addressed only formal issues—letting those issues be conjoined only to other abstract disciplines, in accordance with Maldonado' insightful interdisciplinary reach. While references to symbols, to associative emotions or memories, or to cultural overtones can well be the context of other pedagogic endeavors, those very matters are kept, as far as is possible, from intruding into and watering down the basic design product. It is, then, perhaps not surprising that many who engage in the practical disciplines of design, in both academia and the professions, find even the best examples of the product to be useless—but not pithily "useless" in the way that Anni Albers had meant it; others think them exotic; but worst of all, perhaps, many of those who are uninitiated in respect to involvement in design, find them, if not baffling, to be decorative.

Recently, at my urging, Claudio Guerri of the University of Buenos Aires[119] ran a semiotic analysis on the question of whether basic design (as I see it) can be regarded as a self-contained discipline.[120] This exercise, probing basic design's body parts, as it were, seemed to be warranted at this juncture—more than eight decades after basic design's legendary inception in Weimar. In the course of our joint venture, Guerri remarked that the product of basic design and the kind of tasks that produces it are "hermetic" in the eyes of many design faculties—mostly for the reason that the need for basic design instruction has not been made clear enough. Agreeing with this, my response is that I myself have been consistent in my argument that I have dealt all along, as Albers put it, purely with "form

[105] From "continuous transformation", "The Theory of Transformation, or the Comparison of Related Forms", D'Arcy Wentworth Thompson, *On Growth and Form*, 2nd ed., Vol. 2, Cambridge, 1959, p. 1086 (page numbers from the reprinted edition).

[106] William S. Huff, "The Landscape Handscroll and the Parquet Deformation", in *Katachi U Symmetry*, Tokyo, 1996, pp. 307–314.

[107] "Optical mixing", Josef Albers, *Interaction of Color*, New Haven, 1963, p. 33.

[108] "'Optical illusion' should be replaced with 'optical deception'", Albers, *Search*, p. 21.

[109] Upon the publication of Tomás Maldonado's manuscript, "Concrete Art and the Problem of the Unlimited" (Ramona, 2003), I learned that Maldonado had termed such an effect "vibrating the ground"—a ground that had no discrete figures.

[110] César Jannello, "Texture as a Visual Phenomenon", *Architectural Design* 33, August 1963, pp. 394–396.

[111] Max Bill's *Unbegrenzt und begrenzt/Unlimited and Limited*, 1947.

[112] In many of its usual depictions, the Möbius band appears to be asymmetrical. In fact, the 180° twist that is given to a flat strip before its two ends are joined should be a dead giveaway to the potential of capturing the twofold rotational property in specific rigid pieces.

[113] Wolf and Kuhn, *Gestalt*.

[114] Though not classified as the 32nd Crystal Class, it was the 32nd of the 32 Crystal Classes to be discovered in the mid-nineteenth century.

[115] Molecules have been found to exhibit this trait, but entities with this property have not been a part of the scenery—at the scale of our familiar visual world.

[116] Pawlowski's curriculum at the Academy in Krakow was influenced by that of the HfG.

[117] Martin Gardner, "Mathematical Games", *Scientific American* 243, September and October 1980.

[118] There were three different one-semester formats, under a variety of different names, that covered (1) syntax in 2D, (2) perception in 2D, (3) syntax and perception in 3D.

[119] Professor Titular of *Morfologia* (a version of basic design—i.e., the study of all formal issues) at the Faculty of Architecture.

[120] The methodology of the analysis is realized by the "semiotic nonagon", which is an operative triadic model developed by Guerri from C. S. Peirce's semiotic construct. See Claudio Guerri, "Gebaute Zeichen: Die Semiotik der Architektur", in *Die Welt als Zeichen und Hypothese: Perspektiven des semiotischen Pragmatismus von Charles S. Peirce*, Uwe Wirth (ed.), Frankfurt am Main, 2000, pp. 375–389.

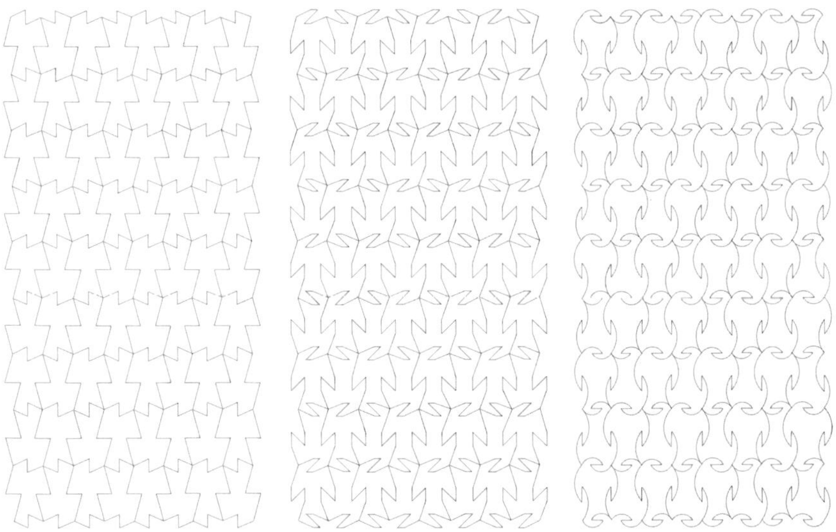

Maurizio Sabini. Basic Design Studio of William S. Huff, Spring 1982, SUNY at Buffalo. © HfG-Archiv/Museum Ulm, HfG-Ar, BDSA, Hu P 06. 002. Assignment: Parquet—3 Variants.

that exists for its own sake",[121] in the confidence that immersion in formal content alone—devoid of cultural, referential, or associative, even physically characterized, overtones[122]—can unleash the sensory capacity. I speak now for myself: My overarching objective has been to elevate, without inordinate distraction, my students' mastery of their own innate aesthetic acuities.

John Weiler. Basic Design Studio of William S. Huff, Fall 1962, Carnegie Mellon University (CIT). © HfG-Archiv/Museum Ulm, HfG-Ar, BDSA, Hu P 02. 032.
Assignment: Symmetry (Version 3 of 3)
(Editor's note: Original orientation is 90° counter clockwise; Original in color).

[121] "'Abstracting,' he wrote, 'is the essential function of the Human Spirit. Abstract Art is the purest art: it strives most intensely toward the spiritual. Abstract Art is Art in its beginning and is the Art of the Future.' He saw abstract art as a natural part of an historical development toward a 'pure art,' as part of a move away from 'imitative aims' that pictured 'nature, stories or sentiments' toward 'non-representative form, form that exists for its own sake, namely for form reasons.'" Mary Emma Harris, *The Arts at Black Mountain College*, Cambridge, MA, 1987, p. 13.

[122] For most of the 1980s, in addition to teaching *basic design* to pre-architectural candidates, I taught *basic architecture* to first-year architectural students. The two courses were markedly different. Basic architecture, instructed by a team, was authored by Alvaro Malo, Richard Cordts, Frances Downing, and myself. Five major "fragments" of architecture, five provinces of performance, were identified: the anthropometric and the ergonomic (the body's relation to itself and to objects in space); the constructional (the smaller and larger joinery of specific materials); the formal or syntactic (emphasizing the void of space and involving aesthetic judgment), the environmental (passive control of natural elements—light, acoustics, climate); the contextual (urban and pastoral landscape). Each fragment was addressed by tasks that strictly minimized, during targeted consideration, the involvement of the other four fragments.

Editorial note

This text was published in *Ulmer Modelle – Modelle Nach Ulm*, Hochschule für Gestaltung Ulm 1953–1968, Ulmer Museum/HfG-Archiv (ed.), Hatje Cantz, Ostfildern-Ruit, 2003. The article is reprinted here with kind permission of William S. Huff and the HfG Ulm Archive; accompanied by new imagery made available by Dr. Martin Mäntele and selected by Werner Van Hoeydonck.

Biography of the Author

William S. Huff attained two degrees from Yale University: Bachelor of Arts, 1949; Master of Architecture, 1952. He was awarded a Fulbright Fellowship (1956) to study at the Hochschule für Gestaltung (HfG) in Ulm, Germany, where he later returned as a Guest Teacher (1953–1968). He held academic positions at the Departments of Architecture of Carnegie-Mellon University from 1960 to 1972 and of The State University of New York at Buffalo from 1974 to 1998, when he was elected Professor Emeritus. In 2008, he received a Doctor Honoris Causa from the Ministry of Science and Education of Ukraine, National University Lvivska Polytekhnyka, Institute of Architecture. He has written on his principal pedagogic discipline, basic design, symmetry, topology and color; with the aid of Claudio Guerri's analytic Semiotic Nonagon, he resolved the age-old problem of a theory of the logic use of color (www.academia.edu/16332326/). Huff has written on Tomás Maldonado, under whom he studied; on Louis Kahn, under whom he also studied and in whose architectural office he worked from 1958 to 1962; and on American artist S. H. Crone. In 1989, Huff was a founding member of the International Society for the Interdisciplinary Study of Symmetry, ISIS-Sym, at Budapest, to which he was elected Honorary President in 2007. He was a honorary member of a number of other international interdisciplinary organizations; he was elected Honorary Member of SEMA (2003) and was an International Fellow and Founding Supporter of Japan's Society for the Science of Design Studies (1998). His studio assignment, the parquet deformation, was recognized by Douglas Hofstadter in Scientific American (July 1983).

Geometry of Structures and Its Philosophical Aesthetic Background

Cornelie Leopold

In this chapter, the design approach at the Ulm School of Design, which is based on the geometry of structures and transformations, will be described and related to the background of the philosophical aesthetic of the school, introduced by the philosopher Max Bense. Max Bill's mathematical approach to art and design coincided fruitfully with the rational philosophy of Max Bense by focusing on the human relationship to a technological world preconditioned by rationality and methodological thinking. Mathematical methods were introduced into the structural analysis and creative design processes. Based on this foundation, aesthetics was developed into an informational aesthetics derived from information theory and semiotics. The redundancies arising from rules such as symmetries were brought into relation with innovation; random and chaotic states were instigating by breaking the preset rules. This was the beginning of the first digital design experiments. Research on different levels of symmetry formed the basis for William S. Huff's programmed design. The roots of his parquet deformation assignments can be found in the structural approach at the Ulm School of Design.

1. Design Approach at the Ulm School of Design

The Ulm School of Design (HfG–Hochschule für Gestaltung) existed for only short a time, between 1953 and 1968, but attracted students and professors from all over the world who later, as professors and practitioners, spread the school's ideas and concepts throughout many countries. One of the school's most important foundations was thinking about structures in relation to mathematical and cybernetic structures as a fundament for design methods. Design had been based on philosophical reflections and theories, especially through the involvement of the philosopher and science theorist Max Bense, who had been professor of philosophy and theory of science at the University of Stuttgart. Bense developed a new definition of aesthetics[1] by starting with Hegel's description of art. In that definition, the aesthetic state of an object is related to distributions of elements or representations of order in the meaning of arrangements. Elisabeth Walther, professor at the University of Stuttgart and lecturer at HfG Ulm, described the role of this new definition:

> Aesthetics, as Bense brings it into play, is the principle of order par excellence. Aesthetics is order, and order on the other hand is describable by mathematics. Therefore, aesthetics is important as structuring the world for techniques as well as architecture, literature, etc., for all what will be created. Whenever we take something out of the chaos of existing and assemble it new, we need an aesthetic foundation.[2]

This background of a new understanding of aesthetics influenced the design approach at HfG Ulm. Bense's aesthetics was in close relationship to Max Bill's mathematical foundation of art and design, as Bill expressed in his essays.[3]

> Now in every work of art the basis of its composition is geometry or in other words the means of determining mutual relationship of its component parts either on plane or in space. Thus, just as mathematics provides us with a primary method of cognition, and can therefore enable us to apprehend our physical surroundings, so, too, some of its basic elements will furnish us with laws to appraise the interactions of separate objects, or groups of objects, one to another.[4]

Max Bill, the founding director of HfG Ulm, found in Max Bense a guest professor for fruitful discussions and interactions in the field of aesthetics between theory and practice. In 1965, at the opening of Max Bill's exhibition in Esslingen, Bense stated, "By coming across Max Bill, I came across a kind of art that could be safely regarded as an object, he provided aesthetic objects for the theory, that could be examined."[5]

The students at HfG Ulm also experienced these interrelationships between design theory and practice as examples for developing a new information aesthetics based on order and chaos and redundancy and innovation. Principles of order as an aesthetic foundation can be looked for in the geometry of tessellations, patterns, their spatial variants and the mathematics of symmetries, developed as a theory of transformations. Bense[6] noted that this corresponds to Paul Valéry's statement[7] that compared with the role of mathematics in the sciences, patterns and ornaments—ornamental drawing—are fundamental to art.

Together with various guest professors, Max Bill and, later, Tomás Maldonado created a curriculum at the Ulm School of Design with mathematical approaches in design and architecture.[8]

2. Geometric Structural Background

A fundamental geometric background was taught in the foundation courses at HfG Ulm. In the first years, from 1953 to 1958, the foundation course was oriented around the experiences of the Bauhaus. It concentrated on a visual training of eye and hand, freehand drawing, and experiments with materials. Max Bill, the first rector of HfG, himself a former student at the Bauhaus, engaged Helene Nonné-Schmidt, Walter Peterhans, Josef Albers, and Johannes Itten as guest teachers for the first course, which started in August 1953. Geometrical transformations like symmetries and proportional transformations were important elements in the Drawing and Paper Folding modules taught by Albers in the 1953/54 and 1955 foundation courses. Max Bill did not teach the foundation course himself but selected the teachers and offered his critiques of some tasks.

The design of the City of Ulm's pavilion for the Baden-Württemberg state exhibition in Stuttgart, 1955, is an example of his architectural design being based on the idea of geometric transformation and pattern. The pavilion was designed by Max Bill, but the graphical appearance of the pavilion was worked out by the students of the visual communication department of HfG Ulm under the guidance of Otl Aicher and Friedrich Vordemberge-Gildewart. The design is based on a fourfold rotation of the fundamental cell module, as shown for the top view of the pavilion in Figure 1. The design is based on the classical development of ornaments based on the root 2 system, which can be also found in HfG students' drawings.[10]

In our 2012 "Structure – Sculpture" summer school in Buenos Aires, we also analyzed the spatial structure that can be produced by a spatial element after a fourfold rotation. Figure 2 shows the 3D analysis and a physical 3D model of the Ulm Pavilion, created by the summer school participants.

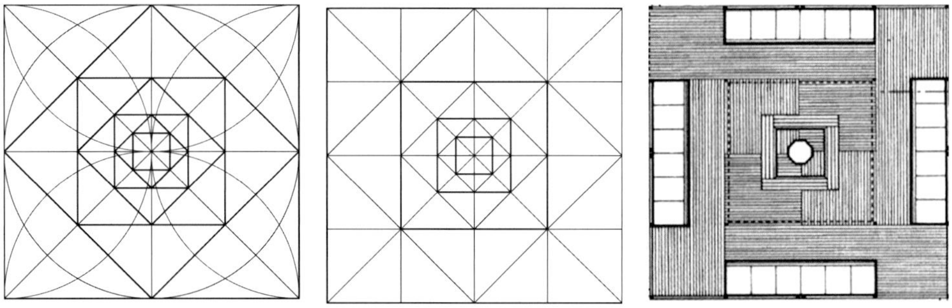

Fig. 1: Development of ornaments based on root 2 system and top view of the Ulm Pavilion.

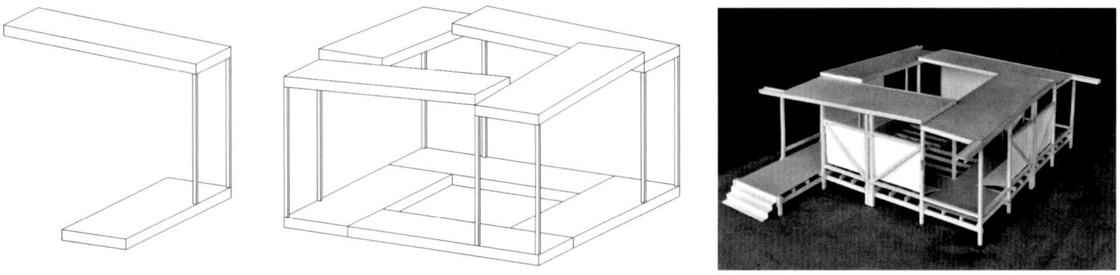

Fig. 2: Spatial element of Ulm Pavilion and result after rotation, physical model.[11]

Fig. 3: Spiral arrangement in the geometric series of squares, regular hexagons, and octagons.[12]

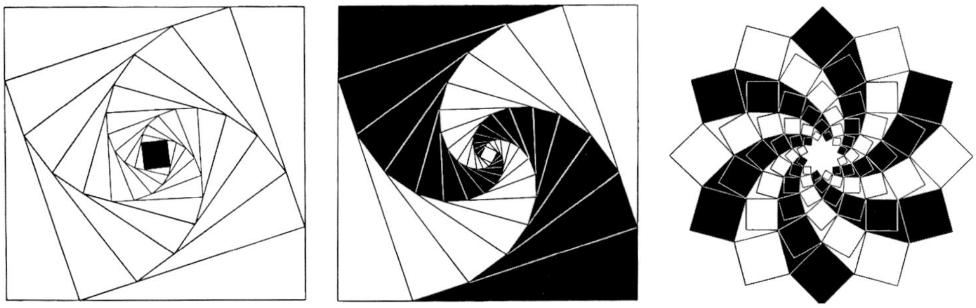

Fig. 4: Geometric series of rotated squares, spiral arrangement, and spiral arrangement of square rings.[13]

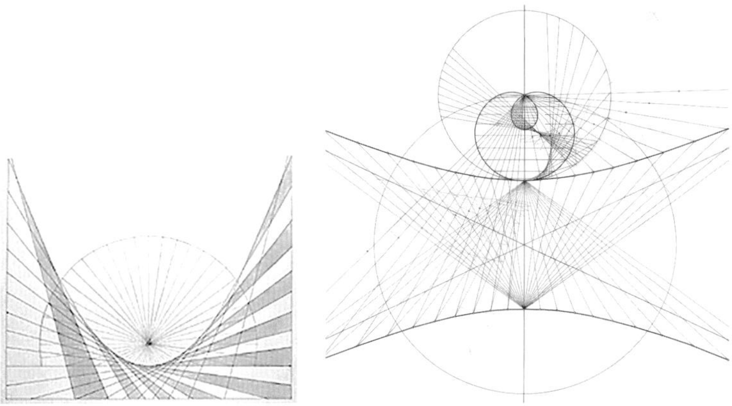

Fig. 5: Creating parabola by moving a right angle, student Dominique Gilliard, 1955/56[14] and Limaçon of Pascal as inversion of a hyperbola, student Hermann Edel, 1956.[15]

More details about the importance of structural thinking at the Ulm School of Design, especially by Max Bill's design approach and Max Bense's philosophy and aesthetics, have been described by Hermann Edel,[16] who studied at HfG Ulm in the Department of Architecture between 1956 and 1960. Later, from 1963 until 1974, Hermann Edel and Max Bill worked together on modular building systems in Darmstadt, Germany.

3. Hermann von Baravalle's Dynamic Geometry

After delivering some guest lectures in the early years of HfG Ulm, Hermann von Baravalle was assigned to teach constructive geometry (1955–1959) in the foundation course. Having strong roots in the tradition of Waldorf education, Baravalle established a dynamic understanding of geometry based on movements of points and lines. His concept of dynamic geometry complemented the Albers action-oriented way of teaching. Baravalle described his dynamic geometry concept in his *book Geometrie als Sprache der Formen*,[17] published in 1957. How fundamental the geometric series of squares are when developed as a root 2 system (as shown in Figure 1) is illustrated in Figure 3, where Baravalle creates spiral arrangements inside the square system by black and white fillings. He constructed corresponding spiral arrangements inside the regular hexagon and octagon.

Baravalle's dynamic understanding of geometry is perfectly illustrated in Figures 4 and 5. These courses must have made a deep impression on William S. Huff,

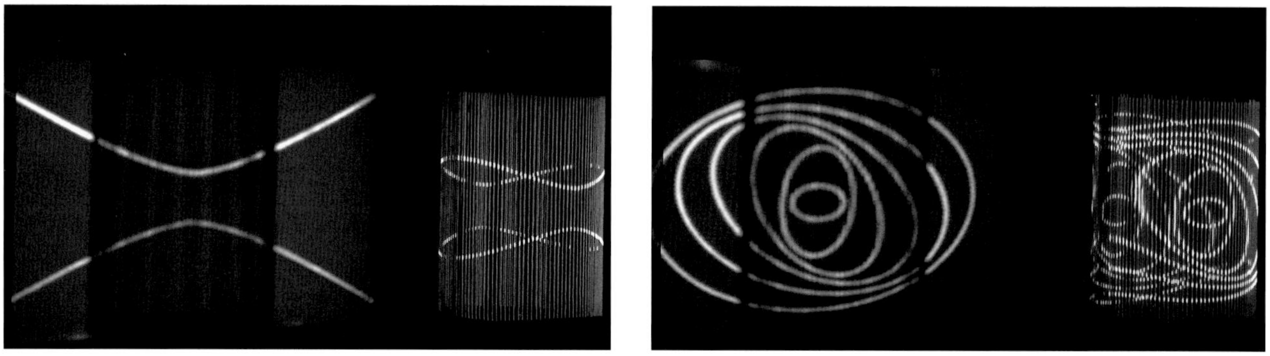

Fig. 6: Two examples of the Baravalle-Kino by Hermann Edel, hyperbola (left) and six ellipses in different sizes and rotated (right).

since many of his students' works take this same dynamic approach.

Hermann Edel was especially impressed by a performance by Baravalle at HfG in 1959. Lines drawn on slides were projected on a string cylinder. A straight line, for example, resulted in an ellipse on the string cylinder. Then the slide projector was moved, which produced changes in the curves on the cylinder. Hermann Edel recreated this performance in 1959, with Baravalle's consent. In 2013, Edel presented a redesigned "Baravalle-Kino" (Figure 6).[18] This dynamic approach to geometry and experimentation using transformational concepts of geometry was fundamental at the Ulm School of Design.

4. Mathematical and Theoretical Background by Tomás Maldonado

A new type of foundation course that took a more scientific approach was conceived by Tomás Maldonado. In his early years in Argentina, he was one of the leading artists and founders of *Arte Concreto-Invención*. In Europe, he contacted the European Avant-Garde, met Max Bill in 1948, and decided to write a monograph on Max Bill's work, which appeared in 1955. Max Bill offered him a position at the newly founded Ulm School of Design, first as his assistant, and he was later given responsibility for the foundation course. Finally, he had been rector and member of the rectorate of HfG for several years. He introduced working and designing on the basis of theoretical knowledge in perception theory and mathematics. "Visual Methodology" played a leading role in the foundation course in this second phase. William S. Huff, an American student and later teacher at HfG Ulm, described the concept of Maldonado's foundation course in an interview:

> Maldonado came to Ulm in the second year. [...] So, he started thinking about better ways of doing the *Grundlehre*. In the third year, 1955/1956, he took on teaching the *Grundlehre*. He carried on what one might call the purification and renovation of the Bauhaus direction. He preserved what Albers had done at the Bauhaus. But at the same time, he introduced something more: He made it interdisciplinary. He brought in some other subjects, such as symmetry and topology and a good dose of Gestalt theory. He introduced information about these subjects into the course, which Albers had not done. [...] But Maldonado was a person who wanted you to know where the different parts of these disciplines came from.[19]

The most important aim was to mediate a way of thinking that could be later used for the applied design tasks. The tasks Maldonado assigned in the foundation course did not have a reference to practical design, though. Instead, the focus was on a methodical approach to connect science and design. Drawing was systematized, and the guiding principle was reflective visualization.[20] In their paper "Wissenschaft und Gestaltung",[21] Maldonado and Gui Bonsiepe listed the following mathematical disciplines as operable for the product designer in the design practice:

1. Combinatorics (for modular construction systems and problems of measure coordination)
2. Group theory (as symmetry theory for construction of patterns and grids)
3. Theory of curves (for the mathematical treatment of transitions and transformations)
4. Polyhedral geometry (for the construction of regular, demiregular, and irregular solids)
5. Topology

Figure 7 shows examples from Maldonado's foundation course related to these topics.

In the section on symmetry, Maldonado integrated different levels of symmetry. In this context, Maldonado

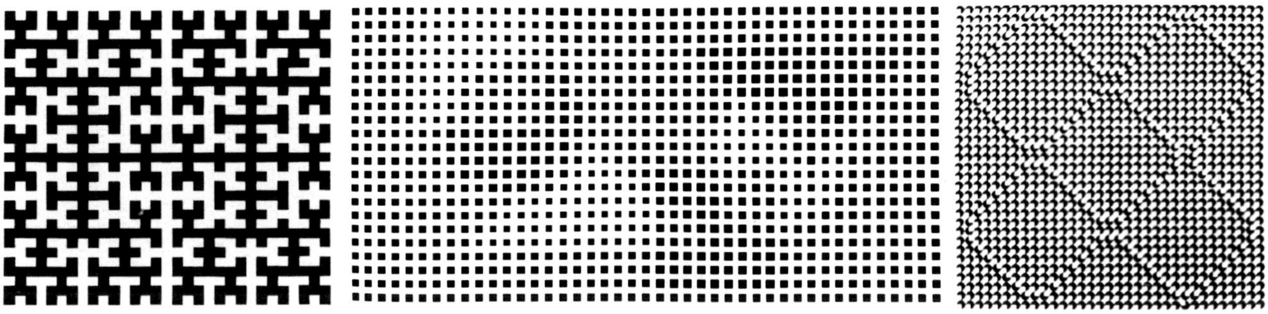

Fig. 7: Peano curve example, student Klaus Frank; inaccuracy with precise means, student Adolf Zillmann; pattern arrangement by student Bertus Mulder; course taught by Tomás Maldonado, 1955/56, 1956/57. © HfG-Archiv, Ulmer Museum, Ulm

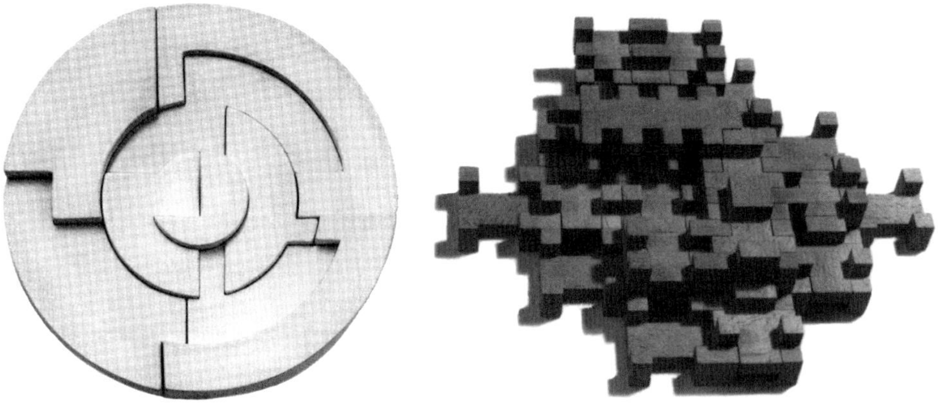

Fig. 8: Form-fitting net of katametric elements by student Klaus Schmitt; grid of katametric elements, student Jan Thylén, 1961/62, teacher Tomás Maldonado. © HfG-Archiv, Ulmer Museum Ulm.

picked up the notion of *katametry*, likely from the publication on symmetries by German chemists Karl Lothar Wolf and Robert Wolff, who were working on molecular structures. Their book is subtitled "Versuch einer Anweisung zu gestalthaftem Sehen und sinnvollem Gestalten"[22] and suggests different levels of symmetric structures (see Chapter 6). Katametry is a low level of symmetric structure, not clearly geometrically defined. Two examples (Figure 8) from Maldonado's course show how he used the notion of katametry as a design method. Kurd Alsleben[23] and William S. Huff[24] analyzed, in detail, the symmetric concepts of Wolf and Wolff (see Chapter 6).

5. Visual Methodology by Anthony Froeshaug

These topics remained important in the following years. A visual methodology was devised in more detail as a key part of the foundation courses. Anthony Froeshaug came from London and taught at the Ulm School from 1957 until 1960 in the Department of Visual Communication. In 1958/59, he took over the foundation course for all departments with the support of Maldonado. Froeshaug further developed Maldonado's concept of visual methodology into the main focus of the general foundation course, with the aim of introducing patterns and grids systematically, first in two dimensions and then in three.

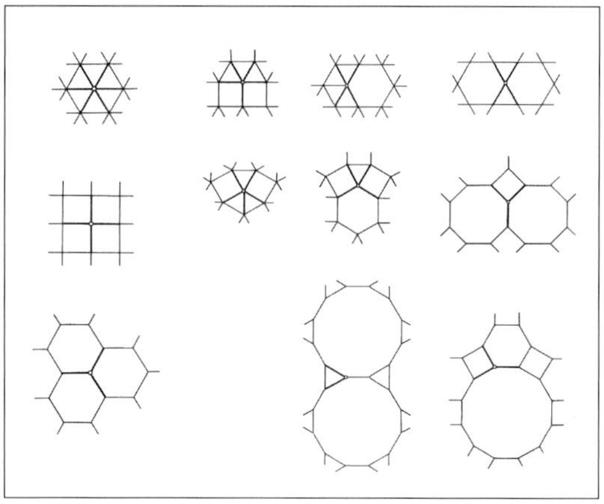

Fig. 9: Regular and semi-regular 2D lattice structures by Anthony Froeshaug, 1959. © HfG-Archiv, Ulmer Museum, Ulm.

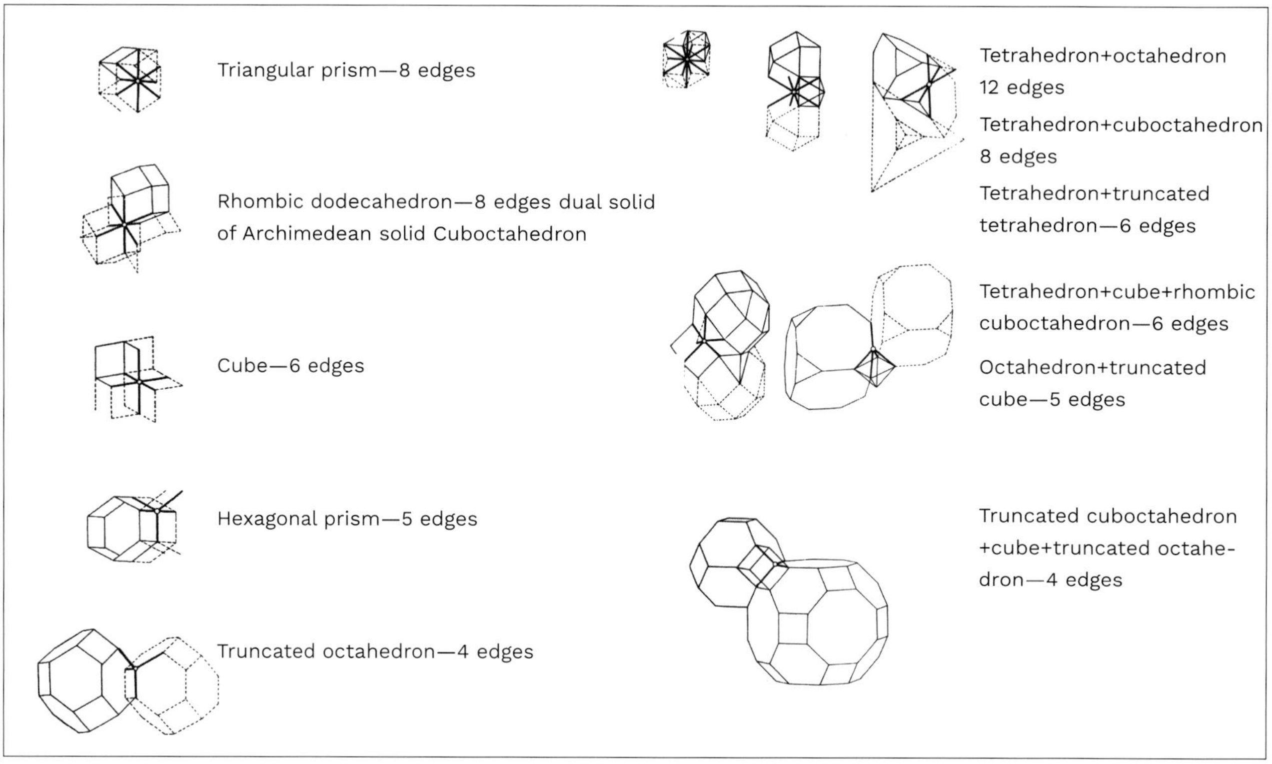

Fig. 10: Regular and semi-regular 3D lattice structures by Anthony Froeshaug, 1959. © HfG-Archiv, Ulmer Museum, Ulm.

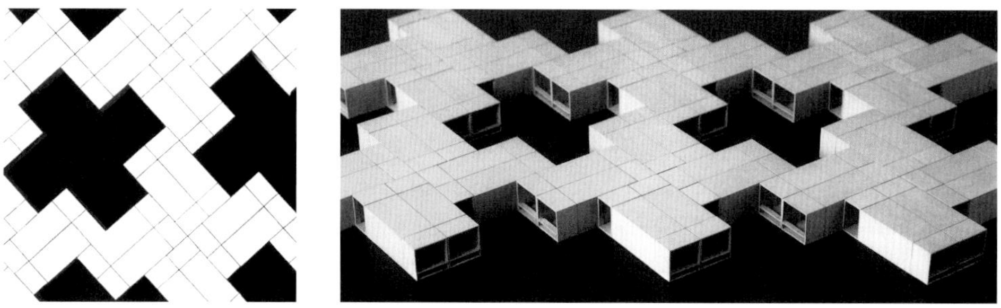

Fig. 11: Space units for residential buildings 1961, design: Bernd Meurer, Herbert Ohl.[25] © HfG-Archiv, Ulmer Museum, Ulm.

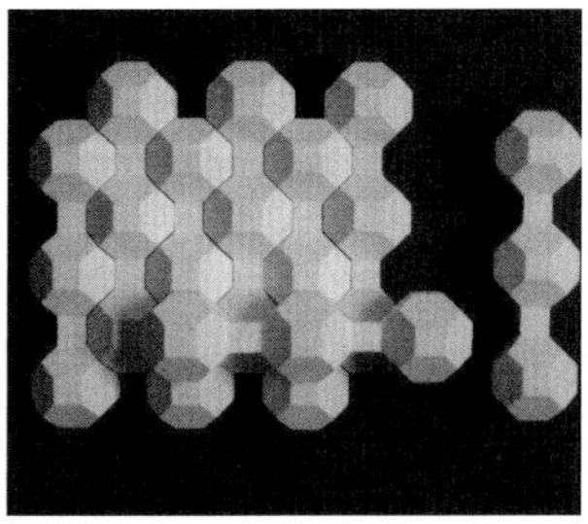

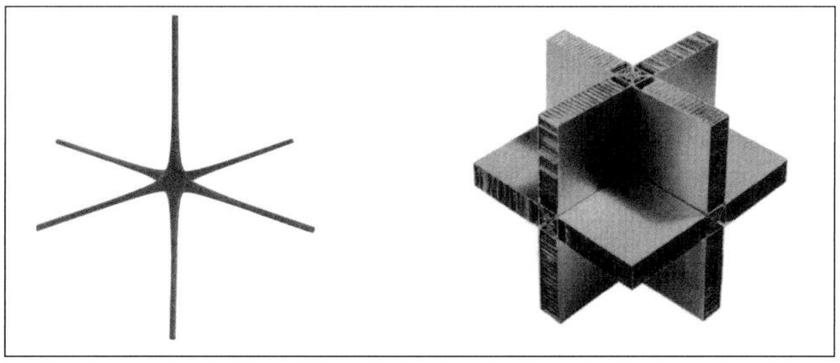

Fig. 12: Use of space without gap, positive-locking stacking solids by student Herbert Falk, teacher Walter Zeischegg, 1959/60;[26] integral building construction, teachers Herbert Ohl, Günter Schmitz, Rupert Urban, 1957–1963; node example, teacher Walter Zeischegg, 1962/63.[27] Photo left: Christian Staub. © HfG-Archiv, Ulmer Museum, Ulm.

These grids were the basis for general ideas about graphs and therefore applicable to many questions. Froeshaug provided an example of a floor plan of Le Corbusier's house in La Plata in 1954, using the graphs as an analysis of circulation paths inside the house. The graphs were understood as a topology—as connections, not forms—but were deduced from possible regular and semi-regular tessellations. In the 1959 visual methodology course taught by Froeshaug,[28] the plane grid versions of regular and semi-regular lattice structures (Figure 9) were studied first.

The 3D versions of regular and semi-regular lattice structures (Figure 10) then followed as a basis for spatial configurations.

Working with patterns in two and three dimensions had also been important later in the application fields, especially in the architecture and design departments. Modular building methods and design nodes followed in the respective specialized departments, where these structural backgrounds in patterns and spatial lattice structures found their usage (Figure 11). The studies of 3D lattice structures are motivated by designing structures, as it had been an important and innovative field of research for Konrad Wachsmann. He was a guest lecturer for industrial building at HfG Ulm between 1954 and 1957. Exercises in spatial tessellations and designing nodes were developed in various courses (Figure 12).

Studies on space fillings with minimal and maximal spatial packings were integrated into the architecture department course by Herbert Ohl in 1957. An example by student Hermann Edel, titled "Kristallographie", is shown in Figure 13.

6. Symmetry Concepts by William S. Huff

In the HfG's later years, the foundation courses were taught separately by each department. William S. Huff taught the basic course in the visual communication

Fig. 13: Studies on minimal, medium, and maximum space fillings by student Hermann Edel, teacher Herbert Ohl, 1957.[29]

department from 1963 to 1966. He referred explicitly to Maldonado's foundation course, as he had taken it as a student, with a Fulbright Scholarship, in 1956/57. Huff further developed the course to feature a concentration on the notion of *structure* and manipulating structures using transformations and deformations. He described his view in 1965:

> By *structure* I strictly mean: the relationship or arrangement of parts of elements. To design, then, is first of all to structure; and for me the study of structure (in the abstract) is the equal of that which has been known as basic design or foundation studies. [...] In the physical manipulation of structure, we are interested in those things that are invariant and those that are variant, with the study of deformations and transformations constituting perhaps the most crucial underlying motif. [...] In our basic design course, then (as it comes from Ulm's Maldonado), my students and I explore, of the physical nature of structure, such groups as can be analysed by symmetry, topology, combinatorial analysis, theories of color and texture.[30]

The examples in Figure 14 illustrate his structural approach, which he described as follows:

> By manipulating an element or group of elements with one or more of the symmetry coverage operations, structures (or systems) are produced. Simple applications result in the higher degrees of symmetry (isometry and homoeometry). More complex combinations of rules, though still rigorously applied, lead to the lower orders of symmetry (syngenometry and katametry). [...] In our studio project, symmetric structures are produced through such a programming process.[31]

The reflections on symmetries and transformations laid the foundations for his unique tasks on net transformations, later termed parquet deformations by Huff.

The parquet deformation exercises became Huff's main student assignment for almost four decades. Figure 16 shows an example of his later teaching in the United States.

Fig. 14: Programmed structures by symmetry operations, student Albrecht Hufnagel 1966/67;[32] symmetry exercises:[33] elements rotate in a combinatorial system involving groups of three and five, student Dennis Becker 1964; groups of rotating and expanding ellipses are arranged on a concentric square module in a complexity of translation, rotation, and mirror operations, student Michael Pollak, 1964, teacher William S. Huff. © HfG-Archiv, Ulmer Museum, Ulm.

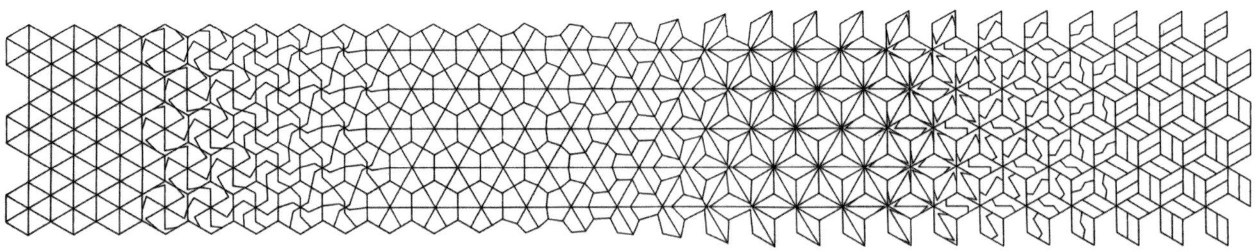

Fig. 15: Net transformation or parquet deformation, student Arno Caprez, teacher William S. Huff, 1965/66.[34] © HfG-Archiv, Ulmer Museum, Ulm

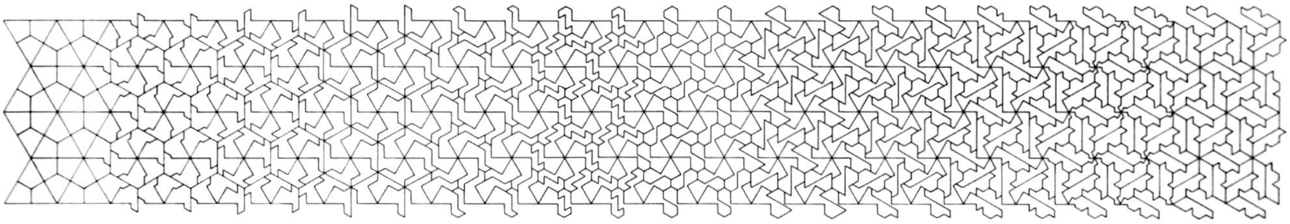

Fig. 16: Parquet Deformation "Wreathes of Holly", by Tina Macica, 19 × 27.88 in, India ink. Fall 1991, State University of New York at Buffalo. © HfG-Archiv/Museum Ulm, HfG-Ar, BDSA, Hu P 01. 042.

Huff's background included intensive studies on the theory of symmetrical structures, as initiated by the input of Maldonado during the foundation course. This topic became Huff's main research topic and resulted in an essay called "Ordering Disorder after K. L. Wolf"[35] in 2000. There, he compared Wolf's system with the typology of mapping after March and Steadman.[36] Katametry, as introduced by Maldonado in designing methods, is integrated into Wolf's system.

	position	size	angle	shape	certainty	rule
autometry	I	I	I	I	I	I
isometry	V	I	I	I	I	I
homoeometry		V	I	I	I	I
syngenometry			V	I	I	I
katametry				V	I	I
hypometry					V	I
heterometry						V
ametry						

Table 1: Levels of structures after Wolf and Wolff (1956). I = Invariant; V = Variant.[37]

mapping / invariant	position	length	angle and ratio	parallelism	cross-ratio	neighborliness
identity	●	●	●	●	●	●
isometry		●	●	●	●	●
similarity			●	●	●	●
affinity				●	●	●
perspectivity					●	●
topology						●

Table 2: Typologies of mapping after March and Steadman.[38]

These typologies of symmetries, which March and Steadman called mappings in a more mathematical concept, correspond with the understanding of symmetry as transformations that had existed since Felix Klein's Erlangen program, in which the invariants of figures characterize the respective transformation. The transformation or mapping, according to March and Steadman, became the fundamental element forming the respective geometry.[39] The Euclidean plane or spatial geometry or congruence geometry can be characterized as a transformation group of isometric and conformal transformations. Similarity transformations are not isometric and allow uniform scaling. Non-conformal transformations that maintain parallelism, but not lengths and angles, are affine transformations. The perspective transformation or projective transformation only maintains collinearity and cross-ratio. Ultimately, only neighborhoods remain in the topological transformation. These typologies correspond with strong geometric concepts, whereas Wolf's levels of structure, shown with examples in Figures 17 and 18, meet more open characteristics relevant for Gestalt-like seeing and reasonable designing, as expressed in the subtitle of Wolf's book.[40]

A profound analysis of Wolf's symmetry classifications can be found in the book *Ästhetische Redundanz* by Kurd Alsleben,[41] published in 1962. Maldonado brought Alsleben to HfG Ulm as a lecturer, where he taught structure theory and Boolean algebra between 1965 and 1968. Together with physicist Cord Passow, he produced and published early programmed computer drawings. The book refers to semiotics, Gestalt psychology, information theory, and aesthetics, all disciplines which formed the fundament of teaching by Max Bense, Abraham Moles, and Tomás Maldonado at HfG Ulm. Alsleben described the symmetry theory of Wolf and Wolff as important for providing rules for image creation, even if the particularly productive low symmetry levels still elude systematics. The symmetry theory shows how the geometric position and shape of signs can be changed according to rules. Then he described the different levels of the used symmetry notions:

- Autometry: Identical
- Isometry: Equality of elements and their uniform repetition
- Homoeometry: Similar, repetition in the same change in size, position, or behavior
- Syngenometry: Shape related
- Katametry: Design related
- Heterometry: Shape different
- Ametry: Unformed, given only in the idea

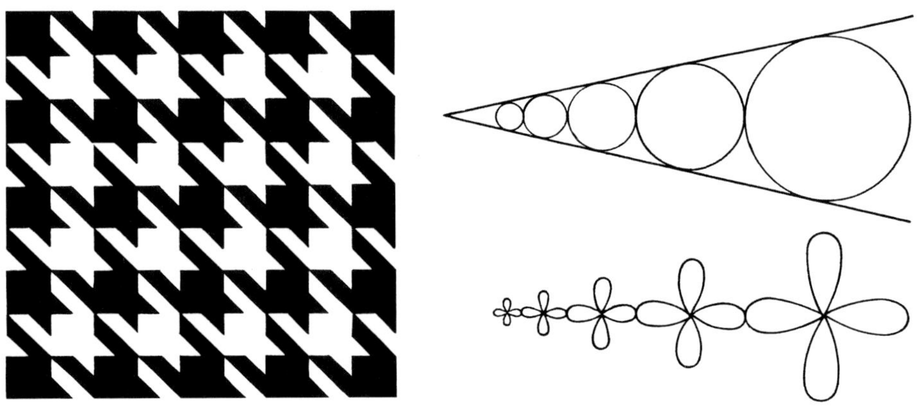

Fig. 17: Isometric surface net and homoeometric strip.[42]

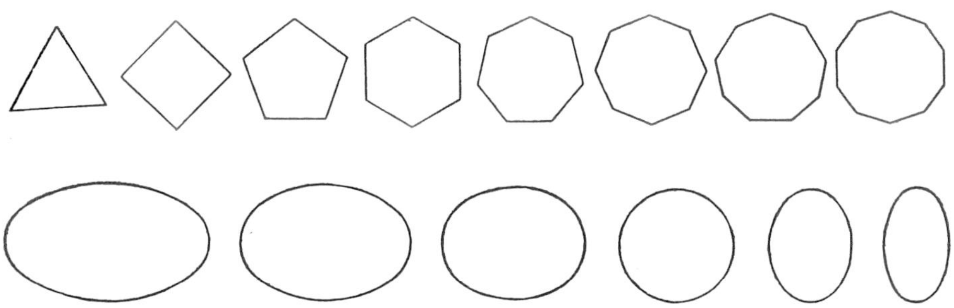

Fig. 18: Syngenometric strip and katametric strip.[43]

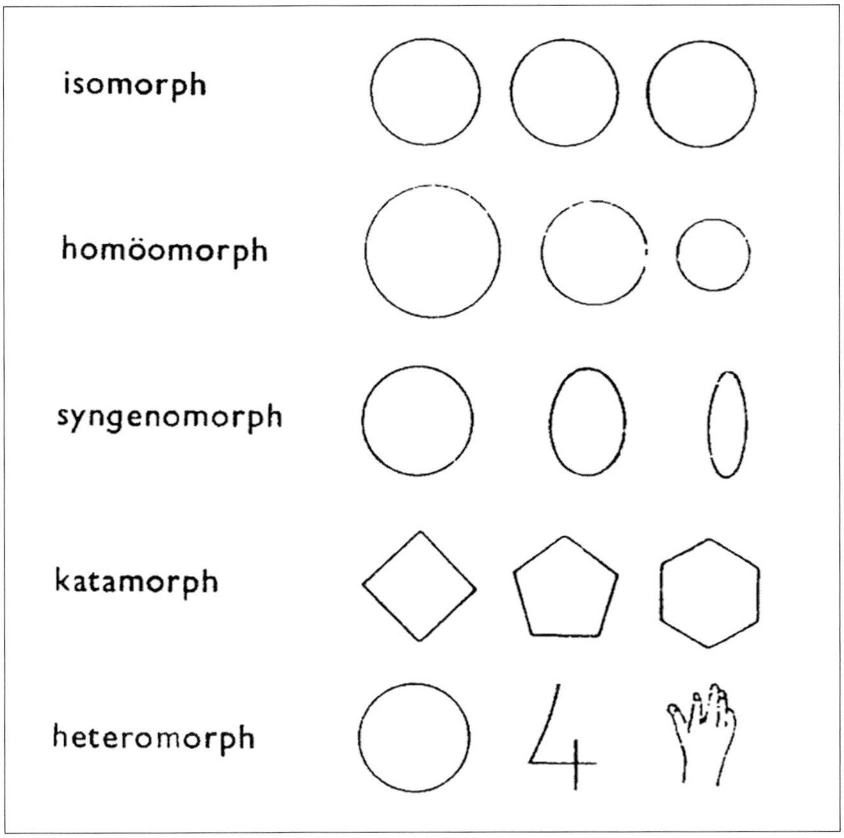

Fig. 19: Examples of degrees of similarity by Kurd Alsleben.[44]

In the examples created by Alsleben, the meaning of the low-level symmetries remains vague. Alsleben characterized symmetry as corresponding to repetitive redundancy. As an artistic device, symmetry belongs to syntactically effective tools.[45] His reflections are embedded in information aesthetics, developed by Max Bense and Abraham Moles[46] in the 1960s and introduced as a relevant theoretical philosophical background at HfG Ulm (see Chapter 7). In his introduction to Alsleben's book, Moles classifies this as part of information aesthetics, which was one of the most significant developments in aesthetics since Hegel. The interplay between redundancy and information is the basis of this theory or, in the words of Alsleben, "Redundancy makes the style of a work of art, information its originality."[47] The artist or creator moves between originality with perfect irregularity and banality with perfect regularity, as shown in Figure 20.

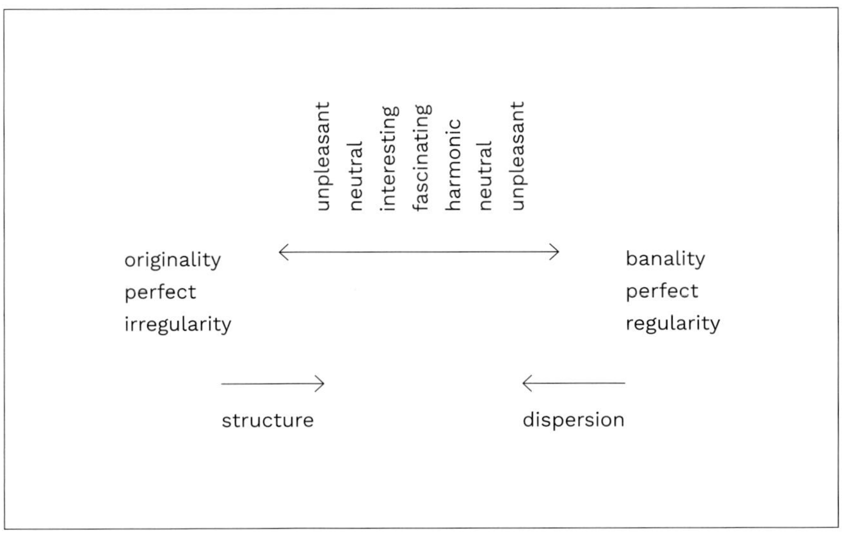

Fig. 20: Originality—banality—scale, according to Alsleben[48] and Moles.

Huff did not refer to information aesthetics in his papers, but his evaluation of the lower levels of symmetric structures in the creation process of design, what he called *programmed design*, coincides with the role of redundancy and innovation in the concept of information aesthetics.

> The programmed design is a staple assignment of my formative design studio in architectural studies. While the succinct brief for the assignment permits anything from isometry on down Wolf's scale of symmetric structures to katametry, the exploration of the lowest level has led to some of the more striking results: designs that, determined by indiscernible, though not overly complex rules—indeed, the leaner the rules, the more fulfilling the provocative outcome—appear to be casual or capricious. Programmed randomness? A contradiction, indeed! That is to say, what is often perceived as random may not be random at all, but wholly programmed.[49]

7. Information Aesthetics and Geometry

Geometric structures and transformations are applied in design processes, as illustrated in the shown examples. The question is, though, how aesthetic results can be achieved and how aesthetics can be substantiated in relation to order structures, rhythms, and—as Bill characterized it—in the individual creative decisions that constitute the difference between art and mathematics.[50] Information Aesthetics developed criteria for aesthetic measures and evaluations. It was initiated by Max Bense and Abraham Moles in the 1960s, mainly in Germany and France, as an aesthetic theory based on a rational mathematical fundament. Frieder Nake, a protagonist of information aesthetics and a student of Max Bense who later became a professor for computer graphics in Bremen, summarized the theory, its applications, and its critics in an article.[51]

There are two roots of this new aesthetic theory: information and aesthetic measures. Information as a root was introduced by Claude E. Shannon[52] during the rise of communication theory and communication technology. His mathematical information model integrated the stochastic nature of news.[53] The possible states of a system can be described in combination with a set of transition probabilities from one state to the next. Bense applied Shannon's information theory to aesthetics. Aesthetic realizations are seen as part of a communication process. The second root is Georg David Birkhoff's aesthetic measure.[54] The aesthetic measure is defined as the function of the order and complexity grade of the viewed configuration: $M = O/C$, where O indicated the number of order relations, symmetries, and harmonies, and C is complexity. The aesthetic measure of an artwork could be calculated as numeric quantities based upon order and complexity. Bense supplemented Birkhoff's numeric aesthetics with information aesthetics. The aesthetic state had been defined by Bense as the relation of an ordered to a not-ordered state. Birkhoff interprets his aesthetic measure M as aesthetic information. The order relation O corresponds to redundancy in finding order relationships and symmetries. Redundant features are necessary for innovation to become recognizable:

> A perfect innovation in which there were only new states as in chaos would not be recognizable. A chaos is finally unidentifiable. The recognizability of an aesthetic state requires not only the recognizability of its singular innovation, but also their identifiability based on their redundant order characteristics.[55]

Therefore, the interplay of redundancy and innovation—order and chaos—must be in an optimal relation to one another to achieve an aesthetic state. The artwork gives aesthetic information as a material carrier of the aesthetic state. Information is always transmitted by signs. Here, semiotics as the science of signs comes into play for the transmission of information. The interrelationships between information aesthetics and semiotics became obvious. Semiotics played an important role in research and teaching at HfG Ulm beyond Bense and Moles; it also played a role in the courses of Maldonado.

The structural approach in designing must be seen in light of the described aesthetic and philosophical background. Huff saw the notion of *structure* and then working on those structures as his fundament. Abraham Moles formulated this comprehension as valid for our relationship to the world, science, and design:

> To grasp the world, we must grasp it. In order to grasp it, we must first structure it. However, there are not structures in themselves, but only perceived structures. Science as an essential form of understanding the world provides us at the same time with measures and forms for this structuring.[56]

Huff's work refers to this general background of perceiving structures. The rules and regularities of the designs of patterns are often not caught directly but are only uncovered by analyses. He describes parquet deformations as being in the "territory between monotony and bewilderment", in other words for between redundancy and innovation and between order and chaos in the concept of information aesthetics:

> We have especially addressed structures, i.e., programmed designs, that are regulated [...] by relatively few elements and relatively few rules and that do not exhibit readily perceived regularities—though the regularities can be uncovered by right analyses. These patterns can engage the visual

sense in territory between monotony and bewilderment, a complexity of experience, achieved through minimal regularization—pattern-distribution that appears in the first instance to be random, yet is distinctly regulated and, thus, sensed to be coherent. Can this be called "hidden harmony"?[57]

References

[1] Max Bense, *Aesthetica*, Agis, Baden-Baden, 1965, 2nd edition 1982.

[2] Elisabeth Walther, "Philosoph in technischer Zeit – Stuttgarter Engagement. Interview mit Elisabeth Walther, Teil 2", in: B. Büscher, von H.-G. Herrmann, C. Hoffmann (eds), *Ästhetik als Programm. Max Bense/Daten und Streuungen*, Diaphanes, Berlin, 2004, p. 72, translated by C. L.

[3] Max Bill, "Die mathematische Denkweise in der Kunst unserer Zeit", *Werk* 36, 3, Winterthur 1949, English version: "The Mathematical Way of Thinking in the Visual Art of Our Time", in: Michele Emmer (ed.), *The Visual Mind: Art and Mathematics*, MIT Press, Cambridge, 1993, pp. 5–9; Max Bill, "Structure as art? Art as structure?", in: György Kepes (ed.), *Structure in Art and in Science*, Braziller, New York, 1965, pp. 150–151.

[4] Bill, "Die mathematische Denkweise", pp. 7–8.

[5] Max Bense, *Artistik und Engagement. Präsentation ästhetischer Objekte*, Kiepenheuer & Witsch, Cologne/Berlin, 1970, p. 92, translated by C. L.

[6] Max Bense, *Konturen einer Geistesgeschichte der Mathematik II. Die Mathematik in der Kunst*, Claassen & Goverts, Hamburg 1949, p. 59.

[7] Paul Valéry, "Introduction à la méthode de Léonard de Vinci", *La Nouvelle Revue Française*, Paris, 1895.

[8] The mathematical approach combined with the philosophical background, especially by Max Bense has been analyzed in two papers: Cornelie Leopold, "Precise Experiments: Relations between Mathematics, Philosophy and Design at Ulm School of Design", *Nexus Network Journal* 15, 2013: pp. 363–380; Cornelie Leopold, "The Mathematical Approach at Ulm School of Design", in: Emmer Michele, Abate Marco, Villarreal Marcela (eds.), *Imagine Maths 4. Between Culture and Mathematics*, Unione Matematica Italiana, Bologna, 2015, pp. 15–28.

[9] Ulmer Museum/HfG-Archiv (ed.), *ulmer modelle – modelle nach ulm. Hochschule für Gestaltung Ulm 1953–1968*, Hatje Cantz, Ulm, 2003, pp. 6–7.

[10] Sketches by Hans G. Conrad from 1954 show examples of such an analysis and creation of ornamental drawings.

[11] Model by the participants of the summer school in Buenos Aires, photo by Willem Roelof Balk, cf. Fachbereich Architektur, Technische Universität Kaiserslautern (ed), *rup'*, Technische Universität Kaiserslautern, Kaiserslautern, 2012.

[12] Ibid., pp. 27–28, Figs. 59, 61, 62.

[13] Ibid., p. 28, Figs. 63, 64, 67.

[14] Exercise in the course by Hermann von Baravalle, photo: Oleg Kuchar. © HfG-Archiv, Ulmer Museum Ulm.

[15] Exercise in the course by Hermann von Baravalle, reproduced by courteous permission of Hermann Edel.

[16] Hermann Edel, “Strukturelles Denken an der Hochschule für Gestaltung Ulm”, in: Joaquín Medina Warmburg, Cornelie Leopold (eds.), *Strukturelle Architektur. Zur Aktualität eines Denkens zwischen Technik und Ästhetik*, Transcript, Bielefeld, 2012, pp. 55–73.

[17] Hermann von Baravalle, *Geometrie als Sprache der Formen*, Verlag Freies Geistesleben, Stuttgart, 1957, 3rd edition 1980.

[18] Hermann Edel, “Geometrische Lichtprojektionen auf einen Fadenzylinder – Baravalle-Kino”, in: Cornelie Leopold (ed.), *Über Form und Struktur – Geometrie in Gestaltungsprozessen*, Springer, Wiesbaden, 2014, pp. 99–102. Video: https://vimeo.com/656511278 (accessed on 12/2021).

[19] Martin Krampen and Günther Hörmann, *Die Hochschule für Gestaltung Ulm/The School of Design. Anfänge eines Projektes der radikalen Moderne/Beginnings of a Project of Radical Modernism*, Ernst & Sohn, Berlin, 2003, pp. 101–103.

[20] Ibid., p. 101.

[21] Tomás Maldonado and Gui Bonsiepe, “Wissenschaft und Gestaltung”, *ulm* 10/11, Hochschule für Gestaltung, Ulm, 1964.

[22] Karl Lothar Wolf and Robert Wolff, *Symmetrie. Versuch einer Anweisung zu gestalthaftem Sehen und sinnvollem Gestalten, systematisch dargestellt und an zahlreichen Beispielen erläutert*, Böhlau-Verlag, Münster/Cologne, 1956.

[23] Kurd Alsleben, *Ästhetische Redundanz. Abhandlungen über die artistischen Mittel der bildenden Kunst*, Verlag Schnelle, Quickborn, 1962.

[24] William S. Huff, “Ordering Disorder after K. L. Wolf”, *Forma* 15, 2000, pp. 41–47.

[25] Ulmer Museum/HfG-Archiv (ed.), *ulmer modelle – modelle nach ulm. Hochschule für Gestaltung Ulm 1953–1968*, Hatje Cantz, Ulm, 2003, pp. 24–25.

[26] Martin Krampen, Günther Hörmann, *Die Hochschule für Gestaltung Ulm/The School of Design. Anfänge eines Projektes der radikalen Moderne/Beginnings of a Project of Radical Modernism*, Ernst & Sohn, Berlin, 2003, p. 120.

[27] Herbert Lindinger (ed.), *Hochschule für Gestaltung Ulm ... Die Moral der Gegenstände.* Ernst & Sohn, Berlin, 1987, p. 60, 202.

[28] Anthony Froeshaug, “Visuelle Methodik”, *ulm* 4, Hochschule für Gestaltung, Ulm, 1959.

[29] Private archive of Hermann Edel, reproduced by courteous permission of Hermann Edel.

[30] William S. Huff, “An Argument for Basic Design”, *ulm* 12/13, Hochschule für Gestaltung, Ulm, 1965, p. 26.

[31] Note 1 by William S. Huff, “Symmetry or Programmed Design”, 1960—after Tomás Maldonado.

[32] Lindinger, *Hochschule für Gestaltung*, p. 57.

[33] Huff, "An Argument", pp. 30, 36.

[34] Ibid., p. 64.

[35] Huff, "Ordering Disorder", pp. 41–47.

[36] Lionel March and Philip Steadman, *The Geometry of Environment*, MIT Press, Cambridge, MA 1974), pp. 24ff.

[37] Huff, "Ordering Disorder", p. 43.

[38] March and Steadman, *The Geometry of Environment*, p. 25.

[39] More on this concept can be found in Cornelie Leopold, "GeometrischeTransformationen als Entwurfsmethodik/Geometric Transformations as Design Methodology", in: Arena A., et al. (a cura di), *Connettere. Un disegno per annodare e tessere. Atti del 42° Convegno Internazionale dei Docenti delle Discipline della Rappresentazione/Connecting. Drawing for Weaving Relationships. Proceedings of the 42th International Conference of Representation Disciplines Teachers*, FrancoAngeli, Milano, 2020, pp. 1221–1240.

[40] Wolf and Wolff, *Symmetrie. Versuch einer Anweisung zu gestalthaftem Sehen und sinnvollem Gestalten*. The subtitle could be translated to "Attempt at instructions for gestalt-like seeing and reasonable designing".

[41] Alsleben, *Ästhetische Redundanz*.

[42] Wolf and Wolff, *Symmetrie*, p. 4.

[43] Ibid., p. 5.

[44] Alsleben, *Ästhetische Redundanz*, pp. 60–61.

[45] Ibid., p. 55.

[46] Abraham André Moles, *Information Theory and Esthetic Perception*, University of Illinois Press, Urbana, 1966. French original 1958.

[47] Alsleben, *Ästhetische Redundanz*, p. 22.

[48] Ibid., p. 23.

[49] Huff, "Ordering Disorder", p. 46.

[50] Max Bill, "Structure as art? Art as structure?", in: György Kepes (ed), *Structure in Art and in Science*, Braziller, New York, 1965, pp. 150–151.

[51] Frieder Nake, "Information Aesthetics: An heroic experiment", *J Math Arts* 6(2–3), 2012, pp. 65–75.

[52] Claude E. Shannon, "A Mathematical Theory of Communications", *Bell Tech J* 27, 1948, pp. 379–423, 623–656.

[53] The development of information aesthetic in relation to the art works of Gerard Caris is explained by the author in: Cornelie Leopold, "Geometric and Aesthetic Concepts Based on Pentagonal Structures", in: B. Sriraman (ed), *Handbook of the Mathematics of the Arts and Sciences*, Springer, Cham, 2019.

[54] Georg David Birkhoff, *Aesthetic Measure*, Harvard University Press, Cambridge, 1933.

[55] Bense, *Aesthetica*, p. 356.

[56] Abraham André Moles, "Produkte: ihre Funktionelle und strukturelle Komplexität", *ulm* 6, Hochschule für Gestaltung, Ulm, 1962, p. 4.

[57] William S. Huff, "On Regulation and Hidden Harmony", in: O. Bodnar (ed.), *Harmony of Forms and Processes: Nature, Art, Science, Society*, International Society for the Interdisciplinary Study of Symmetry, Lviv, Ukraine, 2008.

Biography of the Author

Cornelie Leopold teaches and researches in the field of architectural geometry at fatuk, Faculty of Architecture, Technische Universität Kaiserslautern, Germany, in the position of academic director and head of the Descriptive Geometry and Perspective section. She received her degree in Mathematics, Philosophy, and German Philology at University of Stuttgart, Germany, with specializations in Geometry and Philosophy (Semiotics, Aesthetics, Logic, and Philosophy of Science). She is a member of the Editorial Board of the *Journal for Geometry and Graphics* and of the Scientific Committee of the *Journal Disegno* of UID—Unione Italiano Disegno. Since 2019 she is corresponding editor of *Nexus Network Journal: Architecture and Mathematics*. She was founding president of the Deutsche Gesellschaft für Geometrie und Grafik (DGfGG) and is a member of the board for the Committee of the International Society for Geometry and Graphics (ISGG) as director for Europe/Near East/Africa. She has contributed lectures, papers, and reviews to many international conferences and journals. In the past, she was a guest lecturer in Krakow, Istanbul, Milan, Porto, Venice, and Buenos Aires. In 2017, she was visiting professor at Università Iuav di Venezia, Italy with a research focus on perspective transformations.

Her research interests include the development of spatial visualization abilities, geometry and architectural design methods, structural thinking, the philosophical background of architecture, visualization of architecture, geometry, and representation. Results of her research have been published in conference papers, books, and articles. Her book *Geometrische Grundlagen der Architekturdarstellung*, first published in 1999, was re-published in 2019 in the 6th extended edition by Springer. Research on the interrelations between geometry and her background in philosophy was published in the co-edited book *Strukturelle Architektur. Zur Aktualität eines Denkens zwischen Technik und Ästhetik* at Transcript and in articles focusing on the philosophy of Max Bense and the role of mathematics at Ulm School of Design.

In 2018 she took part in the Conference Chairs Team of RCA, Research Culture in Architecture - International Conference on Cross-Disciplinary Collaboration, organized and hosted by fatuk and co-editor of the connected book, published in 2020 at Birkhäuser. The international conference NEXUS 20/21: Relationships of Architecture and Mathematics organized at TU Kaiserslautern and coordinated by her together with Kim Williams in summer 2021.

https://geometrie.architektur.uni-kl.de
https://www.researchgate.net/profile/Cornelie_Leopold

The Tiles, They Are a-Changin'

Craig S. Kaplan

School of Computer Science,
University of Waterloo, Ontario, Canada;
csk@uwaterloo.ca

Like many people, I first encountered parquet deformations through Douglas Hofstadter's essay, which I read in *Metamagical Themas*[1] in my late teens or early twenties. I was primed to fall in love with them. I have admired the art of M. C. Escher from the earliest days of my childhood; I begged my parents to get me a reprint of his *Metamorphosis II*, which still hangs in my office today. As a PhD student in computer science, I then had the good fortune to be drawn back into this topic from a more informed perspective. In my research, I adapted ideas from the branch of mathematics called *tiling theory* to generate, manipulate, and render tessellations inspired by Escher and by Islamic art. As part of that research, I produced my first parquet deformations, and have continued to experiment with them in the almost 20 years since then. My latest phase of experimentation is a direct result of Werner Van Hoeydonck's invitation to contribute a chapter to this book. I am grateful for the motivation to return to this topic and resurrect my old software.

Every parquet deformation is a tiling—or a finite excerpt of a conceptually infinite tiling, at any rate—and so it is natural to expect that tiling theory would be an ideal tool for studying them and for generating new designs. Of course, one need not be a mathematician to draw beautiful tilings! Escher demonstrated this fact beyond any doubt, and we can assume that most of Huff's students were guided more by intuition and visual rhythm than by mathematical rules. Mathematics is but one possible route to geometric design, albeit a powerful one. In this context, the power of mathematics lies in its ability to map out a design space systematically, categorizing a body of existing work and making sure we have not overlooked any opportunities. A computer scientist can then reduce these mathematical ideas to a practical piece of software, one that allows an artist to focus on creative exploration rather than the execution of the drawing. For my part, I derive as much artistic satisfaction from writing code to produce drawings as I might from executing them by hand. I hope that we live in an age where it is uncontroversial to speak of code as a creative medium.[2]

It turns out that a family of tilings called *isohedral tilings* are particularly well suited to the creation of tessellation-based geometric designs like parquet deformations. In this chapter, I will first give a brief overview of the isohedral tilings, focusing on their mathematical and computational properties that are relevant in a design context. I will then present the results of a number of experiments that use the isohedral tilings as a basis for drawing parquet deformations. I will conclude with a few remarks about the constraints Huff imposed upon this art form, and when it may be appropriate to break them.

1. The Isohedral Tilings

Tilings have been part of art and ornamentation for thousands of years, but only more recently did a formal branch of mathematics develop around their study. Today tiling theory is a beautiful, deep topic that overlaps with many other parts of mathematics. Happily, the sorts of tilings that interest us here tend to be relatively tame in comparison to the frontier of research, and well-established ideas can be used to great effect.

While I wish to provide some intuition for the mathematical machinery that I use to construct parquet deformations, it would be counterproductive to give a full account of the background. Interested readers should consult Grünbaum and Shephard's masterful *Tilings and Patterns*[3]; artists and designers will also find endless inspiration in its pages. *My own book* offers a condensed introduction more focused on algorithms and data structures for writing software to draw tilings.

A *tiling* is a collection of shapes that cover the plane with no gaps and no overlaps. We are often interested in tilings formed from copies of a single shape,

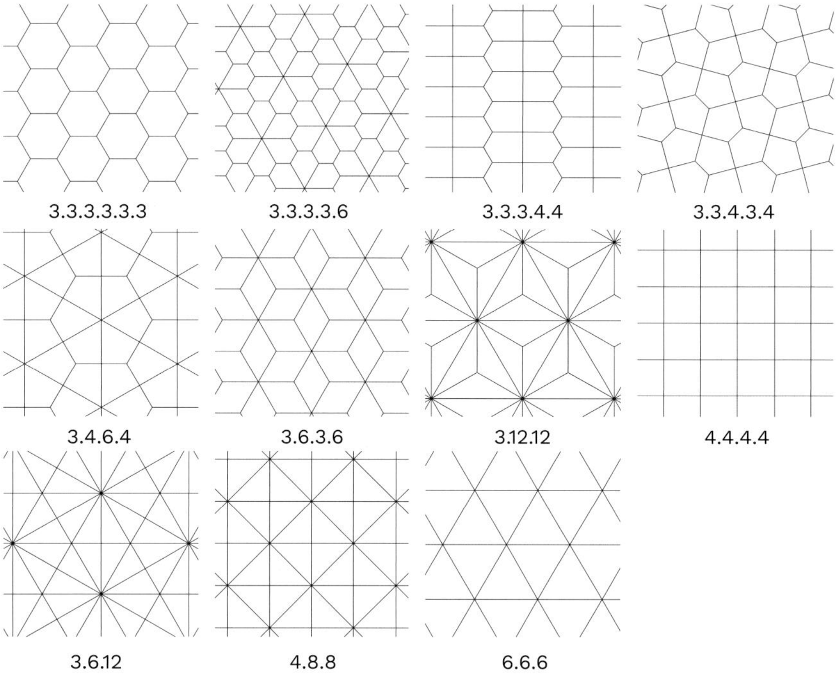

Fig. 1: The eleven Laves tilings, which serve as a basis for constructing isohedral tilings. The symbolic name for each tiling describes the number of edges meeting at every vertex around the boundary of a single tile.

where each copy is transformed by some combination of translation, rotation, and reflection. Such tilings are called *monohedral*, and the single shape is the tiling's *prototile*.

In art and design, we are typically interested in tilings that have a degree of what we can informally call "regularity". By virtue of its single prototile shape, a monohedral tiling has some regularity, but the arrangement of tiles can still be uncomfortably complex, both mathematically and aesthetically. Escher developed a "layman's theory"[5], codifying his intuition for regular division of the plane, after encountering a research article on the subject by Pólya. Later, Heesch and Kienzle formalized regularity in a tiling by requiring that every tile be surrounded by its neighbors in the same way.[6] This local constraint imposes global order, allowing Heesch and Kienzle to divide all such tilings into 28 distinct families.

Grünbaum and Shephard offered the definitive treatment of this notion of regularity in their analysis of the isohedral tilings.[7] Viewed informally, they define an *isohedral tiling* as one in which the individual tiles behave as simply as possible with respect to the tiling's symmetries. As in Heesch and Kienzle's work, this global constraint is equivalent to requiring that every tile be surrounded by its neighbors in the same way. Grünbaum and Shephard develop a compact symbolic notation for describing a tile's internal symmetries and its relationships to its neighbors, and list all possible symbols that lead to valid tilings. The result is a set of 93 families of tilings called the *isohedral tiling types*, which are denoted IH1, IH2 ... all the way to IH93. Each type encompasses a broad range of tilings that are arranged according to a shared set of neighbor relationships. Twelve of these types are less useful for our purposes, because they can only be realized visually with the addition of extra markings to the interiors of tiles. We typically skip over those types and use the other 81 in decorative applications of tilings. Figure 1 shows small sample tilings for each of these 81 isohedral types.

2. Drawing Isohedral Tilings

The isohedral tilings occupy a sweet spot at the intersection of mathematics, computation, and design. They are a good fit for the intuitive notion of regularity adopted by Escher. They are fully and systematically described using simple notation. And this notation can be converted into data structures and algorithms for representing, manipulating, and drawing isohedral tilings efficiently. I created a software library called *Tactile* for this purpose early in my research on this subject, and more recently published an updated version.[8]

To describe an isohedral tiling (or rather, its single prototile), we first select one of the eleven *Laves tilings*, shown in Figure 2. A Laves tiling is the scaffolding upon which we will affix the details of the tile shape: It records the connectivity between tiles and their neighbors, without regard for precise tile shape. The Laves tilings are canonical representatives of all different possible connectivities for isohedral tilings. Each one has a symbolic name that lists the number of edges that meet at the vertices around the boundary of a single tile.

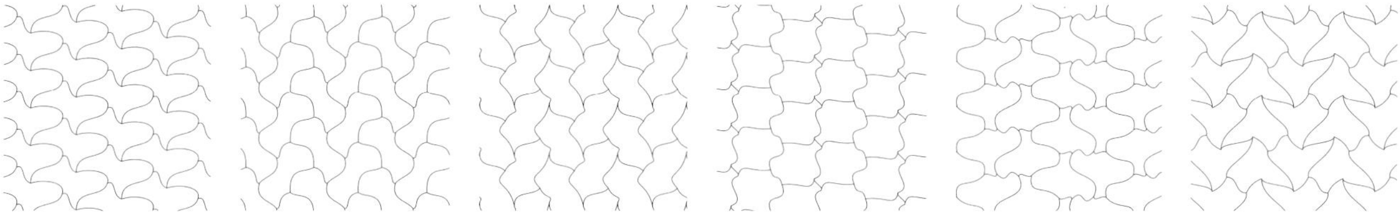

IH1 IH2 IH3 IH4 IH5 IH6

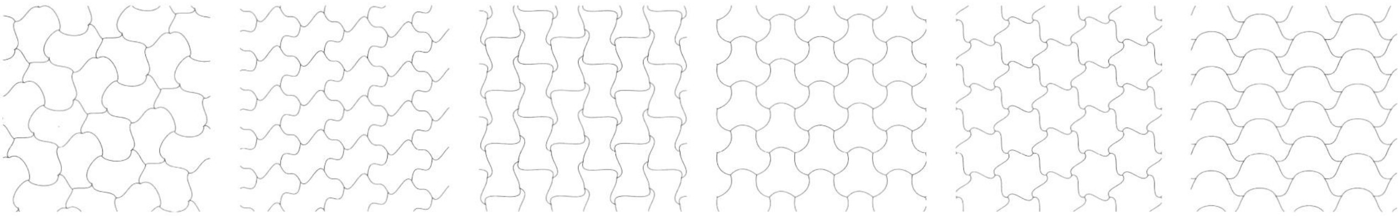

IH7 IH8 IH9 IH10 IH11 IH12

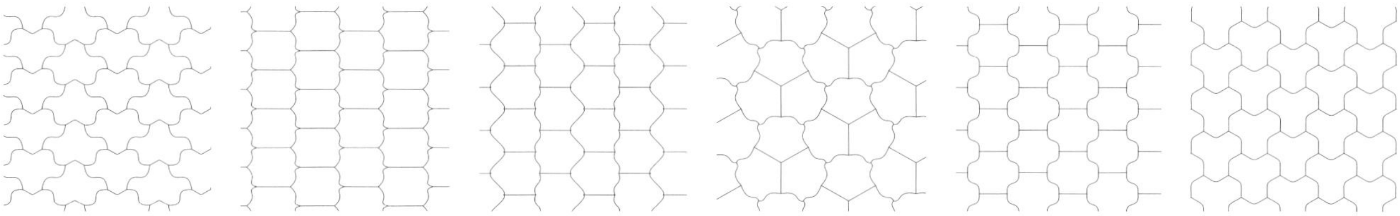

IH13 IH14 IH15 IH16 IH17 IH18

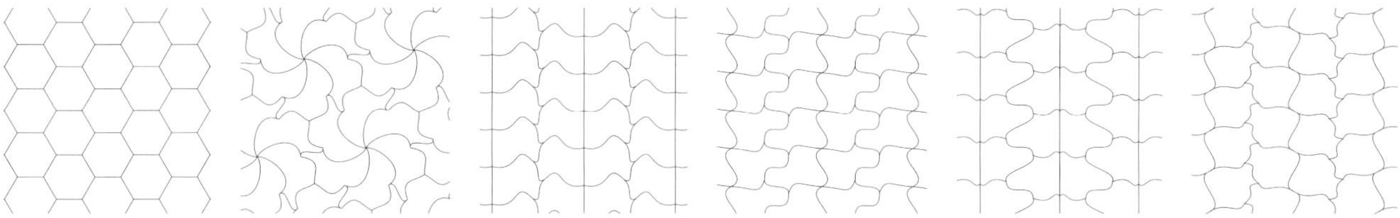

IH20 IH21 IH22 IH23 IH24 IH25

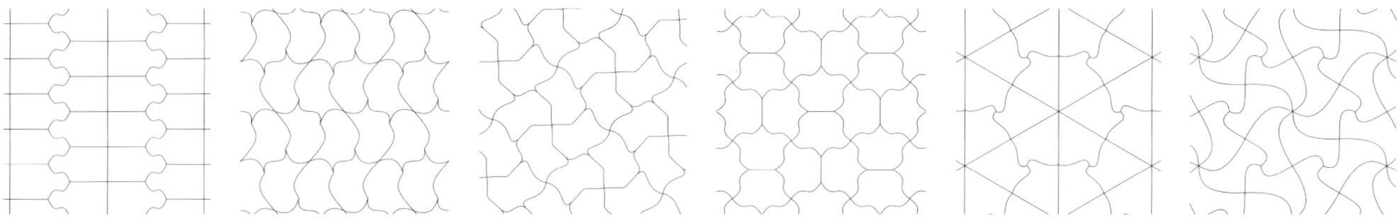

IH26 IH27 IH28 IH29 IH30 IH31

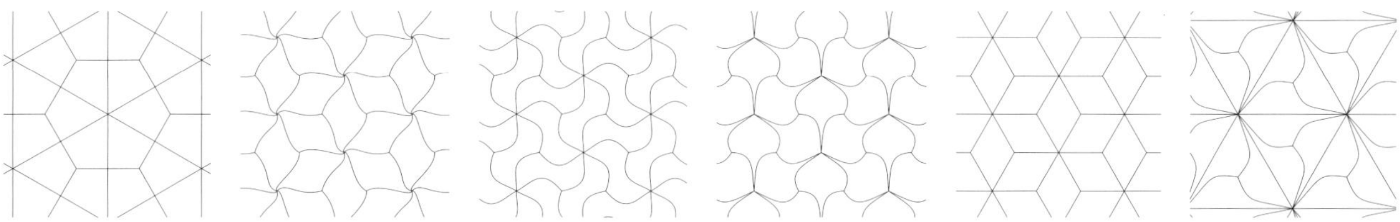

IH32 IH33 IH34 IH36 IH37 IH38

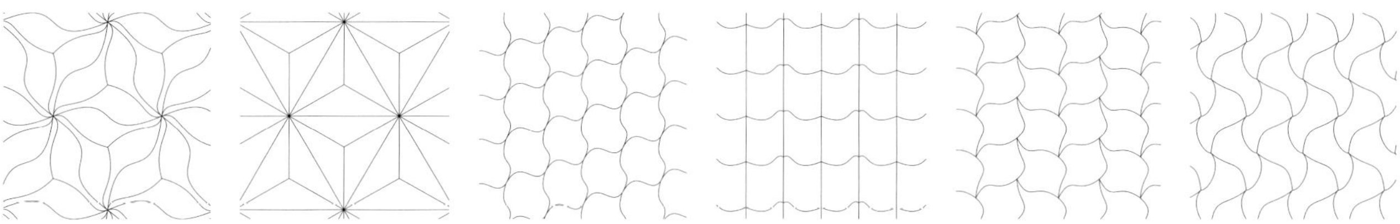

IH39 IH40 IH41 IH42 IH43 IH44

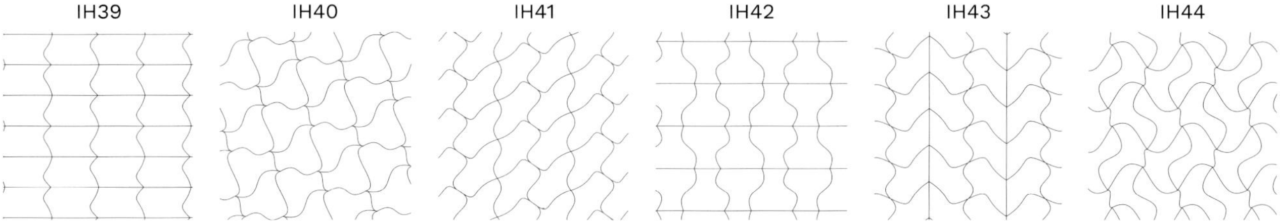

IH45 IH46 IH47 IH49 IH50 IH51

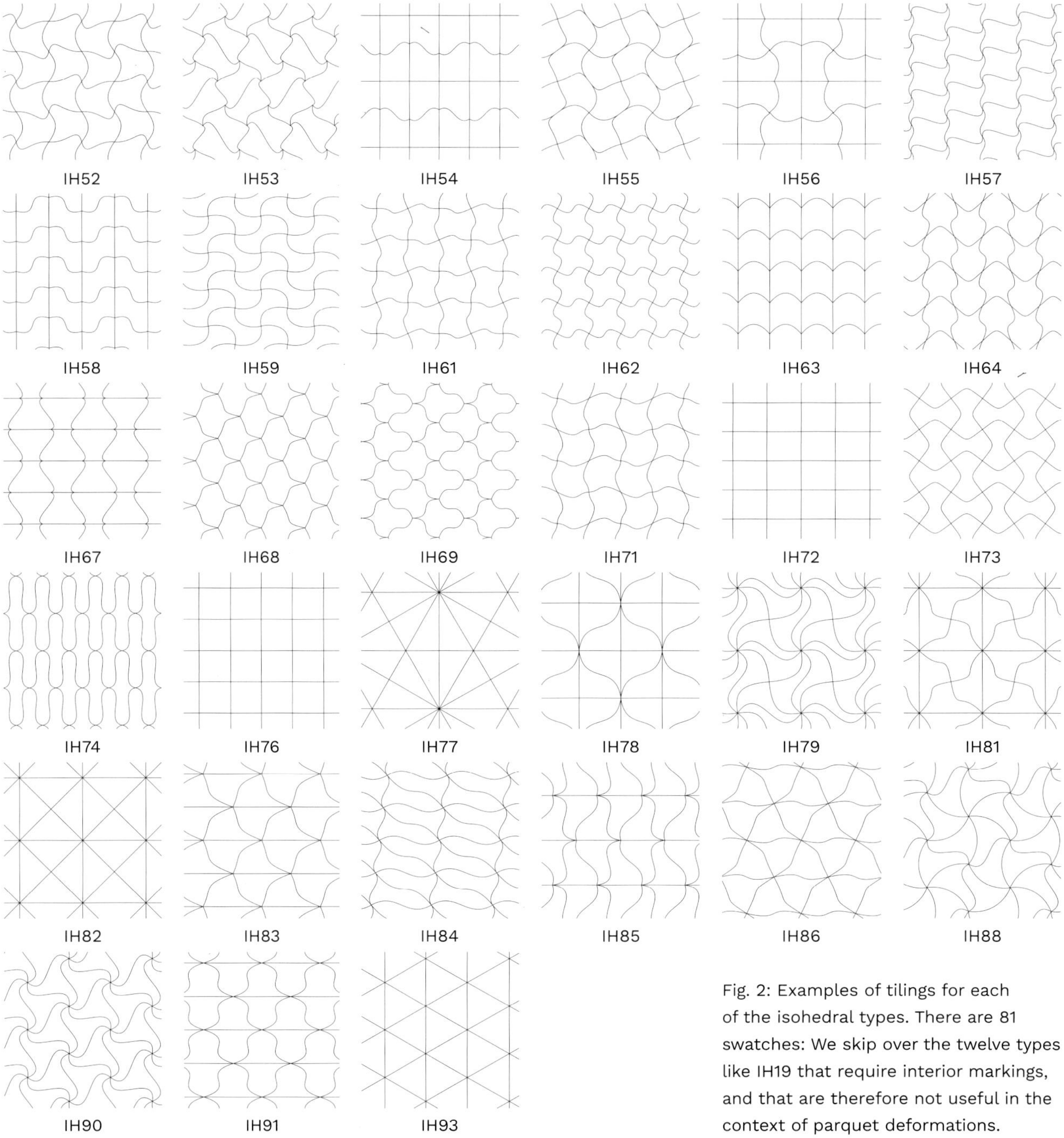

Fig. 2: Examples of tilings for each of the isohedral types. There are 81 swatches: We skip over the twelve types like IH19 that require interior markings, and that are therefore not useful in the context of parquet deformations.

Depending on the isohedral tiling type, we might have the opportunity to alter the shape of the Laves tile. For example, 36 different isohedral types are all based on 4.4.4.4, the regular tiling by squares. In different types, those squares can be deformed into rectangles, or parallelograms, or other kinds of quadrilaterals. Every isohedral type is equipped with a *tiling vertex parameterization*, a set of numbers that can be chosen freely to determine an alteration to the initial Laves tile. Different types have different numbers of parameters, from zero (a type with no degrees of freedom in its vertex locations) up to six. I refer to this modified Laves prototile shape as the *base tile*.

Of course, we often wish to draw the edges of tiles not as straight lines, but as more expressive curves. We complete the description of a prototile by supplying a set of distinct paths that will be used to join the vertices of the base tile. A given prototile tile may re-use the same path multiple times, whether because of internal symmetries or to allow it to interlock with a translated neighbor. Any path that can be expressed computationally may be used here; the most common choices in digital graphic design are piecewise polygonal paths (made up of straight line segments) and smooth cubic curves.

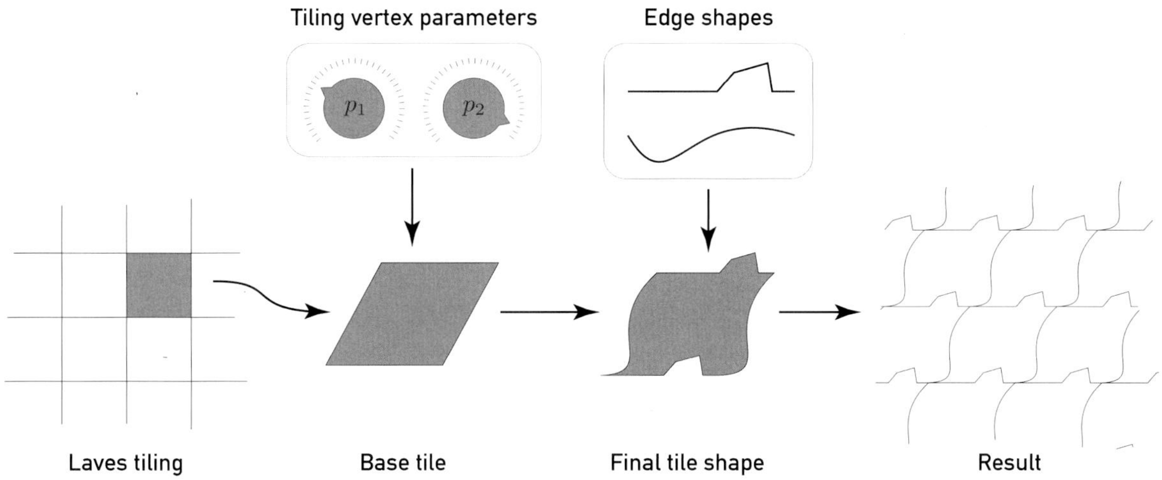

Fig. 3: The construction of a prototile for an isohedral tiling. On the left, we select the Laves tiling 4.4.4.4. The square prototile is then modified into a parallelogram based on the values of two tiling vertex parameters. The parameters p1 and p2 can be thought of as controlling the x and y coordinates of the upper-right corner of the prototile, thereby allowing us to choose any parallelogram as the base tile. We then apply two distinct paths to define the shapes of the edges. The resulting shape produces a tiling of isohedral type IH41.

My *Tactile* library serves as a simple means of collecting all the information above and combining it to determine the shape of the prototile and the arrangement of tiles in an isohedral tiling. Figure 3 illustrates the construction of one particular isohedral tiling, of type IH41, based on a choice of Laves tiling, values for a tiling vertex parameterization, and paths for the edges.

3. Parquet Deformations as Spatial Animations

In traditional cell animation,[9] a lead animator would draw a relatively sparse set of *keyframes*, showing the most important poses taken by a character in motion. Other animators called *in-betweeners* would then fill in the intermediate frames to depict the full motion of the character, usually at 24 frames per second. When the frames are projected back in sequence, the eye fuses these discrete snapshots into smooth motion. Computer animation offers the promise of alleviating the burden of in-betweening by replacing it with *interpolation*, the direct calculation of intermediate values for pose parameters like joint angles. In practice, this promise has its limits: Automated interpolation looks too rigid, and the most expressive animated characters are still meticulously posed frame by frame.

Previously, I demonstrated how to create temporal animations of isohedral tilings by analogy with traditional animation.[10] We can regard a parquet deformation as a kind of spatial animation, depicting the evolution of our "character" from one side of the canvas to the other rather than through time. We describe the animation by specifying a sparse set of keyframes, each of which associates an isohedral prototile with a position along one axis of the canvas. The computer can then smoothly interpolate the numbers controlling the tile's shape, producing a patch of tiles with shapes that evolve gradually in response to the keyframes. Here the rigid nature of mathematical interpolation is perhaps a virtue, as it plays into the already geometric aesthetic of this art form.

As a simple example, consider the diagram in Figure 4. The squares represent a fragment of a tiling that we wish to elaborate into a parquet deformation. For each square edge, we use the x coordinate of the midpoint of that edge (marked with a dot) to look up an interpolation amount between 0 and 1. A value of 0 tells us to draw tiles resembling a keyframe at the left side of the canvas, and 1 tells us to draw the right keyframe. Intermediate values should interpolate smoothly between the keyframe shapes. We can visualize this lookup process by drawing a vertical line downward from the midpoint and finding its intersection with the linear ramp D(*x*). Figure 5 shows the parquet deformation that results from using these values of D(*x*), where the left keyframe is a square and the right keyframe has zigzag edges. A single evolving edge is shown underneath for reference.

In practice, D(*x*) can be a more general function than a linear ramp, allowing us to control the speed at which tile shapes evolve, or even to move back and forth between two keyframes multiple times. We can also chain together more than two keyframes, producing longer animations with more intermediate steps.

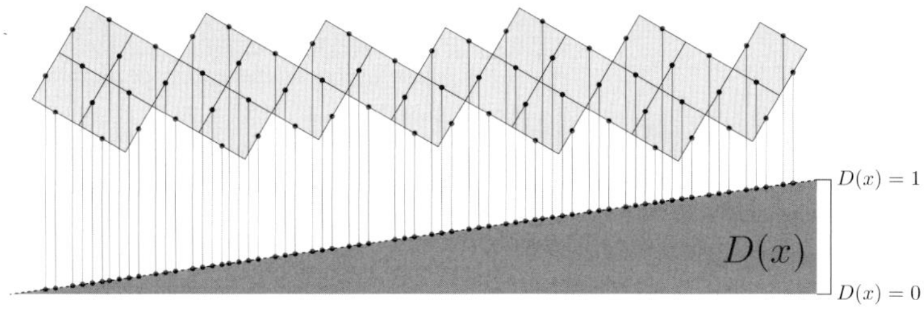

Fig. 4: A visualization of how interpolation values are calculated in a linear parquet deformation. Each edge midpoint (marked with a dot) is projected downward onto an interpolation function D(x), which yields a value between 0 and 1.

Fig. 5: A parquet deformation constructed using the tilted squares of Figure 4. Keyframes are defined at the left and right edges of the canvas, both of isohedral type IH62. The left keyframe has straight edges, and the right keyframe has zigzag edges.

4. Evolving Edge Shapes

In many of the parquet deformations produced in Huff's studio, a single base tile is used for the duration of the drawing, and only the edge shapes are permitted to evolve. This constraint is natural to adopt in the context of hand drawing—it becomes easier to conceive of the layout of tiles, while still permitting a wide space of creative exploration. It also fits with Huff's use of square and isometric lattices as a basis for geometric design. Over the years I have conducted a number of experiments based on this simplified framework. In several of them I restrict my attention purely to the unmodified Laves tiling of squares (4.4.4.4) and consider different strategies for evolving the paths that define the edges.[11] I will present three such strategies here, and then discuss a more general system for interpolating paths in all isohedral tiling types.

4.1 Grid-Based Evolution

The first evolution strategy is typified by a drawing like that shown in Figure 6, produced in Huff's studio. Here, the squares of the tiling are each subdivided into finer grids, and at each evolutionary step the edge shape shifts to enclose or liberate one grid cell. Hofstadter refers to deforming a path by "introducing a 'bump' or 'pimple' or 'tooth'"; I will refer to this device less viscerally as "grid-based" evolution.

A grid-based system is ideal for interactive design in software. I developed an interface in which the artist clicks on grid squares, defining a sequence of discrete shifts to be taken by the edge paths. The software renders the final parquet deformation by constructing each edge in the tiling with a number of shifts based on the edge midpoint's horizontal position in the drawing. The interpolation is "snapped" to the nearest whole number of shifts—edges do not evolve continuously, even in principle. Figure 7 illustrates the definition of a single edge evolving according to a grid-based method, and a parquet deformation constructed from that edge. Figure 8 shows two additional examples that use grid-based evolution.

Fig. 6: "Memory Chip Meander", by Frank W. Dunn, 19 × 27.88 in, India ink. Basic Design Studio of William S. Huff, State University of New York at Buffalo, 1983. © HfG-Archiv/Museum Ulm, HfG-Ar, BDSA, Hu P 06. 015. An example of grid-based curve evolution.

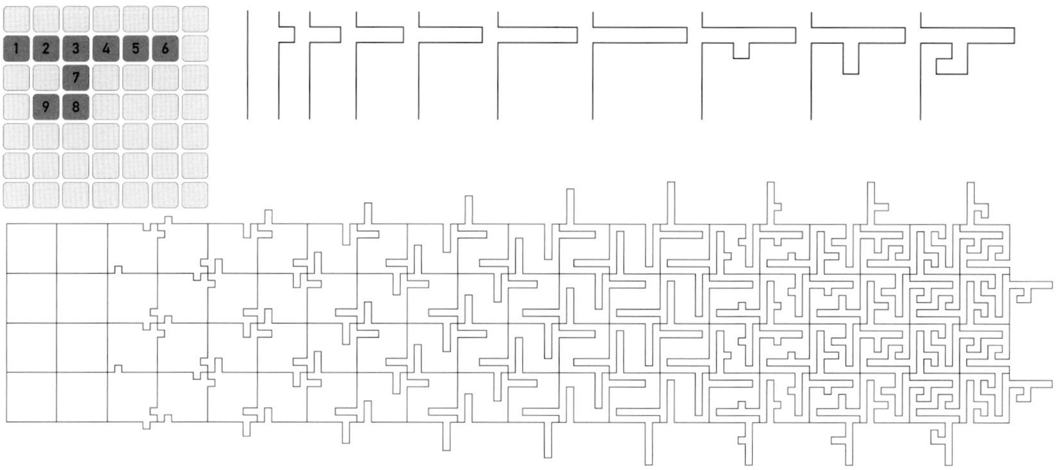

Fig. 7: A demonstration of grid-based path evolution. The top-left grid defines a sequence of shifts for an evolving path, which grows to wrap around each numbered square in turn. The paths can then be distributed across a patch of tiles to define a parquet deformation, here of type IH61.

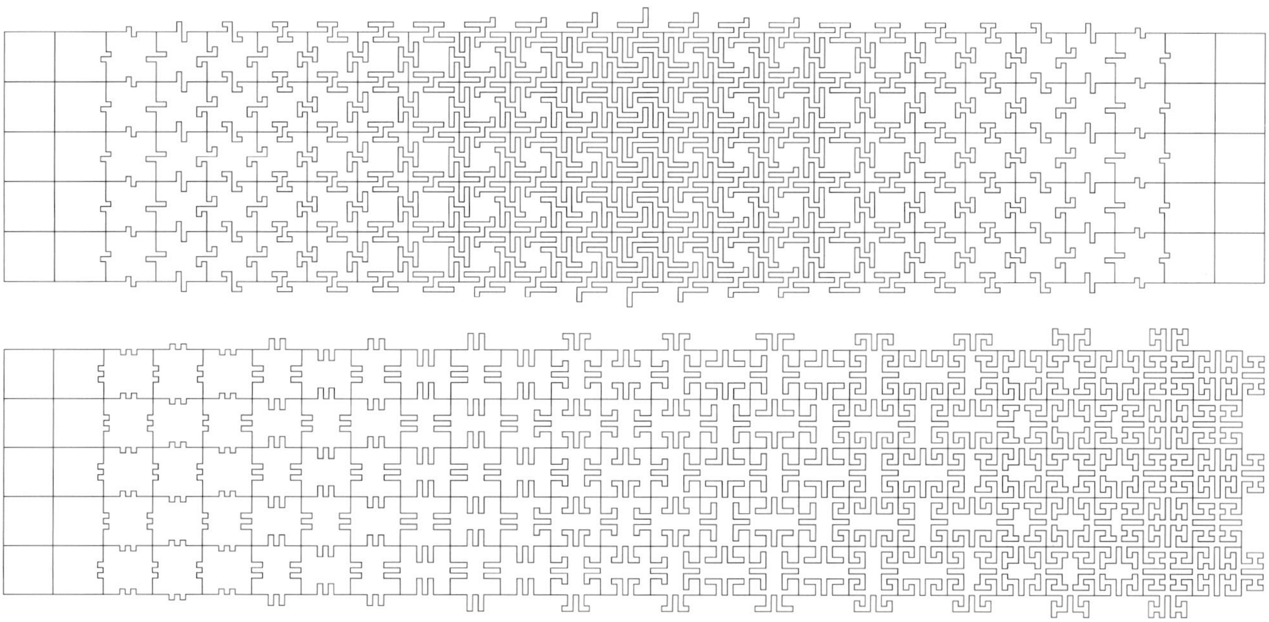

Fig. 8: Two examples of grid-based evolution, of types IH62 (top) and IH73 (bottom). The top example uses a mountain-shaped deformation function D(x), which interpolates from the first tile shape to the second and then back again.

4.2 Organic Evolution

Computer graphics researchers and artists have experimented with approaches for evolving organic forms using physical or biological simulations. In my work I adapted an algorithm by Pedersen and Singh,[12] in which a curve undergoes random perturbations while attempting to remain smooth and holding other parts of the curve at a fixed distance. I adapt the algorithm so that multiple copies of the curve may attract and repel each other around the boundary of a prototile, while the vertices of the underlying Laves tiling remain fixed. The sequence of time steps in this simulation forms a temporal animation of an evolving shape, which always tiles the plane. I harness this animation to draw a parquet deformation by replacing the edges of the base tiling with snapshots of edges from different points in time. The simulation deforms the tile gradually enough that these snapshots produce a continuous parquet deformation. Figure 9 shows two examples of parquet deformations based on organic evolution. I used this technique to design low-relief parquet deformations for the entrance of the National Museum of Mathematics in New York City, two small sections of which are shown in Figure 10.

Fig. 9: Two examples of organic evolution, of types IH61 (top) and IH74 (bottom).

4.3 Fractal Evolution

Fractals have been a mainstay of mathematical art for decades, and so it is natural to investigate their use in parquet deformations. I have conducted a few visual experiments using simple fractal curves based on iterated function systems.

Suppose that P is a polygonal path. We can construct a slightly more elaborate path by replacing every line segment in P by a scaled, translated, and rotated copy of P itself. We can iterate this process, yielding a sequence of ever more detailed paths. The hypothetical limit of repeating this process infinitely many times is a fractal curve, assuming that we started with a path P that is reasonably well-behaved.[13]

We might try to take the first few curves produced in this sequence and distribute them across a design, but in practice they exhibit poor behavior when used as-is. In the first few steps, the difference between consecutive paths is too large and abrupt; later, changes are invisibly small. I mitigate this problem by interpolating smoothly between consecutive refinement steps using a linear blend, producing a more continuous evolution of form. Here, *blending* refers to a class of algorithms that interpolate smoothly between paths. A blend algorithm might take two paths P_1 and P_2, together with a number t between 0 and 1, and produce a new path. We expect that $t = 0$ produces a copy of P_1, $t = 1$ produces a copy of P_2, and other values of t will carry out a continuous progression between these two limiting shapes. Software for illustration and animation often includes tools for constructing blends. Figure 11 shows two examples of parquet deformations based on fractal evolution.

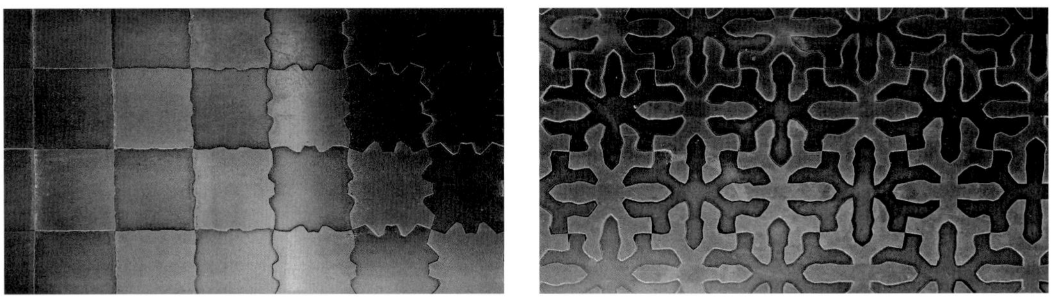

Figure 10: Two fragments of a long organic Parquet Deformation of type IH73, executed in bas-relief bronze at the entrance of the National Museum of Mathematics in New York City. Photographs courtesy of of National Museum of Mathematics (momath.org).

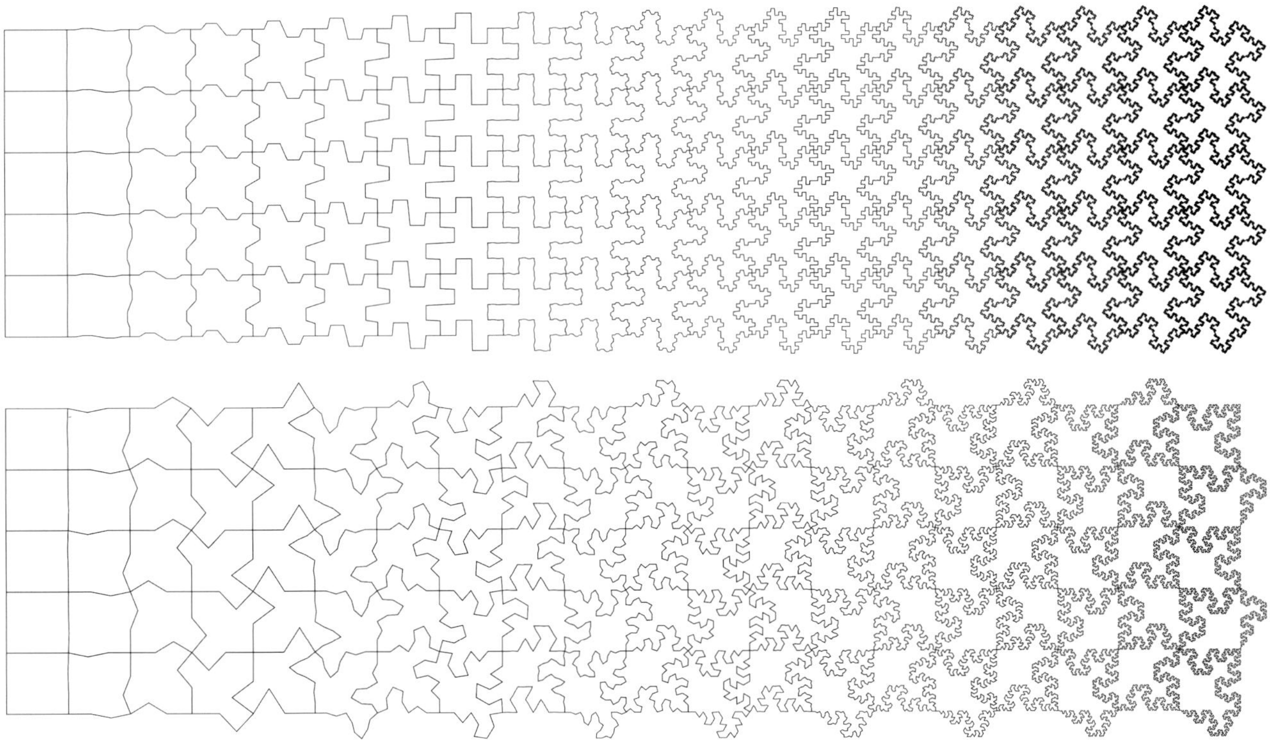

Fig. 11: Two examples of fractal evolution, of types IH62 (top) and IH71 (bottom).

Fig. 12: Two examples of generic path blending, of types IH29 (top) and IH18 (bottom). Both examples use edges that start straight and grow in complexity. The bottom example passes through multiple intermediate keyframes to produce a smoother progression of form.

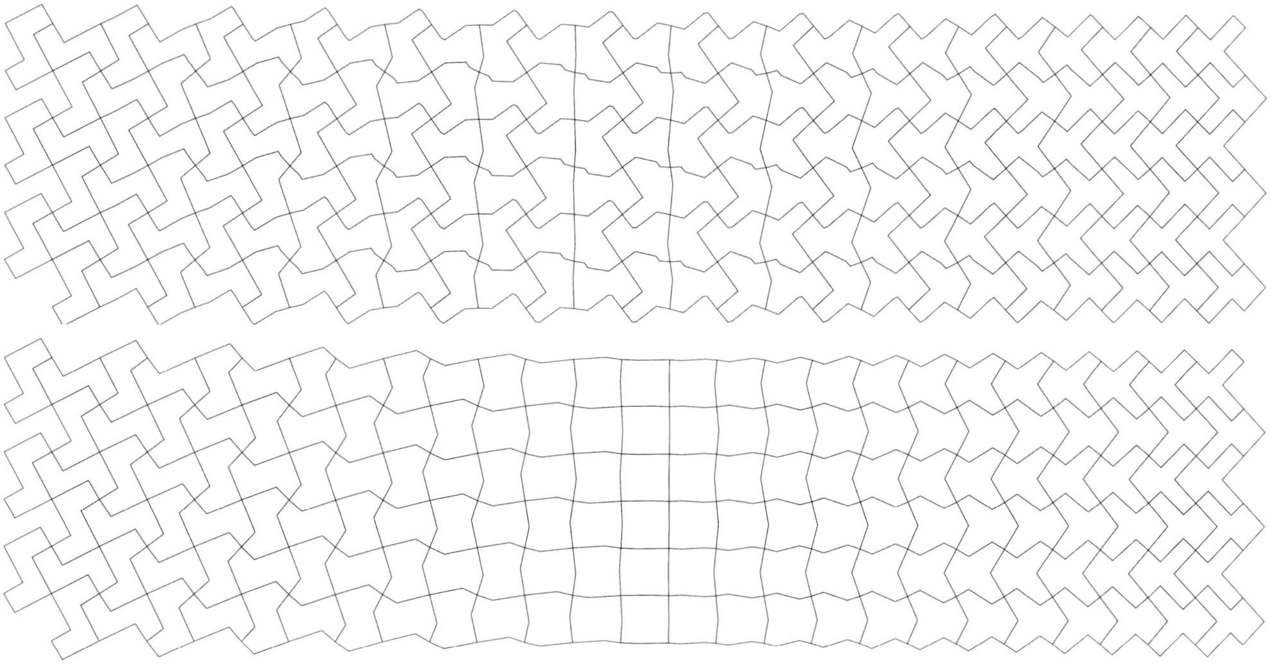

Fig. 13: Two designs based on keyframes, of types IH61 (left) and IH66 (right). If the tiles are left to interact directly, their different patterns of orientations will produce multiple distinct tile shapes. If desired, we can avoid this interaction by passing through the square tiling shared by these two isohedral types.

4.4 General Interpolation of Edges

The blending process described in the previous section suggests a general scheme for producing parquet deformation based on keyframes. Recall from Section 2 that an isohedral prototile can be described by choosing a Laves tiling, a set of tiling vertex parameters that modify the initial shape of the Laves tile, and edge shapes to join its vertices. Suppose that two keyframes are defined at the ends of a drawing, using the same base tile (that is, the same combination of Laves tiling and tiling vertex parameters). A tiling by the base tile provides a common ground for interpolating between the two keyframes. Each base edge carries two paths, one from each of the keyframe tilings. As in Figure 4, we can use the midpoints of an edge to look up an interpolation amount D(*x*) between 0 and 1. These values can then be plugged into a blending algorithm, together with the two paths that share that edge, to yield an intermediate path. As we move along the length of the canvas, the values of D(*x*) change gradually, producing tiles that morph smoothly from the first keyframe to the second.[14] Figure 12 shows two examples that interpolate between general paths.

A problem can arise with this approach when two keyframes share a Laves tiling but do not use the same isohedral type. Although the tiles in a given isohedral tiling must all be copies of the same shape, they need not all have the same orientation. Furthermore, different isohedral types can place tiles in different combinations of orientations. For example, consider the tilings at the left and right sides of the design in Figure 13. On the left, the tiles are arranged in a checkerboard of two distinct orientations; on the right, the orientations form alternating rows. When those two tiling types collide, different combinations of paths will meet at different edges of the shared Laves tiling, leading here to intermediate tilings made from two distinct tile shapes. Huff's rules for parquet deformations required that each position in the drawing have an implied monohedral tiling, a requirement that is violated here. We could ignore this rule and accept the drawing. But if we wish to adhere to Huff's constraints, one option is to introduce a third keyframe at the center of the drawing in which all edges are straight, as shown at the bottom of Figure 13. This straight-edged tiling is representable within the space of every isohedral type based on it, and so we can always pass through it monohedrally on the way from one isohedral type to another.

5. Evolving the Laves Tiling

In the techniques of the preceding section, we assumed that keyframes share the same base tile. The tilings associated with two keyframes can therefore be brought into perfect alignment, and interpolation is purely a matter of deforming edges relative to a fixed lattice of vertices. When using isohedral tilings as a basis for constructing parquet deformations, allowing two keyframes to have different Laves tilings, or different tiling vertex parameters, will necessarily require more sophistication.

If two keyframes have the same Laves tiling but different tiling vertex parameters, then interpolation becomes less reliable. In principle we can still establish a one-to-one correspondence between the vertices of the two tilings and use that to smoothly interpolate vertex positions. Unfortunately, such compositions are often stretched or skewed in unappealing ways. In some cases, however, this approach can succeed. In the parquet deformation of Figure 14, for example, half of the tiling vertices remain fixed, while the other half flex around them. The fixed vertices lock the pattern in place, permitting a stable composition to emerge.

The most extreme type of change is what I call a "topological transition", in which the keyframes are based on different Laves tilings altogether.[15] How might we build a parquet deformation from, say, 4.4.4.4 (squares) to 3.3.3.3.3.3 (hexagons), or 3.4.6.4 (kites) to 3.6.3.6 (rhombs)? In my research on this subject I have begun to articulate principles that make such transitions possible. Often, a transition can be achieved by having an isohedral tile based on one Laves tiling masquerade as another Laves tiling. We might adjust the tiling vertex parameters so that some edges shrink down to points, or deform edge paths until they meet each other, subdividing tiles. I offer two specific examples of topological transitions in Figure 15; many others are possible. Note that by concatenating multiple topological transitions and edge deformations, it may be possible to build a parquet deformation whose endpoints are any two isohedral tilings.

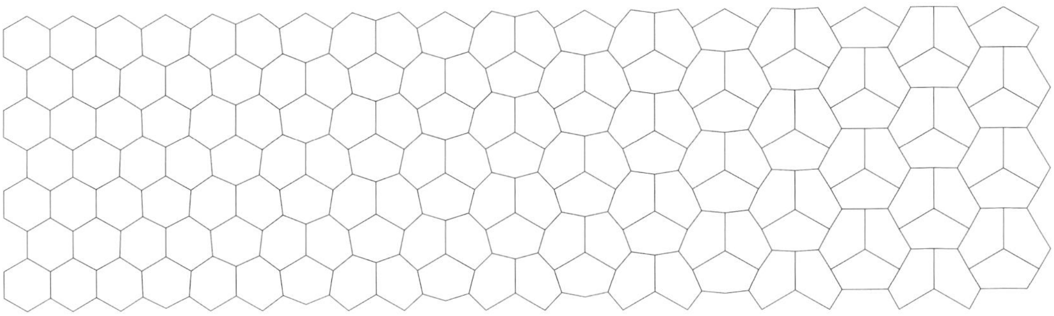

Fig. 14: A computer-generated reproduction of "Dizzy Bee" by Richard Mesnik, 1964. © HfG-Archiv/Museum Ulm, HfG-Ar, BDSA, Hu P 01. 023. This design demonstrates a case where tiling vertex parameters can vary between two keyframes, but nevertheless produce a stable composition.

Fig. 15: Two examples of topological transitions. The top transition moves from 3.3.3.3.3.3 (hexagons) to 4.4.4.4 (squares, here oriented diagonally). The bottom transition moves from 3.6.3.6 (rhombs) to 3.4.6.4 (kites).

6. Limitations and Opportunities

Huff imposed narrow constraints on the structure of parquet deformations. These constraints are entirely understandable given his interest in basic design and the need to offer a feasible exercise to students. Of course, when freed from the classroom, and accelerated by software, we can re-evaluate these constraints and choose which ones to retain.

6.1 Color

Huff intended parquet deformations to be an exercise in the manipulation of shape and line. Filling tiles with color would have been a time-consuming distraction; in a basic design studio, color might best be studied in isolation.

When drawing parquet deformations in software, we can fill tiles with color with almost no extra work. *Tactile*'s representation of an isohedral prototile already includes an assignment of colors to tiles. Given two keyframes with different color assignments, intermediate tile colors can be interpolated even more easily than edge shapes. Figure 16 gives an example of a parquet deformation with colored tiles. I find that color adds a rich aesthetic dimension that could allow these drawings to be applied in a broader range of art and design contexts.

Fig. 16: An example of a colored parquet deformation, based on isohedral type IH21.

6.2 Two-dimensional Deformations

Most of the designs produced in Huff's studio showed a progression along one dimension of space. But some students inevitably experimented with two-dimensional developments, in which tile shapes evolved along multiple axes.

The keyframe-based approach I have developed here can be extended to two dimensions in a natural way. A keyframe still consists of an isohedral prototile assigned to a fixed position on the canvas. But rather than restricting keyframes to a single axis, we allow them to be placed anywhere on the canvas. In the final drawing, we expect tiles near a keyframe to closely resemble that keyframe's prototile, and to evolve smoothly between prototiles everywhere else.

This approach entails two challenges. First, in the one-dimensional case, every edge midpoint falls somewhere between two keyframes, allowing us to compute the proportions of those prototiles to use when blending. In two dimensions, there is no obvious notion of betweenness. Instead we adopt a more general view that at every point in the plane, we can compute a set of "weights", one for each keyframe. The weights must be nonnegative and sum to 1. A given keyframe's weight should be close to 1 in its immediate neighborhood and fall off to 0 as we move away from it. The problem of computing continuously varying weights from keyframe locations can be seen as an instance of *scattered data interpolation* in computer science.[16]

The second challenge is that in general, any number of the weights computed above may be positive, potentially requiring us to blend between more than two paths for a given tiling edge. Most blending algorithms operate on exactly two paths, and must be generalized to handle this case. I extended the linear blending I use in one dimension to handle arbitrary numbers of paths and their weights.

Figure 17 shows two examples of two-dimensional parquet deformations, one monochromatic and one colored.

Fig. 17: Two examples of two-dimensional parquet deformations.

6.3 Monohedrality and Handedness

Huff required that a parquet deformation never contain "*A* and *B* elements", two different interlocking tiles. Expressing this constraint in a mathematically rigorous way is surprisingly difficult—every parquet deformation will necessarily include tiles of a wide variety of distinct shapes! I interpret this rule to mean that a given design is like a coarse sampling of a space of monohedral tilings, with prototile shapes that vary continuously across the canvas. In principle we could query any point on the canvas and be shown the associated tiling.

Figure 13 has already illustrated that there is no mathematical impediment to drawing parquet deformations with two (or more) distinct shapes, arising from interpolation between inconsistent tile orientations in keyframes. Of course, many of Escher's metamorphoses use multiple tile shapes. I have also previously experimented with Islamic geometric patterns that evolve in the manner of parquet deformations,[17] which almost inevitably involve more than one shape. Jay Bonner's chapter in this book discusses the connections to Islamic patterns in detail. When aiming to emulate Huff's style, I tend to respect the monohedral constraint: It produces a greater sense of visual unity and inevitability across a design.

Huff also prohibited "*A* and *A′* elements", by which he meant tilings containing both a shape and its mirror reflection, or equivalently, left- and right-handed versions of the same shape (he did allow tiles with internal bilateral symmetry, which do not change under mirror reflection). I consider this restriction to be too heavy-handed. Many designs produced in Huff's studio contain lines of mirror symmetry that pass through bilaterally symmetric tiles, with an aesthetic outcome comparable to that produced by reflections between adjacent tiles. It is true that if a left-handed tile reflects directly across an edge to its right-handed counterpart, then that edge must be a straight line and hence a possible distraction. But we can construct many parquet deformations in which left- and right-handed tiles are related by *glide reflections* (combinations of reflections and translations), which I find aesthetically pleasing. Figure 18 gives an example of a design that uses glide reflections to good effect. Indeed, a few drawings produced in Huff's studio also contain glide reflections, whether in conscious or unconscious violation of this constraint.

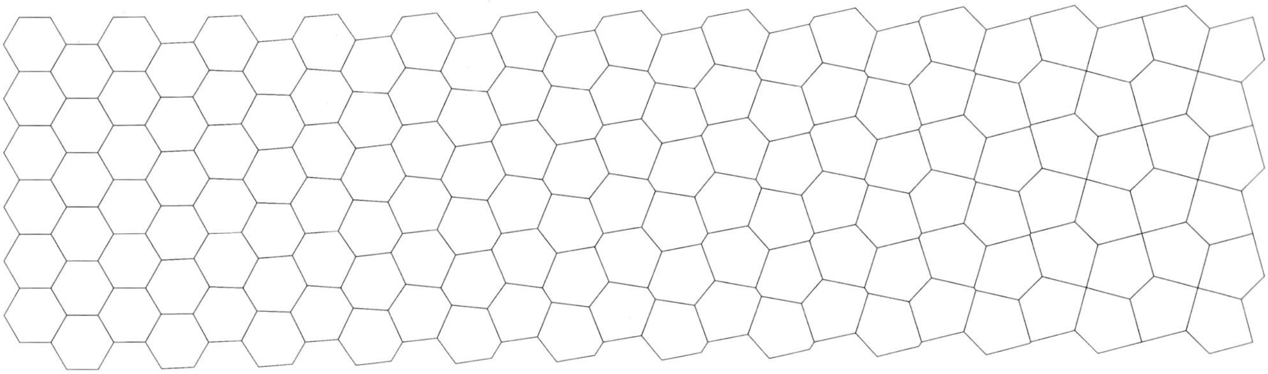

Fig. 18: A topological transition from 3.3.3.3.3.3 (hexagons) to 3.3.4.3.4 (Cairo tiles). The Laves tiles on the left and right edges of the design are mirror symmetric, but all other tiles come in left- and right-handed pairs related by vertical glide reflections.

6.4 Other Opportunities

The experiments presented here represent just a small sampling of the application of mathematics and compute science to the creation of parquet deformations. Many opportunities await for incorporating new mathematical ideas, or for translating these designs to new realms. Some, such as three-dimensional designs, designs based on aperiodic tilings, or the fusion of parquet deformations with Islamic geometric art, you will find elsewhere in this book. Others will inevitably arise over time, by those seeking inspiration at the intersection of mathematics and art.

References

[1] Douglas Hofstadter, *Metamagical Themas: Questing for the Essence of Mind and Pattern*, Bantam Books, 1986.

[2] Golan Levin and Tega Brain, *Code as Creative Medium: A Handbook for Computational Art and Design,* The MIT Press, 2021.

[3] Branko Grünbaum and G.C. Shephard, *Tilings and Patterns*, Dover, 2nd edition, 2016.

[4] Craig S. Kaplan, *Introductory Tiling Theory for Computer Graphics*, Morgan & Claypool, 2009.

[5] Doris Schattschneider, *M.C. Escher: Visions of Symmetry*, Harry N. Abrams, second edition, 2004.

[6] Heinrich Heesch and Otto Kienzle, *Flächenschluss: System der Formen lückenlos aneinanderschliessender Flachteile*, Springer-Verlag, 1963.

[7] Grünbaum and Shephard, *Tilings*, chapter 6.

[8] Available at: github.com/isohedral/tactile.

[9] Frank Thomas and Ollie Johnston, *The Illusion of Life: Disney Animation*, Disney Editions, 1995.

[10] Craig S. Kaplan, "Animated Isohedral Tilings", in: Susan Goldstine, Douglas McKenna, and Kristóf Fenyvesi (eds.), *Proceedings of Bridges 2019: Mathematics, Art, Music, Architecture, Education, Culture*, Tessellations Publishing, Phoenix, AZ 2019, pp. 99–106. Available online at http://archive.bridgesmathart.org/2019/bridges2019-99.pdf.

[11] Craig S. Kaplan, "Curve Evolution Schemes for Parquet Deformations", in: George W. Hart and Reza Sarhangi (eds.), *Proceedings of Bridges 2010: Mathematics, Music, Art, Architecture, Culture*, Tessellations Publishing, Phoenix, AZ 2010, pp. 95–102. Available online at http://archive.bridgesmathart.org/2010/bridges2010-95.html.

[12] Hans Pedersen and Karan Singh, "Organic Labyrinths and Mazes, in: NPAR *'06: Proceedings of the 4th International Symposium on Non-photorealistic Animation and Rendering*, ACM Press, 2006: pp. 79–86.

[13] Jeffrey J. Ventrella, *Brain-Filling Curves—A Fractal Bestiary*, Eyebrain Books, second edition, 2012. Available online at fractalcurves.com.

[14] Craig S. Kaplan, "Metamorphosis in Escher's Art", in: Reza Sarhangi and Carlo H. Séquin (eds.), *Bridges Leeuwarden: Mathematics, Music, Art, Architecture, Culture*, Tarquin Publications, London, 2008, pp. 39–46. Available online at http://archive.bridgesmathart.org/2008/bridges2008-39.html.

[15] Ibid.

[16] Richard Franke and Gregory M. Nielson, "Scattered Data Interpolation and Applications: A Tutorial and Survey", in: Hans Hagen and Dieter Roller (eds.), *Geometric Modeling*, Springer, Berlin/Heidelberg, 1991, pp. 131–160.

[17] Craig S. Kaplan, "Islamic Star Patterns from Polygons in Contact", in: GI *'05: Proceedings of the 2005 Conference on Graphics Interface*, Canadian Human-Computer Communications Society, 2005: pp. 177–185.

Biography of the Author

Craig S. Kaplan is an associate professor in the David R. Cheriton School of Computer Science at the University of Waterloo in Waterloo, Ontario, Canada. Originally from Montreal, he earned a bachelor's degree in Pure Mathematics and Computer Science from Waterloo in 1996 and a PhD in Computer Science from the University of Washington 2002. Kaplan's research focuses on relationships between computer graphics, art, and design, with an emphasis on applications to graphic design and illustration. He explores the mathematical theories of symmetry and tilings as a means of creating patterns, as well as the perceptual basis for our aesthetic appreciation of those patterns. This work frequently leads him into the broader world of computer graphics, particularly non-photorealistic rendering. He also occasionally ventures into related areas such as computational geometry and human-computer interaction. Kaplan is the author of the short textbook *Introductory Tiling Theory for Computer Graphics*, published by Morgan & Claypool, as well as numerous papers in the Computer Graphics and Mathematical Art literature. He helps organize the annual Bridges conference on art and mathematics, and serves as an Associate Editor of the *Journal of Mathematics and the Arts*.

Parametric Modeling of Parquet Deformations: A Novel Method for Design and Analysis

Tuğrul Yazar

Introduction

Introducing students of architecture to systems thinking in the form of patterns and their deformations is becoming a significant research topic.[1] Alejandro Zaera-Polo depicts a history of pattern studies in architecture, emphasizing a conceptional shift in the "Computational Design Era".[2] This conceptional shift can be explained with the development of digital design technology, which makes it "possible to process multiple layers of patterns such as social, economical, cultural, formal, etc., and their deformations simultaneously with desired precision".[3] In contemporary architectural geometry, deformation is defined as "an alteration of shape which is based on an underlying mathematical principle".[4] Today, the static pattern of configurations, tessellations, or any form of structural order can be mediated into a system of both generative and differentiated potential.[5] This paper is about a special studio exercise of architectural education named "Parquet Deformation". The exercise was derived from a special educational discourse in the mid-twentieth century and reached today with the contributions of various researchers and instructors. This paper aims to explain an alternative parametric modeling workflow and test it via re-constructing typical parquet deformations. The Parquet Deformation exercise is about the tessellations of the plane that gradually shapeshift in two dimensions without gaps or overlaps (Figure 1, Figure 2, and Figure 3). The exercise encourages students of architecture to think about the geometric relationships between sequences of continual shape-shifting while developing reasoning about a pattern as a structural whole. This is expected to be explored by morphing the cells of a pattern while sustaining its visual continuity and rhythm.[6]
This study is a continuation of a previous study on the re-construction of parquet deformations via contemporary parametric modeling tools.

The Parquet Deformation exercise is generally attributed to William S. Huff, who introduced and conducted it at several schools of architecture starting in the 1960s. Huff defines the exercise as rooted in two analytical disciplines; monohedral tilings in geometry, and the continuous deformations in biological morphology, generally exemplified by D'Arcy Thompson's and Albrecht Dürer's studies.[7] Huff emphasizes its temporal quality by describing the exercise as a form of visual music with themes, events, intervals, rhythm, and repetitions,[8] and harmony of figuration,[9] defining the designer's role as being similar to that of a composer. In his later writings, Huff mentions the temporal and spatial variation of Sino-Japanese landscape handscrolls[10] and symmetry studies in chemistry[11] concerning the exercise. These relationships and definitions verify the artistic and scientific backgrounds of the exercise. To better investigate these backgrounds, we can examine the academic environment in which the Parquet Deformation exercise has emerged.

William Huff's educational discourse began with his visits to the Ulm School of Design (The Hochschule für Gestaltung Ulm, HfG) as a graduate student between 1956 and 1957, and as a visiting instructor for the Basic Course (*Grundkurs*) between 1963 and 1968[12]. The educational doctrine of the HfG had an important role in the development of this exercise. HfG was founded in 1946 by educationalist Inge Scholl and graphic designer Otl Aicher, with the aim of rebuilding the social structure of post-war Germany. The school went through different periods in its short life. The timeline at the HfG Ulm Archive website (www.hfg-archiv.ulm.de), produced from a review with Otl Aicher in 1975, summarizes the periods HfG has gone through. In that diagram, William Huff's name appears under the course names "Value-based Design" and "Programmed Design" (*Wertbestimmtes Design and Programmdesign*). The first rector of the school was

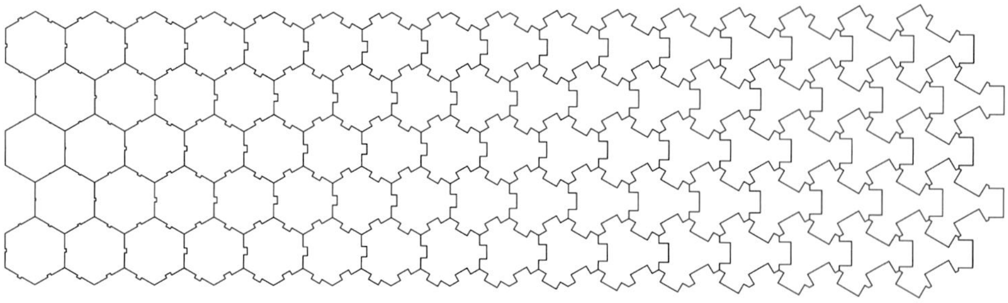

Fig. 1: "Trifoliolate", designed by Glenn Paris in 1966.[13] Redrawn by the author.

Fig. 2: "I at the Center", designed by David Oleson in 1964.[14] Redrawn by the author.

Max Bill, who led the school's claim to be the continuation of the Bauhaus in Weimar. According to Bill, design education should be a combination of science, technology, and fine arts. As quoted by Peter Kapos; for Bill, design work should proceed following the "spiritual substance" of modern art.[15]

William Huff's first visit to HfG was during Bill's administration. However, it is possible to claim that the administration that Huff was more influenced and benefited from intellectually was the period of "scientific operationalism" introduced by Tomás Maldonado. In some sources, Maldonado is introduced as the director of the school after the resignation of Bill.[16] However, the timeline of the HfG Archive indicates that a Rector's College (*Rektoratskollegium*) was in charge; including Aicher, Gugelot, Vordemberge-Gildewart, and Maldonado. However, it is possible to indicate that Tomás Maldonado became an influential figure in the new period of the school after Max Bill. Unlike Bill, Maldonado was more interested in production, consumption, exchange systems, and multi-disciplinary approaches. He criticized Bill's thoughts on aesthetics as the natural basis of function. According to Maldonado, function includes historicity, and it is possible to see it

Fig. 3: "Crossover", designed by Richard Long in 1963.[17] Redrawn by the author.

in production-consumption systems. Peter Kapos summarizes this idea as: "Building form, for example, would be principally determined by methods of prefabrication and techniques of systematic construction. [...] No longer directing production by decree according to artistic principles from an external position, it had become necessary for the designer to become fully integrated within the production process."[18] Maldonado claimed that a designer's success is related, among other things, to the precision of thinking and doing methods, and the adequacy of scientific and technical knowledge. During Maldonado's influence, the educational program of HfG has changed, to a new method called "scientific operationalism". This method is also known as the "Ulm Model" at the international level.

The first-hand resource of the Ulm Model is the Ulm Journal (*Journal of the Hochschule für Gestaltung*), published between 1958–1968. The philosophical and pedagogical background of the Ulm Model can be studied from Maldonado and Bonsiepe's paper in the Journal.[19] According to Peter Kapos; in this period, the school opened new positions for cybernetics, game theory, and mathematics.[20] Today, this interdisciplinary approach is still regarded as an original example for the discussion on the education of science and mathematics in the schools of architecture.[21]

There were other exercises at HfG that were designed for similar purposes with parquet deformation. For example, Herbert Kapitzki's "Spatial Operations in the Plane" (Räumliche Operation in der Ebene), "The Symmetry Exercise", and Maldonado's "Raster" approach similar educational purposes from different angles.[22] Several design exercises including "The Programmed Design", "The Conflicting Depth Cues", "The Figure-Ground Figure without Ground", and "The Parquet Deformation" are described as derivations of Maldonado's previous studio experiments.[23] In an article in the Ulm Journal, Huff explains Maldonado's influence on his exercise designs.[24] Moreover, in the article titled "Defining Basic Design as a Discipline", Huff describes the influences of Maldonado, Albers, and Chernikov on his "Formative Design Studio".[25] These confirm that the initial development of the Parquet Deformation exercise was one of the collective results of a special academical atmosphere. However, it was William Huff who described the exercise clearly, conducted it continuously at his design studios, and continued to publish his opinions and studies long after the closure of the HfG.[26]

In 1983, Douglas Hofstadter published and commented on some of the parquet deformations in one of his journal papers and a chapter of the book titled *Metamagical Themas: Questing for the Essence of Mind and Pattern*.[27, 28] Hofstadter describes the temporal qualities of the student works, created in William Huff's studios. Shortly after these publications, the exercise started to capture a wider multi-disciplinary interest. Another key personality in the development of the exercise was Louis Kahn. Huff worked at Kahn's office between 1958 and 1960. This coincides with his two visits to HfG, as a student and as a teacher. Hofstadter addresses their connection by quoting Kahn's admiration of Huff's Basic Design discourse.[29] Besides, Huff often mentions Kahn's ideas on "order, disorder, change, and chaos" while explaining his point of view on the relationships between geometry and design.[30] Although any direct effect of Kahn on the particular studio exercise is questionable, this connection indicates the theory of structuralism that influenced a generation of architects and educators when studio exercises such as Parquet Deformation were developed.[31]

It is possible to find pattern studies similar to parquet deformations in various fields of art since the beginning of the twentieth century. One of the earliest examples of systematic pattern deformations can be seen in Lewis Foreman Day's studies on textile ornaments in his books titled *Pattern Design, A Book for Students Treating in a Practical Way of the Anatomy, Planning & Evolution of Repeated Ornament and The*

Anatomy of Pattern. Day was a painter and industrial designer, and an important figure of the Arts and Crafts movement. In these books, Day does not directly address or name pattern deformations, but introduces various patterns by drawing several variations near each other, denoting them "varieties of the same pattern".[32] The most well-known and mentioned examples of the systematic and methodical deformation of patterns are the artworks of M. C. Escher, especially *Metamorphosis and The Day and Night*.[33] In *Metamorphosis*, Escher created many deformations of a square tessellation and manipulates the image by using shading and color.

The recent studies on parquet deformations are mostly based on geometric principles. Craig Kaplan studied the mathematical underpinnings of pattern deformations in his dissertation and various publications.[34] He also studied Escher's artworks and the continuous deformations of Islamic patterns.[35] Parallel to Huff's exercise, John Sharp studied similar compositions he named *Morphing Tilings*.[36] In 2006, Andrew Cooke developed *BulliEpu*, a computer application in Java that generates parquet deformations. Although the Parquet Deformation and similar exercises are still being conducted in design studios, the academic studies on the topic remain limited. Karen Li is one of a few former students of Huff who succeeded her background into an academic publication about the exercise.[37] For further reading and bibliography, readers are referred to David Bailey's website (http://www.tesselation.co.uk/parquet-deformations) which shows one of the most comprehensive sources on the literature of Parquet Deformation exercise.

Methodology

This study is a continuation of the author's previous study[38] on the contemporary approaches for the parametric modeling of parquet deformations. An original generative design approach and a computer tool will be introduced and tested. As the testing case studies, two student works supervised by William Huff will be analyzed and reconstructed by utilizing the aforementioned tool. This is expected to help provide a framework for a contemporary interpretation of the exercise and its potential connections with today's popular design tools and methods. This framework is believed to be an example of how today's architects can use computer-aided tools not only in drawing but also in design exploration.

Since the first students of William Huff at Ulm had no computer access, these geometric computations were probably made by extensive work of sketching on tracing papers. These compositions are generally based on a regular tessellation (square, triangular, or hexagonal grids). It would be possible for the students to use several layers of tracing papers while trying to figure out a transformation rule by considering the symmetry operations. The transition from one shape to another requires a repeated modification on the edges and vertices. In most examples, the continuous shapeshifting starts from a simpler shape on the left side and becomes increasingly complex while deforming to the right side. In some of the designs, it is possible to identify several steps, or phases, where the deformation process changes. In this study, such key moments will be identified and used as the geometric base of the parquet deformations. The major components of a parquet deformation can be defined as follows:

› Lattice: Lattice represents the underlying structure of a parquet deformation. The term is also used by Huff while describing the types of tessellations that a parquet deformation might be constructed onto.[39] In the original exercise, lattices are generally monohedral (Figure 4).

› Prototile: A prototile is a key cell that the parquet variations are generated from. A regular systematic parquet deformation has at least two prototiles, from which the parquets are generated while the shapeshifting from one prototile to another (Figure 4).

In this study, more components are added to better identify the proposed methodology:

› Fundamental Curve: In most cases, the prototiles of parquet deformations are symmetrical. This reduces the problem into the deformation of one or several curves. In this study, these curves will be defined as the "fundamental curves" since they contain the minimum information about a parquet deformation. In the shapeshifting of a fundamental curve, new vertices and edges can be created (Figure 4). If the transformation process of a fundamental curve is examined closely, it can be seen that generally, there are linear interpolations between the vertices of these curves. During these interpolations, the appearance and disappearances of the vertices can be observed.

› 3D Prototile: In the proposed approach, a three-dimensional abstract object is created digitally, to embed the variations of many two-dimensional prototiles. This object includes the sequential interpolations between the prototiles, represented in the XYT space (Figure 4d). Every section taken from this object would return a parquet variation. The design of the 3D Prototile should be done depending on the underlying lattice, as in the original parquet deformations. This would require sketch modeling and feedback, just like the original design process.

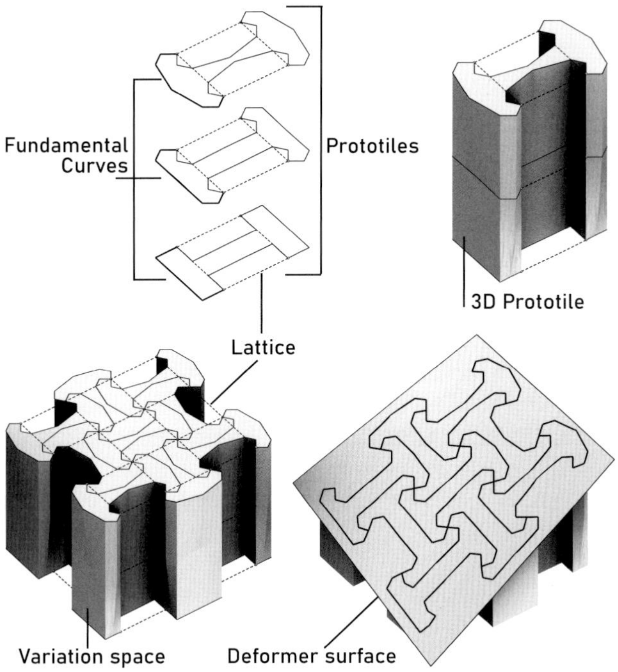

Fig. 4. Anatomy of a typical Parquet Deformation ("I at the Center"). Image by the author

› Variation Space: After defining the 3D Prototile, it is copied on the lattice, by specified numbers. This three-dimensional waffle-like structure is named "variation space" in this study. This set, as the name suggests, contains all the possible parquet deformation compositions that can be derived from given prototiles and fundamental curves (Figure 4).

› Deformer Surface: After the preparations explained above, design outputs can be produced. Projection of each section taken from the variation space on the XY plane would generate a two-dimensional parquet deformation design. If sufficient attention has been paid to the relationship with the lattice during the prototile design phase, no gaps or intersections would occur between the inner surfaces of the variation space. Thus, the sections produced from this structure wouldn't contain any gaps or overlaps. In most of the original examples, the deformer surface is usually an inclined flat plane. This enables a parquet deformation to progress at a steady rate of change, being evenly distributed among the prototiles. However, the method proposed in this study makes it possible to experiment with various surfaces with different curvatures. If the surface is derived from a polynomial function, this would sustain the surface continuity, and the rate of change of the derived parquet deformation will be more consistent and connected. These surfaces can be derived in parametric or explicit forms, or they can be created with different approaches such as vector fields. The way these surfaces are created and the data sources they use will provide a controlled environment for the designer. Any digital input and surface creation method would be related to the design process of a parquet deformation (Figure 4).

The method described above provides fast results by utilizing the basic functions of CAD such as surface modeling, intersection, and projection operations, without revealing the complex mathematical calculations underneath. The deformer surface can be defined independently from the lattice, prototile, and 3D prototile. Therefore, the data source that constitutes the deformer surface can be defined independently. Moreover, the geometric properties of the deformer surface would give information about the parquet deformation it creates. These properties include topological connectedness, draft angle, curvature, and critical points.[40] For example, the Gaussian curvature of a deformer surface represents a mathematical basis for explaining the local and overall regularities of a parquet deformation. If the Gaussian curvature of a deformation surface is zero at every point, the surface is flat. This would result in a parquet deformation in which the amount of change in every step of the deformation is constant. If the deformation surface has no Gaussian curvature and it is parallel to the projection plane of the pattern, then there would be no deformation on the pattern. While moving across two points on a deformation surface, a positive or negative change in the Gaussian curvature results in a variable rate of change in the deformation. Similarly, the projection of the critical points on the deformer surface would give the center points or attractor points of a parquet deformation. More studies are needed to utilize these properties of the deformer surfaces.

Toolset

The methodology explained above belongs to the design process of a generalized parquet deformation. It doesn't represent a fully automated design process. As in the original compositions, a sketching process with a feedback cycle is still necessary. However, since the proposed method includes digital data and three-dimensional digital models, it is not possible to perform it by using hand tools. In turn, it is better suited to be fed by digital data, thus being used in generative design systems. In this study, it was decided to develop a simple computer tool to increase the usability of this method and to facilitate the modeling process. Currently, the tool is being developed for the *Grasshopper* in *Rhinoceros Computer-aided Design* (CAD) software. *Grasshopper* is a visual programming language specialized in generating algorithmic designs and the analysis of geometric forms. The dataflow programming concept is utilized in *Grasshopper* by introducing graph-like algorithms, composed of components (nodes), and the connections between the components (directed edges). The algorithms created in this environment enables designers to construct and explore geometric forms in real-time. *Grasshopper* also offers an infrastructure open to enrichment with new components prepared by the experts of the field. Currently, the Parquet Deformation add-on includes two prototype components for testing purposes.

The add-on does not aim to generate random parquet deformations automatically. Instead, it aims to support designers in creating and analyzing these compositions by solving several geometric construction problems which are the essential parts of the methodology presented in the previous section. This is why the components of the add-on are not closed systems, but rather small problem-solving tools, intended to be used in regular *Grasshopper* algorithms. The components were developed in *Python* Scripts and *Grasshopper* clusters and added to *Grasshopper* as user objects. In the future, these prototype components would be further developed with C#.

The first component, *Loft Aligned*, aims to help designers in the construction of the 3D prototiles. The main problem of this geometric construction is the determination of the transitions between the vertices of the fundamental curves. Figure 5 shows that the regular surface-creating commands such as loft, and sweep does not have enough inputs to automatically create such surfaces. It is possible to model these surfaces manually in CAD by adding more vertices. However, the *Loft Aligned* component presents a general solution and helps designers in this modeling process. It takes two input curves from the user, analyzes them, and matches their vertices so that they correctly create the surfaces necessary for a 3D prototile. The vertex matching algorithm is derived from the observations made on the original parquet deformations. The component can generate new vertices, if necessary. It is an essential phase of the methodology presented in this study

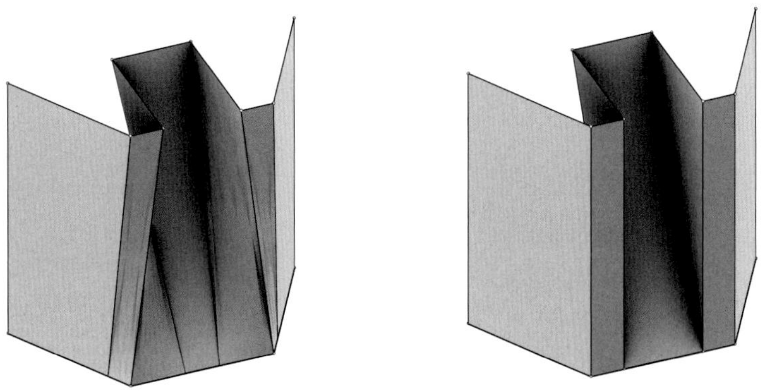

Fig. 5: The *Loft Aligned* component's functionality and difference from a standard surface modeling command, especially in protrusions. The object on the left is the result of a standard Loft operation in Rhinoceros. Since the command does not have enough information about the general shape-shifting style of parquet deformations, it adds random edges along the surface. The object on the right is the result of the Loft Aligned component. This component calculates naked and overlapping vertices and generates new edges according to the general rule of orthogonal foldings in parquet deformations. Image by the author.

because the outputs of this component return two sets of points that are aligned and ready to be lofted as a surface geometry. Currently, the *Loft Aligned* component is under the component group of the add-on named Utilities.

The second component is called "p31m" and is under the component group named Symmetry. This component helps designers to explore not only parquet deformations but many pattern systems by enabling the application of symmetry groups. Currently, only one symmetry group called p31m was developed for testing purposes. This component is developed as a native *Grasshopper* cluster, which means it is still under the development phase. It takes geometric objects to be transformed, and two points to determine the size of the hexagonal lattice of the symmetry transformation. These inputs are organized to match the outputs of the *Loft Aligned* component so that an efficient parquet deformation modeling workflow could be established quickly. In the future, the other symmetry groups could also be implemented to the add-on. In the next section, the tool and the approach introduced in this section will be tested on the reconstruction of two original parquet deformations.

Strange Start, Startling Stop

"Strange Start, Startling Stop" was designed by student Mary Purdy at the State University of New York in 1985. The composition is based on a hexagonal lattice (Figure 6). There are four prototiles, marking the four key moments in the shape-shifting process. The first prototile is a regular hexagon, which is also the first tile of the composition. This prototile morphs into a shape that is a composition of four smaller hexagons, creating the second prototile. This morphing process finishes at the 9th tile from the left. The third prototile is then, slowly erected by enlarging a portion of every edge. This morphing process finishes at the 17th tile from the left. The fourth and last prototile is a continuation of the previous one. It expands the parts and creates snowflake-like spikes to finalize the composition.

This final prototile expands the edges and changes their directions, and the opposing edges merge into single vertices at the end. These prototiles are created

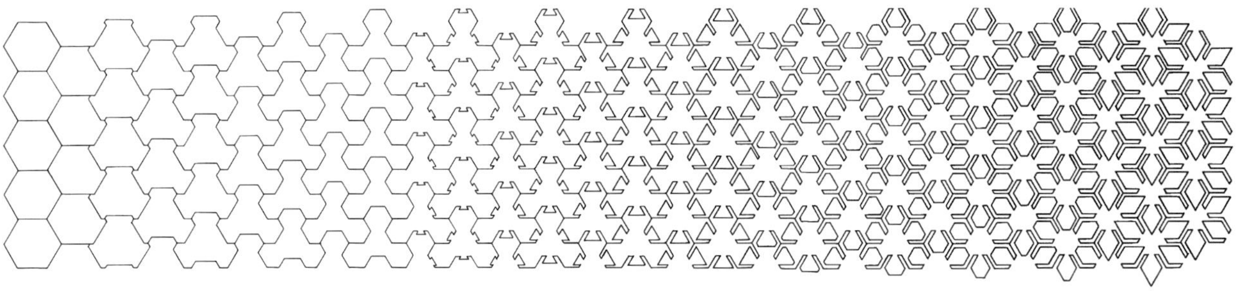

Fig. 6. "Strange Start, Startling Stop". Redrawn by the author. The original drawing made by the student, Mary Purdy. © HfG-Archiv/Museum Ulm, HfG-Ar, BDSA, Hu P 06. 017.

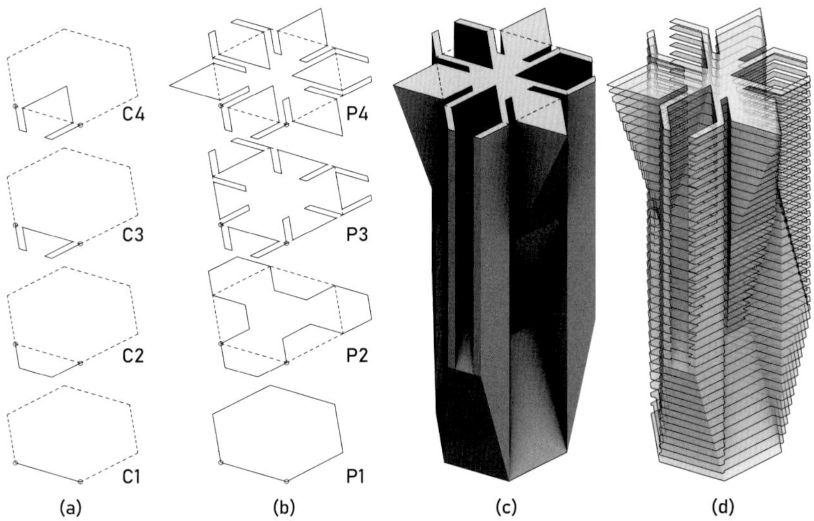

Fig. 7. "Strange Start, Startling Stop". (a) Fundamental curves, (b) prototiles, (c) the 3D prototile, and (d) several slices of the 3D prototile, creating the tiles of the deformation. Image by the author

by four fundamental curves. The fundamental curves and corresponding prototiles are shown in Figure 7a and Figure 7b. The designer would probably think of these four prototiles while designing "Strange Start, Startling Stop". One of the important qualities of parquet deformations is that they allow partial deformations on single tiles. In the example, the 10th and 18th tiles from the left show this kind of partial deformations. The proposed methodology is expected to simulate this behavior. After the definition of prototiles, their vertices are matched to create the lofting operation (Figure 7c). Then, the 3D prototile is created by utilizing the p31m symmetry operation. This operation repeats several rotation and reflection transformations to create the closed polyhedron.

The geometric construction described above is tested in *Grasshopper* (Figure 8). This algorithm can also be regarded as a generalization, which means, it can generate not only the particular case study but many other alternative designs by providing it with different fundamental curves. The first part of the algorithm (Figure 8a) takes the fundamental curves of the four prototiles. Then, these curves are fed to the *Loft Aligned* component to match their correct vertices. The outputs P1

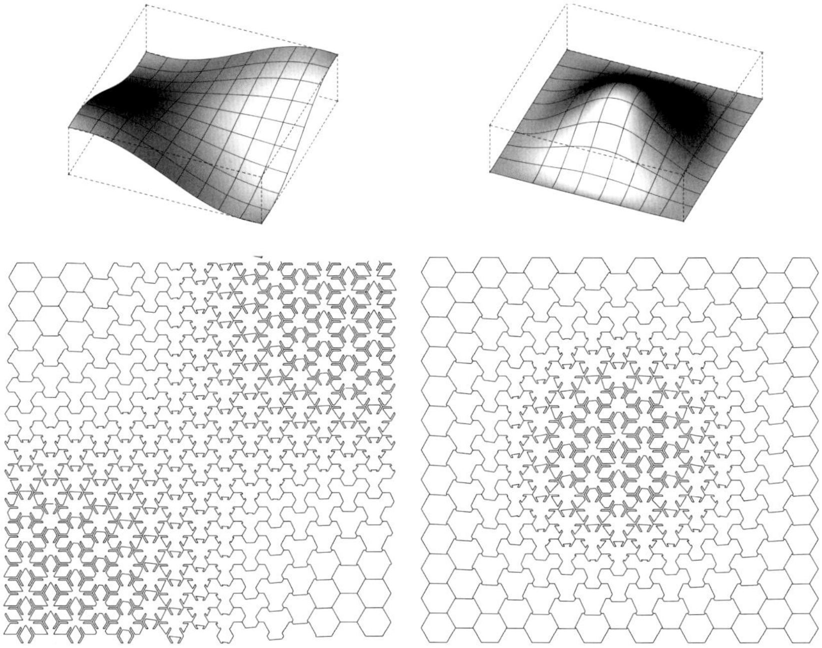

Fig. 9. New interpretations of "Strange Start, Startling Stop", created by different sections of the variation space. Image by the author.

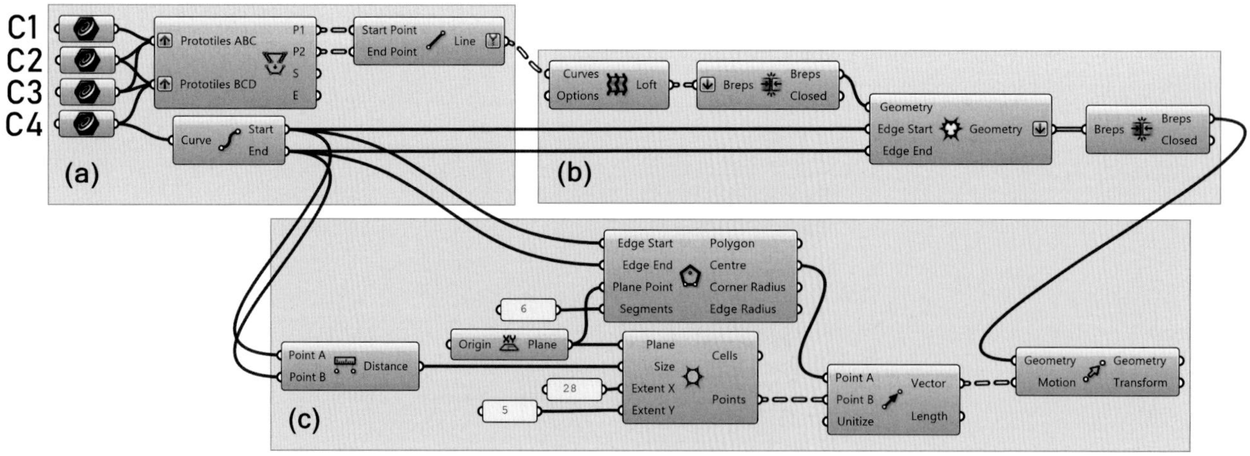

Fig. 8. Parametric model of the variation space of "Strange Start, Startling Stop". (a) Utilizing the "Loft Aligned" component to align the vertices of the fundamental curves. (b) The application of p31m symmetry transformation to create the 3D prototile. (c) The array of the 3D prototile on the hexagonal lattice, creating the variation space. Image by the author

and P2 are used to draw line segments of the matching vertices on the prototiles. In the second part (Figure 8b), these line segments are used to create a surface shape by using regular modeling components of *Grasshopper*. Then, the symmetry transformation is applied to this surface to create the 3D prototile. In the last part (Figure 8c), a hexagonal grid is created, and the 3D prototile is copied to this grid to finalize the variation space. The result of this algorithm is a waffle-like structure of many copies of the 3D prototile, capturing all possible parquet deformations that could be generated from the given fundamental curves.

In the last part of the reconstruction, various deformer surfaces are used to cut the variation space and generate new alternatives. In general, Huff's studio works utilize a continuous deformation on either one or two axes. The methodology presented in this study adds many different ways to it. Figure 9 shows two of these re-constructions. One of the main qualities of parquet deformations is the seamless continuity of all parquets. This is why it is possible to see variations even within a single parquet. The proposed methodology enables this quality to be implemented since any continuous deformer surface would result in a continuously varying set of parquets. The rate of change of the deformation is related to the change in the curvature of the deformer surface. Also, the local minimum and maximum points of the deformer surface mark the points or regions where the parquet deformation is attracted to Wiry Wonder.

The parquet deformation named "Wiry Wonder" was designed by Michael Cuttita in William Huff's studio at the State University of New York in 1989. Figure 10 shows the original drawing made by the student. Similar to the previous one, this composition is based on a hexagonal lattice. In this composition there are three major prototiles, marking the three key moments in the shape-shifting process. There is also one hidden prototile, which is created to accommodate the transition between the last two prototiles. The first prototile is similar to the second prototile of "Strange Start, Startling Stop", composed of four small hexagons.

This prototile morphs into a shape that has extensions inside and outside, creating the second prototile. This morphing process finishes at the 8th tile from the

Fig. 10. Michael Cuttita, "Wiry Wonder". Basic Design Studio of William S. Huff, Spring 1989, SUNY at Buffalo. © HfG-Archiv/Museum Ulm, HfG-Ar, BDSA, Hu P 01. 037.

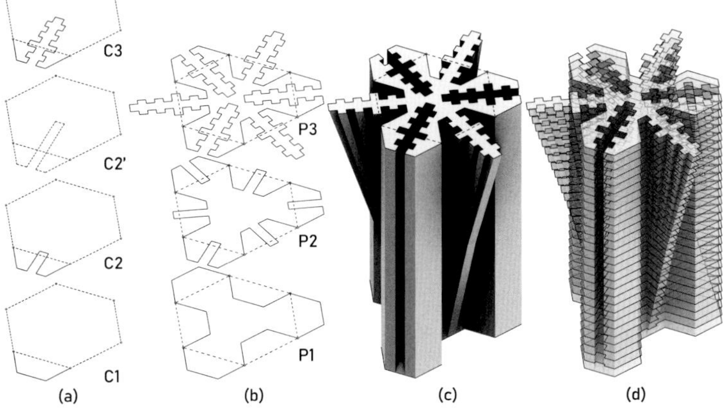

Fig. 11. "Wiry Wonder". (a) Fundamental curves, (b) prototiles, (c) the 3D Prototile, and (d) several slices of the 3D prototile, creating the tiles of the deformation. Image by the author

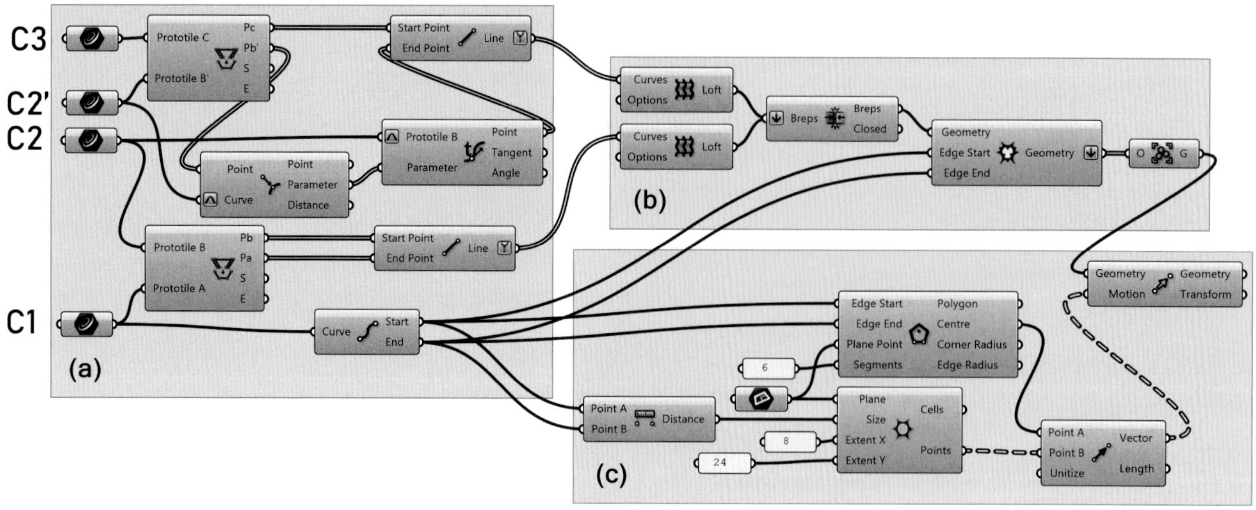

Fig. 12: Parametric model of the variation space of "Wiry Wonder": (a) utilizing the *Loft Aligned* component to align the vertices of the prototiles, and the utilization of a hidden prototile to achieve the transition between prototiles, (b) the application of p31m symmetry transformation to create the 3D prototile, (c) the array of the 3D prototile on the hexagonal lattice, creating the variation space. Image by the author.

left. The third and the last prototile creates saw-like details on the newly created edges in the second prototile. This morphing process finishes on the right end. These prototiles are created by fundamental curves, shown in Figure 11a. It is the same symmetry operation with "Strange Start, Startling Stop", that creates the prototiles shown in Figure 11b. After the definition of prototiles, the *Loft Aligned* component developed for this study was used to match the vertices of the prototiles. This returns the one-to-one morphings of the line segments of the fundamental curves, creating the 3D prototile (Figure 11c).

Figure 12 shows the *Grasshopper* algorithm to generate the setup of "Wiry Wonder". The first part of the algorithm (Figure 12a) takes the fundamental curves of the three prototiles. The difference of this composition from the previous one is the usage of a hidden prototile curve, which is between the second and third prototile. When analyzed, the transition from the second prototile to the third prototile includes two different transformations. One of them is the extension of the protrusions generated in the second prototile. These protrusions are becoming much longer while approaching the third prototile. At the same time, another transformation occurs. This second transformation creates saw-like edges on the protrusions. This is why the transition between second and third prototiles is a composite transformation. Since the current code of the *Loft Aligned* component can only process one transformation at a time, this required the definition of a hidden prototile. This is why the *Grasshopper* code has four fundamental curves, instead of three. The hidden prototile is the extended version of the second prototile, creating a basis for the transition between the second and third prototiles. The operations shown in Figure 12a use the *Loft Aligned* component twice. One of them is the actual matching of the vertices of the fundamental curves. The other component creates a temporary matching to add the information coming from the hidden prototile. A parametric evaluation was required to transfer this information to the actual vertex-matching process. match their correct vertices. In the second part (Figure 12b), a surface shape was created by using regular modeling components of Grasshopper. Then, the symmetry transformation is applied to this surface to create the 3D prototile. In the last part (Figure 12c), a hexagonal grid is created, and the 3D prototile is copied to this grid to finalize the variation space. The result of this algorithm is a waffle-like structure of many copies of the 3D prototile, capturing all possible parquet de-formations that could be generated from the given fundamental curves. Finally, various deformer surfaces are used to cut the variation space and generate new alternatives. Figure 13 shows two of these reconstructions.

Conclusion and Discussion

Architectural education must continue to redefine its interdisciplinary role with the help of newly developing technologies. This study focused on a historical studio exercise that is still valid for today's parametric modeling approaches. A novel methodology was

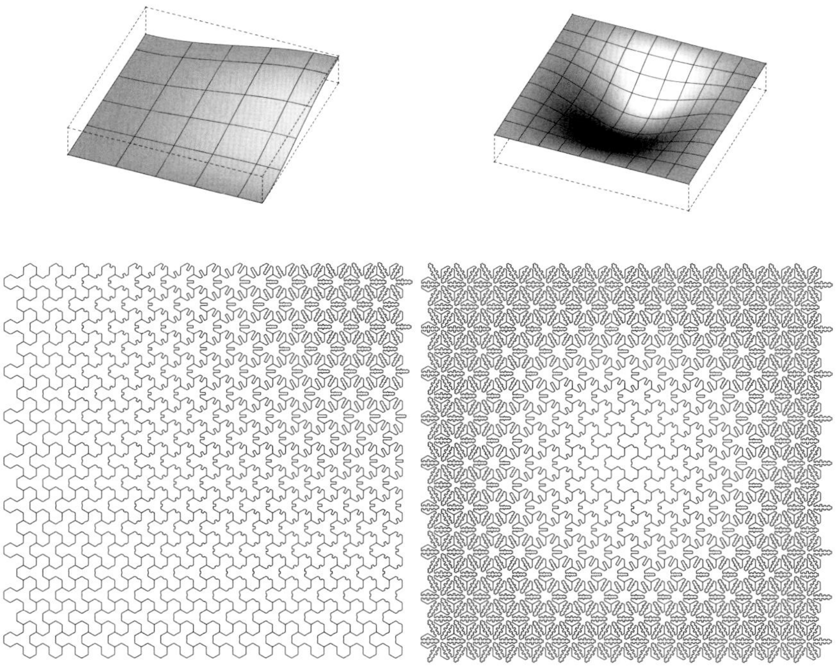

Fig. 13: New interpretations of "Wiry Wonder", created by different sections of the variation space. Image by the author.

introduced and tested. Different from the traditional two-dimensional drawing, the usage of a three-dimensional variation space and a deformer surface was introduced as visual ways of making complex calculations in the creation of parquet deformations. The toolset developed for this purpose should be further advanced and better tested in the future. In the proposed toolset, fundamental curves, and symmetry groups were defined as the primary components of parquet deformations. The methodology presented in this study helps designers in executing complex and repeating geometric constructions of parquet deformations. When the geometric construction of such patterns is no longer a problem, it can be enhanced by additional inputs of any design domain. The code package being developed can be used as an example in the current parametric modeling and coding-related design courses and transformed with different data inputs. This would break the limitation of the tool and widen the educational perspective. It would also be appropriate to consider hybrid studio setups in which both traditional and digital tools are used to better understand the underlying mathematics and to speed up creative thinking at the same time. It is not possible to state that the developed code can automatically generate all possible parquet deformations. Human creativity can always get out of the box and reveal unique patterns of thought that cannot be predicted by pre-made code sequences. In this respect, the code presented in this article is no different from a compass. It can be used in new ways for different purposes in the hands of the new generation of designers trained in this field. More studies and studio experiences are needed to clarify these potential uses.

One of the common starting points of many digital design theories is based on the relationship between complexity and harmony. In the broadest sense, most computer-aided design tools are developed to help designers deal with the increasing complexity of design problems efficiently, and open new ways of studying harmony. On the other hand, it should be noted that the intellectual basis of these methods has been establishing before the development of computer technologies. The Parquet Deformation exercise is a perfect example of the non-computerized basis of a contemporary digital design method, called parametric modeling. Although the Ulm Model has no major impact on today's architectural theories, the element that still makes the Parquet Deformation exercise useful and meaningful is the bridge it hosts between art and mathematics, similar to one of the prominent intentions of parametric modeling. Both parquet deformation and parametric modeling are the reflections of modern thought in science, art, and philosophy, in which a choreography of continuity, flow, dynamism, and evolution are at the forefront.

The modeling approach presented in this paper increases the speed of formal exploration. Using this method, a parquet deformation that would take several hours to be designed and drawn by hand can be discovered in minutes. However, speed is not necessarily a positive factor for design exploration.

Appearing to be a major advantage, at first sight, it is also esoteric and limiting from a wider perspective. Besides, the inevitable result of this point of view is the necessity of digitalization. Again, the digitization of architectural information raises the ontological and epistemological criticisms of reduction. This criticism is based on the fact that architectural knowledge cannot tolerate reduction. Similar to the reduction of architecture into "building science" in HfG, this educational experience showed us that it is not possible to leave architectural education to a single point of view. If a lesson is to be learned from the history of HfG, it would be the importance of addressing different perspectives from a holistic and pluralist perspective, and being able to stay together by understanding the value of those differences and benefiting from all. This is why the methodology presented in this study can be regarded as an alternative aiming to enrich the constructivist pedagogy of parquet deformations. It is believed to emphasize the power of keeping diverse attitudes together and keeping communication channels open between them.

In Basic Design education, it is possible to see that the constructivist perspective still lays the groundwork for short-term and contextually limited studio exercises. But even Constructivism itself is not a broad enough framework to include all the possibilities of architectural education. The contextual limitations proposed by Constructivism should not turn into reduction. For this reason, these exercises should be carefully linked to the general objectives of contemporary architectural education and professional responsibilities. The integration of these exercises with the interdisciplinary roles of the architect continues to be one of the issues of every curriculum, studio, and instructor. It is an open question how the future design studios will take over this issue from the point left by William S. Huff and the parquet deformation.

Acknowledgments

The author would like to thank Werner Van Hoeydonck for providing the original drawings of the Parquet Deformations which were analyzed in this study.

References

[1] Tuğrul Yazar, "Revisiting Parquet Deformations from a Computational Perspective: A Novel Method for Design and Analysis", *International Journal of Architectural Computing* 15(4), SAGE Publishing, 2017, pp. 250–267.

[2] Alejandro Zaera-Polo, "Patterns, Fabrics, Prototypes, Tessellations", *Architectural Design* 79, Wiley, United Kingdom, 2009, pp. 18–27.

[3] Rivka Oxman and Robert Oxman, "The New Structuralism: Design, Engineering, and Architectural Technologies", *Architectural Design* 206, Wiley, United Kingdom, 2019, pp. 15–24.

[4] Helmut Pottman, Andreas Asperl, Michael Hofer, and Axel Killian, *Architectural Geometry*, Bentley Institute Press, United States, 2007, p. 451.

[5] Mark Garcia, "Prologue for a History, Theory, and Future of Patterns of Architecture and Spatial Design", *Architectural Design* 79, Wiley, United Kingdom, 2009, pp. 6–17.

[6] Yazar, "Revisiting Parquet Deformations", pp. 250–267.

[7] William S. Huff, "The Parquet Deformation", *Best Beginning Design Projects*, The University of Wisconsin-Milwaukee, United States, 1979, pp. 30–33; D'Arcy Wentworth Thompson, *On Growth and Form*, Cambridge University Press, United States, 1945 edition, pp. 1026–1095.

[8] Huff, "The Parquet Deformation", pp. 30–33.

[9] William S. Huff, "On Regulation and Hidden Harmony", *Harmony of Forms and Processes: Nature, Art, Science, Society*, International Society for the Interdisciplinary Study of Symmetry, Ukraine, 2008.

[10] William S. Huff, "The Landscape Handscroll and the Parquet Deformation", *Katachi U Symmetry*, Springer-Verlag, Japan, 1996, pp. 307–314.

[11] William S. Huff, "Ordering Disorder after K. L. Wolf", *Forma 15, Proceedings of the 2nd International Katachi U Symmetry Symposium*, Scipress, Japan, 2000, pp. 41–47.

[12] William S. Huff, "Defining Basic Design as a Discipline", *The Quarterly of the International Society for the Interdisciplinary Study of Symmetry: Symmetry, Art and Science* 2, ISIS-Symmetry, Belgium, 2002, pp. 91–98; Carnegie Mellon University, "William Huff, Buildings by Pedagogs", exhibition catalog, Carnegie Institute, United States, 1965, p. 8; William S. Huff, "An Argument for Basic Design", *Journal of the Ulm School for Design* 12–13, Germany, 1965, pp. 25–38; Dénes Nagy, "Architecture, Mathematics, and a Symmetric Link Between Them", The Quarterly of the International Society for the Interdisciplinary Study of Symmetry: Symmetry, Art and Science 2, ISIS-Symmetry, Belgium, 2002, pp. 31–64.

[13] Ibid.

[14] Yazar, "Revisiting Parquet Deformations", pp. 250–267.

[15] Peter Kapos, "Art and Design: the Ulm Model", exhibition at Raven Row, London, 2016, http://www.ravenrow.org/texts/83/, accessed: 28 January 2021.

[16] Isabel Clara Neves and João Rocha, "The Contribution of Tomás Maldonado to the Scientific Approach to Design at the Beginning of Computational Era, The Case of The HFG of Ulm", *Future Traditions: 1st Regional International Workshop*, ECAADE, Portugal, 2013, pp. 39–50; Isabel Clara Neves, João Rocha, and José Pinto Duarte, "Computational Design Research in Architecture: The Legacy of the Hochschule für Gestaltung, Ulm", *International Journal of Architectural Computing* 12(1), SAGE Publishing, 2014, pp. 1–25.

[17] Yazar, "Revisiting Parquet Deformations", pp. 250–267.

[18] Kapos, "Art and Design".

[19] Tomás Maldonado and Gui Bonsiepe, "Science and Design", Journal of the Hochschule für Gestaltung, *Ulm* 10/11, Germany, 1964, pp. 10–29.

[20] Kapos, "Art and Design".

[21] Cornelie Leopold, "Precise Experiments: Relations between Mathematics, Philosophy and Design and Ulm School of Design", *Nexus Network Journal, Architecture and Mathematics* 15(2), Kim Williams Books, Italy, 2013, pp. 363–380.

[22] Yazar, "Revisiting Parquet Deformations", pp. 250–267; Huff, "An Argument for Basic Design", pp. 25–38; Neves and Rocha, "The Contribution", pp. 39–50.

[23] William Huff, "Students' Work from Basic Design Studios of William S. Huff", *Intersight 1, The Journal of the School of Architecture and Planning*, University of Buffalo, United States, 1990, pp. 80–83.

[24] Huff, "An Argument for Basic Design": pp. 25–38.

[25] Huff, "Defining Basic Design", pp. 91–98.

[26] Yazar, "Revisiting Parquet Deformations", pp. 250–267.

[27] Douglas Hofstadter, "Parquet Deformations, A Subtle, Intricate Art Form", *Metamagical Themas: Questing for the Essence of Mind and Pattern*, Basic Books, United States, 1983, pp. 191–199.

[28] Douglas Hofstadter, "Parquet Deformations, Patterns of Tiles that Shift Gradually in One Dimension", *Scientific American Magazine*, Springer Nature, United States, 1983, pp. 14–20.

[29] Hofstadter, "A Subtle, Intricate Art Form", pp. 191–199.

[30] Huff, "Ordering Disorder", pp. 41–47.

[31] Yazar, "Revisiting Parquet Deformations", pp. 250–267.

[32] Lewis Foreman Day, *The Anatomy of Pattern*, B.T. Batsford, United Kingdom, 1887, p. 16; Lewis Foreman Day, *Pattern Design, A Book for Students Treating in a Practical Way of the Anatomy, Planning & Evolution of Repeated Ornament*, B.T. Batsford, United Kingdom, 1915, pp. 28–47.

[33] Craig Kaplan, "Curve Evolution Schemes for Parquet Deformations", *Proceedings of Bridges Conference, Mathematics Music Art Architecture Culture*, Tessellations Publishing, Hungary, 2010, pp. 95–103; Hofstadter, "A Subtle, Intricate Art Form": pp. 191–199; Elaine Krajenke Ellison and John Sharp, "Tiled Torus Quilt with Changing Tiles", *Proceedings of Bridges Conference, Mathematics Music Art Architecture Culture*, Tessellations Publishing, Hungary, 2010, pp. 67–74; Yazar, "Revisiting Parquet Deformations": pp. 250–267.

[34] Craig Kaplan, "Computer Graphics and Geometric Ornamental Design", Ph.D. dissertation, University of Washington, Seattle, 2002, pp. 75–76, 208–212; Craig Kaplan, "Metamorphosis in Escher's Art", *Proceedings of Bridges Conference, Mathematical Connections in Art, Music, and Science*, Tarquin Publications, The Netherlands, 2008, pp. 39–46.

[35] Craig Kaplan, "Islamic Star Patterns from Polygons in Contact", *Proceedings of Graphics Interface GI'05*, Canada, 2005, pp. 177–185.

[36] Ellison and Sharp, "Tiled Torus Quilt", pp. 67–74.

[37] Karen Li, "Programmed Design, The Systematic Method and the Form of Pattern", *The Quarterly of the International Society for the Interdisciplinary Study of Symmetry: Symmetry, Art and Science 1–4*, ISIS-Symmetry, Belgium, 2002, pp. 85–89.

[38] Yazar, "Revisiting Parquet Deformations", pp. 250–267.

[39] Huff, "The Parquet Deformation", pp. 30–33.

[40] Yazar, "Revisiting Parquet Deformations", pp. 250–267.

Biography of the Author

Tuğrul Yazar is an architect and computational design researcher. He received an M.Arch degree in 2003, and a PhD in 2009 in the field of Computer-Aided Architecture. His dissertation is a computational perspective on the short-term design exercises conducted in the early years of architectural education. He has published on architectural geometry and design technologies. In a recent publication, he explained the methodology of drawing Bézier curves and B-Splines using only a compass. Since 2010, he has taught Architectural Geometry, Design Mathematics, Parametric Modeling, and Digital Fabrication at İstanbul Bilgi University Faculty of Architecture. In the Parametric Modeling and Design Mathematics courses, he has been teaching *Grasshopper* and *Python* languages to design students. In the Digital Fabrication course, he is introducing robot technologies to design students. In addition to these technical courses, he has also been a studio instructor at the first-year computation-based basic design studios of the same faculty. This studio is based on a combination of computational thinking and physical material performances. Between 2010 and 2018 he shared a portion of his studies on his blog at designcoding.net. In 2016, he published the first Turkish book in this field, *Parametric Modeling with Grasshopper*. In a recently completed scientific project, he was a member of a team that developed specialized computer software based on the principles of space syntax theory. In a current scientific research project, he is studying the effects of different geometric qualities on the physical performances of rammed-earth structures. Apart from the academic studies, he is a computational design consultant and a workshop tutor. The works of the POTPlus design/research group, which he established with Fulya Akipek, have been exhibited in various exhibitions and biennials. In 2018 their rammed-earth structure exhibited at the Antalya Architectural Biennial received the Sustainable Architecture (S-ARCH) Award.

Pattern Manipulation through Hinged Tessellations

Jay Bonner

Introduction

In 1948, Buckminster Fuller discovered polyhedral "jitterbug" transformations, whereby specific vertices of a uniform polyhedron act as hinges, allowing the faces of the polyhedron to rotate in a progressively increasing angle.[1] This progressive angular increase causes the overall size of the polyhedron to expand. At the zenith of this expansion, the continued rotation of the faces draws them gradually back together through the decreasing angles of the opposite side of each rotating vertex, thereby shrinking the size of the polyhedron until it is back to its original form. In 2018, I published a paper titled "Doing the Jitterbug with Islamic Geometric Patterns" in the *Journal of Mathematics and the Arts*.[2] This paper described how the geometry of jitterbug transformations can be used to apply geometric designs with Islamic characteristics onto spherical surfaces, and by setting the degree of rotation of the transformation to conform with the angles associated with specific polygons, one can create spherical geometric designs that exhibit the uniform distribution of unexpected regular star forms. In that paper, I demonstrate two examples: a design with a uniform distribution of regular 7-pointed stars; and one with regularly placed 13-pointed stars. Each of these employs the jitterbug transformation of the octahedron, with the eight triangular faces rotated to angles associated with the heptagon and tridecagon, respectively. Rotating the octahedron's triangles to these specific angular conditions creates interstice regions comprised of isosceles triangles that are edge to edge with one another upon their short edges. The spherical design is created by applying carefully constructed pattern lines to the triangular and isosceles triangular faces and projecting these decorated faces to the surface of the sphere (Figure 4b). On the two-dimensional plane, the same edge-to-edge isosceles triangles produce a rhombus, and this paper also demonstrates a two-dimensional corollary pattern with 7-pointed stars that makes use of the same triangular faces and rhombic interstice regions (Figure 5).

This chapter expands upon this two-dimensional corollary by examining the use of progressively rotating hinged tessellations to modify existing geometric patterns and, with greater and greater angles of rotation, creating altogether new designs.

When asked by Werner Van Hoeydonck to contribute a chapter for this publication, and knowing that a prime focus of this book would be the pioneering work of William S. Huff and others who have contributed so significantly to the remarkable study of parquet deformations, including the works of my co-authors of this book, I chose to write about the metamorphic potential of pattern manipulation that can result with the use of hinged tessellations. Even if somewhat tangential to the primary subject of parquet deformations, I believe my contribution is nonetheless relevant, if for no other reason than the fact that the groundbreaking and beautiful works of such luminaries as Huff, Hofstadter, and Escher[3] have directly inspired my exploration of hinged tessellations as a means of creating new geometric designs.

My focus upon hinged tessellations as a means of creating geometric designs through the gradual vertex rotation of the polygonal modules of a tessellation is in marked contrast to the gradual modification of a grid through the process of parquet deformation. Parquet deformations involve a spatial evolutionary metamorphosis that is either one-dimensional (linear) or two-dimensional (e.g., radial) in symmetrical makeup. The changes in angular growth of hinged tessellations are more a function of time than space and are best represented through animation, such as examples by the Dutch geometric artist Rinus Roelofs,[4] rather than fixed illustrations. However, for the medium of the printed page I am herein representing this process of seamless angular expansion as a series of isolated, or one might say frozen sequential angular intervals. These illustrate the gradual metamorphosis of the initial tiled design with 0° rotation of the polygonal module. (Of course, it is worth noting that it is entirely possible to also represent the gradual changes that result from parquet deformations through the vehicle of animation.)

Parquet Deformations and Islamic Geometric Patterns

As a visual artist and specialist in Islamic geometric design, I enjoy exploring new methodological approaches to creating geometric patterns. When I first saw Craig Kaplan's parquet deformations of Islamic geometric patterns,[5] I was both excited by their aesthetic impact and beauty, but also disappointed for not having thought of the idea myself! He and I have both worked extensively with the use of polygonal tessellations as the substructure for generating Islamic geometric patterns, and when I saw his parquet deformations of Islamic geometric design, I immediately comprehended his gradual opening and closing of the angular conditions of the crossing pattern lines that are located at the midpoints of the generative, but not shown, polygonal tessellation. Along with a more general interest in parquet deformations, this work sparked my own interest in working with geometric designs that are characterized by gradually changing rotational conditions.

It is worth mentioning that the examples of such gradually changing Islamic geometric designs do not strictly adhere to the two criteria for parquet deformations as set by Huff.[6] In particular, the patterns that are being modified are comprised of many distinctly different polygonal shapes that lock together to create a larger repeat with translation symmetry, rather than each modified cell of a parquet deformation having the ability to fill the two-dimensional plane on its own. And yet the aesthetic character of these gradually changing Islamic geometric designs, as well as the modifying process itself, is close enough to be regarded, at least in my opinion, as a loose interpretation of Huff's criteria.

In order to better differentiate parquet deformations of Islamic geometric designs with patterns that are modified via the process of hinged tessellations, I have prepared a couple of examples of the former. I have also included additional visual information that illustrates some of the principles used in their construction.

The gradually changing geometric design in Figure 1 is derived from the 3.4.6.4 – 4.6.12 two-uniform, or demi-regular grid of regular triangles, squares, hexagons, and dodecagons. The angular conditions change by 10° increments from 12-pointed stellar center to the adjacent 12-pointed stellar center, yet the control points for these rotational changes remain fixed upon the midpoints of the formative tessellation throughout. As these changes move from left to right, the angles of the pattern move from being more acute to becoming more obtuse. The progressive design in Figure 2 employs two points upon each polygonal edge of the formative tessellation and starts with the formative tessellation itself (A) before rotating the edges both clockwise and anti-clockwise in increments of 6°. Throughout this gradual process, several distinct designs emerge that are noteworthy. The pattern at (D) is characterized by two sizes of regular decagon; the pattern at (G) includes regular pentagons and is, in fact, a well-known Islamic geometric pattern; the example at (J) shares characteristics with a variety of fivefold historical patterns; the pattern at (M) has parallel lines leading to the 10-pointed stars, and lines that converge upon a single point at the center of the initial formative pentagons (see A); design (P) has parallel lines that connect the 5- and 10-pointed stars; the pattern in (S) is characterized by regular pentagons and is also a historical Islamic pattern; and example (V) includes regular decagons. The use of two points of contact between the edges of the formative tessellation and the applied pattern lines in this sequence is in keeping with the two-point historical pattern family associated with the tradition of Islamic geometric design. The method for placing and rotating these pattern lines is demonstrated in Figure 3. The horizontal line in (A) represents any one of the polygonal edges that make up the initial tessellation. This edge line shows the two points in contention, and the diagram above this line shows how the division of these lines is based upon the golden section. This is a purely arbitrary decision on my part. In the subsequent illustrated edge conditions, the dashed lines represent the original polygonal edges, while the two sets of crossing pattern lines can be seen at the two division points. These sequentially increase with 6° rotations until they become perpendicular with the formative polygonal edge (P).

As these illustrations demonstrate, parquet deformations of Islamic geometric designs involve the rotation of the crossing pattern lines where they intersect with the midpoints of the polygonal edges of the formative tessellation. This rotational process is similar to, but nonetheless distinct from, the rotational process used in modifying designs with hinged tessellations. They both have their own aesthetic merits and are both worthy of further exploration.

Hinged Tessellations

Hinged tessellations are essentially the two-dimensional corollaries of three-dimensional jitterbug transformations. By way of example, the octahedron is comprised of eight triangular faces with a 3^4 configuration

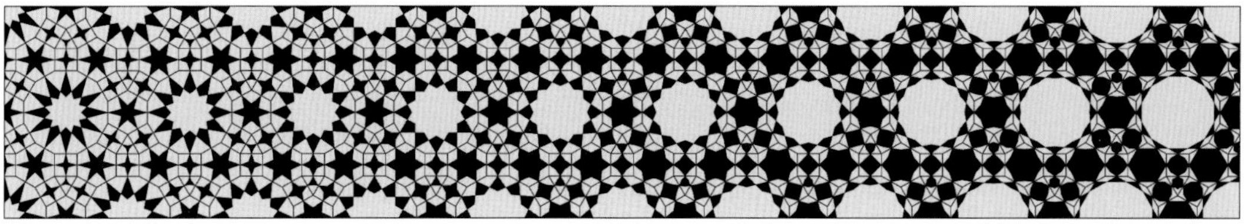

Fig. 1: Progressive 10° angular transformations of an Islamic geometric design constructed from the 3.4.6.4. – 4.6.12 2-uniform tessellation of triangles, squares, hexagons and dodecagons.

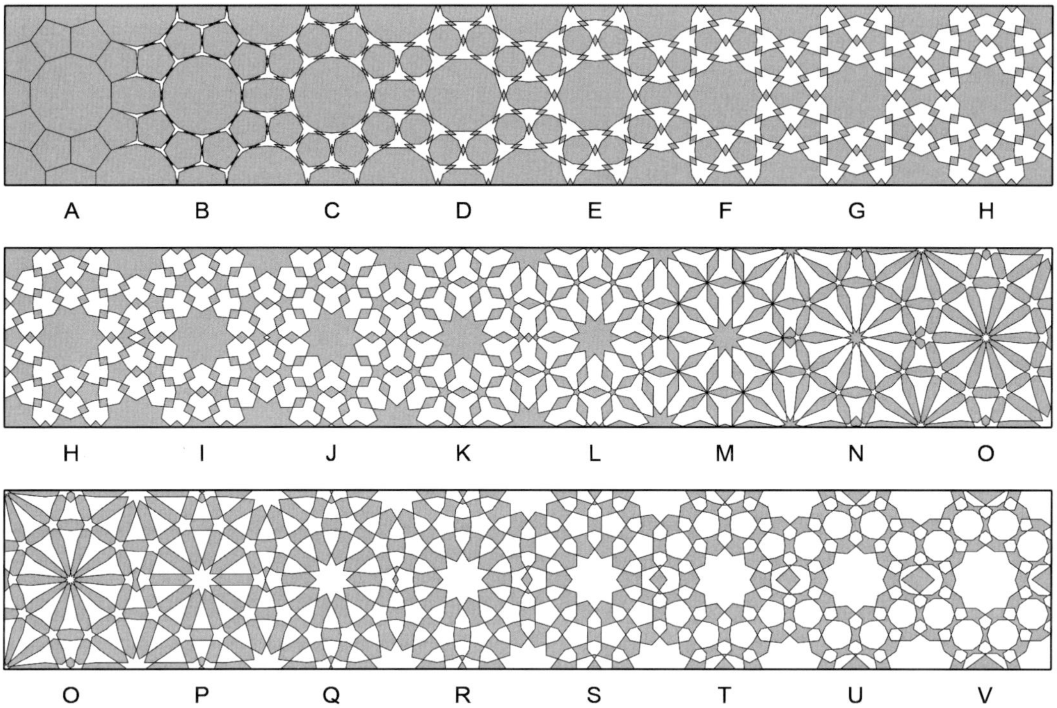

Fig. 2: Progressive angular transformation of a two-point Islamic geometric pattern.

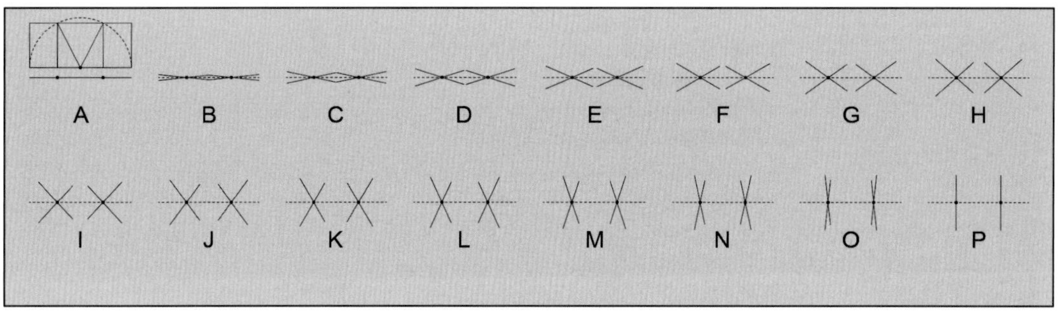

Fig. 3: The sequential modification of the initial polygonal edges (A) uses two points of rotation, thereby creating the progressive angular transformations of the two-point geometric patterns.

at each of the six vertices. By rotating each of the faces by 60° at the vertices, the angular openings conform to the geometry of the icosahedron with a 3^5 configuration at each vertex. With a 90° rotation at the vertices, the angular opening creates the cuboctahedron with the 3.4.3.4 vertex configuration. Similarly, the 120° vertex rotation of the equilateral triangles of the 3^6 regular two-dimensional grid transforms this tessellation into the 3.6.3.6 semi-regular grid of triangles and hexagons (Figure 8).

The two images in Figure 4 were both published in my 2018 paper[7] concerning jitterbug transformations as a vehicle for spherical Islamic geometric patterns. These demonstrate how a specific rotation of the octahedron's triangular faces by an amount associated with the heptagon (25.7142...°) allows for the construction of a geometric pattern that is characterized by a regular distribution of 7-pointed stars. The yarn *temari* in Figure 4b is a spherical projection of the jitterbug polyhedron in 4a. This lovely object was made by my friend Maude Rayburn in Santa Fe.

Since their discovery by Buckminster Fuller in 1948, jitterbug transformations have received considerable scholarly study.[8] Similarly, the science of two-dimensional hinged tessellations has been explored extensively and is well understood as an accordion-like expansion and contraction mechanism applicable to a diverse variety of polygonal tessellations, including regular grids, semi-regular grids, and grids made up of non-regular polygons.[9]

Vertex rotations of polyhedral tessellations invariably increase in area as the angle of opening increases. This is a distinctive feature that differs from parquet deformation structures. The shape and geometric character of the interstice regions are a product of the rotating polygonal modules and their degree of rotation. As with jitterbug transformations, after the rotation has reached its zenith, continued rotation draws the polygonal modules back toward themselves. This expansion and contraction takes place as a temporal continuum; to illustrate its properties for the printed page, I have arbitrarily selected specific rotational sequences. However, the reader is encouraged to keep in mind that the sequences of rotating tessellations, along with their associated geometric patterns, that are represented in this chapter are merely snapshots of a continuously changing geometric structure. As demonstrated herein, this rotational process has a dramatic effect on the overall visual quality of the geometric patterns.

Pattern Application

The application of the pattern lines onto the hinged polygonal modules that make up the tessellation involves the placing into each polygonal module that makes up the initial non-rotated tessellation a repetitive design with lines that either flow seamlessly and identically into the lines of the adjacent module or reflect into the adjacent module along their shared edge. Theoretically, these pattern lines can have any degree of geometric complexity, but for the purposes of this demonstration, I have kept the applied pattern lines very basic. Even with these simple repetitive motifs, and the resulting simplicity of the basic overall pattern with 0° of rotation, once the process of hinged rotation takes effect, the resulting changes to the basic pattern can become quite interesting.

The manner I have chosen to populate the interstice regions that open up as the hinged tiles progressively rotate employs one of two stratagems: Either the lines along the edges of the rotating modules extend into the interstice regions until they meet with another extended line, or the lines along the edge of the rotating modules are mirrored into the interstice regions. In either case, the lines are cleaned up by either extending them until they meet with other lines or are trimmed at a place that is aesthetically pleasing. Invariably, this process of introducing pattern lines into the interstice regions requires a degree of aesthetically driven decision-making, and the examples illustrated in this chapter are a combination of the

A B

Fig. 4: A jitterbug transformation of the octahedron with angular openings set to 25.7142...° rotation, thereby allowing for the equal distribution of 7-pointed stars. The spherical projection.

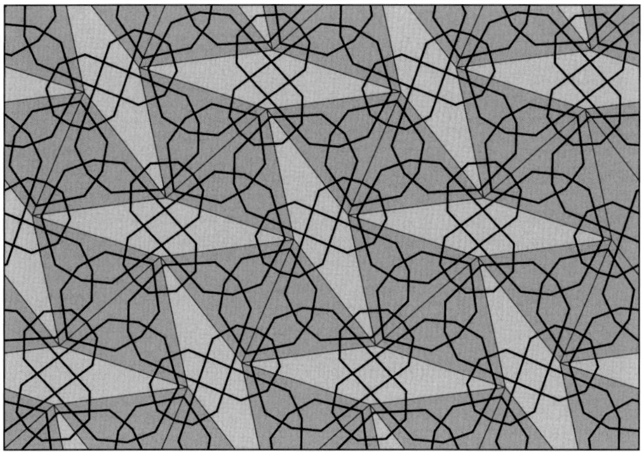

Fig. 5: A two-dimensional pattern with 7-pointed stars that also employs a rotation of the repetitive double-triangles by 25.7142...° (1/14 of 360°), thereby allowing the placement of regular 7-pointed stars.

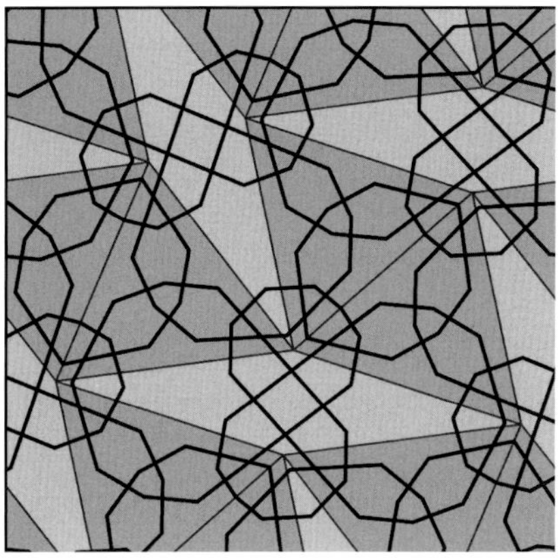

22.5° rotation

25.7142° rotation (1/14 of 360°)

Fig. 6: Two historical patterns that employ the principle of modular rotation.

obvious, the more interesting, and the aesthetically pleasing. In other words, the rotated designs depicted herein are, to a lesser or greater extent, arbitrary, even if constructed using established formulae.

Figure 5 shows a two-dimensional design, originally from my 2018 paper,[10] that rotates the congruent edge-to-edge double-triangle modules by an amount that also corresponds to the heptagon, thereby creating a rhombic interstice region that allows for the construction of a geometric design with regular 7-pointed stars. There are a number of historical Islamic geometric patterns that exhibit this form of rotation symmetry, and I have examined multiple examples in my book on Islamic design methodology.[11] Two particularly interesting historical examples from this book are shown in Figure 6.

Despite such historical examples of patterns with rotated repetitive modules, it is important to emphasize that the use of hinged tessellations to create geometric designs is not being proposed as a historic design methodology. The methods used to construct geometric patterns by the countless Muslim geometric artists of the past is debated by specialists in this field. My own belief is that the predominant method used traditionally was the polygonal technique (sometime referred to as "polygons in contact"). Unlike other proposed methods, this highly refined design methodology is capable of producing all levels of complexity found throughout this discipline, and is ideally suited to producing patterns in each of the recognized pattern families associated with Islamic geometric art. Moreover, there is an abundance of historical evidence for the use of the polygonal technique, something that other proposed methods of construction lack. However, one thing that most specialists agree on is the fact that an individual design can frequently be created identically with multiple methodological techniques—whether historical or not. In the case of the two historical examples in Figure 2, these can easily be produced without using an approach that involves the willful rotation of a primary repetitive module to an arranged angle as per hinged tessellations. These two examples are included because they closely resemble designs created with hinged tessellations, and their underlying geometry is essentially identical.

A Selection of Geometric Patterns Created with Hinged Tessellations

Figure 7 illustrates the progressive hinged rotation of the 44 regular tessellation made up of squares. The squares are rotated in 5° increments—from 0° to 90°. After 90°, further 5° increases in the rotation angle (not shown) cause the formerly obtuse angles of the interstice rhombuses to sequentially decrease, and the resulting patterns and tessellations are mirror images of the 5° increasing progression. In this way, the rotation to 95° is the mirror image of the rotation to 85°. For this reason, I have only demonstrated the rotation of the hinged tessellations in this chapter up to their rotational zenith.

The applied pattern lines on each of the square modules are an 8-pointed star, with every other point intersecting the midpoints of each edge of the square. This repetitive module was well known to the historical record, producing the classic "star and cross" design. The applied pattern lines extend into the interstice regions to create the modified designs. Setting the incremental increases to every 5° is an arbitrary determination that was chosen as it is a divisor of 45°, 60°, and 90°, and therefore works nicely with the symmetry of the square. It is worth noting that the 60° rotation creates the angular conditions of the 3.3.4.3.4 semi-regular tessellation of triangles and squares. Once the rotation reaches 90°, the square modules are once again in an orthogonal arrangement, and the geometric design is identical in every respect save its surface coverage to that of the initial unrotated tessellation.

Figure 8 shows a progressive rotation of the 36 tessellation of regular triangles. This also employs an angular increase of 5°, thereby allowing for the demonstration of designs with 30°, 60°, 90°, and 120° rotational conditions.

The applied pattern lines are a simple hexagon placed so that three of the vertices of the hexagon are

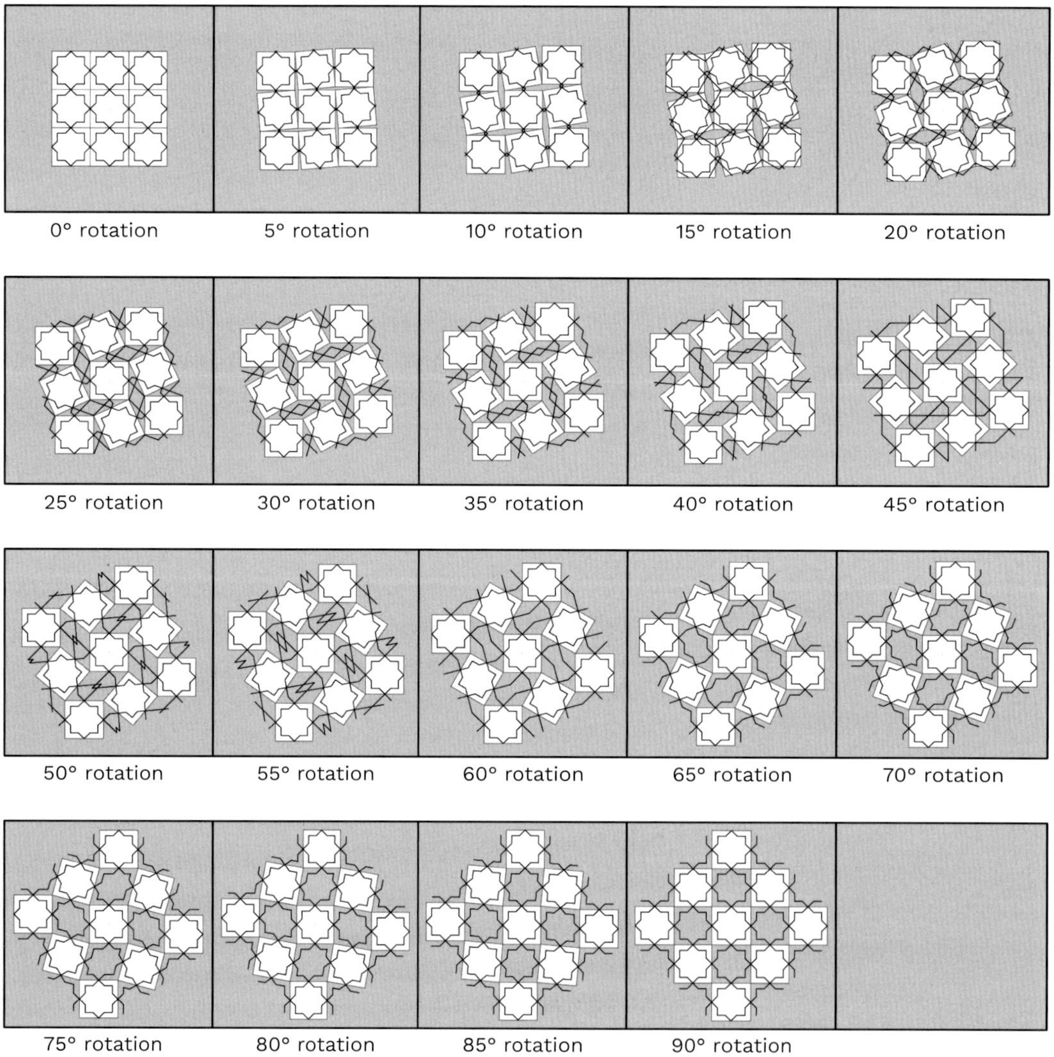

Fig. 7: A sequence of 5° rotations of the 4^4 tessellations of squares. Each square is decorated with an 8-pointed star.

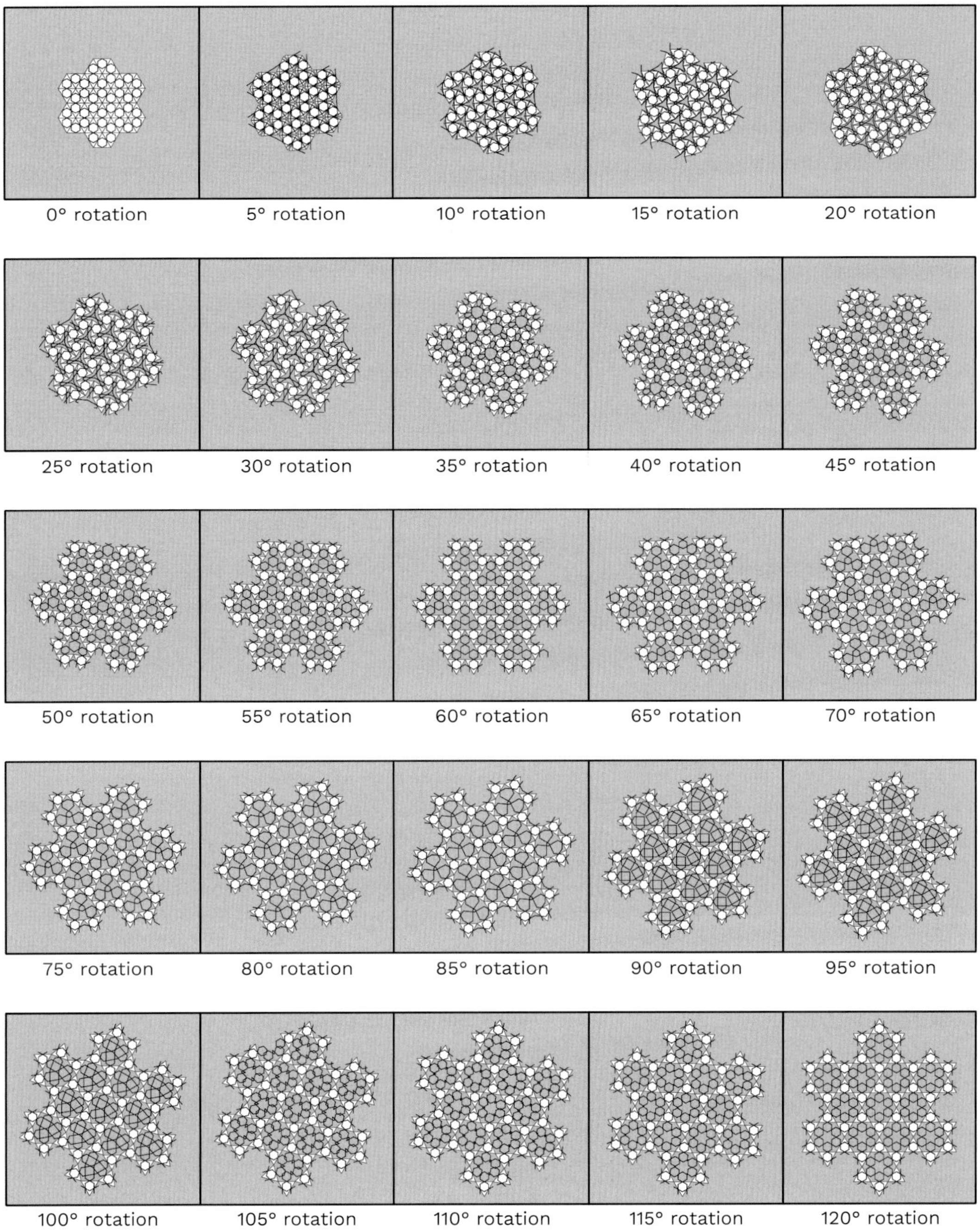

Fig. 8: A sequence of 5° rotations of the 36 tessellation of triangles. Each triangle is decorated with a simple hexagon.

located at the midpoints of the triangle's edges. On the 3^6 tessellation without rotation this produces the classic threefold Islamic geometric pattern comprised of 6-pointed stars and hexagons. It is interesting to note that the 60° rotation produces a pleasing tessellation of small equilateral triangles separated by larger equilateral triangles with edges that are double in length. The tessellation with 90° rotation separates the triangular modules with ditrigons that have three 90° internal angles, and the tessellation with 120° angles is the 3.6.3.6 semi-regular grid of triangles and hexagons.

Figure 9 demonstrates a series of patterns created by the sequential rotation of the 3.6.3.6 semi-regular tessellation. In a sense, this can be regarded as a continuation of the previous example in its 120° rotation. However, in this hinged tessellation the hinged

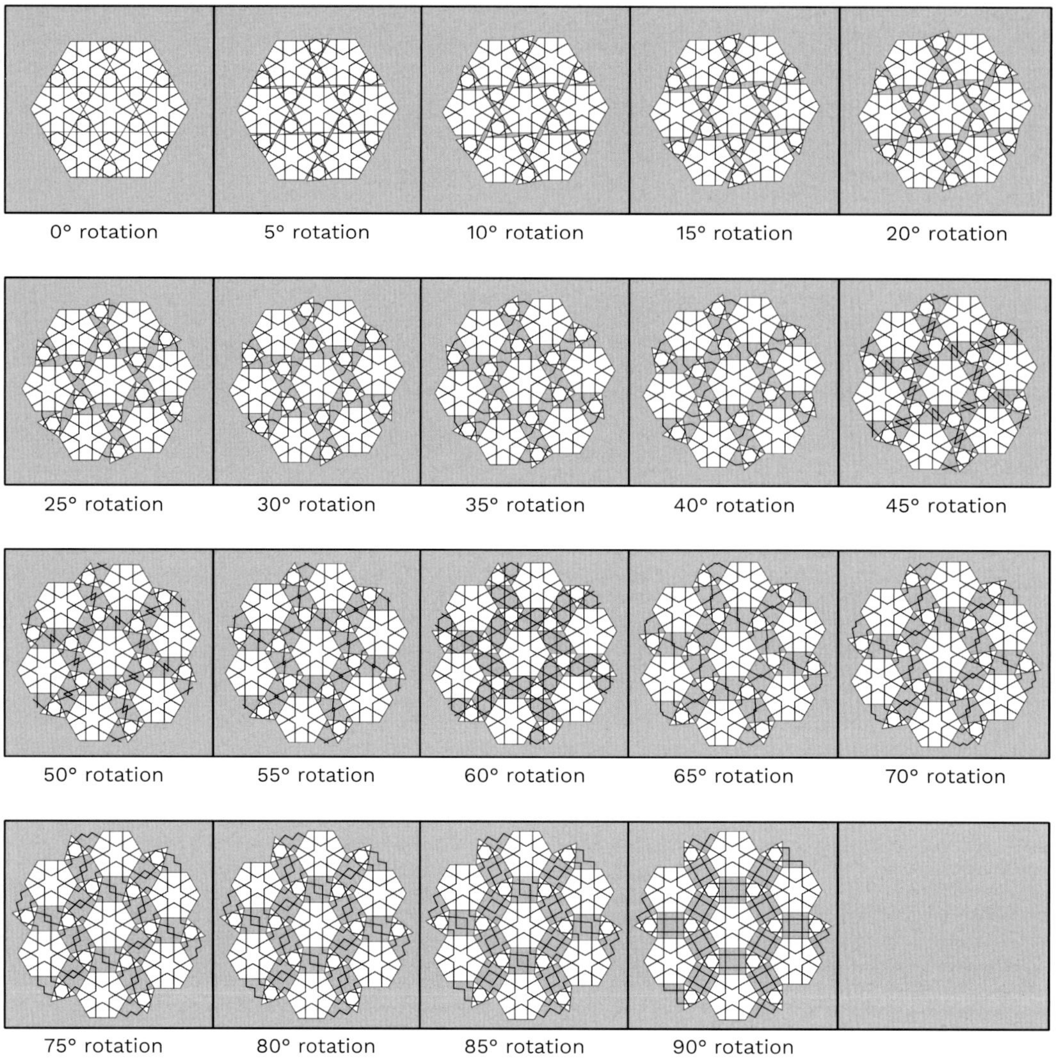

Fig. 9: A sequence of 5° rotations of the 3.6.3.6 tessellation of triangle and hexagons. The applied pattern lines are perpendicular to the edges of the grid.

vertices are not the same as those of the previous 120° example. These patterns are also derived from a 5° sequence of rotations, from 0° to 90°, after which the triangular and hexagonal modules close back into themselves, with resulting mirror images as discussed previously.

The applied pattern lines are perpendicular to the edges of both the hexagonal and triangular modules and are located at 1/4 divisions of the polygonal edges. This produces a 6-pointed star within the hexagonal module and a hexagon with extended edges within the triangular modules. The patterns in this set are particularly pleasing.

The 60° tessellation produces the conditions of the 3^{4}.6 semi-regular tessellation of triangles and hexagons, and the 90° rotation produces the 3.4.6.4 semi-regular tessellation of triangles, squares, and hexagons.

Figure 10 is a variation of the examples in Figure 9, with different applied pattern lines to the same 3.6.3.6 rotating tessellations. This demonstrates the range of diversity that can be achieved through varying the applied pattern lines, and anyone interested in working with hinged tessellations as a means of producing geometric designs should play with all manner of pattern line applications to a single rotating tessellation. As this illustrates, changing the applied pattern to the repetitive modules will result in very different, and sometimes very satisfying, designs. Both the triangular and hexagonal modules in this set of designs have hexagons as their applied pattern lines. These applied hexagons connect the midpoints of each edge of the

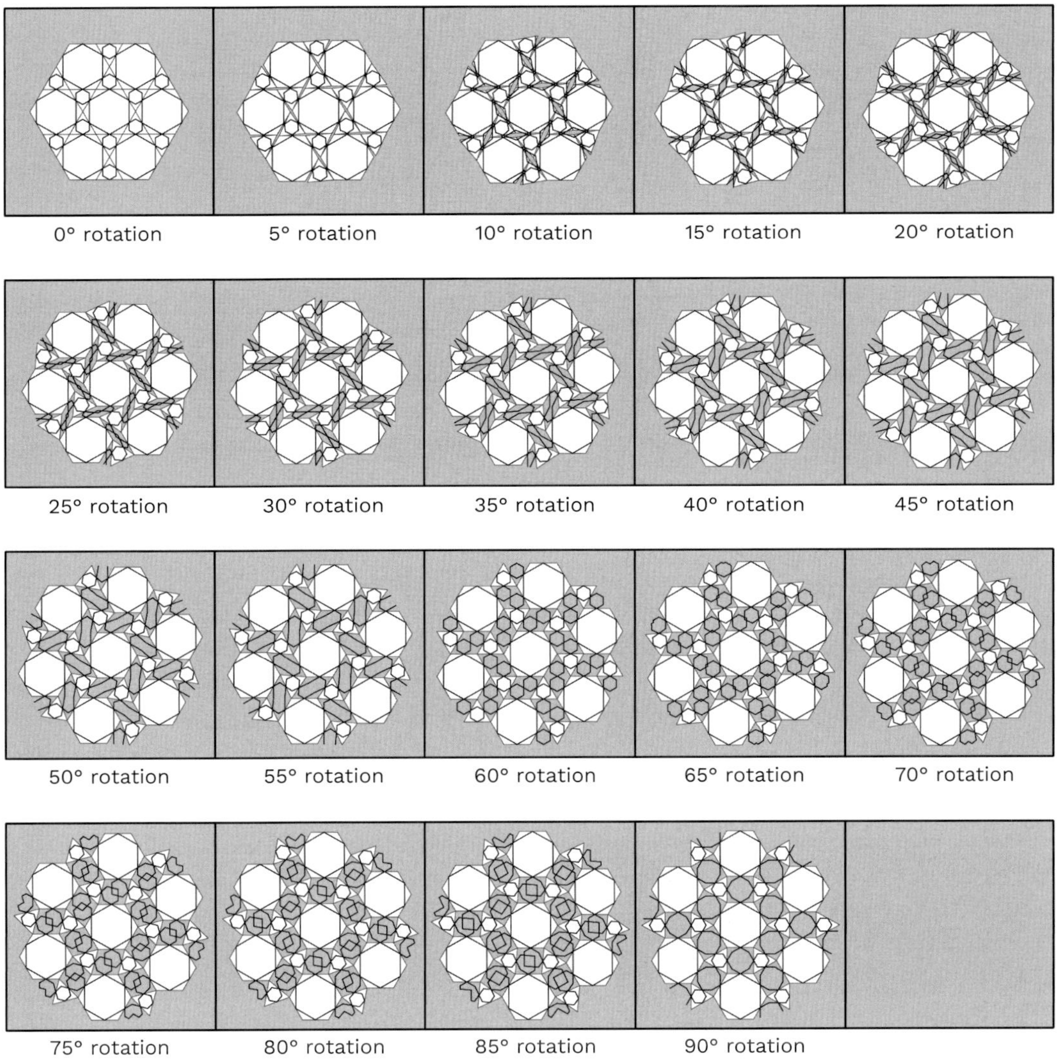

Fig. 10: A sequence of 5° rotations of the 3.6.3.6 tessellation of triangles and hexagons. Each triangle and hexagon is decorated with a simple hexagon.

modules. The patterns produced with this alternative pattern line application are likewise very successful.

The designs in Figure 11 are also produced from the same 3.6.3.6 semi-regular tessellation in 5° rotational increments. The applied pattern lines of the triangular module simply connect adjacent midpoints of each triangle's edges, producing a 60° triangle within each triangle. These 60° angles within the hexagonal modules produce a 6-pointed star. Once again, the unrotated 3.6.3.6 tessellation with this specific application of pattern lines produces a design that is known to the historical record.

The design produced from the 90° rotated tessellation, with its combination of 6-pointed stars, 4-pointed stars, and triangles is, once again, known to the historical record (Figure 21).

The rotational tessellations in Figure 12 stem from the semi-regular 3.4.6.4 grid comprised of triangles, squares, and hexagons. In these hinged tessellations only the square and hexagonal modules are hinged, with the triangles of the initial tessellation (0° rotation) gradually morphing into new trifold shapes with each sequential 6° rotation. These centers of threefold rotation produce distinctive rotational design features within the applied pattern lines.

Figure 13 applies a different set of pattern lines to the same sequential 6° rotations of the 3.4.6.4 semi-regular tessellation that was used in Figure 8. In this series of designs only the square modules have applied patterns lines. These consist of a simple cross of two perpendicular lines that connect opposite corners of each square. The pattern that these applied pattern

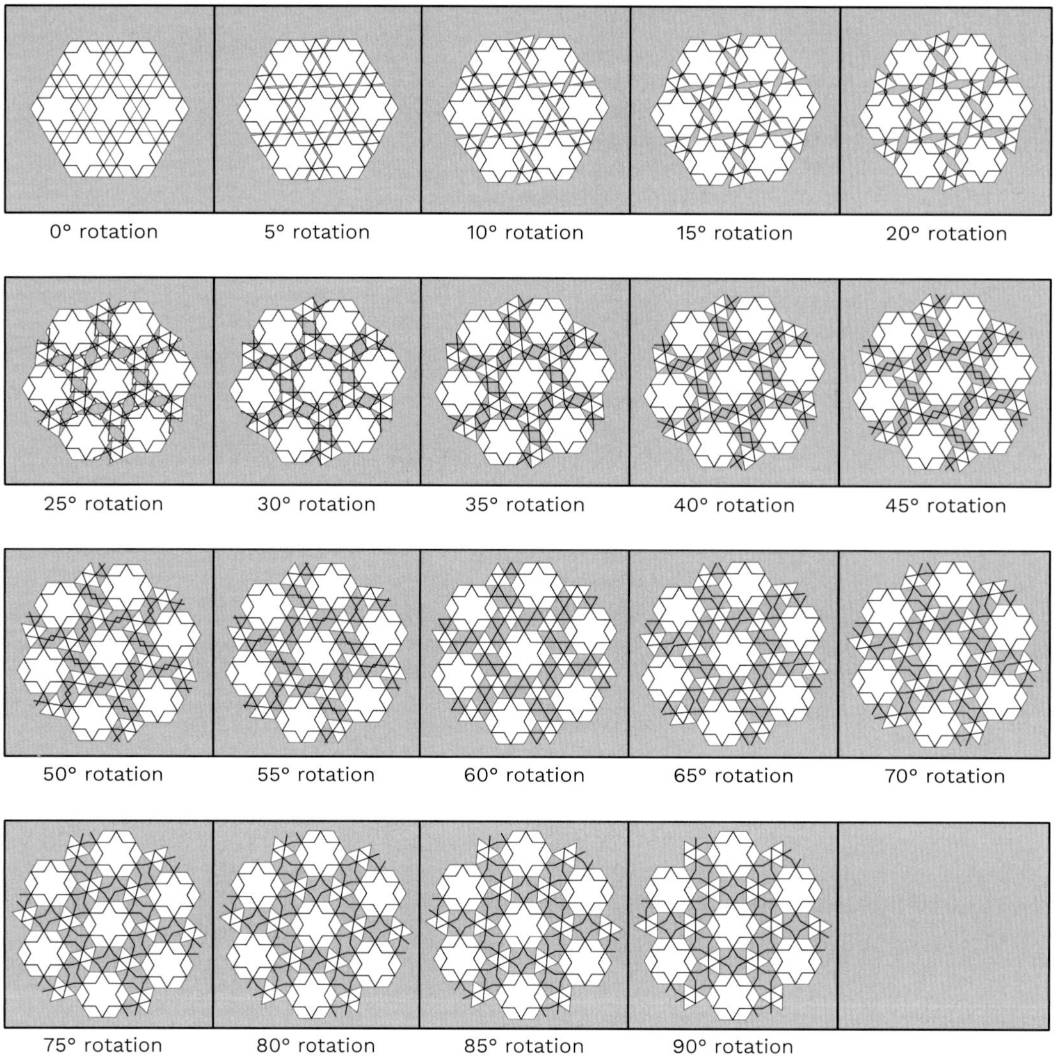

Fig. 11: A sequence of 5° rotations of the 3.6.3.6 tessellation of triangles and hexagons. The triangles are decorated with a simple triangle and the hexagons with a 6-pointed star.

lines produce on the initial tessellation with 0° rotation is a well-known historical design comprised of 6-pointed stars that have 90° angles at their points, surrounded by ditrigons with three 90° internal angles. As with the previous example, the regions of threefold rotation symmetry in the rotated tessellations produce very obvious and interesting design features with this simple application of crossed pattern lines. The design created by the 90° rotation is a superimposition of the regular hexagonal grid with its dual triangular grid.

Figure 14 is a third design variation based upon the same 3.4.6.4 initial tessellation. The pattern lines in this set of rotational tessellations place regular octagons into each square module. Four of the vertices of these octagons are located at the midpoints of each edge of the squares. The 135° interior angles of the octagons are mirrored into the hexagons and, in the initial tessellation with 0° rotation, into the triangles. Within the hexagons, this mirroring is further elaborated with the introduction of a 6-pointed star. Within the triangle, the mirroring produces a ditrigon. This particular design set within the unrotated tessellation was popular among Mamluk artists in Egypt.[12]

Figure 15 is a departure from the previous eight sets of rotational designs in that the rotating module is not a regular polygon. Rather, it is the well-known rhombus associated with fivefold symmetry that has

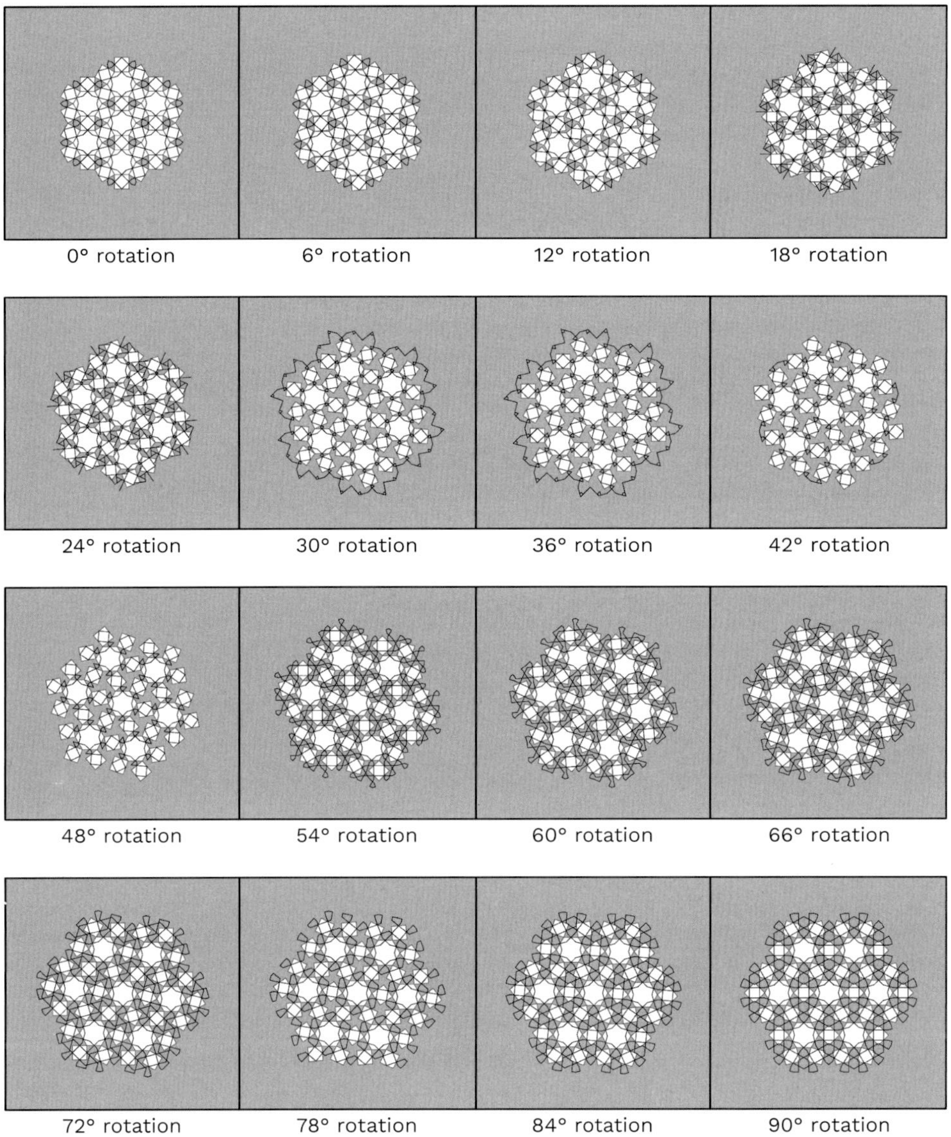

Fig. 12: A sequence of 6° rotations of the 3.4.6.4 tessellation of triangles, squares and hexagons. The decoration places 90° pattern line upon the midpoint of each polygonal edge.

72° and 108° interior angles. The translational unit of many fivefold Islamic geometric patterns employ this rhombus, and indeed, the depicted initial design with 0° rotation is very well known to the historical record. I have chosen to illustrate the increased growth of rotation at 6° intervals. This allows for 18°, 36°, 54°, 72°, and 90° increments, each of which is associated with fivefold symmetry. Once again, continued rotation beyond 90° (not shown) causes the hinged tessellation to close back into itself, with further 6° increments being mirror images of the depicted designs. For example, the design produced from a rotation of 108° (not shown) will be a mirror image of the design produced from 72° rotation. The 36°, 72°, and 90° tessellations are particularly interesting. The interstice rhombuses of the 36° rotated tessellation have 36° and 144° interior angles. This rhombus is likewise associated with fivefold symmetry and was also used historically as a translational unit in Islamic geometric design. It is also worth noting that both of these two rhombuses provide the basis for Sir Roger Penrose's aperiodic rhombic tiling with matching rules. It therefore stands to reason

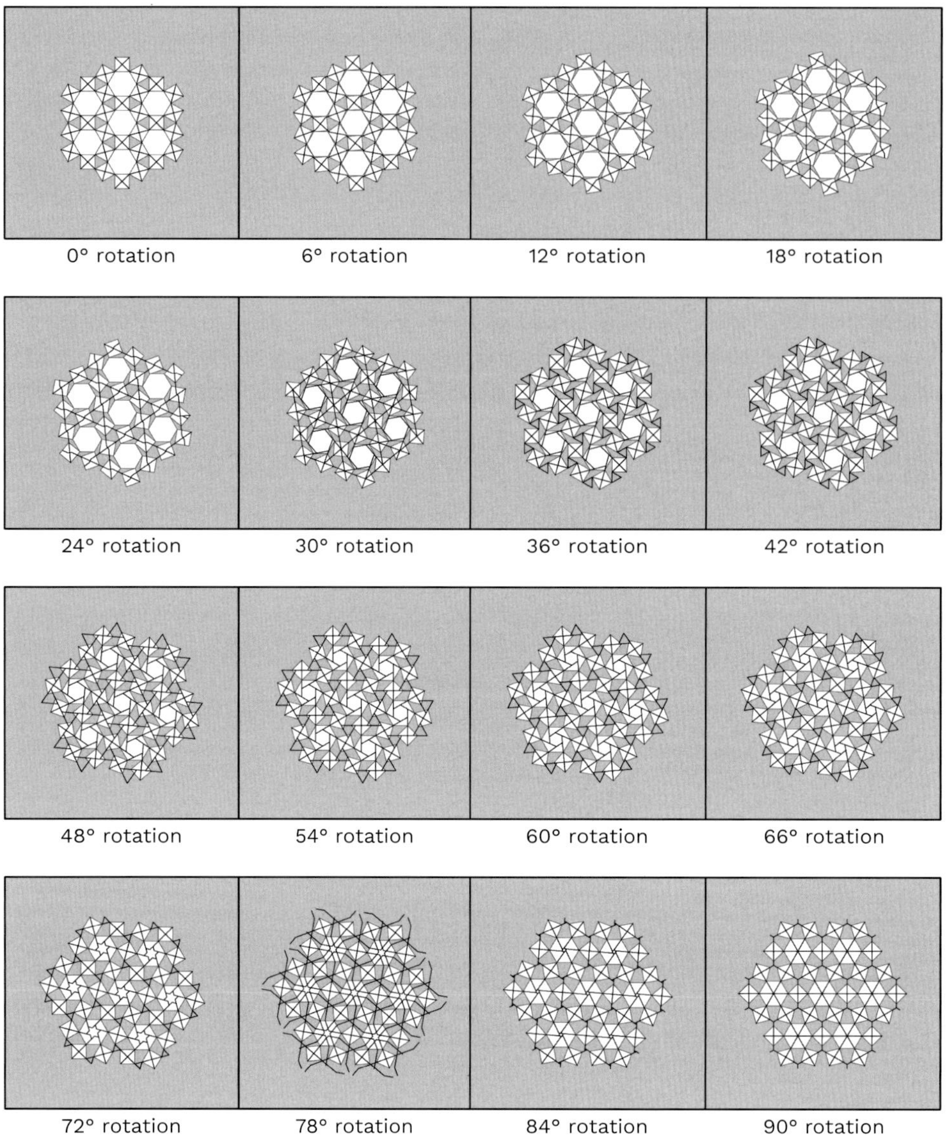

Fig. 13: A sequence of 6° rotations of the 3.4.6.4 tessellation of triangles, squares and hexagons. The decoration places corner-to-corner pattern lines within each square of the tessellation.

that the extended pattern lines that populate the interstice regions of this 36° hinged tessellation produce a particularly satisfactory geometric pattern (see Figure 25). Somewhat surprisingly, this does not appear to have been used historically. The tessellation of the 72° rotation of the rhombic module creates an interstice rhombus that is identical to the rotating module itself, with 72° and 108° interior angles. In this example the geometric design results in regular 10-pointed stars located at each vertex of the tessellation. Despite the non-regular stars at each vertex, the example with 90° rotation is interesting in that it combines features associated with fivefold symmetry (such as the regular pentagons) within an orthogonal repetitive structure.

The formative initial tessellation with 0° rotation in Figure 16 is comprised of pairs of edge-to-edge pentagons that connect with other pairs at their vertices. This network of pentagons has two varieties of rhombic interstices. It is worth noting that these two rhombuses are the same fivefold rhombuses discussed previously (with 72°/108° and 36°/144° interior angles). The applied pattern lines for these pentagonal modules are a simple pentagon that connects each adjacent midpoint of the pentagonal module. The unrotated initial tessellation with its applied pattern lines provides a good, if rather simple, example of the polygonal technique whereby key points of an underlying polygonal grid (most frequently the midpoints of the polygonal edges) are used to apply pattern lines. This discipline is made more elaborate by the use of four historical conventions for applying such pattern lines—each varying the angular conditions of the pattern lines, thereby creating distinct pattern families. Within fivefold Islamic geometric patterns, the application of 108° crossing pattern lines at the polygonal midpoints produces patterns in the *obtuse* family. (For those interested in historical Islamic geometric design methodology, please refer to my book on this subject.[13]) The absence of 10-pointed stars in the fivefold non-rotational initial design that is produced from this underlying tessellation identifies this as a *field* pattern, and although it does not appear to have been used historically, is shares multiple aesthetic characteristics with the many fivefold field patterns used by Muslim geometric artists during the Seljuk Sultanate of Rum in Turkey.

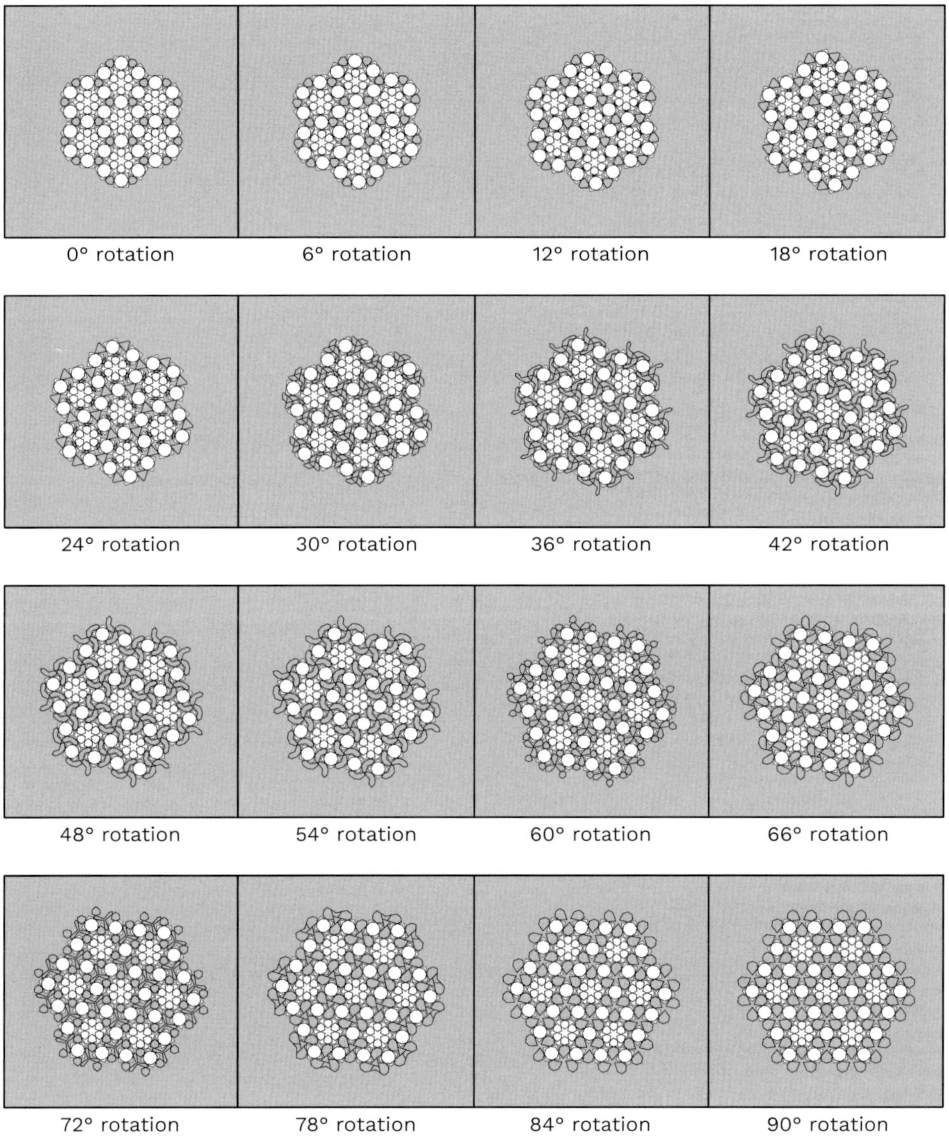

Fig. 14: A sequence of 6° rotations of the 3.4.6.4 tessellation of triangles, squares and hexagons. The decoration places 135° crossing pattern lines at each polygonal midpoint of the tessellation.

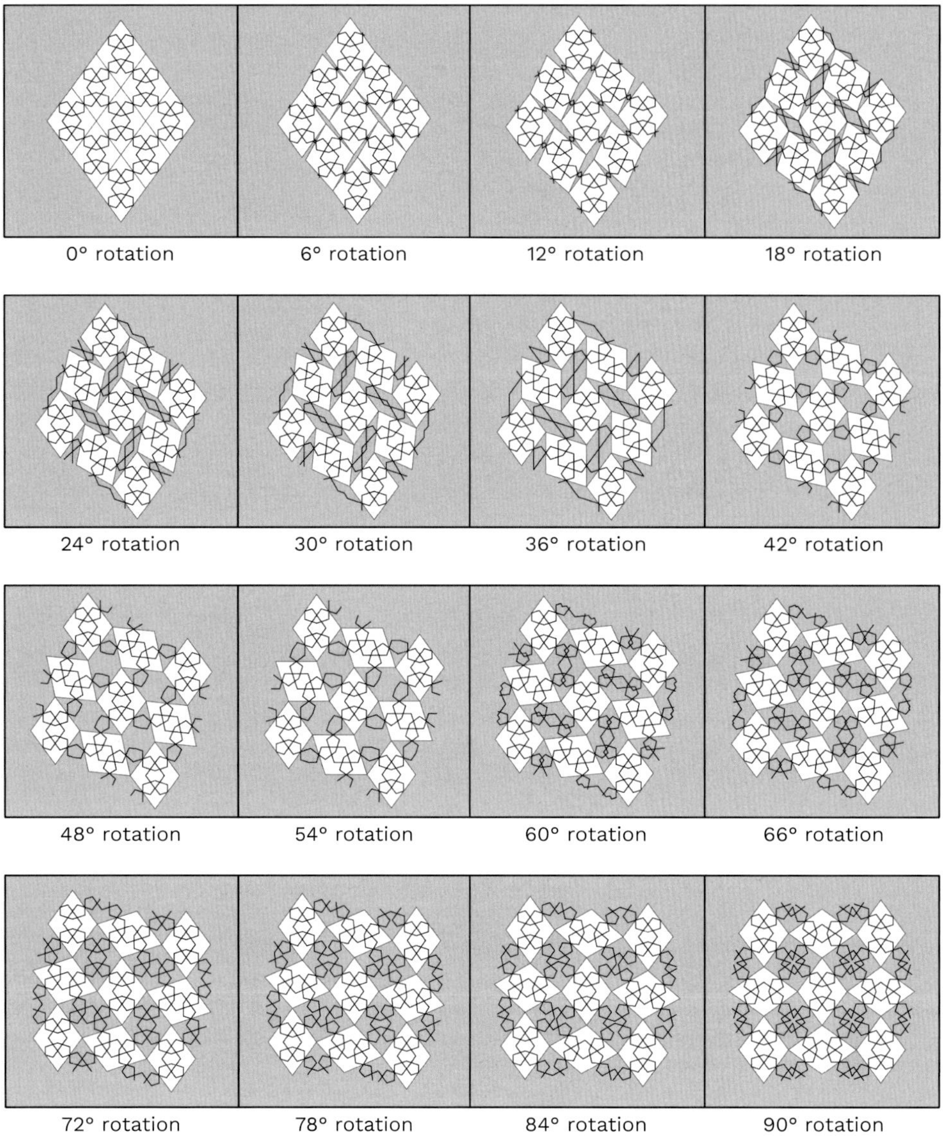

Fig. 15: A sequence of 6° rotations of a grid of rhombuses comprised of 72° and 108° angles. The decoration places 108° crossing pattern lines at the midpoint of each rhombic edge.

This rotational sequence is also set at 6° intervals and the brevity of incremental examples is due to an interesting and unusual phenomenon: at 36° rotation the tessellation becomes identical to its 0° starting point except that the overall tessellation is now rotated 90°. Concomitantly, the geometric pattern that results from the 36° rotation of the pentagonal modules is identical to that of the 0° rotation, except that it is now rotated 90°. A further 36° of rotation of the pentagons would bring the tessellation and pattern back to its original starting point. It is also worth noting that the conditions of the 18° rotation create an orthogonal tessellation and geometric pattern that repeats upon the square grid (Figure 26).

Particularly Successful Designs Created from These Hinged Tessellations

The many geometric patterns created by the hinged tessellations shown in the previous figures are rather small and, in some cases, difficult to appreciate. In order to emphasize how successful this method of pattern manipulation can be, I have selected examples from each of the previous sets that I find particularly interesting and appealing for further aesthetic elaboration. Specifically, I have increased the scale, dispensed with the underlying formative tessellations, widened the pattern

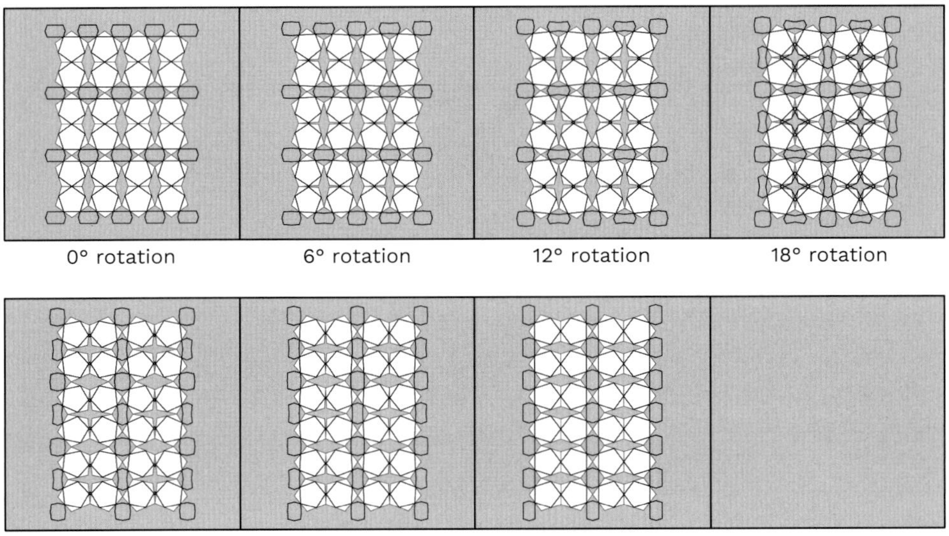

Fig. 16: A sequence of 6° rotations of a grid made up of pentagons and two varieties of rhombuses. The decoration places a simple pentagon within each pentagon of the grid.

lines, provided the widened lines of most examples with an interweave, and introduced color. These examples are intended to help demonstrate the design potential of hinged tessellations for generating new and original geometric patterns with interesting symmetrical characteristics.

Conclusion

A fascinating feature of the contents of this book is the expansion of two-dimensional parquet deformations into the realm of their three-dimensional corollaries. Such gradually changing three-dimensional space tessellations have very real potential for application to architectural expression, including the architectonics of spatial layout, vaulting designs, and especially spaceframe structures. Perhaps ironically, my contribution to this discussion moves from the three-dimensionality of jitterbug transformations to their two-dimensional corollary: hinged tessellations. Despite my work with kinetic architectural features such as open-and-closing shade structures and domes that slide into an open or closed position, it is difficult to imagine a practical architectural application of such hinged tessellations. Could their gradually increasing and decreasing interstice regions serve as a means to increase or decrease light penetration into a building—either as window screen or shade structures? And if so, what would one do with the ever-changing pattern lines within the interstice regions? Such questions of real-world relevance should not hinder one's inspiration while working with new ideas. It is often a fact that inspiration precedes application, and this is how I am approaching my explorations into hinged tessellations as a means of developing new geometric designs.

It is, therefore, my intention that the material in this chapter should demonstrate how the process of applying pattern lines into the interstice regions that result from hinged rotations of polygonal modules is a highly flexible method of creating original geometric patterns. Such designs will frequently bear the hallmark of individual creativity, and potentially idiosyncratic aesthetic sensibilities. When the as-yet-unrotated tessellations have applied pattern lines that are typical of historical Islamic geometric patterns, as per the examples in this chapter, the patterns created through the hinged rotation process will exhibit varying degrees of traditional Islamic aesthetic standards. While I do not suggest that the use of hinged tessellations was a historical methodology, or for that matter, a particularly effective means of producing "traditional" Islamic geometric designs, it is through innovative experimentation that the exceptional range of stylistic and geometric diversity found within the Islamic geometric arts flourished. In short, experimenting with new approaches to design methodology such as parquet deformations and hinged tessellations is both enjoyable and frequently highly worthwhile. And just as innovative flexibility was undoubtedly an aspect of the historical discipline of Islamic geometric design, so also can contemporary artists and designers find great satisfaction in working with these somewhat unusual methodological variants. Parquet deformations and hinged tessellations are certainly avenues that can lead to worlds of further design exploration.

30° rotation | 45° rotation | 70° rotation

Fig. 17: Three patterns from Figure 07 with widened interweaving lines.

25° rotation | 80° rotation | 90° rotation

Fig. 18: Three patterns from Figure 08 with widened interweaving lines.

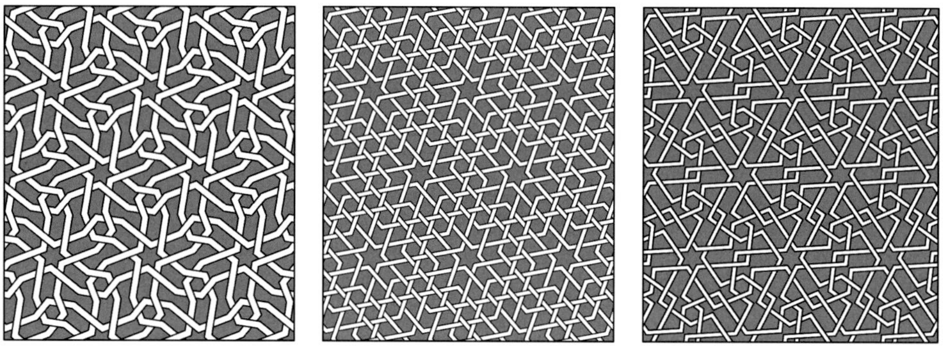

30° rotation | 60° rotation | 80° rotation

Fig. 19: Three patterns from Figure 09 with widened interweaving lines.

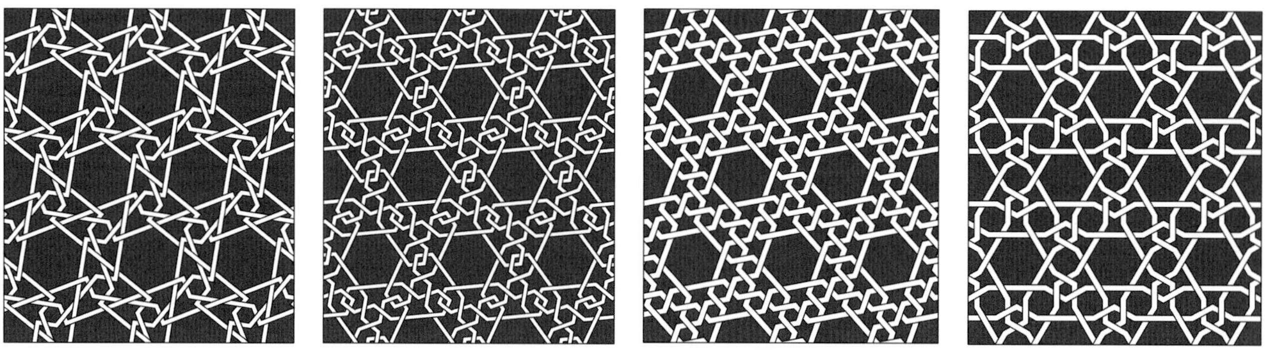

30° rotation | 75° rotation | 60° rotation | 90° rotation

Fig. 20: Four patterns from Figure 10 with widened interweaving lines.

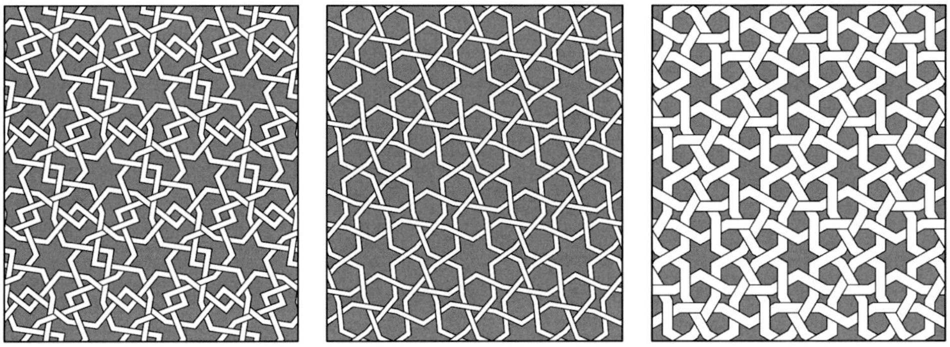

30° rotation | 75° rotation | 90° rotation

Fig. 21: Three patterns from Figure 11 with widened interweaving lines

48° rotation | 72° rotation

Fig. 22: Two patterns from Figure 12 with widened interweaving lines.

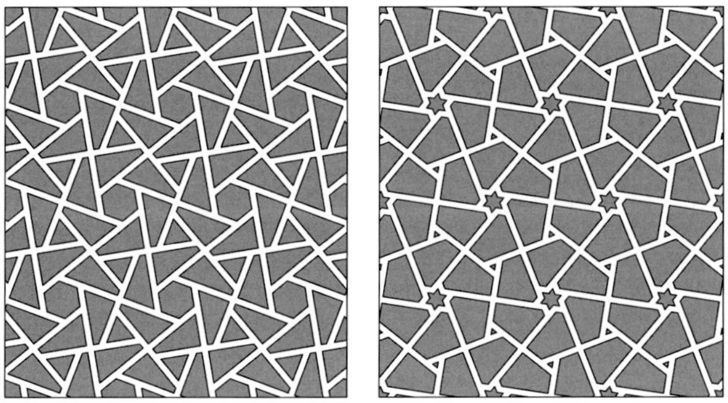

48° rotation | 72° rotation

Fig. 23: Two patterns from Figure 13 with widened lines.

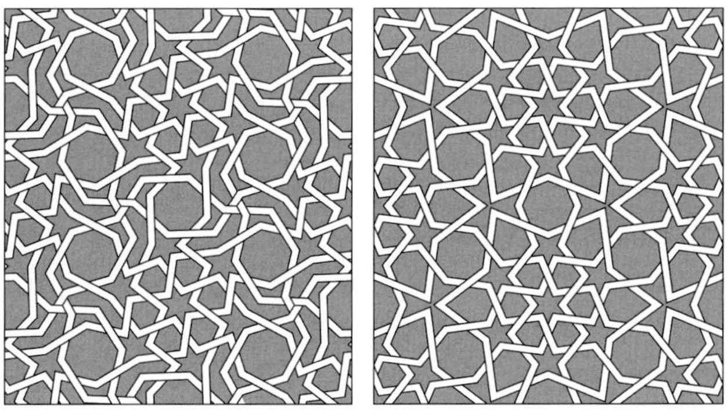

48° rotation | 90° rotation

Fig. 24: Two patterns from Figure 14 with widened interweaving lines.

36° rotation

72° rotation

90° rotation

Fig. 25: Three patterns from Figure 15 with widened interweaving lines.

0° rotation

18° rotation

Fig. 26: Two patterns from Figure 16 with widened interweaving lines.

References

[1] Joachim Krausse and Claude Lichtenstein, *Your Private Sky: Discourse R. Buckminster Fuller*, Lars Muller, 2001.

[2] Jay Bonner, "Doing the Jitterbug with Islamic Geometric Patterns", *Journal of Mathematics and the Arts* 12, 2–3, pp. 128–143.

[3] William S. Huff, Parquet Deformations *"Best Problems" from Basic Design*, State University of New York, 1979; Douglas Hofstadter, "Parquet Deformations: A Subtle, Intricate Art Form", *Metamagical Themes*, New York, 1985; Doris Schattschneider, *Visions of Symmetry: Notebooks, Periodic Drawings, and Related Works of M. C. Escher*, New York, 1990.

[4] Rinus Roelofs: http://www.rinusroelofs.nl/animation/avi-dyn-tilings/avi-dyn-tilings.html.

[5] Craig Kaplan, *Islamic Patterns*, ACM SIGGRAPH Art Exhibition, 2008; Craig Kaplan, "Curve Evolution Schemes for Parquet Deformations", *Bridges Proceedings 2010, Mathematics, Music, Art and Culture*, 2010.

[6] Huff, *Parquet Deformations*.

[7] Bonner, "Doing the Jitterbug", pp. 128–143, Figures 14 and 15.

[8] Hugo F. Verheyen, "The Complete Set of Jitterbug Transformation and the Analysis of their Motion", *Computers & Mathematics with Applications*, 17, 1989, pp. 203–250; Duncan Stuart, "Polyhedral and Mosaic Transformations", *Student Publications of the School of Design*, University of North Carolina, Raleigh, NC, 1963.

[9] David Wells, *The Penguin Dictionary of Curious and Interesting Geometry*, Penguin: p. 199; Robert Williams, T*he Geometrical Foundation of Natural Structure: A Sourcebook of Design*, Dover (reprint, 1979), Joseph Clinton, "Let's Make a (36)D (36)L Chiral Tessellation Dance", *Bridges Proceedings 2012, Mathematics, Music, Art and Culture*, 2012.

[10] Bonner, "Doing the Jitterbug", pp. 128–143, Figure 9.

[11] Jay Bonner, *Islamic Geometric Patterns: Their Historical Development and Traditional Methods of Construction*, Springer, New York, 2017.

[12] Bonner, *Islamic Geometric Patterns*.

[13] Ibid.

Biography of the Author

Jay Bonner is a specialist in multiple Islamic design disciplines, including geometric patterns, muqarnas, rasmi star-vaulting, as well as the floral idiom. He has an international reputation for his work with Islamic geometric patterns, including particularly complex designs that meet the modern mathematical criteria for self-similarity and quasi-periodicity. As an independent scholar of Islamic geometric design, Jay Bonner has published multiple peer-reviewed papers. He is the author of *Islamic Geometric Patterns: Their Historical Development and Traditional Methods of Construction*, with a contributing chapter from Craig Kaplan and a foreword by Sir Roger Penrose, Springer, 2017. At 595 pages, with over 100 photographs and over 500 illustrations, this book is a significant contribution to this field of study. Jay Bonner has taught design workshops and given lectures on the topic of Islamic geometric patterns in North America, Europe, North Africa, and Asia. He was the opening keynote speaker at the 2003 Bridges Conference in Granada, Spain (Three Traditions of Self-Similarity in Fourteenth and Fifteenth Century Islamic Geometric Ornament). Jay Bonner is currently working on a series of online Islamic geometric design courses that will be available very soon. He is also a professional design consultant specializing in Islamic architectural ornament, with some 38 years of experience working on projects in the Middle East, Asia, Europe, and the United States. The many projects he has participated on include: the expansion of the Masjid an-Nawabi (Prophet's Mosque) in Medina; the expansion of the Masjid al-Haram (Grand Mosque) in Mecca, including the minbar for the Kabba courtyard; the Abraj Al-Bait Clock Tower in Mecca; the International Medical Center in Jeddah; the Tomb of Sheikh Hujwiri in Lahore; the New Senate House in Rawalpindi; and the Ismaili Centre in London.

Parakeet3D: Algorithmic Re-Envisioning of Geometrical Pattern Morphogenesis

Esmaeil Mottaghi and
Arman Khalil Beigi Khameneh

1. Introduction

Computational tools have created new linguistics in different disciplines related to design and fabrication. The algorithmic nature of these tools offers a critical possibility to encode the form-generation process and embed various constraints, which results in a rich and dynamic platform for early exploration of design possibilities. Furthermore, the innate procedural notion in these tools coupled with tracking methods and maintenance of the associated data of each alternative facilitates the process of evaluation and optimization using real-time feedback. Algorithms enable the designer to explore the design space interactively and efficiently.

The computational approach is a relevant discourse under the subject of morphological methods for geometrical pattern generation. There is a notable gap in the research on [traditional] geometrical patterns. What is being accumulated and studied for most geometrical patterns is simply the outcome or final product of the generation process. The data we have today on the progression of these patterns is minimal. Barring a few exceptions, what has been gathered to date are mere morphs and shapes without associated data or algorithms. The missing link is the logic behind these morphological processes, forming the idea behind *Parakeet3D*. This research aims to decode or approximate the generation process behind some of the old and authentic patterns in an algorithmic syntax. This approach enables the designer to generate, apply, and analyze patterns not only for ornamental designs, but also for modern architectural purposes, such as thin shells, free-form surfaces, and performative envelopes.

Parakeet3D is a cross-platform design tool. Parts of it have been released for *Grasshopper3D*™, an algorithmic modelling tool associated with McNeel *Rhinoceros*™. In addition, *Parakeet3D* offers methods of creating and modifying patterns and biomimetic patterns (Figure 1), and some geometrical processes inspired by computer science are also included.

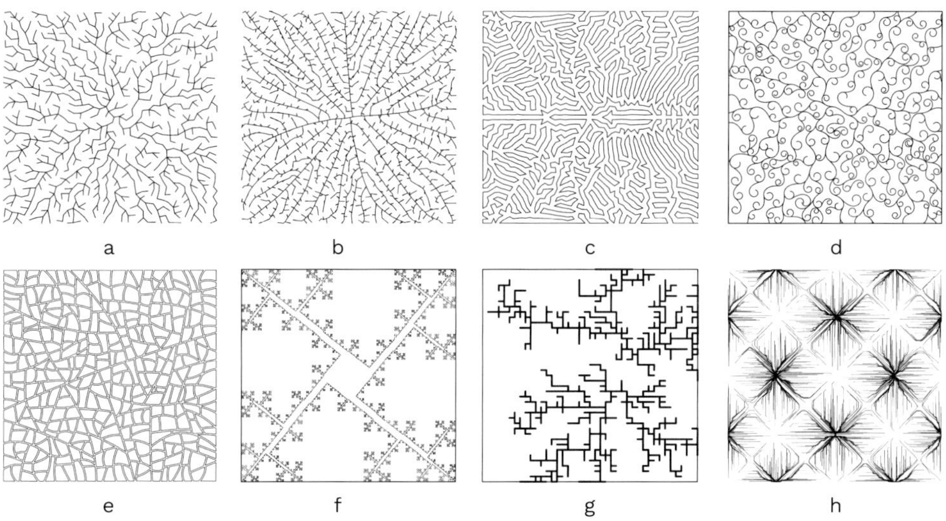

Fig. 1: Examples of bio-inspired patterns generated using *Parakeet3D*:

a) Venation algorithm I
b) Venation algorithm II
c) Differential growth algorithm
d) Floral (arabesque) patterns
e) Fracture (crack) pattern
f) Fractals
g) Diffusion-limited aggregation
h) Flow-path patterns

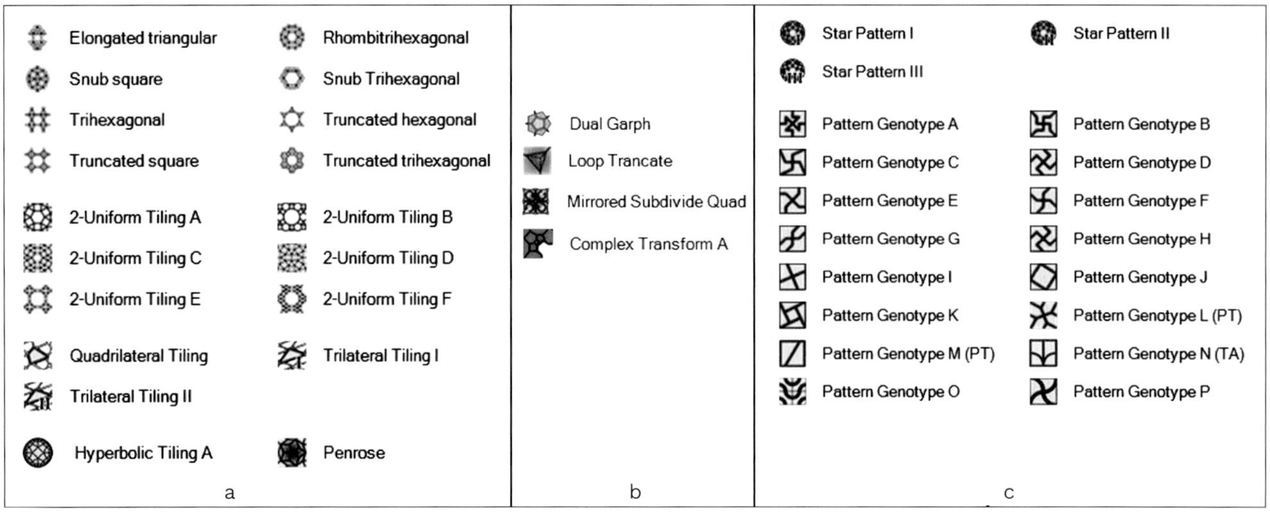

Fig. 2: Basic concepts and methods for geometric pattern generation using *Parakeet3D*:
a) Tilings (base grids)
b) Modification methods
c) Pattern generation methods (Genotypes)

2. Heterogeneous Pattern Generation via *Parakeet3D*

To create parquet deformations or heterogeneous patterns with *Parakeet3D*, a number of basic concepts must be considered, namely tilings, modification methods, and pattern genotypes (Figure 2). To obtain a simplified design method, the generation procedure of networks is divided into four discrete steps: first, selecting the base grid or tiling; second, selecting modification methods which can optionally be applied on the base grid; third, deciding the pattern-generation method applied on each cell; and fourth, applying optional modification or post-processing methods upon the resulting network.

This approach simplifies the process for intermediate users and offers numerous possibilities for custom interventions by advanced designers. The intention was to design the pipeline not in a black box, but in an adaptable manner. Aligned with a generic interpretation of these patterns, the methods for generating patterns are called "genotypes". This approach is highly valuable for multiple reasons, including the ability to keep track of each outcome via "identifiers" or "genes", to substitute some of the time-consuming geometrical processes with simpler textual operations, and to achieve an enhanced optimization process.

To design patterns or, in particular, parquet deformations, the base grid or tiling must first be selected. The tiling category of *Parakeet3D* currently consists of a variety of tilings, such as uniform and semi-uniform tilings, (some) k-uniform and irregular filings, and pentagonal and non-edge-to-edge space-filling networks.

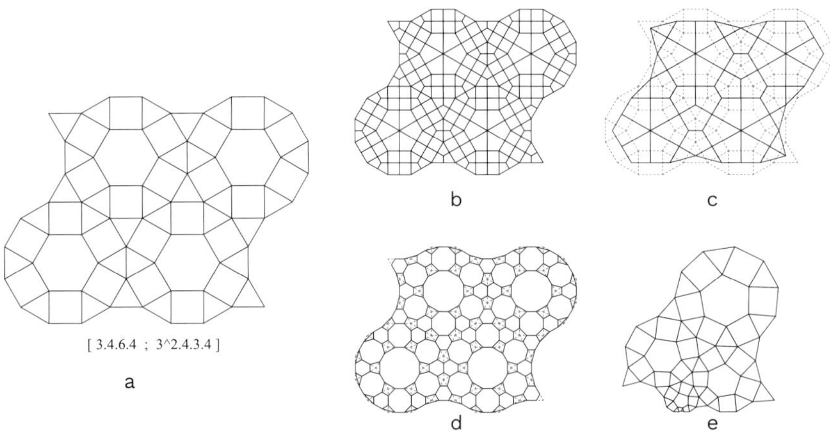

Fig. 3: A *Parakeet3D* 2-Uniform Tiling;
a) Basic tiling (with vertex configuration of [3.4.6.4 and 3^2.4.3.4]
b) Tiling after mirroring quad subdivision
c) Dual graph of the tiling
d) Tiling after truncation
e) Tiling after complex transformation A.

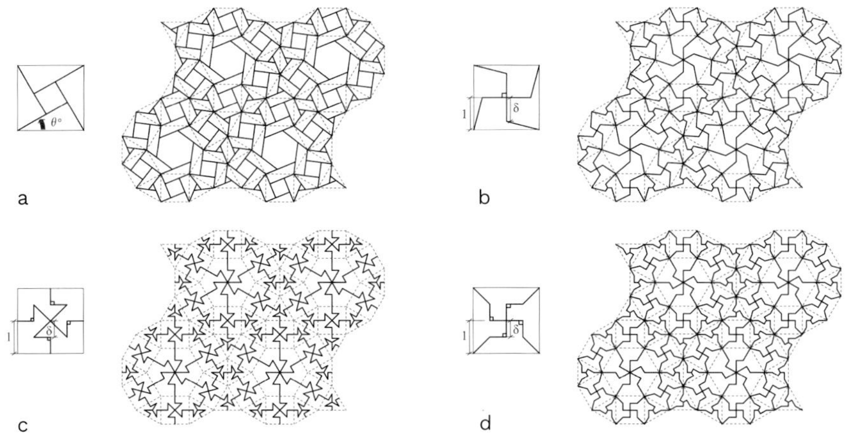

Fig. 4: Application of different *Parakeet3D* genotypes and a tiling:
a) Genotype K
b) Genotype C
c) Genotype A
b) Genotype B

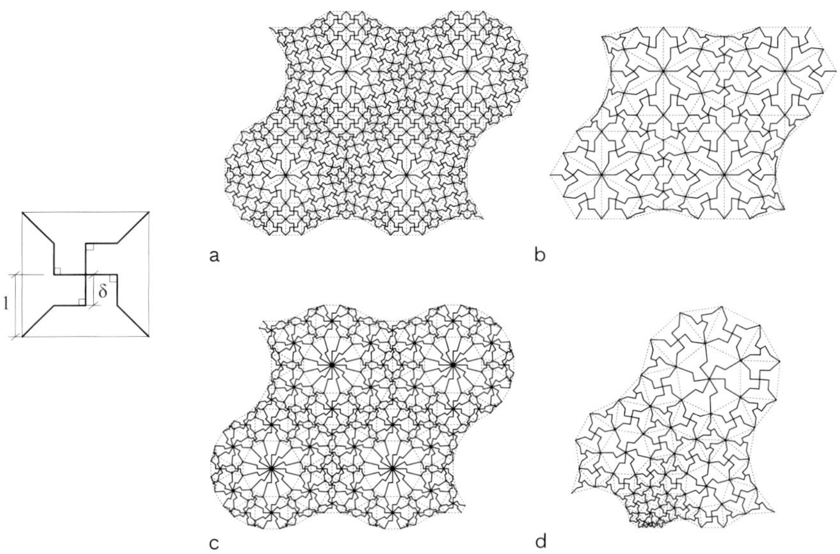

Fig. 5: Application of a *Parakeet3D* genotype on modified tilings:
a) Genotype B on a tiling with mirroring quad subdivision
b) Genotype B on a tiling's dual graph
c) Genotype B on a tiling with truncation
d) Genotype B on a tiling with complex transformation

At this point, an opportunity for post-processing is offered, or for modifications that can be applied to the grid. These modifications increase the complexity and diversity of the results (Figure 3).

The modification methods—including truncation, mirroring quad subdivision, dual graph, and complex (non-Cartesian) operations—can be applied on any type of network consisting of closed polylines. Each method is detailed below.

› Mirroring quad subdivision: Derived from some traditional geometric patterns, mirroring quad subdivision is a particular method for subdividing the base grids. Though the subdivision itself is based on the common method of drawing the perpendicular bisector on each edge, the key resides in the order of the points in resulting shapes (Figure 3b). Thus, points on each sub-cell are ordered so that horizontal and vertical mirroring axes are created. This particular order of points makes seamless patterns when used with the majority of *Parakeet3D*'s pattern genotypes.
› Dual graph: Based on a notion in graph theory, a dual graph is a graph (network) in which the nodes are located inside the faces (closed polylines) of the initial network (in this case, at the centroid of the existing polylines). The connectivity is derived from the topological relation of the initial cells. As the dual graph of any base grid results in different and diverse cells, it expands the options for the base network (Figure 3c).
› Truncation: Commonly perceived to be similar to the concept of Archimedean solids in 3D space, truncation refers to essentially shrinking the endpoints of each linear element towards its midpoints, which creates a new cell (closed polyline) at each node with several segments equal to the node's valency. This process can be repeated recursively, as needed, which also smoothens the angles among elements (Figure 3d).
› Non-Cartesian operators: Several numerical methods can be applied on geometries for complex

transformation, namely Möbius and hyperbolic transformation. For instance, a simple method is converting the Cartesian coordinates to non-Cartesian coordinates, followed by processing the result with complex operators and returning the results to Cartesian space again. This is not an affine transformation, meaning that the parallelism, angles, and distances will not remain constant (Figure 3e). After the optional application of the modifications, pattern genotypes are subsequently selected (Figure 4). The majority of genotypes are designed to create seamless networks. The logic can be applied on any closed polygon and therefore applies to every type of tiling (Figure 5). After this point, the designer can perform the modifications again, if needed.

By selecting the base grid or tiling, the generation method or genotype, and optional modifications on each step, a homogenous pattern can be created (Figure 6). Though changing the input genotype parameters generates various patterns, all cells are associated with

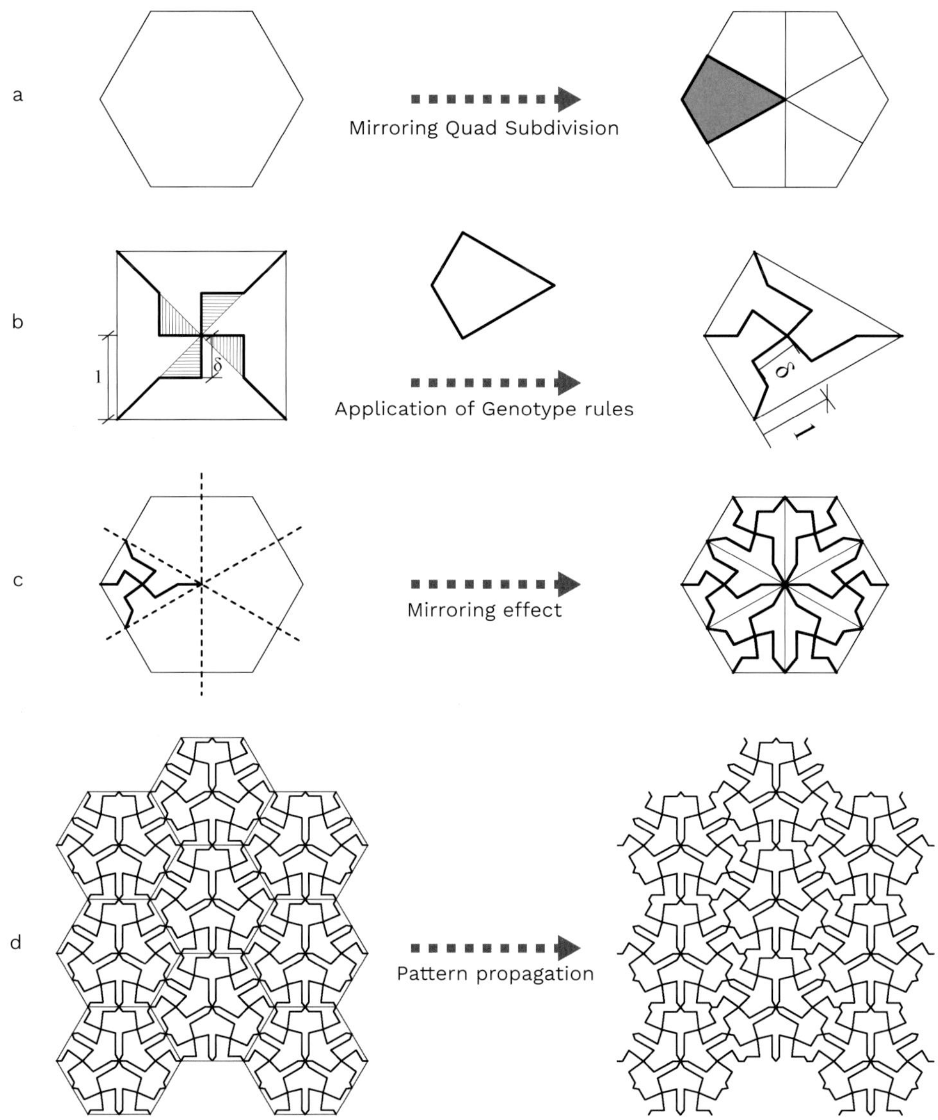

Fig. 6: Homogenous pattern generation procedure using Parakeet3D Genotype B and mirroring quad subdivision on a hexagonal tiling: a) Subdivision of a cell into quadrilateral sub-cells, b) Application of genotype rules, c) Alteration of point orders in adjacent cells to create mirroring effect, d) Pattern propagation.

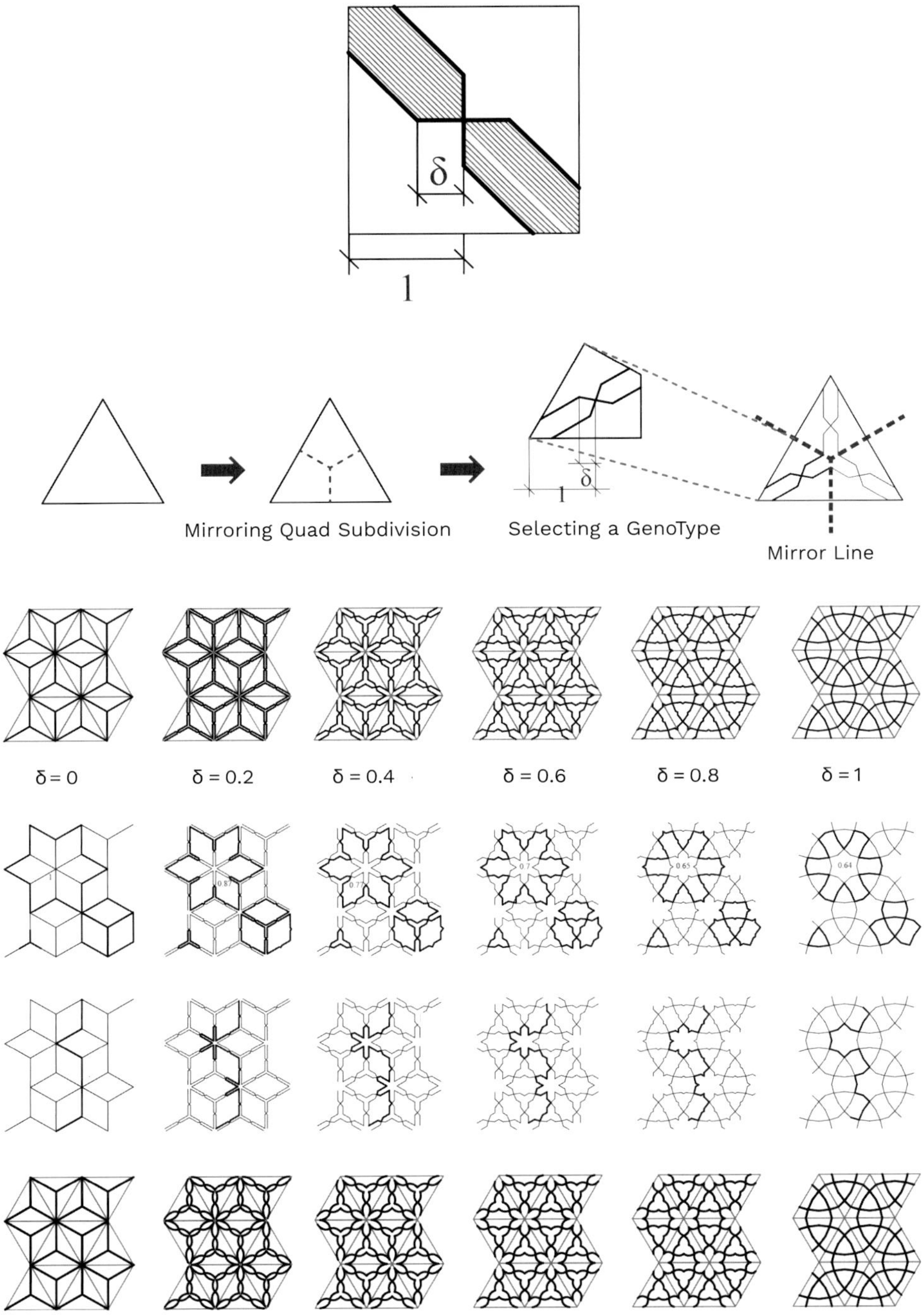

Fig. 7: Variation of (homogenous) patterns created using a sample genotype (G) on subdivided base grids.

a constant state of genotype; therefore, the resulting shapes are uniform and unvarying (Figure 7).

In order to create heterogeneous variations, the genotype input parameters have to vary. Therefore, instead of associating all of the cells with a single state of a genotype, each cell is linked with a unique number. To achieve a unique value for each cell, several simple techniques can be used. Widely used methods include using X or Y coordinates for each cell's centroid (Figure 8) or the distance from each cell to certain distinct geometries in space. More advanced users may create unique values for each cell based on numerical equations, graphs, or values derived from the design environment.

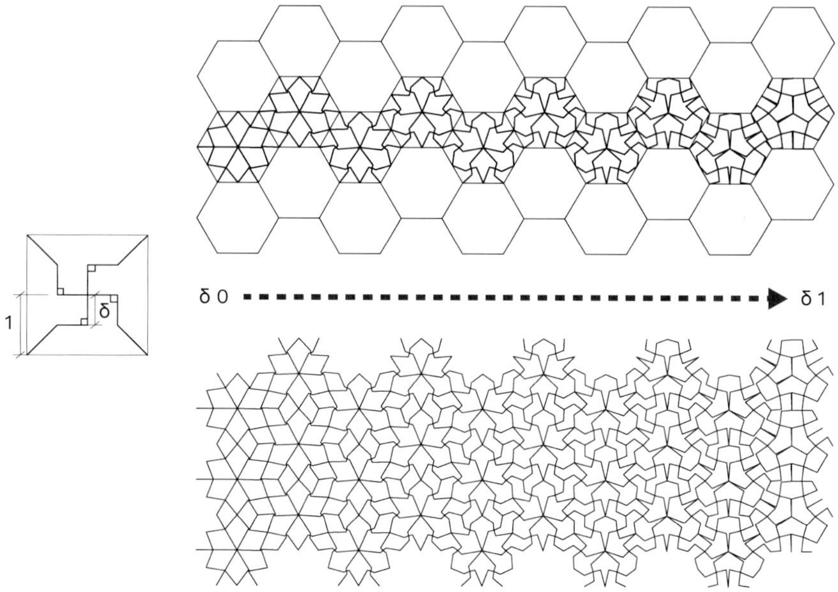

Fig. 8: Parquet deformation generation by a continuous change in genotype inputs.

Fig. 9: Parquet deformations based on *Parakeet3D* genotypes.

To summarize, having selected tilings, genotypes, and modifications, homogenous geometrical patterns are generated. Then by associating different values for each cell, heterogeneous networks, or parquet deformations, emerge. At this point, as most of the *Parakeet3D* genotypes are standardized, numerous variations of parquet deformations can be generated (Figure 9).

3. Beyond Linear Deformations

The computational approach in *Parakeet3D* pattern genotypes aligned with the generative context of *Grasshopper*™ enables the designer to easily explore advanced types of interpolation. The linear transition between the cells to create a metamorphosis outcome has been widely explored. Conventional linear deformation parquets can be generated using *Parakeet3D*. Moreover, algorithmic complexity augments the resulting patterns with tools embedded in *Parakeet3D* or methods from the host environment.

Non-linear deformations are exemplary outcomes of this approach. Thus, utilizing integrated digital tools can push conventional limitations. Examples include transitions of higher degrees, polynomial or spline-based (graph-based) transitions (Figure 10), or transitions based on characteristics of initial surface or mesh, such as Gaussian or mean curvature. Another method for creating patterns with non-linear propagation is the use of specific tilings, for example, hyperbolic tilings such as the Poincaré disk model or substitutional tilings such as Penrose (Figure 11).

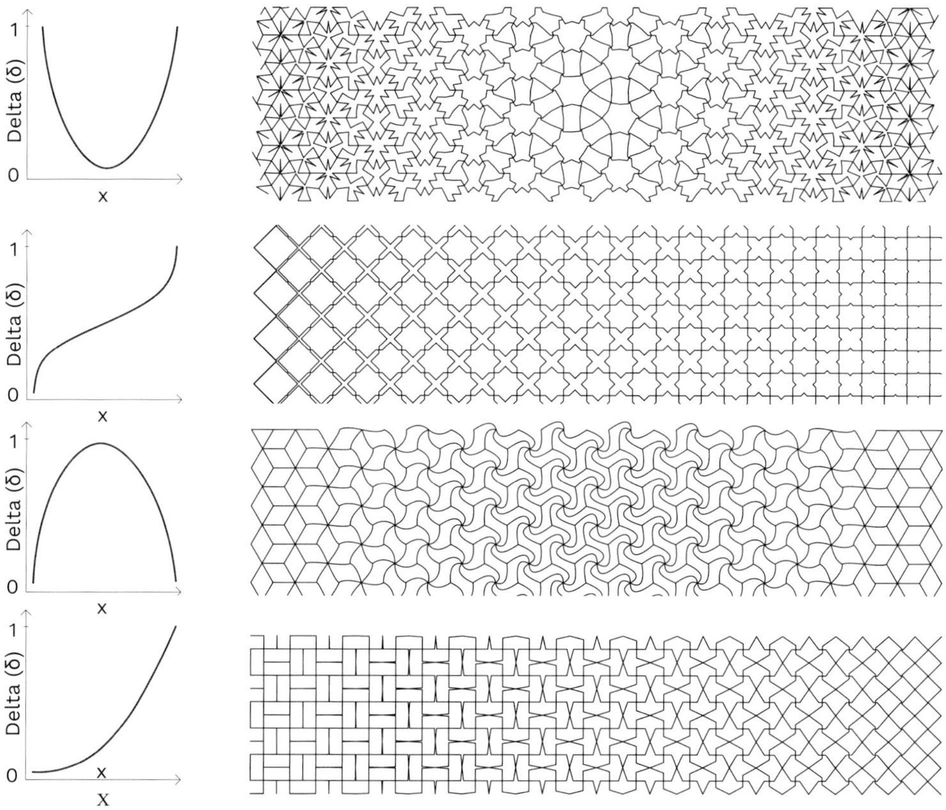

Fig. 10: Effect of non-linear interpolation of genotype values.

Fig. 11: Parquet deformations on non-linear tilings:
a) Parquet deformation on hyperbolic disk,
b) Parquet deformation on a transformed variant of regular square tiling,
c) Parquet deformation on Penrose tiling.

4. Towards New Dimensions

Several approaches can be used to investigate geometries derived from patterns beyond the two-dimensional plane. One widely studied method is stacking shapes inside each cell upwards to create a 2.5-dimensional shape. A more profound approach, though, comprises using a non-Cartesian coordinate system—that is, mapping coordinates to cylindrical or spherical systems.

4.1. [Pseudo] Three-Dimensional Geometries

This method substitutes linear propagation in a two-dimensional plane with a horizontally assembled order. In this widely investigated approach, the third dimension is not actively generated and lacks the amount of data embedded in other dimensions. (It is a plain accumulation of two-dimensional shapes.) Therefore, this category may more accurately be called 2.5D (two-and-a-half dimensional) or pseudo-three-dimensional geometries.

In this method, a number of issues are still under-studied, including "transition rate" and "desirable phenotypes". Desirable phenotypes are a set of characteristics resulting from the interaction of their genotypes. These phenotypes (expression or emergent outcomes of genotypes) can offer beneficial architectural/design features. For example, some genotypes have regions that maintain a fixed inner area. Therefore, the corresponding three-dimensional shape has sections with a constant area (Figure 12).

The transition speed (rate) between various sections is a further parameter for examination. Non-linear transformation of input parameters forms various three-dimensional geometries. The transformation speed is not constant, and the conversion is performed using non-linear interpolations. For instance, interpolation may be based on arbitrary graphs, trigonometric functions, or polynomial equations (Figure 13).

4.2. Non-Cartesian Geometries

Excluding the Cartesian methods and transformation rates that can generate complex and novel patterns, we conducted extensive research using various coordinate systems with *Parakeet3D*. The logic behind this tool enables designers to explore geometric designs in different coordinate systems. Genotypes are designed to work with simplified numerical inputs. Therefore, these parameters can easily be interpreted as non-Cartesian coordinates. The generator parameters can be translated into polar coordinates in two-dimensional space or cylindrical and spherical coordinates in three-dimensional space (Figure 14). This novel approach generates greater complexity than the conventional method of stacking 2D layers of geometries upon each other to create 3D geometries (Figure 15).

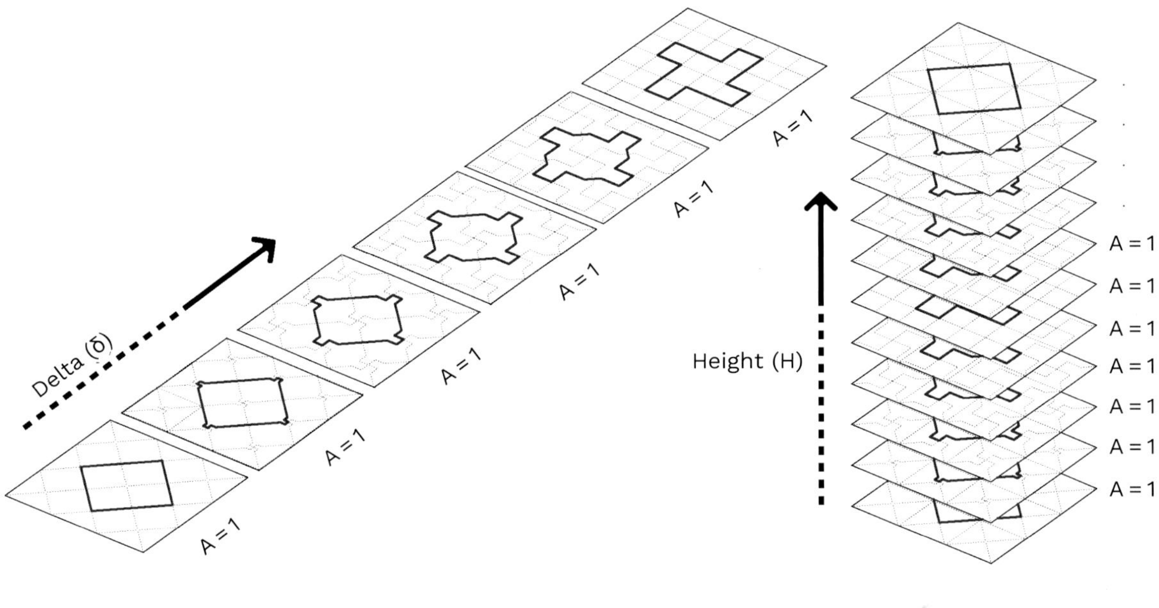

Fig. 12: [Pseudo] three-dimensional geometries created by the accumulation of 2D patterns. Depicting an emergent phenotype of maintaining a constant area throughout the transformation.

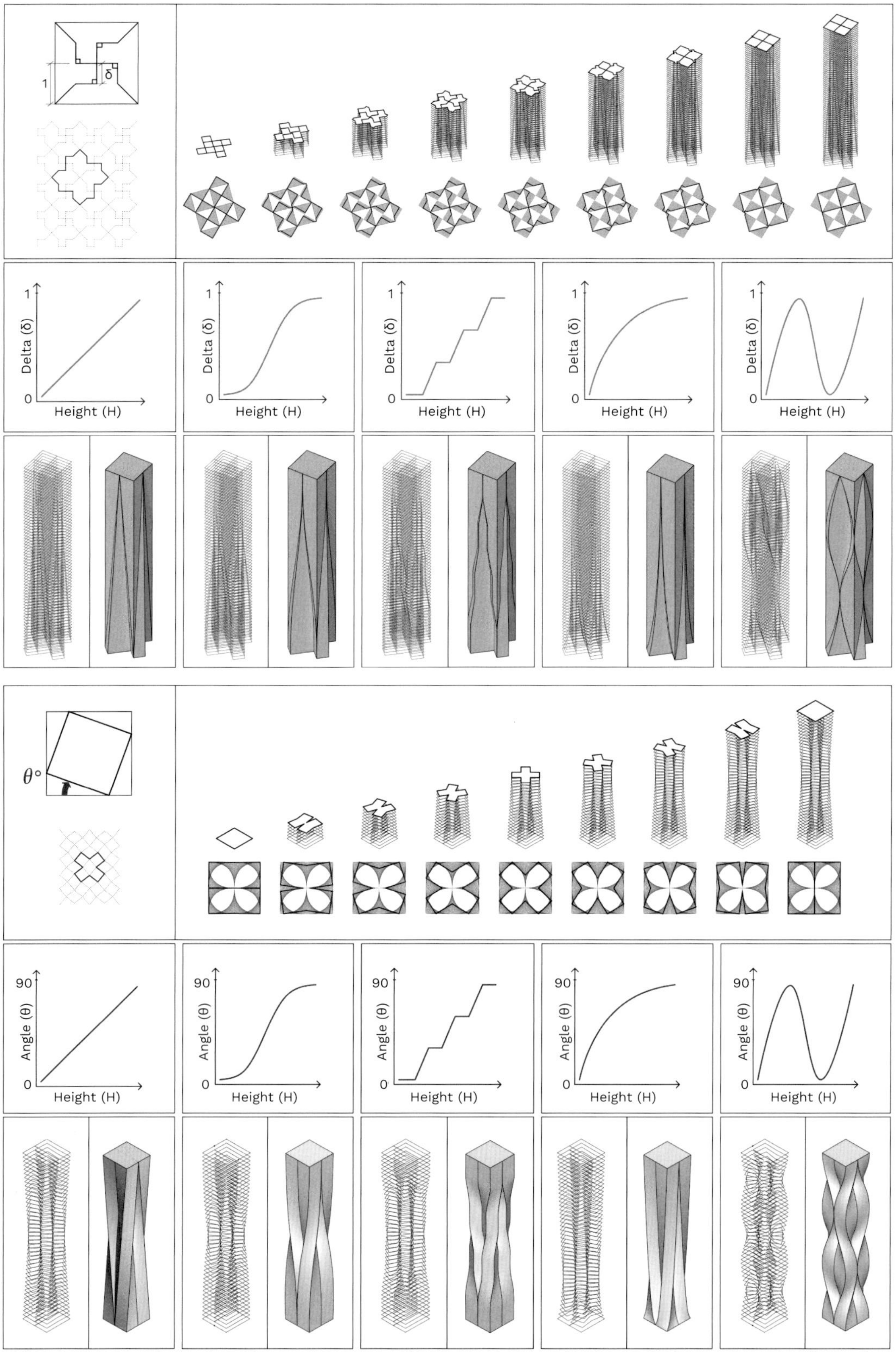

Fig. 13: [Pseudo] three-dimensional geometries created by the accumulation of 2D patterns. Depicting the effect of non-linear transition rate.

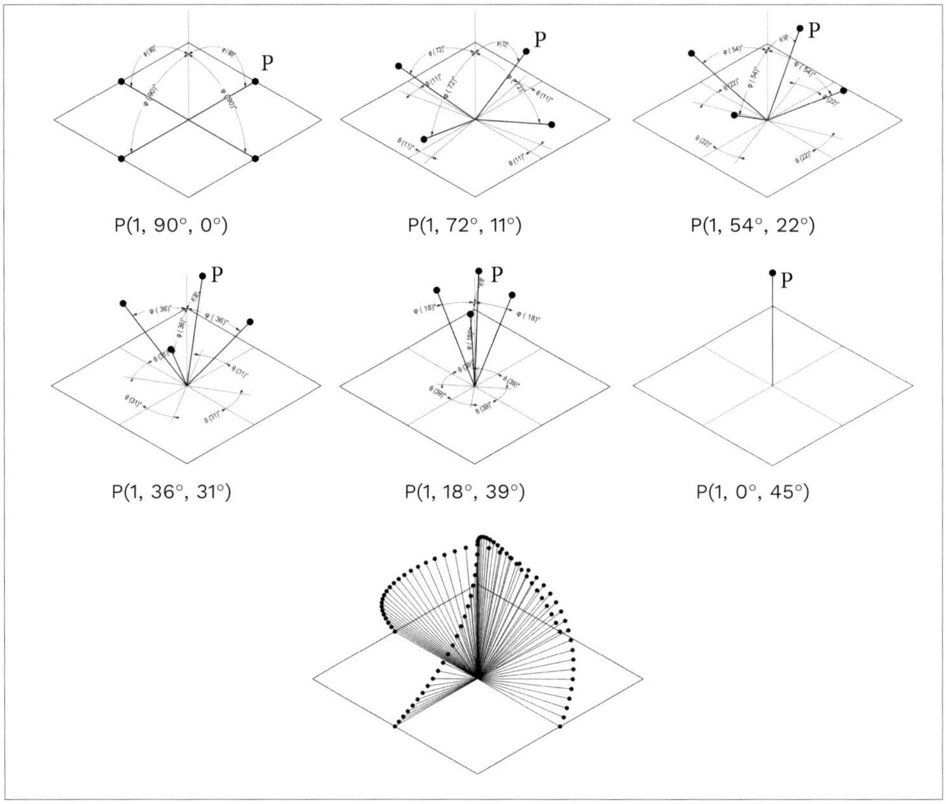

Fig. 14: Interpretation of input parameters of a genotype (I) to spherical coordinates.

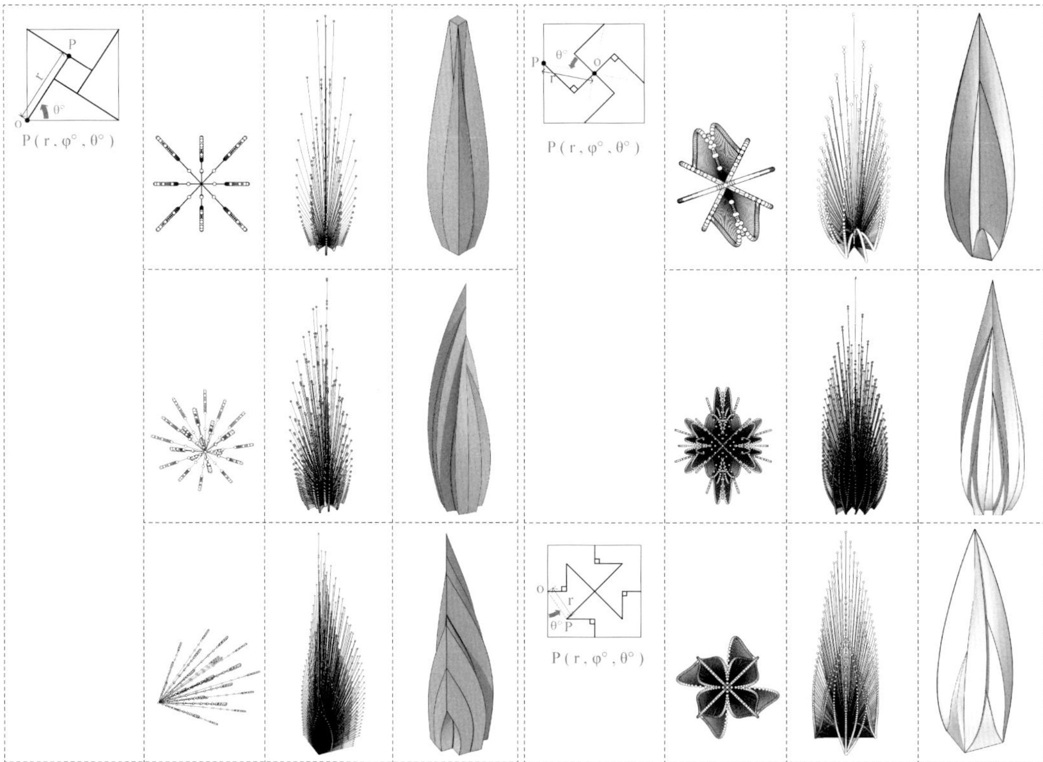

Fig. 15: Interpretation of input parameters of different genotypes to spherical coordinates.

5. Discussion: Limitations and Opportunities

Through the radical advancement in personal computers and the emergence of advanced computational tools at designers' disposal in the last several decades, a conspicuous tendency towards building free-form geometries or projects with augmented performative capabilities has developed. These phenomena reflect the urge of designers to solve increasingly complex problems. The level of complexity and the integrated data in modern projects require an inevitable shift in design tools and problem-solving methods. The algorithmic context offers possibilities to tweak and develop for advanced users. Digital tools have even greater potential in their integration with tools from other disciplines. Digital tools can be adjusted with the requirements and constraints of complementary fields. For instance, with a generative tool like *Parakeet3D*, data for digital fabrication can be generated directly from the generation platform or optimization criteria can be considered to optimize the fabrication process of waste or time management.

Geometry is a small portion of what a competent digital tool must offer a computational designer. At the lowest level, generating morphs and shapes is expected from such tools. Integration and coherence is another significant feature. Using standard protocols and methods for storing or transferring data enables digital tools to create a powerful gestalt. For example, instead of saving the geometric components in simple plain data, *Parakeet3D* handles data in more advanced data structures, such as half-edge data structures. This practice allows *Parakeet3D* to keep topological data associated with morphological data and thus tightly integrated with other major computer science libraries, which makes future developments much more manageable.

One of the concerns regarding digital tools is at the level of user intervention. On one hand, tools like *Parakeet3D*, which are usually referred to as "high-level" tools, need to limit the number of user inputs/modifications to keep the tool user-friendly and simple. On the other hand, "low-level" tools offer a higher degree of freedom for more competent users. Thus, a limitation in digital tool development is managing a trade-off between being user-friendly and at the same time providing intervention possibilities. Another limitation of morphological tools is the coordinate system. Current studies on pattern generation methods primarily use a Cartesian coordinate system and then morph, map, or project the outcome shapes onto arbitrary geometries. These transformations are problematic in many cases, for instance, in mapping a flat pattern onto a manifold mesh. A possible solution is using local coordinates systems, such as using parametrized UVW coordinates of a surface or mesh instead of using Cartesian positions and calculations. This approach requires a major revision of generation procedures, as even the simplest methods of calculating intersections, angles, and distances are fundamentally different in local UVW coordinate systems.

Parakeet3D represents an effort to revise pattern generation methods. Algorithmic thinking can be used to re-code the generative process. The subject of geometrical patterns began long before computational tools were in designers' toolkits, yet the geometrical and mathematical concepts behind it make it highly compatible with modern computational geometry syntax. Computational tools offer a vast opportunity for designers to effortlessly generate, represent, and evaluate their designs.

Biographies of the Authors

Arman Khalil Beigi Khameneh is a digital architect. He holds a master's degree in architectural technologies. He is a design technician, and his teaching focuses on design computation and integration of cutting-edge or customized fabrication technologies into the design process. He pushes the boundaries of his designs to the intersection of computational geometry, digital fabrication, and material technologies. He is a co-founder of Paragen creative studio, where he provides algorithmic solutions for complex design and fabrication.

Esmaeil Mottaghi is a computational designer, architect, and computational geometry researcher based in Tehran, Iran. He graduated with a master's degree in computational design from the University of Tehran and has experience as an expert in digital manufacturing and as a computational design tutor. He has also been a director of multiple digital fabrication and algorithmic design workshops organized by Tehran University and other architectural centers. He is a co-founder of Paragen creative studio.

Presenting the Experiments' Outcomes

Editor's note

Approximately 450 students completed the experiment in each of the two years—a selection of their works form the core of this book and are displayed in the following chapters carrying the names of the respective experiments: "3D Parquet Deformation" (winter semester 2017–2018) and "Cellular Space Sequences" (winter semester 2018–2019).

Both chapters progress chronologically so that readers can follow the logic of the assignments given to students. In both cases, initial two-dimensional exercises are shown, leading to a selection of three-dimensional models built at the end of the semester.

Following the notion of the artistic experiment, this book focuses on presenting investigations rather than judging the results obtained by students as right or wrong. The topics investigated by the students' final presentation model overlap in many instances, and they have been grouped accordingly during the editing process of the book.

The "3D Parquet Deformation" chapter features works that explore "Composition", "Dissolving", "Gradual Changes", "in Motion", "Materiality Matters", "Multiplication", and "On Stage".

The "Cellular Space Sequences" chapter collects works examining "Balance", "Crystalline", "Gradual Changes", "Materiality Matters", "Multiply", and "Opening Up the Inside".

Themes do not follow any (scientific) criteria chosen beforehand; instead, they have arisen from carefully studying the students' works and distilling ideas from them—ideas that reoccur, that blur into one another, and that do not present a systematic evaluation regarding a particular direction, be it materiality or geometric rule sets. Rather, the topics extracted from the works do not follow any given order; they stand next to one another to build relationships.

The models were realized with many different materials and processing types, the drawings were created partly by hand, partly digitally. This and also the exact size is not always documented and is therefore not indicated. Short explanations offer the reader some background information about the design process and essential features of its structure.

The Tiling and The Whole

Christian Kern

As the person responsible for the "three-dimensional design and model making" research field at the Vienna University of Technology and as one of the editors of this book, I would like to begin with a few cursory notes on the task, the process, and the results presented here.

Our research center is affiliated with the Institute for Art and Design, part of the Faculty of Architecture and Spatial Planning. We train architecture students, among others, in fundamental questions of form. Due to its size and durability, architecture is a very visible and permanent symbol of culture; it is "building culture". As a creative achievement of a community, it interacts with other artistic, intellectual, and creative disciplines. It may hurry ahead or lag behind or even be self-referential or consciously take itself out of the temporal context in which it repeats. An essential difference from other creative cultural achievements lies in architecture's sheer dimensionality.

As a rule, it is not possible to conceptually grasp the future effect of architecture before it is physically represented in any way. In the development of a design, visual media and other tools, are therefore necessary to convey an impression and allow the assessment of design approaches. This process does not happen at the real scale of architecture; this would be too slow, too complex, and would allow too few variants. As such, the design is scaled down, and work is carried out at this smaller scale—in the sketch, the plan, or the model. Shapes and surfaces are necessarily abstracted, bodies initially represented in monolithic form.

In the 1:1 implementation, depending on the material and its processing, contiguous seamless surfaces as found in the model are not possible. A discretization of the surfaces is necessary—that is, a division into elements of limited size that can be produced and assembled. The geometry of these elements and their interaction produce an aesthetic effect that either supports the form of the architecture or space or disturbs and questions it. The division and the structure of these elements should therefore not be decided in a technical-pragmatic manner in implementation, but should be related to the aesthetics of the building.

Perhaps this discretization of surfaces is already shaped by rhythms, by rules that live from many or a few complex variations of the repetition and which can be easily described mathematically. In this case, it would be obvious to apply these rules also in the sub-level of the form, in the design of elements. Yet perhaps the architecture is complexly curved or dissolved into objects with different geometries and directions, as in the work of Zaha Hadid, Frank Gehry, or Daniel Liebeskind. In such cases, the development of the division becomes an exciting design task in its own right, a task that we approached with students over two semesters as part of the subject "three-dimensional design" in architecture training at the Vienna University of Technology.

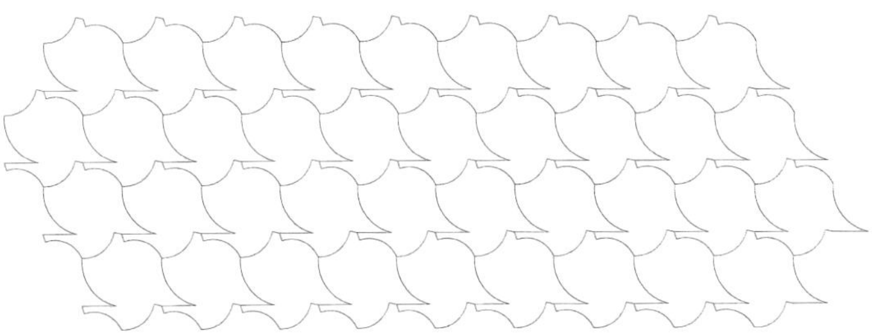

Fig. 1: Cinthia Anton, 2017; overlapping effects.

Legato and crescendo in the deformation of the parquet

Let us consider the parquet in more detail. In mathematics, a parquet is defined as the gap-free, overlap-free division of an area or plane. For functional reasons, this definition does not have to exclusively apply in architecture. Gaps can be interesting as perforations (light, ventilation), and overlaps can be useful for technical reasons (e.g., with shingles). Nevertheless, it makes sense to first stick to the mathematical definition in order to be able to develop design rules and to start experiments in which not only results are assessed, but targeted changes are made with increasing knowledge gain.

A wide variety of often surprising patterns can be accomplished within these rules. With small changes in the geometry of the elements, there are sometimes decisive changes in the appearance of the whole. In the spirit of experimentation, the following design questions can be asked: What if convex shapes are chosen? What if partial shapes become expressive? We explored these questions with a large number of students, and it was amazing how different and enriching the results were, even with simple specifications. On the basis of these investigations, the experiments, as described in more detail elsewhere in this book, became more complex. We advanced from legato to crescendo, from a sequence to a deformation and thereby to an increase in the effect. The elements were continuously changed, or the grids in which the elements developed were warped. This was initially a two-dimensional development with a three-dimensional effect. At the end of the discussion, however, there was a need to think about and apply tiling in three dimensions as an abstract principle of order for sculpture and architecture.

Three-dimensional effects were observable even in the first drawings. Overlaps, and thereby depth, could be interpreted depending on the geometry of the elements, because human perception automatically simplifies shapes for reasons of effectiveness. Shapes are completed even if the corresponding area is not visible or is mentally overlaid by another element. If one was aware of this principle, one could consciously increase the depth effect by, for example, using convex shapes together with an additional expressive shape, leading to an incision in the adjacent field. The latter was ignored in the perception as an essential feature of the actual shape and interpreted as an overlapping element of an adjacent element.

A paradox emerges here. When the shape develops outwards, it turns inside out on the opposite side at the same time, since all parts used are congruent in a tiling. The creative impact of these effects is difficult to predict, even with some experience. The design process involves emergences, appearances, and effects that arise in the making and that were not considered in advance. Good examples are directions, rotation effects, and depth effects, which become visible when a sufficient number of elements work together.

If there are more elements, the effect does not fundamentally change, but may repeat or lengthen. This outcome can be useful if a designer does not want to distract from the geometry, the area being played on, or the architectural context. If parquet may be effective as a design element, the deformation becomes interesting: a continuous change in the basic structure or the protocell in which these interventions become more and more expressive and complex. This process can occur radially or linearly, for example, and a curve or a centric effect is created accordingly. The students' examples

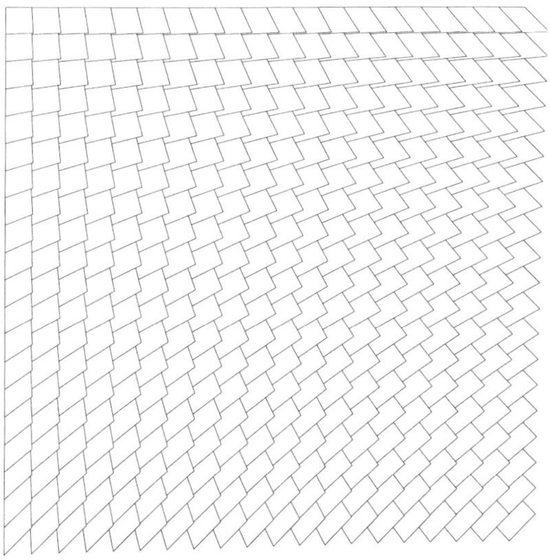

Fig. 2.a: Sarah Reithofer, 2017, depth effect through overlapping effects.

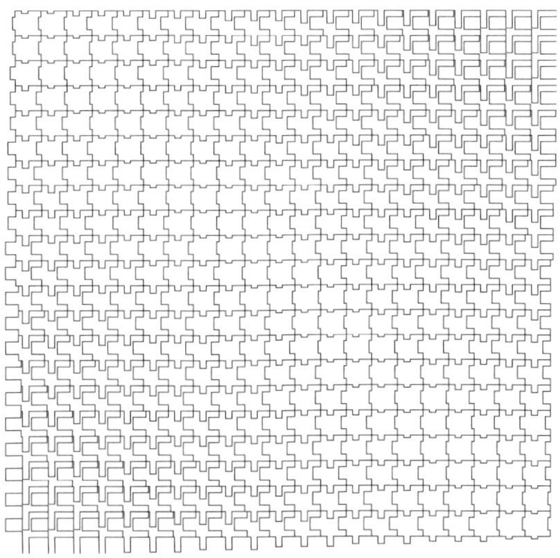

Fig. 2.b: Daria Lanina, 2017, depth effect through different densities.

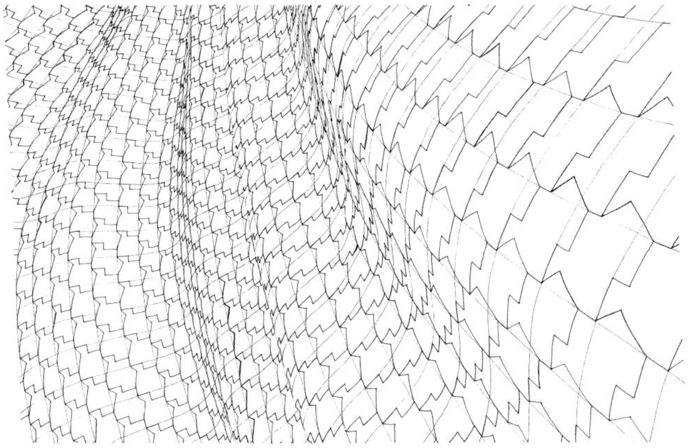

Fig. 3: Anja Bezjak, 2017, wave motion due to grid distortion.

appear particularly dynamic when the changes take place in two directions at the same time. For various reasons, in these cases the three-dimensional effect tends to be stronger than with simple tiling in only one direction. Overlapping effects can occur again, though. Another cause is the depth perception due to the so-called "aerial perspective". Based on experience, the assumption is that objects further away are seen as brighter, as the contrasts decrease due to reflective floating elements in the air (aerosols, dust, water vapor). Through a compression and thus a change in the gray value, the corresponding areas are interpreted as closer. With alternating gray values, three-dimensional wave movements can be perceived.

The deformation of the basic grid had a dramatic effect (Exercise 3). Due to these distortions, elements are interpreted as lying diagonally in space. A strong depth effect can be expressed by means of a parquet deformation in the plane. The French Op Art artist Victor Vasarely has often used this effect in his pictures and justified the use of such optical effects with the statement: "Art is artificial and by no means natural: creating does not mean imitating nature, but equaling it and even her by means of an invention which, among all living things, only humans are capable of surpassing it"[1].

As previously noted, this examination of the rules and design possibilities of tiling formed the basis for a three-dimensional, object-like, and spatial investigation. It was important to us that we not only use this principle for the design of surfaces, but also for the shaping and configuration of solids. For functional and efficiency reasons, architecture is often thought of as a "tight package". Residential buildings, for example, primarily consist of a three-dimensional arrangement of rooms. These spaces, together with their envelopes, can also be understood as stacked solids, as in the case of North American pueblo architecture.

What if these spaces are not just orthogonal? What if they change in the sense of a "parquet deformation" and break away from the monotony of 3D parquet? Yet, what if important rules like the absence of gaps and the exit from a basic grid still apply? As is always the case with the transition from a two-dimensional to a three-dimensional design investigation, the effort involved in exploring this question is significantly greater than in a pure drawing experiment. Form studies have to be built and material processed. Furthermore, gravity is of great relevance in the process, as joints must be form-fit or force-fit.

A particular problem arises in the visual or haptic detection of the configuration or the deformation. If made from opaque surfaces, the solid packs are initially invisible. As such, strategies had to be developed to look inside or to present elements in such a way that an interesting composition did not just appear as an undefined collection. One way was to break up the bodies into edges. Another method was the definition of gaps, which—together with the solids—were subject to a rule. In some cases it was sufficient to show the basic solids detached so that an observer constructed the spatial representation of the geometry in his or her head, even though it was not directly visible.

The wish that individual elements and their configuration could be experienced tends to lead to additive "element swarms". These can have any effect or, as a whole, can acquire a meaning and become "gestalt" (form + meaning = gestalt). Students developed basic design ideas so that a sculpture could be created that is more than the sum of its parts. This idea was often a development or transformation of basic elements and thus the overall form, partly linear, partly radial. There were variations of bodies that remained similar in size, but there were also works with a dramatic crescendo. Others exhibited little or no variation and lived off a rhythm that is made interesting by light and shadow. There were works that seemed self-contained and others that represented an excerpt from something larger. Deliberately chosen locations, the decision for or against a base, and elevations or suspensions supported or weakened the design intent. Color, gloss, and strong

Fig. 4: Victor Vasarely, *Vega*, 1956. © Bildrecht, Wien 2021.

material structure occurred, but could distract from the shape. In their conception and implementation, the works were very enriching and impressive. What they have in common in a positive sense is a mathematical, geometric logic with individual characteristics and high design quality.

Staccato of the objects and legato of the spaces and the space sequence

For the initiators of the previous exercise, an important question of perception remained open, which was reflected in the work described above. The objects are generally viewed from the outside as sculptures, particularly because of their dimensions. There are sometimes gaps, when the solids are broken up into bars or transparent surfaces so that insights are possible. However, the spatial quality of the interior is not easy to grasp and was not particularly addressed. In architecture, it is not only the formal quality of the object that is essential, but also the space inside the solid or the spaces in between.

This aspect became formative for the program in the following year for the "Cellular Space Sequences" exercise. Here, too, the basic assumption was taken from tiling and its geometrical-mathematical fundamentals, but interior and intermediate spaces were considered from the start. Although these spaces were geometrically related to the outer shape, they were not necessarily identical in terms of their formal characteristics. The topic was expanded by connecting the spaces, a sequence that can be walked through or flown through.

Emergences, phenomena that were not considered in advance, again arose from the mathematical-geometric principles. A conscious and high-quality choreography in the spatial sequence, the sequence, and the transitions between the spaces was required—a conscious design within the rules and a commitment to individual authorship. The shape should be edited

Figure 5: Peter G. Auer, 2018; Example of a solution.

and defined on four levels: the shape of the cell, then the overall shape resulting from the combination of cells, the space inside the cell, and the spatial continuum resulting from the connection. With some results, there is another form that requires attention, which is the spaces between the cells (i.e., spaces in between).

This makes judgements as well as predictions within this design exercise a complex and demanding task, especially because it is extremely difficult for human perception. Not least for evolutionary reasons, people usually concentrate on objects (or subjects). Like interior spaces, these are delimited, while spaces in between often expand without limits in one or more directions. In the two-dimensional graphic representation, this perception problem can be avoided by reversing it, keeping the cut surfaces of the bodies dark (e.g., by hatching). This approach makes the spaces more visible as a form. However, concentration is required to be able to perceive the shapes of the objects in this type of representation.

As in a tilt image by psychologist and phenomenologist Edgar John Rubin, the space or the object appear alternately. In such a situation, design is only possible iteratively. A person works on one and checks the effects on the other. If the changes are assessed negatively, this intervention is withdrawn and a different approach is attempted. Only with increasing knowledge about the impact can a more targeted and holistic approach be taken. This task is therefore very close to an architectural problem in which different parameters have to be mutually dependent, although they are subject to different requirements. A basic design exercise in our faculty is also a basic exercise in architectural thinking.

The three-dimensional development or investigation of the topic of cellular spatial sequences leads to different design priorities than with the previous parquet deformation. The focus, as indicated in the title of this exercise, was on the sequence of spaces, the choreographed transition from one space to the next. The solids themselves were mirrored or rotated, but basically retained their geometric features. This continuity resulted in compositions in which a staccato of the objects was accompanied by a legato of the spaces.

These “tilting solids”, in which the viewer’s perception constantly fluctuates between two basic characteristics, required a critical number of elements in order for the composition and sequence to be effective. It therefore took some effort to physically manufacture them. In addition, openings, resolutions, or distances had to be developed and implemented with reference to a higher-level aesthetic so that the spatial sequence could be sufficiently perceived. The selection of the resulting objects presented here deals with these demanding requirements in different ways. However, as in the previous exercise, all examples achieved a very high quality of design. They are able to intensively occupy the observer, but—due to the inherent geometric logic—they can be grasped both as overall compositions and on the level of the individual elements, a sculptural achievement that is also a fundamental characteristic of architecture.

References

[1] Victor Vasarely, Gespräche mit Victor Vasarely, Jean-Louis Ferrier, *Spiegelschrift 8*, Verlag Galerie der Spiegel, Köln 1971, p. 155.

Biography of the Author

Christian Kern was born in 1964 in Wipperfürth, West Germany. Apprenticed as a machine fitter, studied architecture at the TU Stuttgart and the Curtain University Perth, West Australia. Collaboration at Stirling and Wilford Stuttgart, Ken Yeang Malaysia, Behnisch and Partner Stuttgart, Auer + Weber Stuttgart, Meier-Scupin & Petzet Munich. Scientific assistant at the chair for building theory and product development, Prof. Richard Horden, TU Munich. Since 1998 own office in Munich, 2001 founding of BLAUWERK Architects with Michael Schneider, since 2008 with Tom Repper. Board member of Europan Germany e.V. Since 2007 Professor at the Vienna University of Technology, head of the department for three-dimensional design and model making.

3D Parquet Deformation

The aim of this exercise was to extend the discussion of 2D tiling and 2D parquet deformation (William S. Huff), which is well anchored in systematized basic design theory, to the concept of 3D tiling and 3D parquet deformation. Students were to become familiar with the groups of congruent figures filling a plane or space, their topological relationships, and the principles of continuous deformation (see, for example, Dürer and D'Arcy Thompson), but also to develop a coherent and aesthetically pleasing 3D composition. Finally, a three-dimensional form study was developed based on the principle of parquet deformation. The semester-long exercise was divided into four individual exercises, the results of which are presented in the following pages.

Exercise 1
2D Parquets and 2D Parquet Deformation

The first exercise started with lattice structures based on regular/platonic polygons (triangle, square, and hexagon) and other simple polygons (e.g., rhombus, rectangle, isosceles triangle), and their transformation possibilities were studied. Based on one of the simple polygons (basic element), a grid was created by hand drawing. In three steps, students "breathed life" into the grid by deforming or transforming it in different ways.

1. Transformation of the Basic Element

The goal was to develop new protocells apt for tiling, based on a constant grid structure. This goal could be achieved by different operations: shortening or lengthening a line; introducing a "kink", a "bump", or a "nub" (penetrating or protruding a simple shape); subdivision (subdividing); assigning a different location for a corner point; changing a straight edge to a curved one; or drawing a diagonal or circles. These newly developed cells were cut out of cardboard to playfully explore their possible combinations (study of symmetry groups based on rotation, translation, reflection).

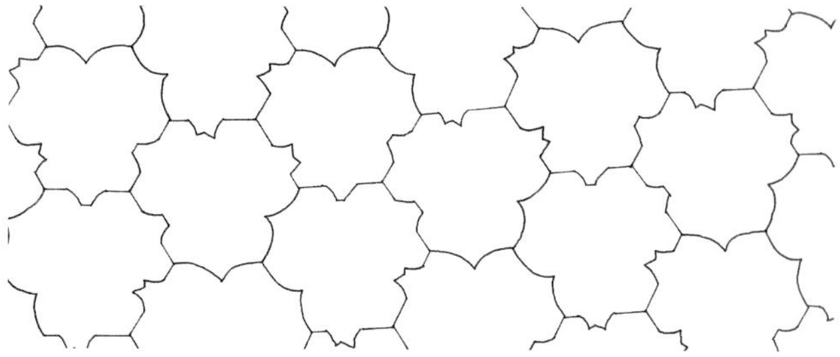

Marijana Zivkovic
Tutor: Werner Van Hoeydonck

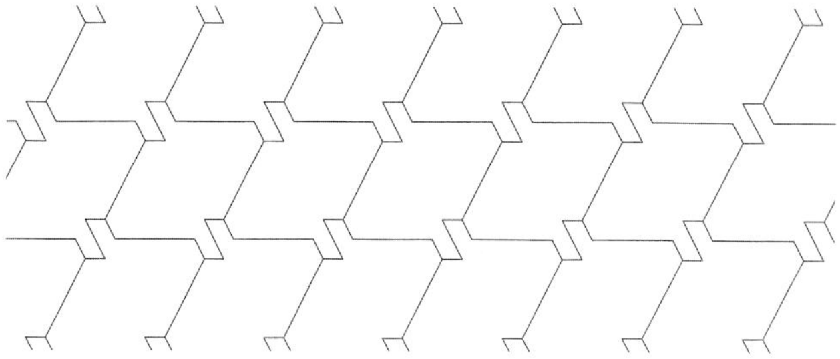

Mehmet Semih Özcelik
Tutor: Martina Kögl

Mehmet Semih Özcelik
Tutor: Martina Kögl

Irem Akcay
Tutor: Manuela Fritz

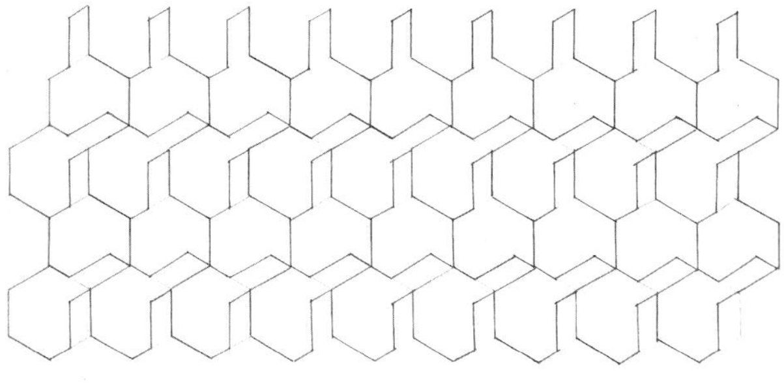

Zeynep Dikmen
Tutor: Manuela Fritz

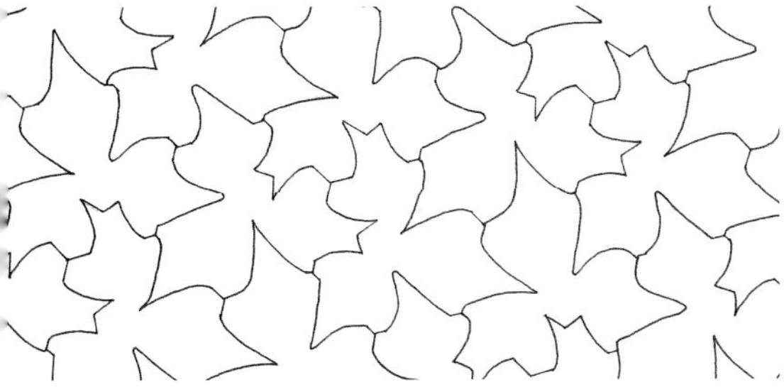

Jakob Kandelsdorfer
Tutor: Christoph Meier

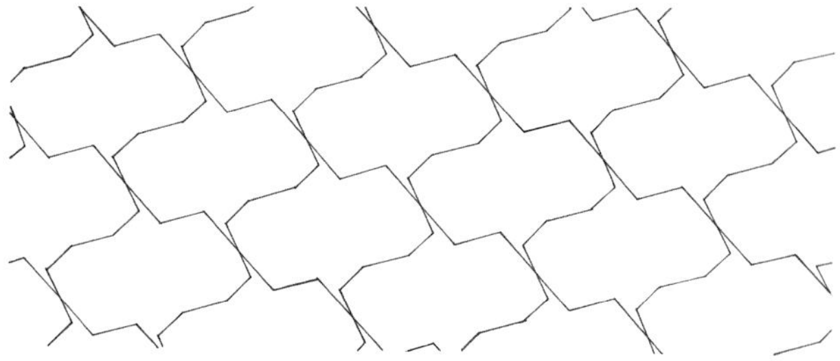

Leonardo Haglmüller
Tutor: Christian Kern

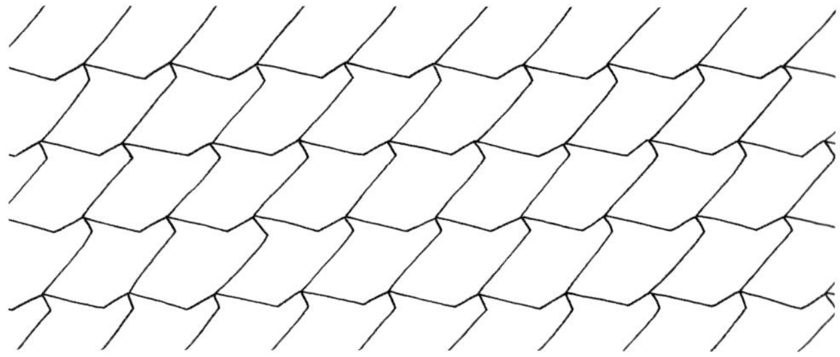

Michael Robert Jimenez
Tutor: Christian Kern

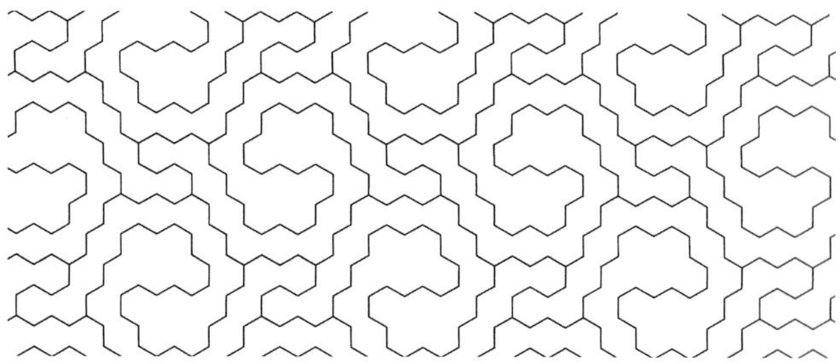

Eunice Gomes Alexandre
Tutor: Fridolin Welte

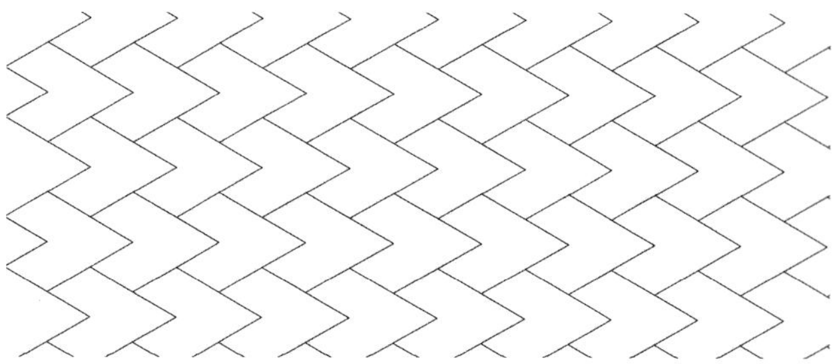

Sarah Bochis
Tutor: Fridolin Welte

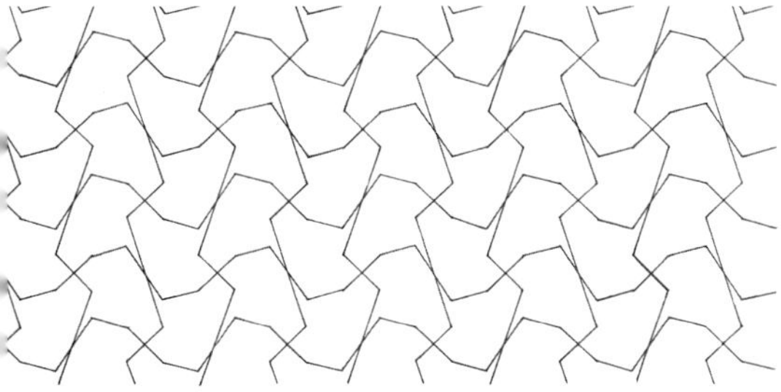

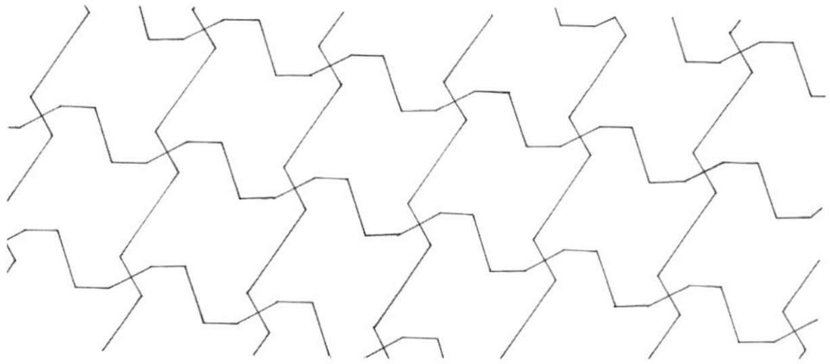

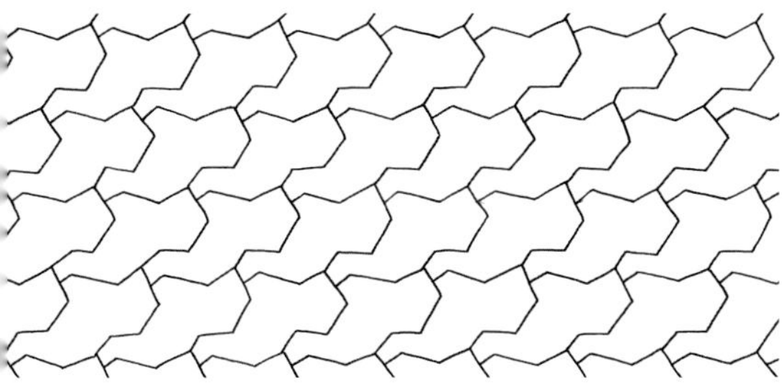

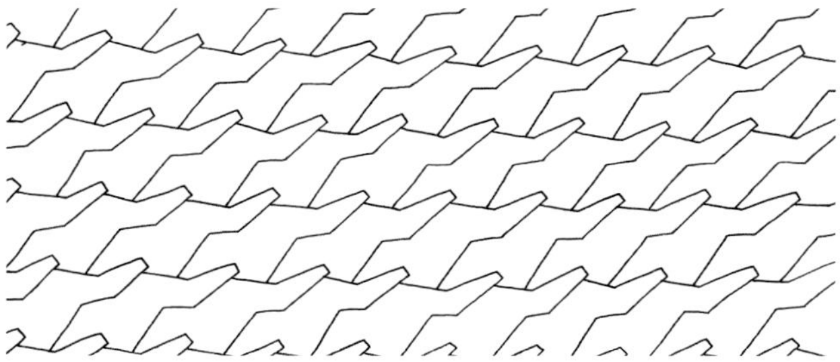

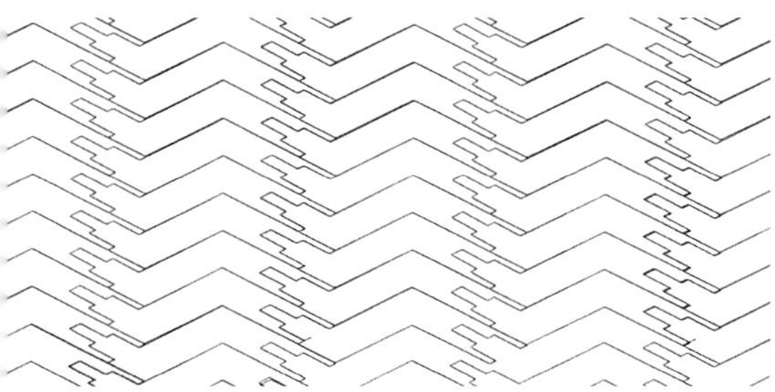

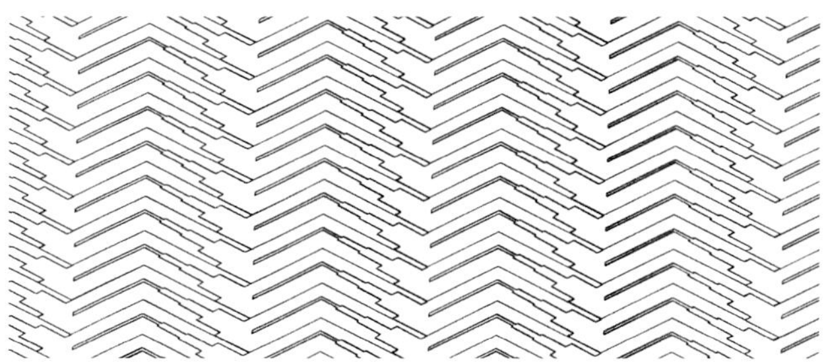

Sarah Bochis
Tutor: Fridolin Welte

Noura Omar
Tutor: Nora Fröhlich

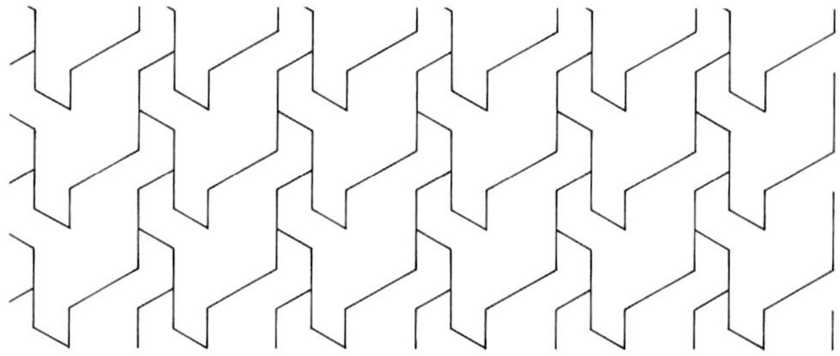

Johanna Himmelbauer
Tutor: Fridolin Welte

Daniel Koller
Tutor: Fridolin Welte

Niklas Hörburger
Tutor: Fridolin Welte

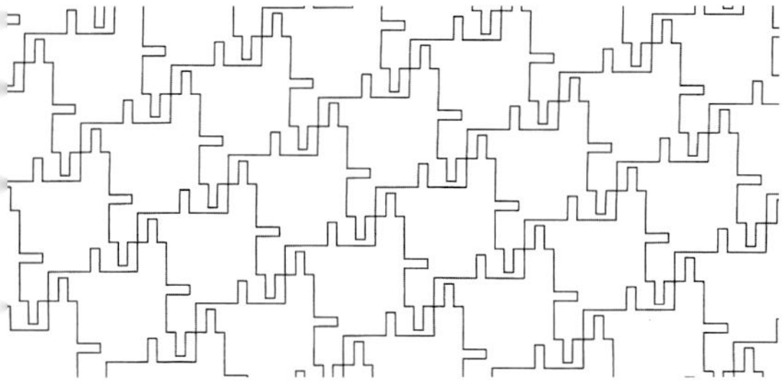

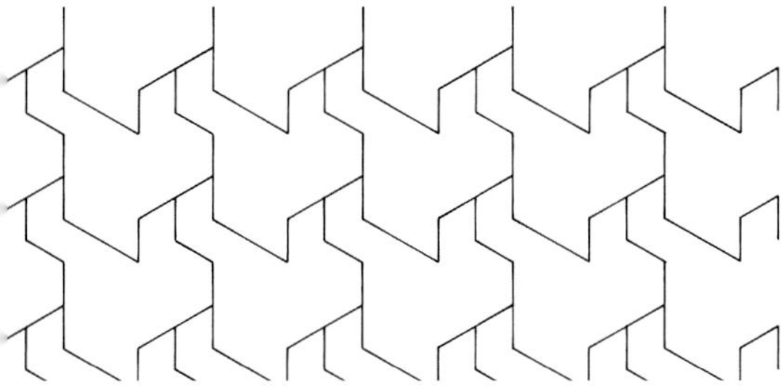

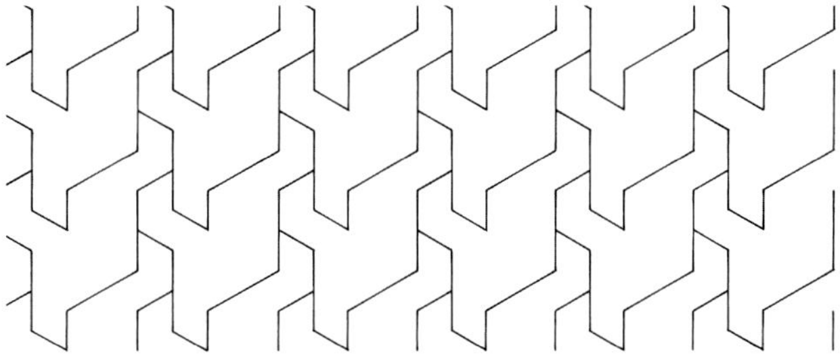

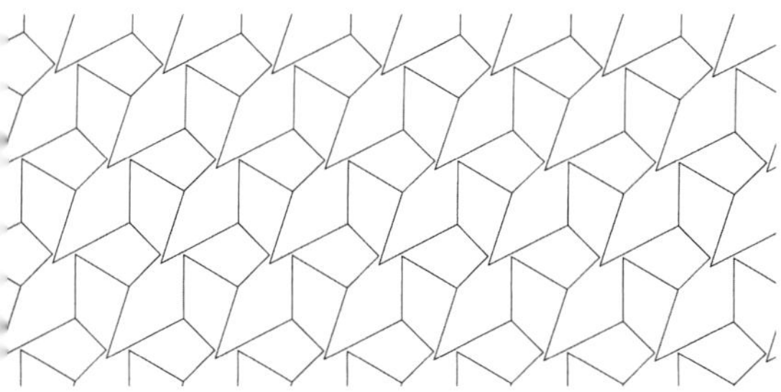

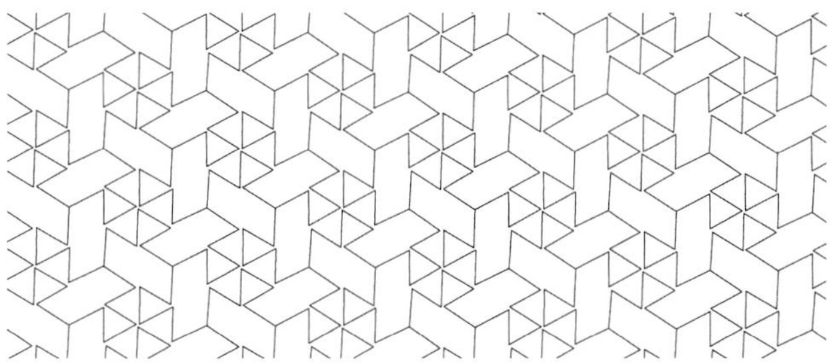

Cinthia Anton
Tutor: Fridolin Welte

Jan Wucherpfennig
Tutor: Fridolin Welte

Ruben Mahler
Tutor: Fridolin Welte

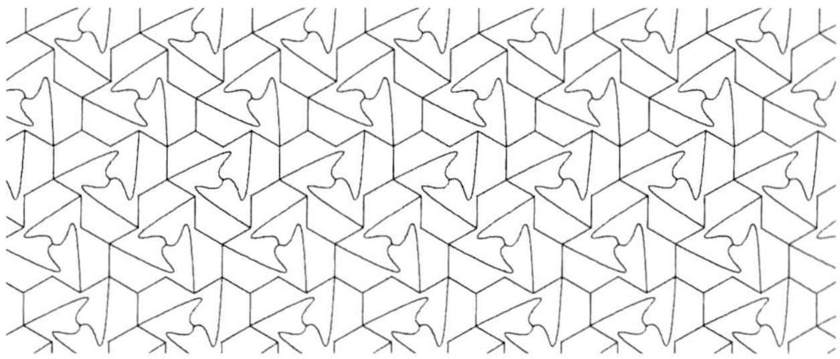

Laurenz Katamay
Tutor: Anita Aigner

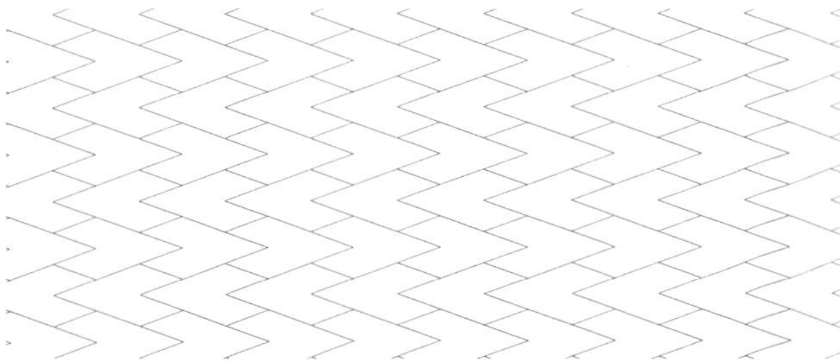

Ye-Ryun Kim
Tutor: Anita Aigner

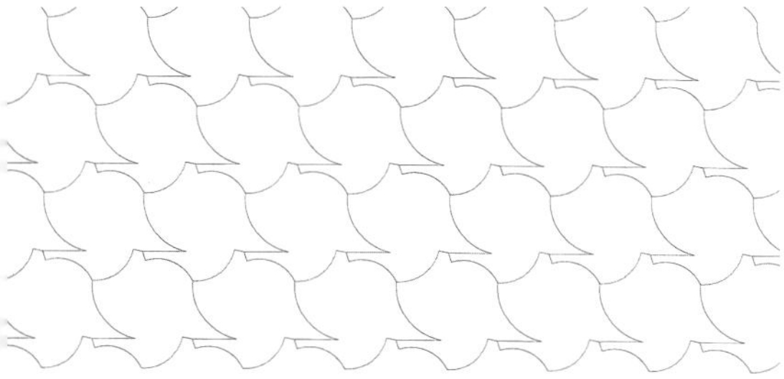
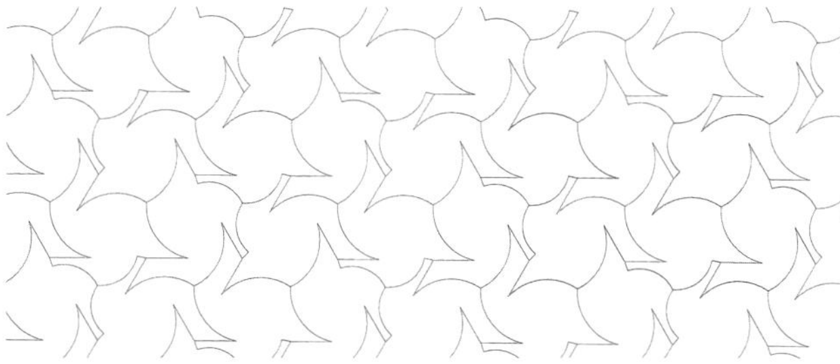

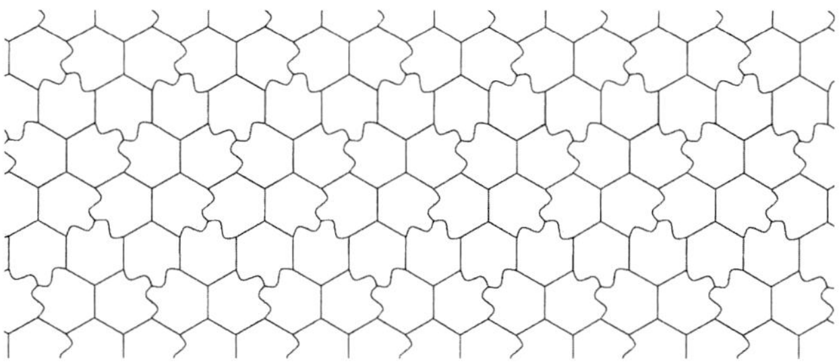

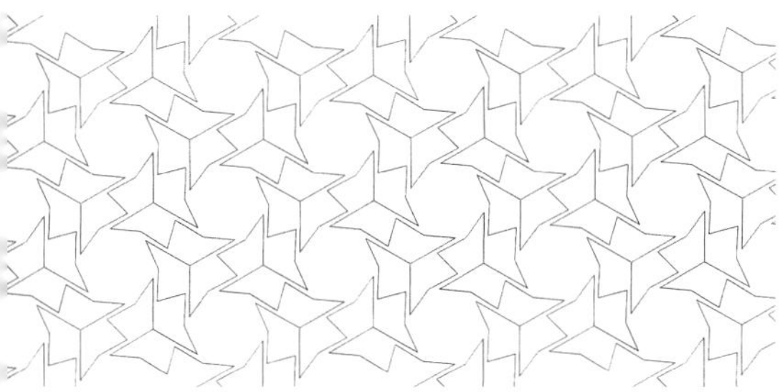

Ye-Ryun Kim
Tutor: Anita Aigner

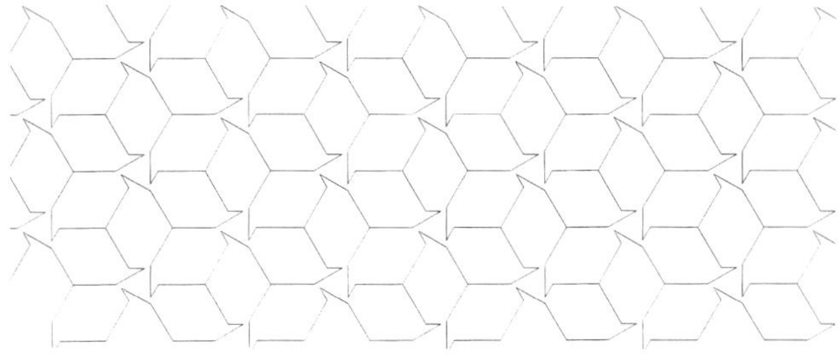

Ye-Ryun Kim
Tutor: Anita Aigner

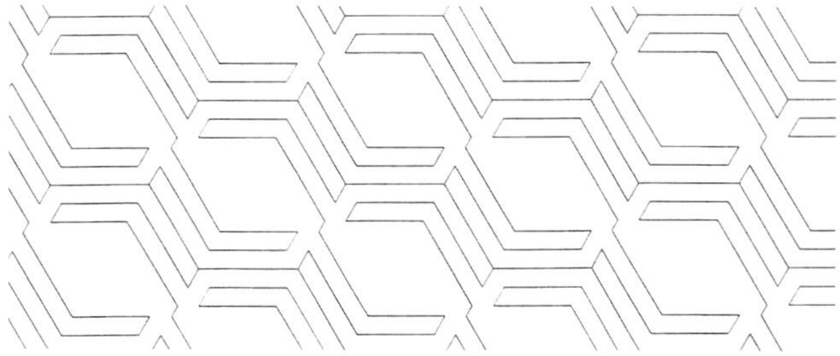

Tobias Dirsch
Tutor: Anita Aigner

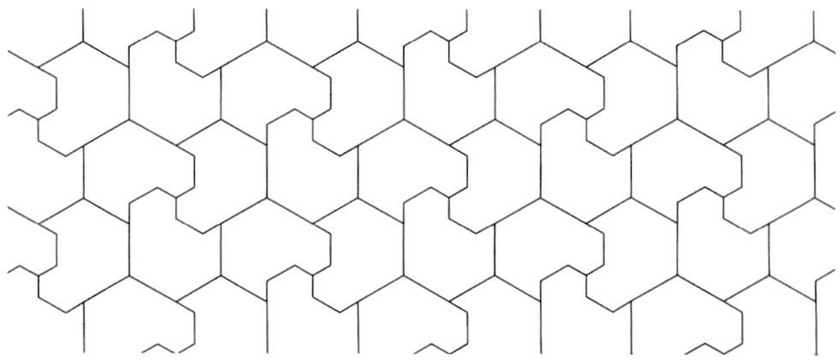

Ceylan Elenor Ergelen
Tutor: Martina Kögl

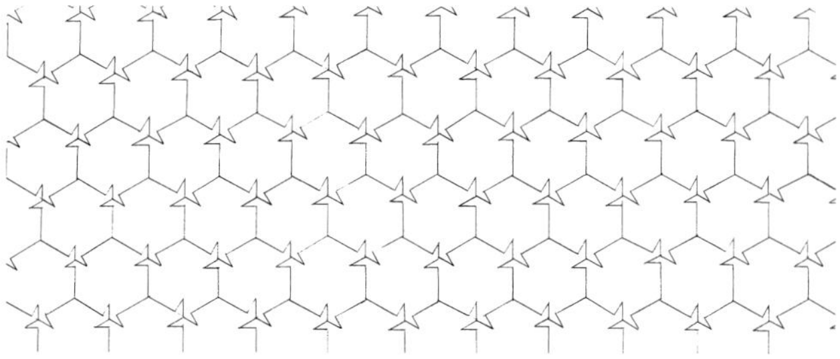

Maximilian Wolfram
Tutor: Anita Aigner

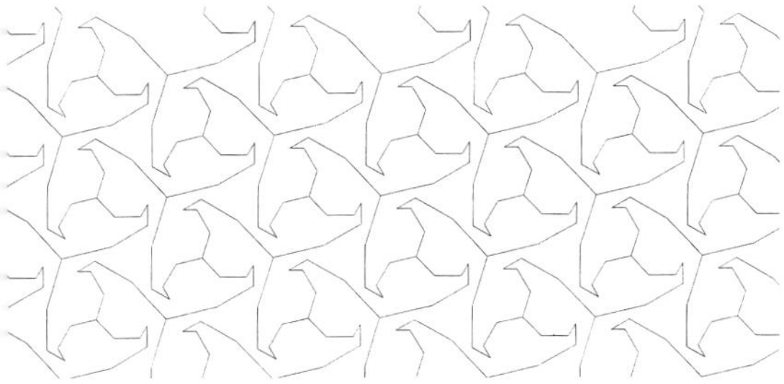
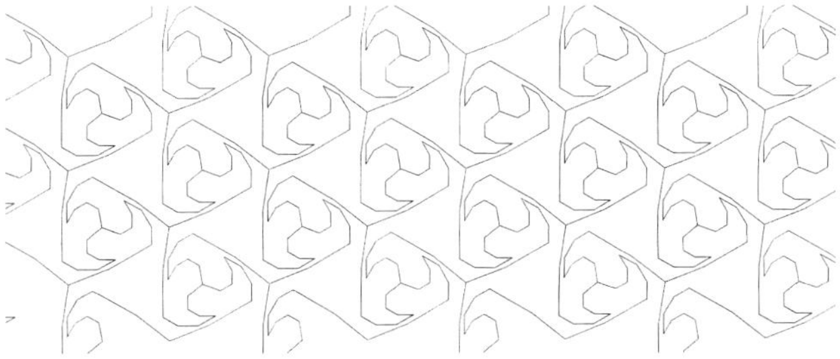

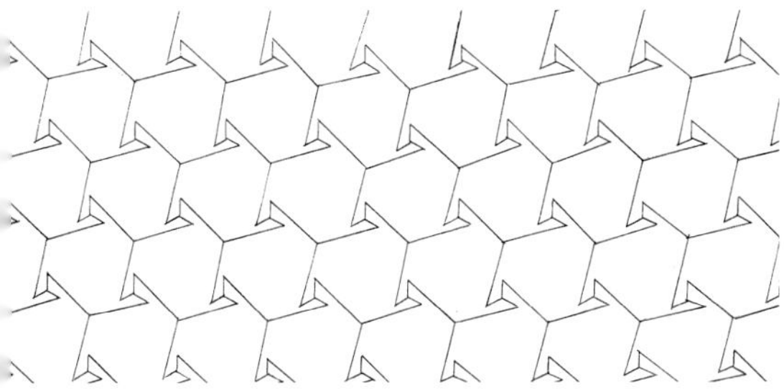
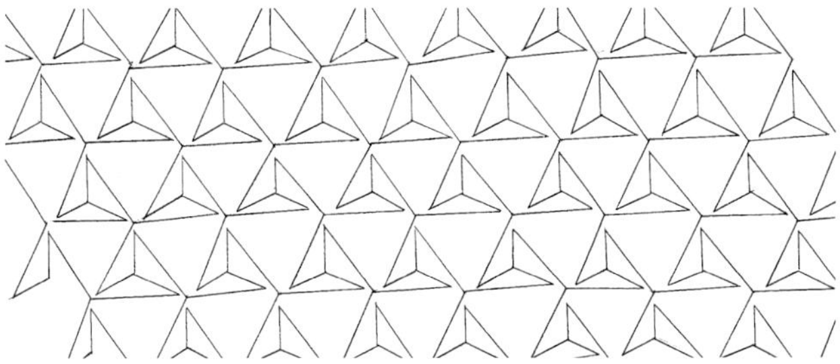

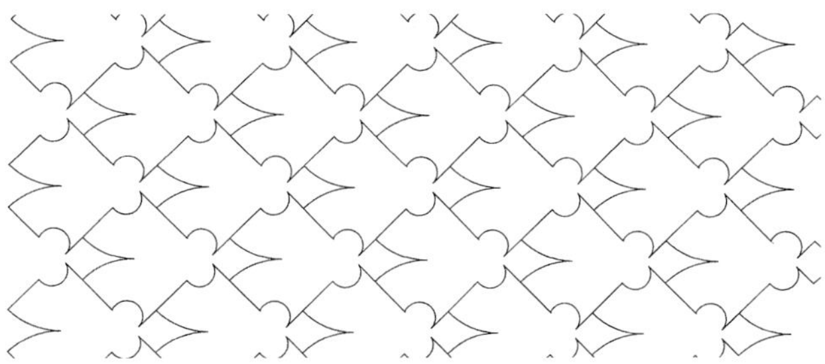

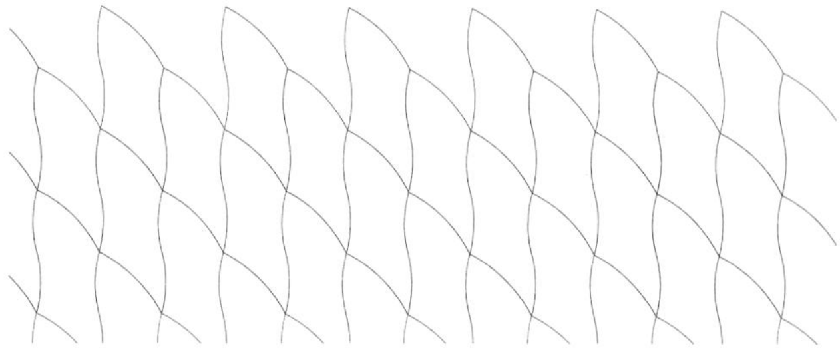

Laura Huber
Tutor: Anita Aigner

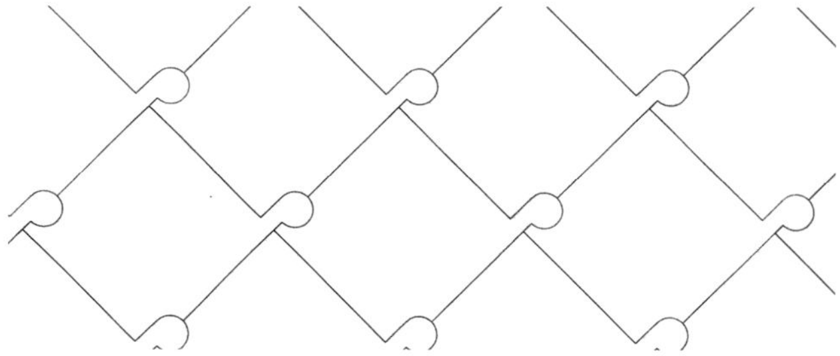

Laura Huber
Tutor: Anita Aigner

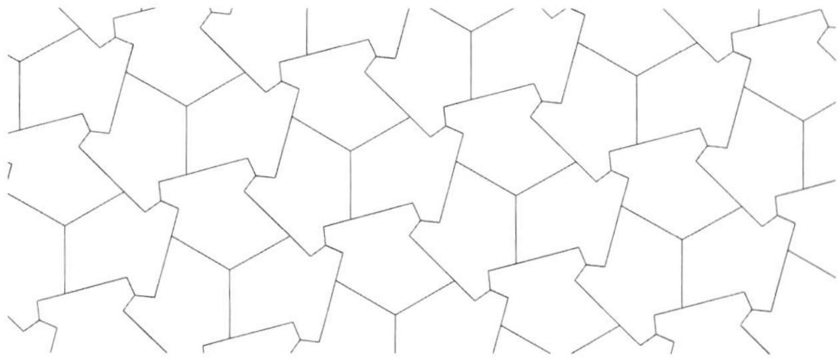

Markus Biel
Tutor: Anita Aigner

Daria Lanina
Tutor: Anita Aigner

Alexander Ladentrog
Tutor: Martina Kögl

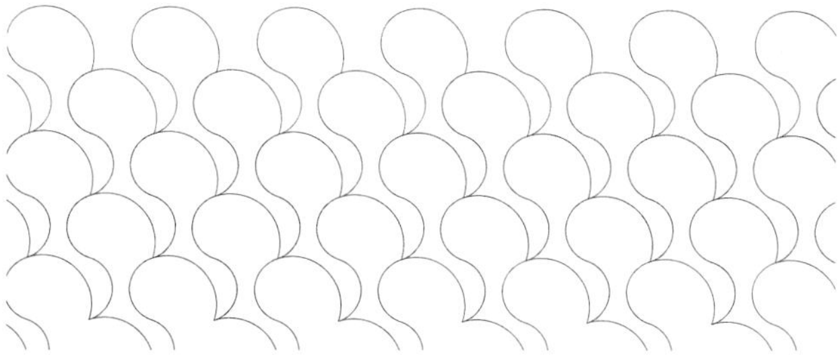
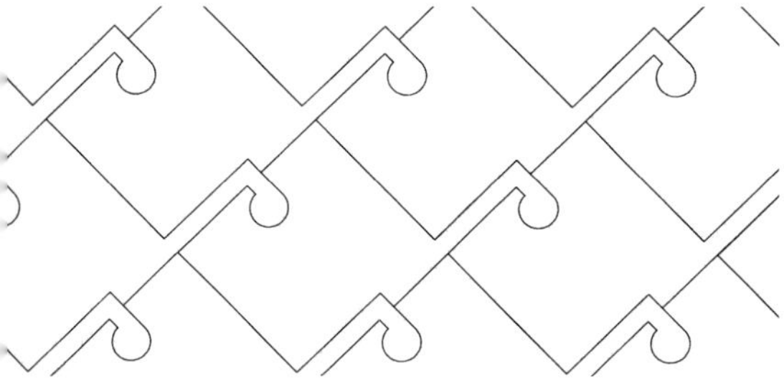

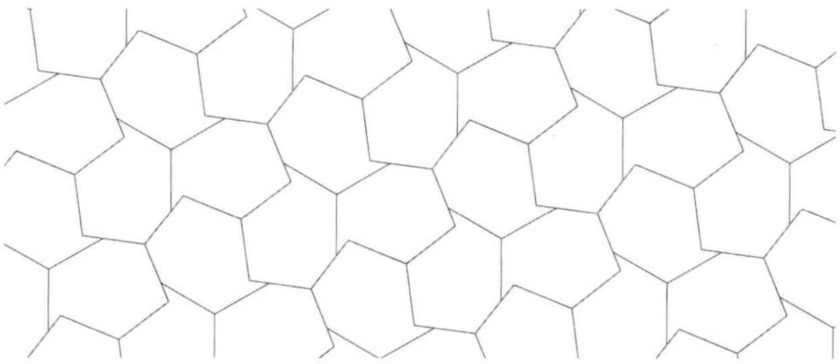
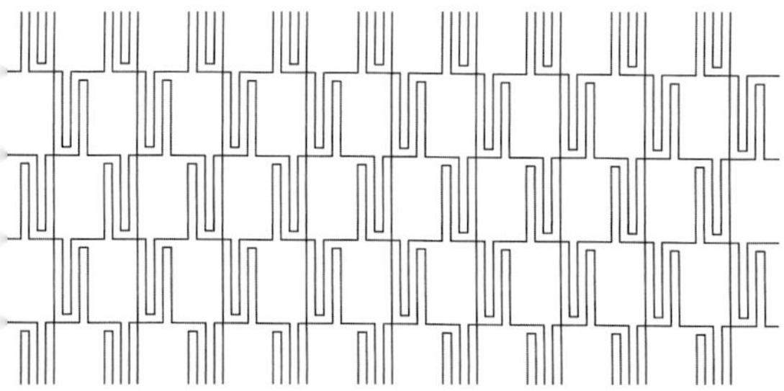
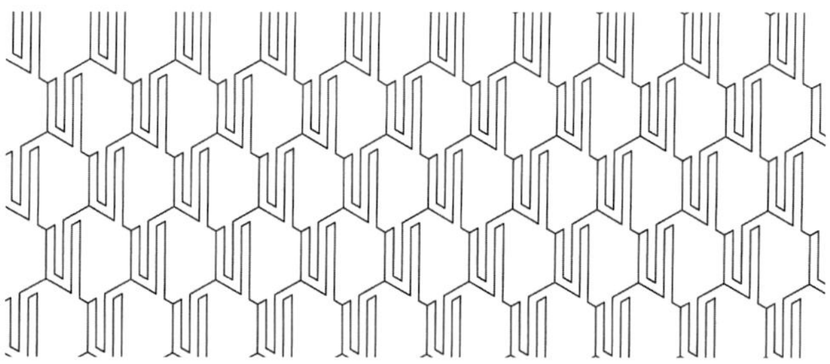

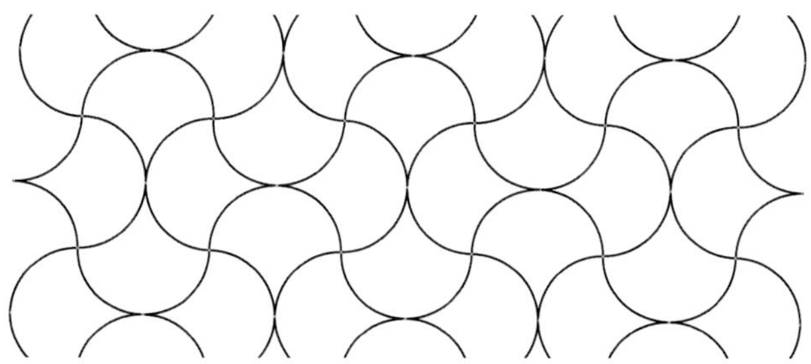

Exercise 1
2D Parquets and 2D Parquet Deformation

2. Continuous Deformation

Within the existing basic structure, the cells could be transformed in one or two directions or even from a center. The considerations of transforming the basic element in Step 1 often already included an approach to "movement" and suggested a stepwise transformation of the individual elements. However, a transition between two (or more) periodic tilings could also be created (i.e., an interpolation between initial patterns).

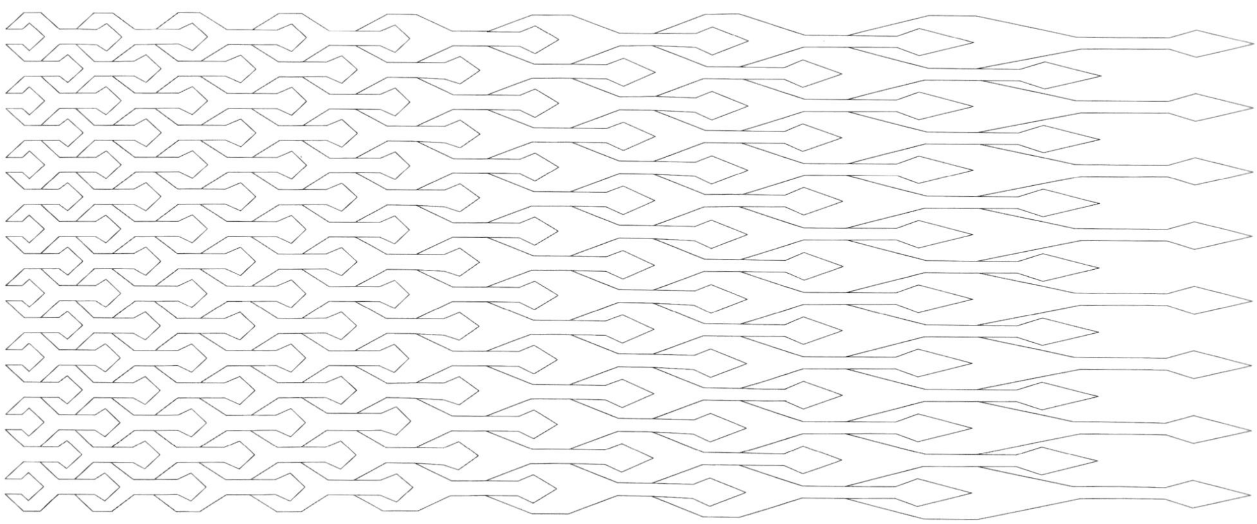

Alexandra Konstantinova
Tutor: Anita Aigner

Leonidas Peithner
Tutor: Anita Aigner

Damjan Veličković
Tutor: Judith P. Fischer

Tobias Speckner
Tutor: Werner Van Hoeydonck

Alexander Keil
Tutor: Anita Aigner

Tobias Dirsch
Tutor: Anita Aigner

Anja Bezjak
Tutor: Christian Kern

Alexandra Konstantinova
Tutor: Anita Aigner

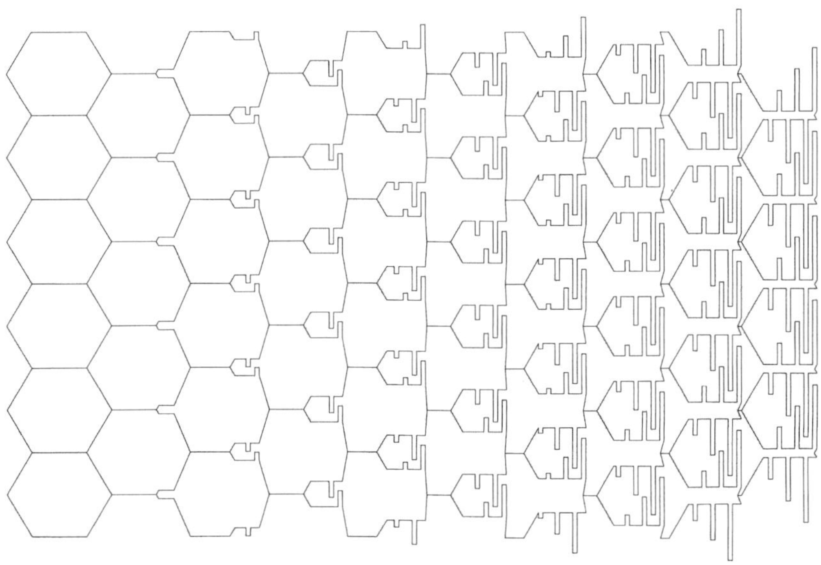

Ye-Ryun Kim
Tutor: Anita Aigner

Theresa Thaler
Tutor: Peter G. Auer

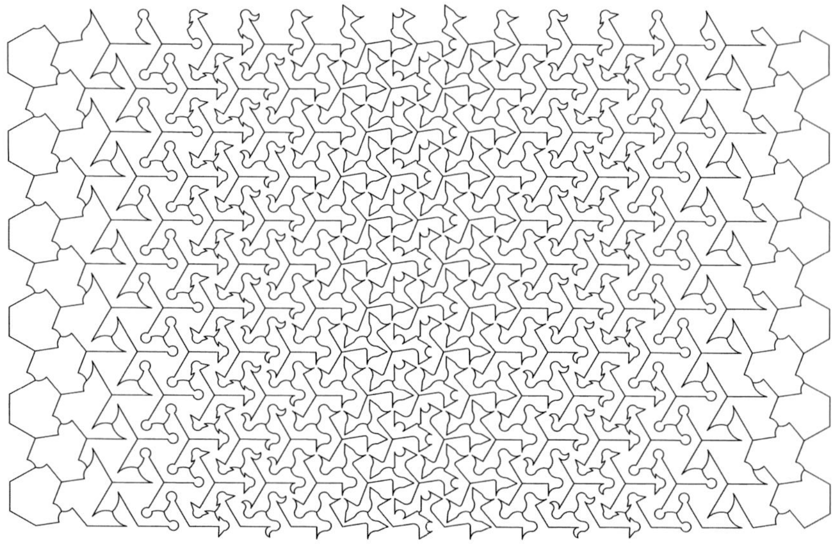

Karlo Keca
Tutor: Peter G. Auer

Sana Halimovic
Tutor: Manuela Fritz

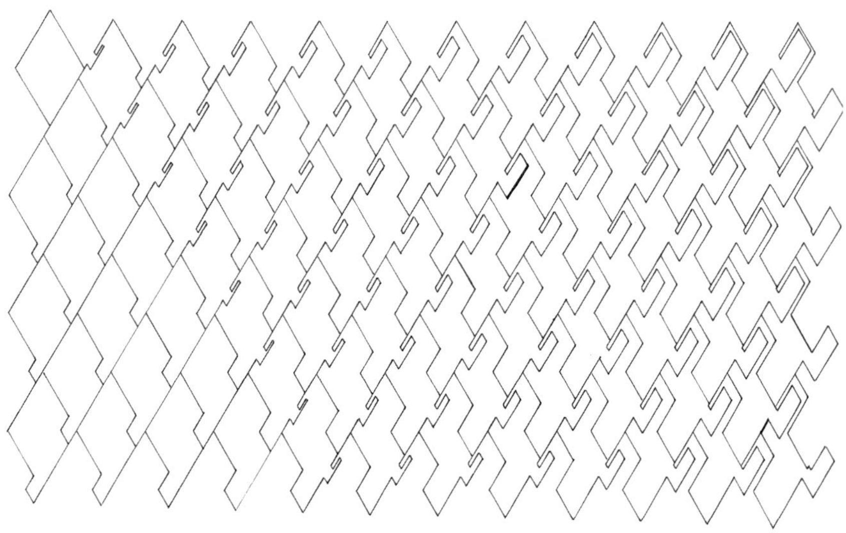

Merve Vural
Tutor: Peter G. Auer

Moira Ruppert
Tutor: Fridolin Welte

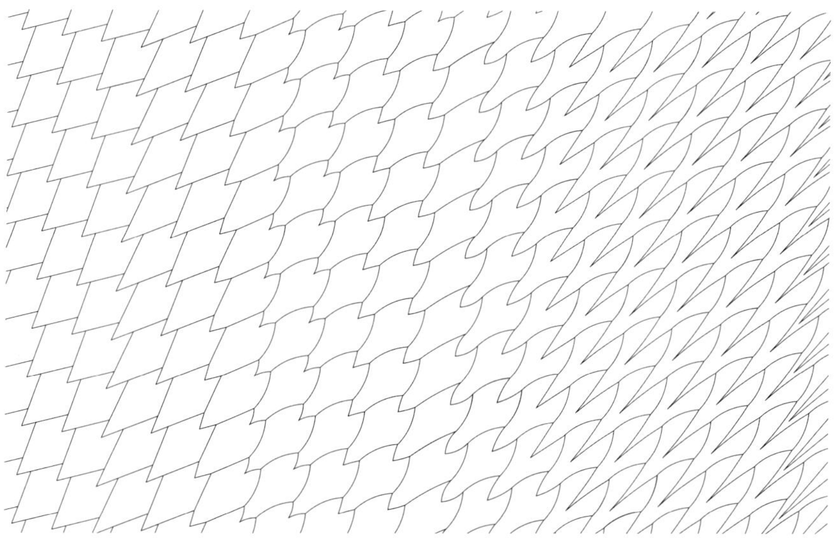

Mahir Kurtalić
Tutor: Christoph Meier

Christian Mitschdörfer
Tutor: Judith P. Fischer

Valentina König
Tutor: Fridolin Welte

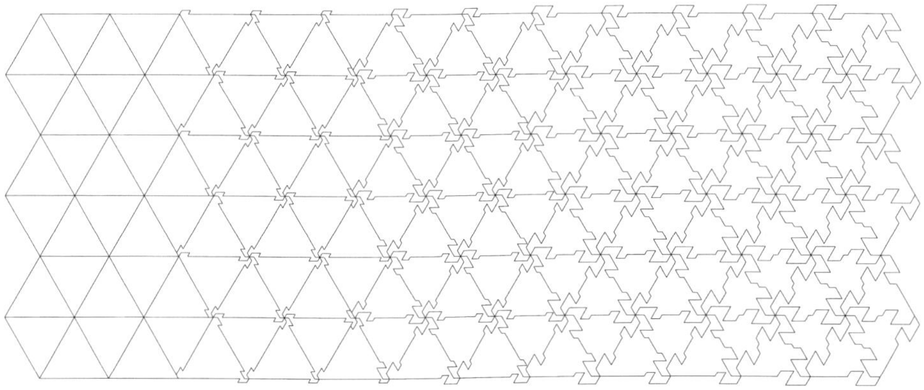

Roman Morozow
Tutor: Manuela Fritz

Chiara Huf
Tutor: Martina Kögl

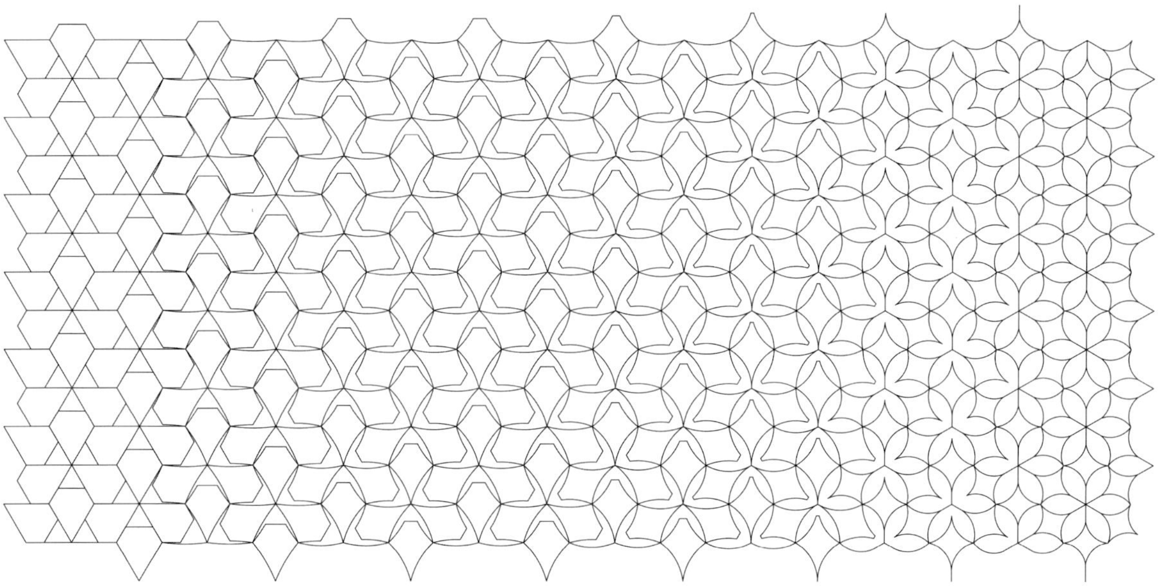

Andreas Frank
Tutor: Werner Van Hoeydonck

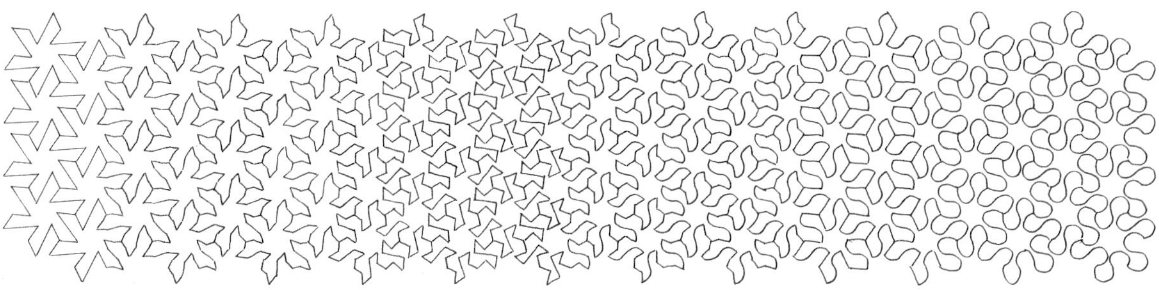

Damjan Veličković
Tutor: Judith P. Fischer

Christoph Paul Hofmann
Tutor: Anita Aigner

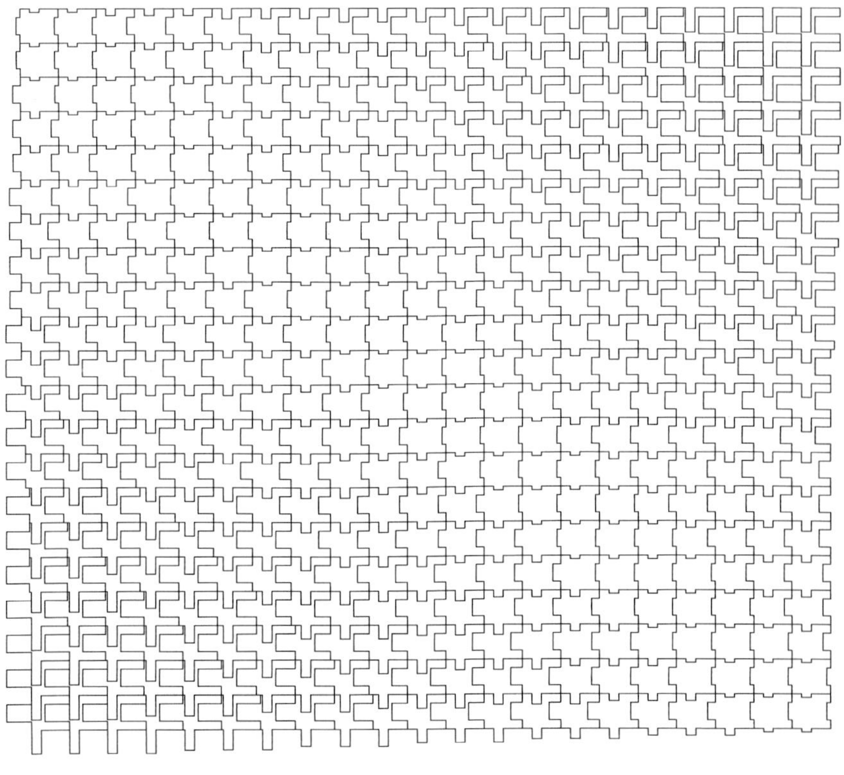

Daria Lanina
Tutor: Anita Aigner

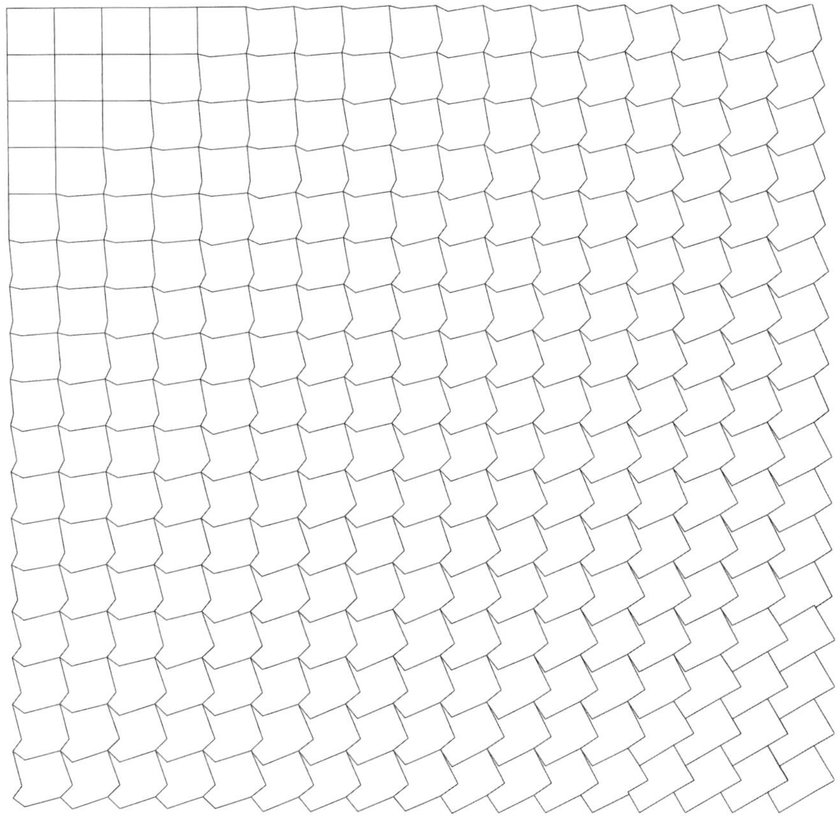

Sarah Reithofer
Tutor: Fridolin Welte

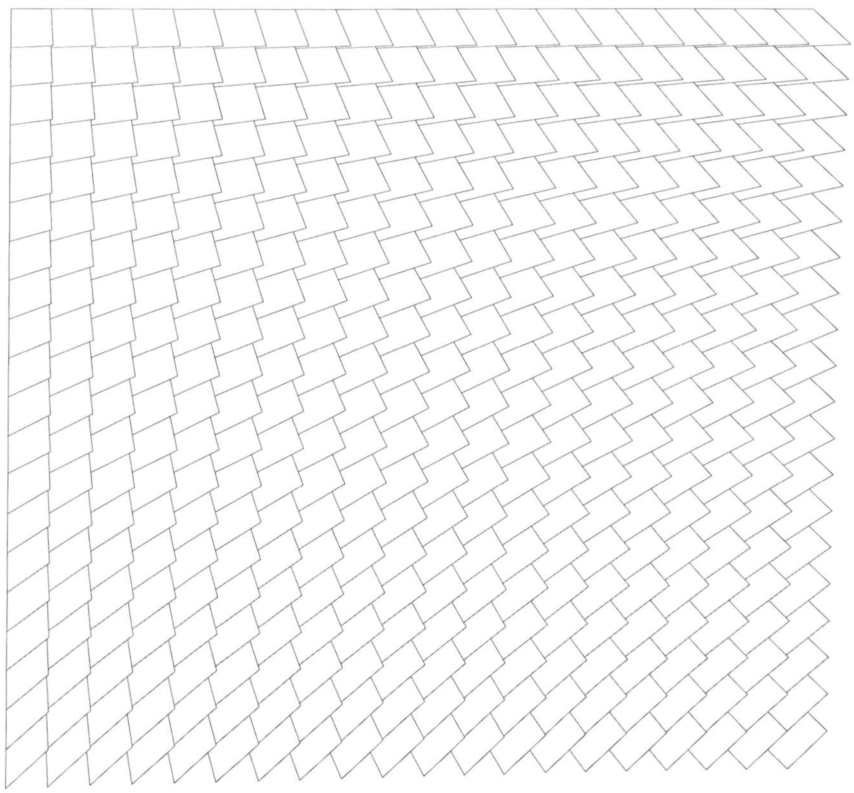

Michael Bachmeier
Tutor: Peter G. Auer

Exercise 1
2D Parquets and 2D Parquet Deformation

3. Deformation of the Basic Structure

A "moving" tiling could also be achieved by transforming the constituent lattice structure. Different possibilities were explored for this purpose.

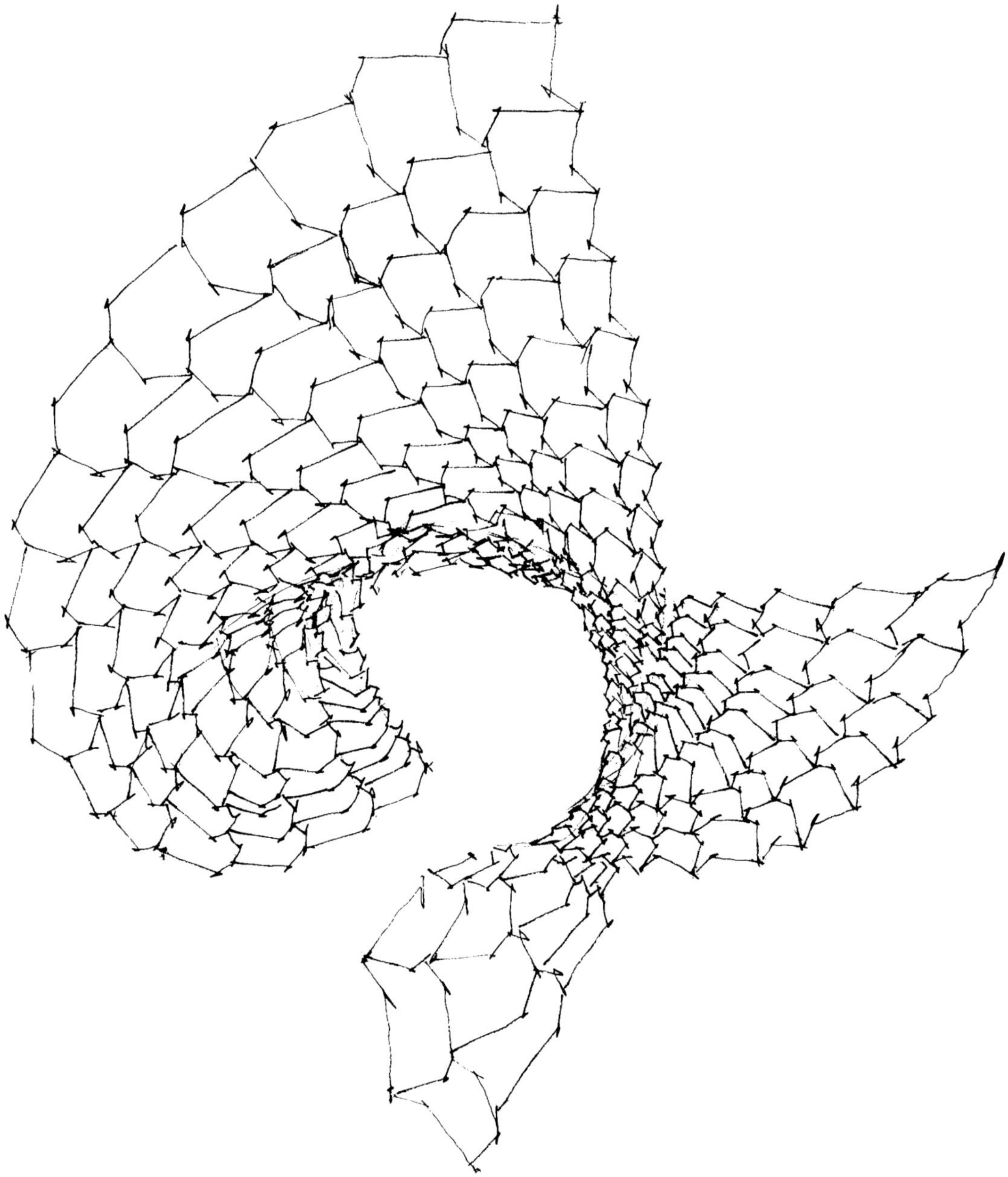

Zorana Sotirov
Tutor: Fridolin Welte

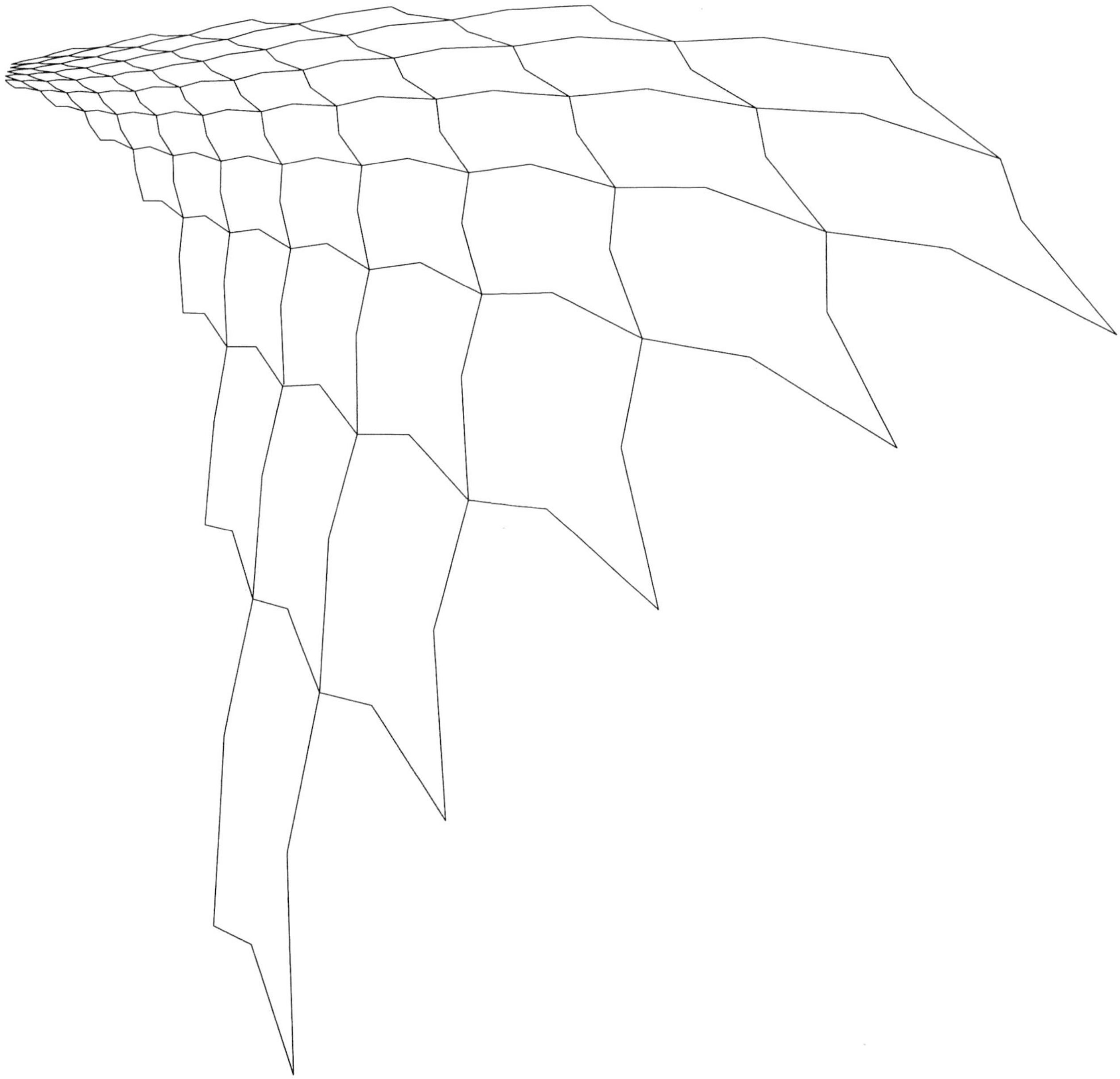

Steffen Alexander Blickle
Tutor: Fridolin Welte

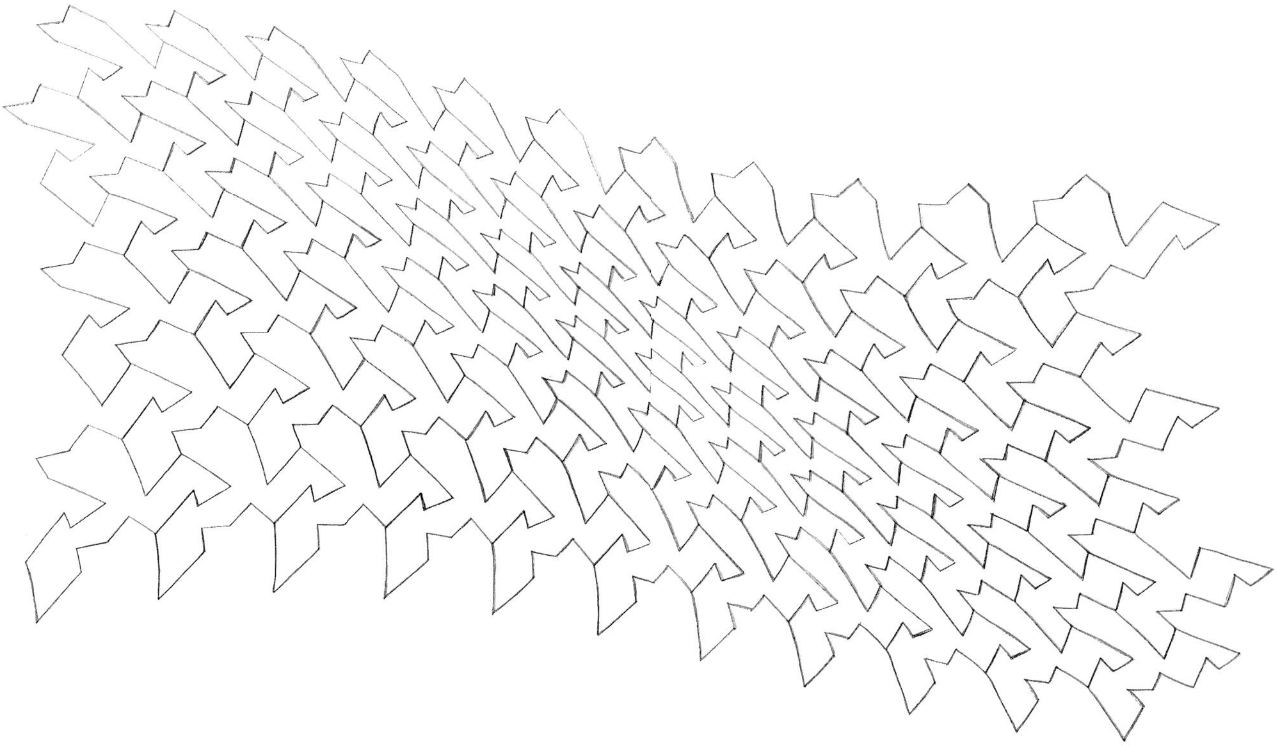

Susanne Stampf
Tutor: Markus Bauer

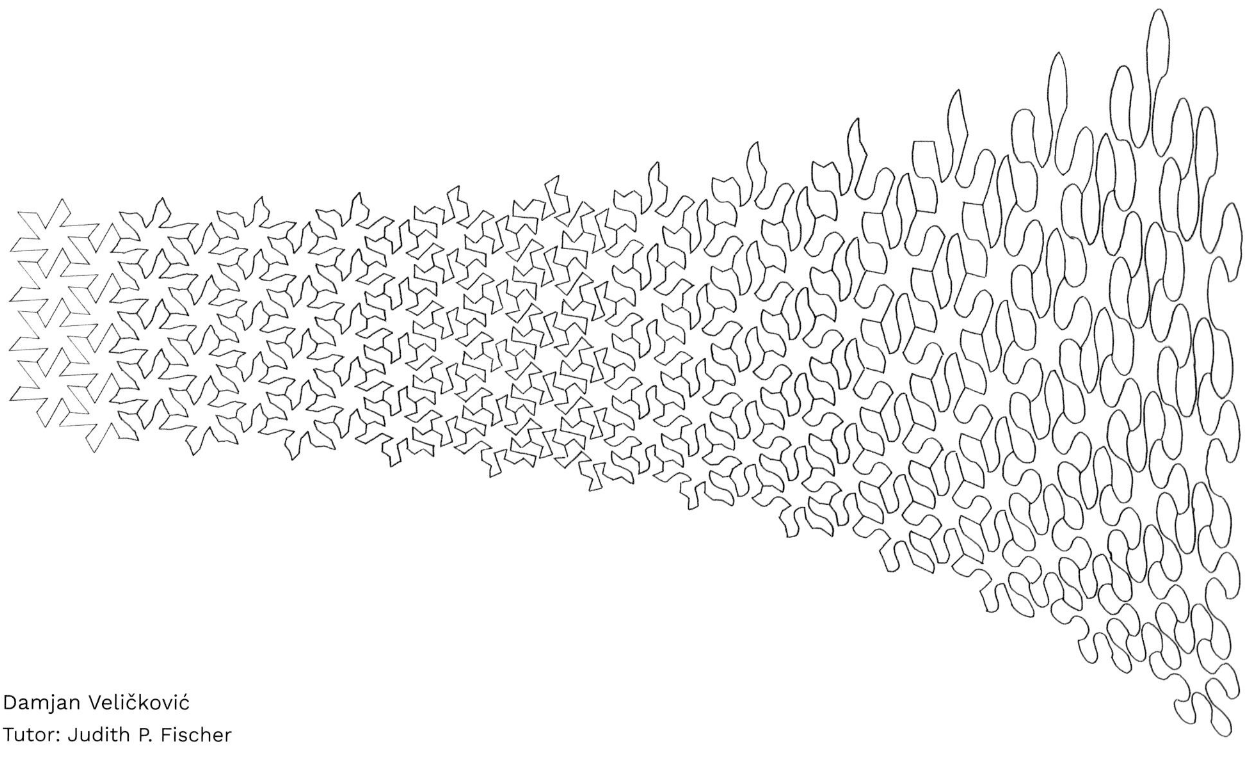

Damjan Veličković
Tutor: Judith P. Fischer

Andrea Di Tommaso
Tutor: Peter G. Auer

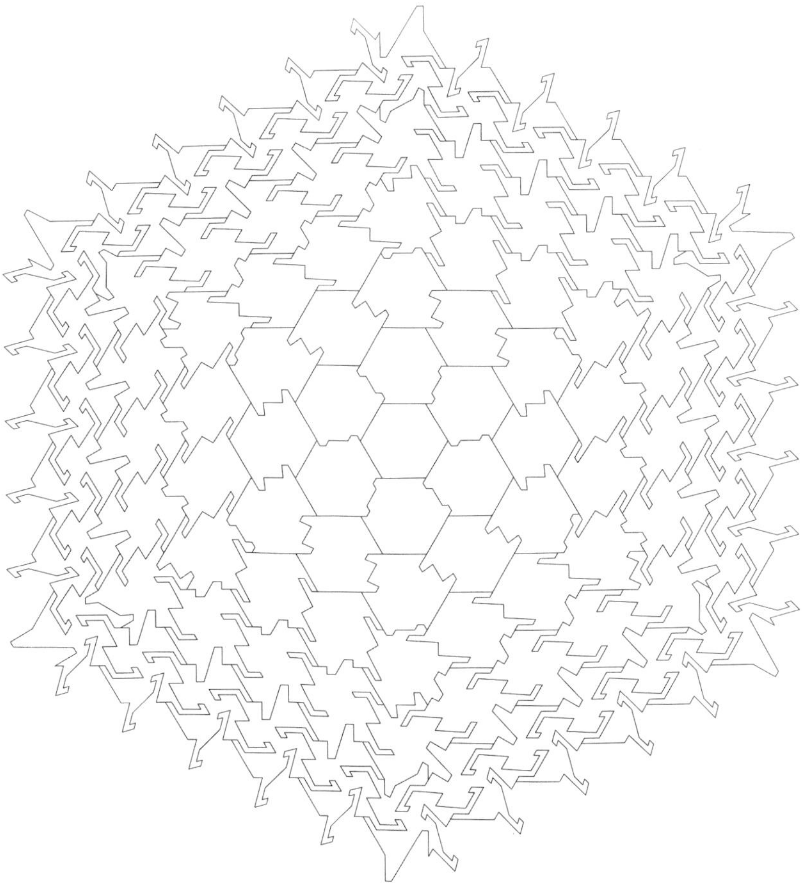

Ye-Ryun Kim
Tutor: Anita Aigner

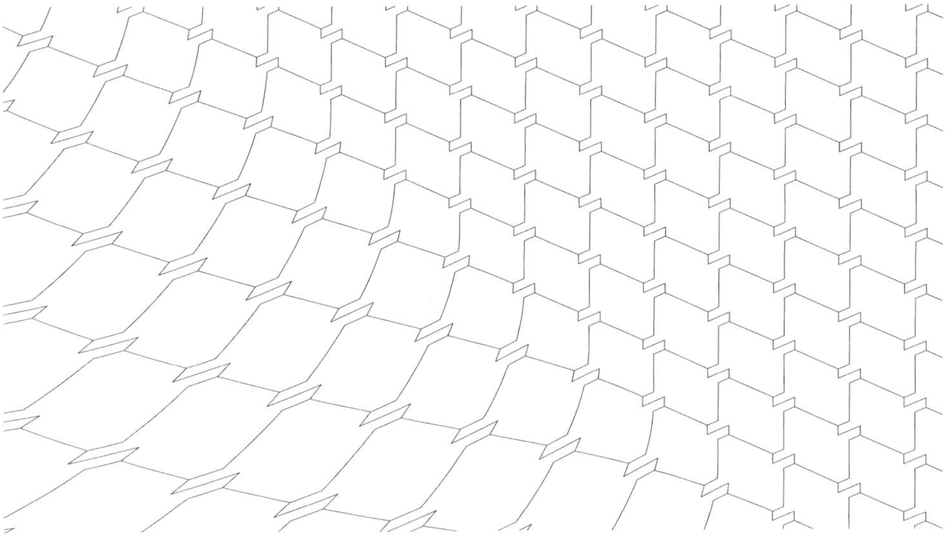

Mehmet Semih Özcelik
Tutor: Martina Kögl

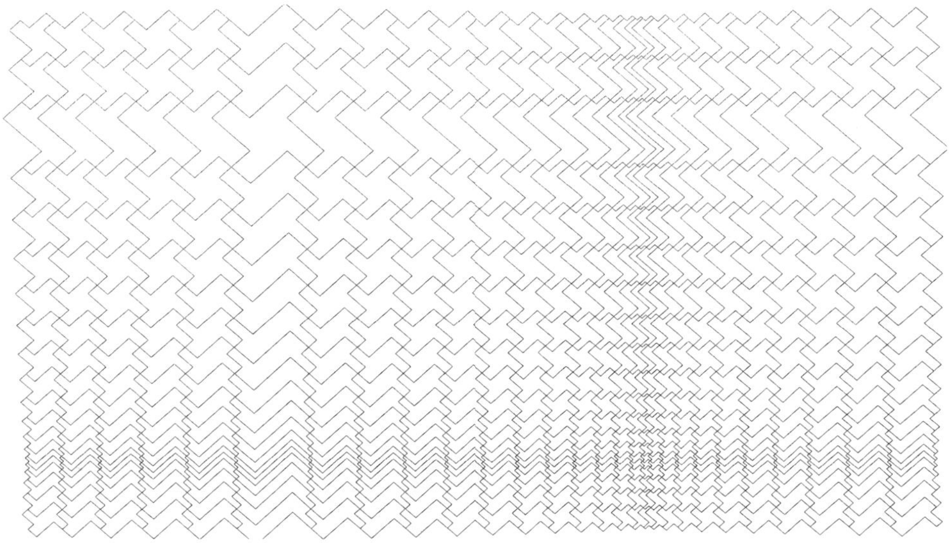

Samuel Huber-Huber
Tutor: Peter G. Auer

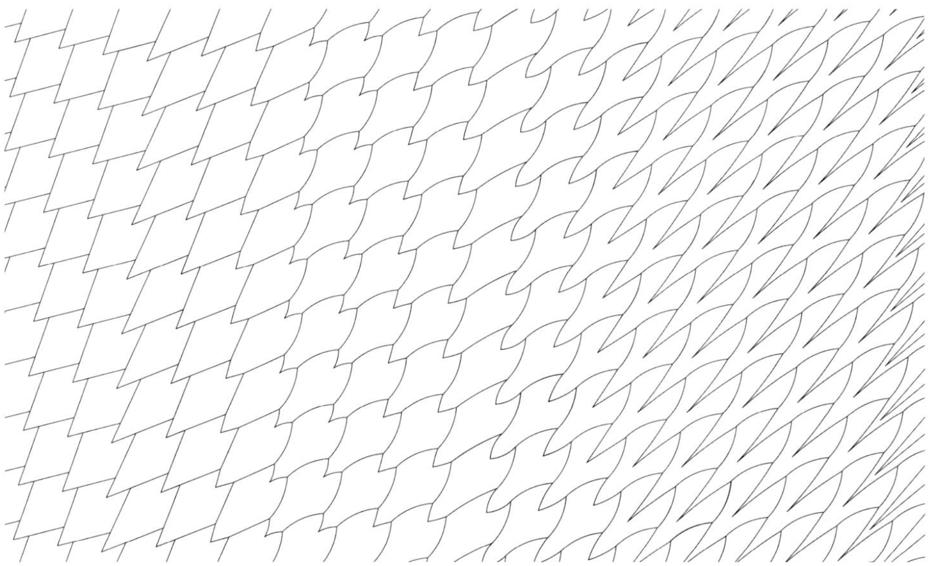

Mahir Kurtalić
Tutor: Christoph Meier

Karlo Keca
Tutor: Peter G. Auer

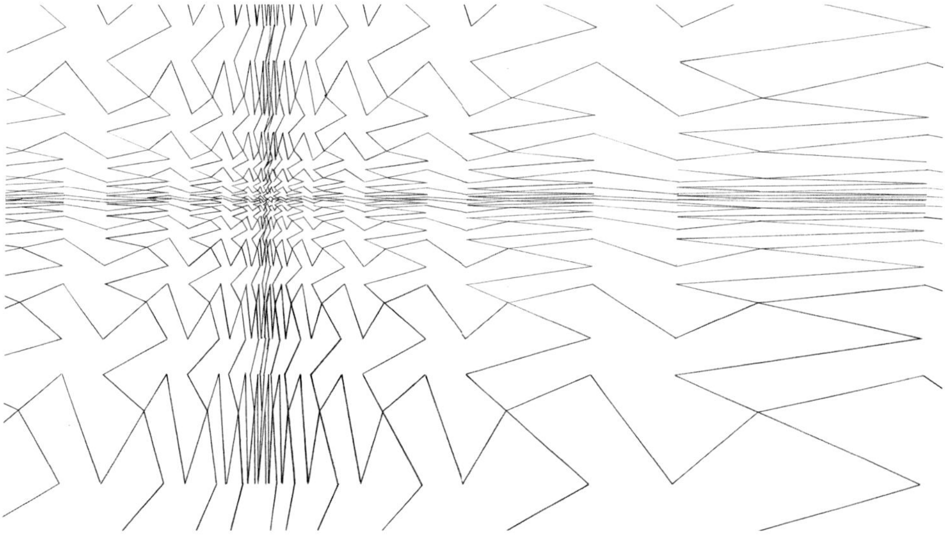

Patrik Marchhart
Tutor: Christoph Meier

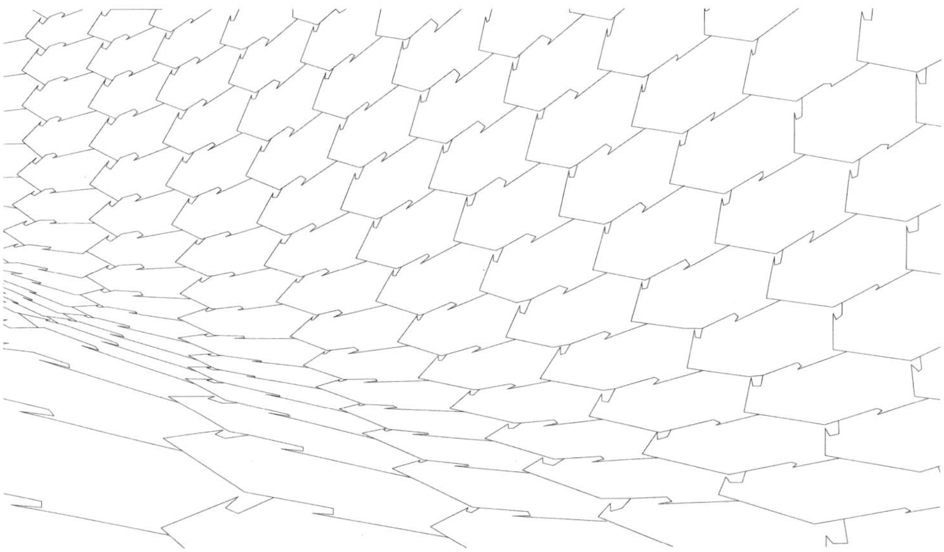

Roman Morozov
Tutor: Manuela Fritz

Claudia Pitterle
Tutor: Manuela Fritz

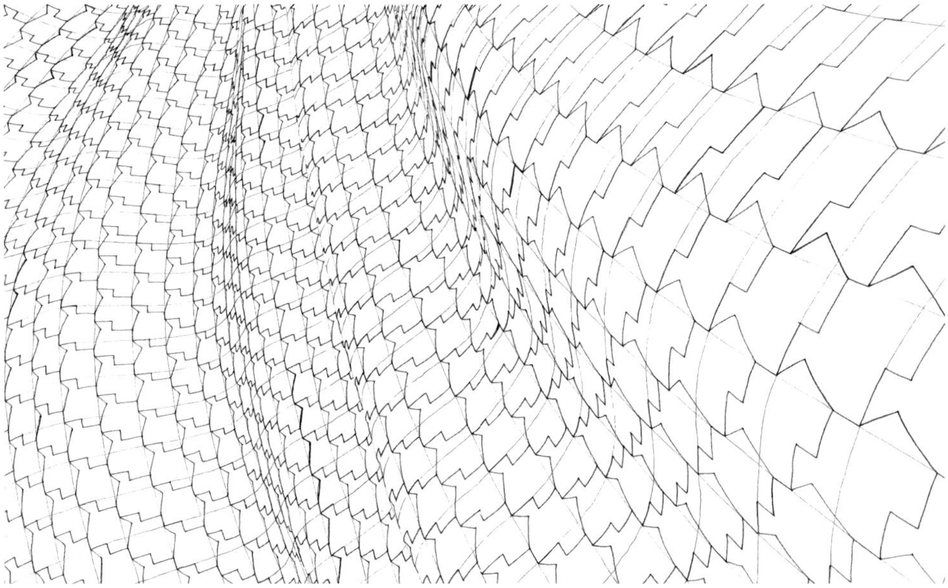

Anja Bezjak
Tutor: Christian Kern

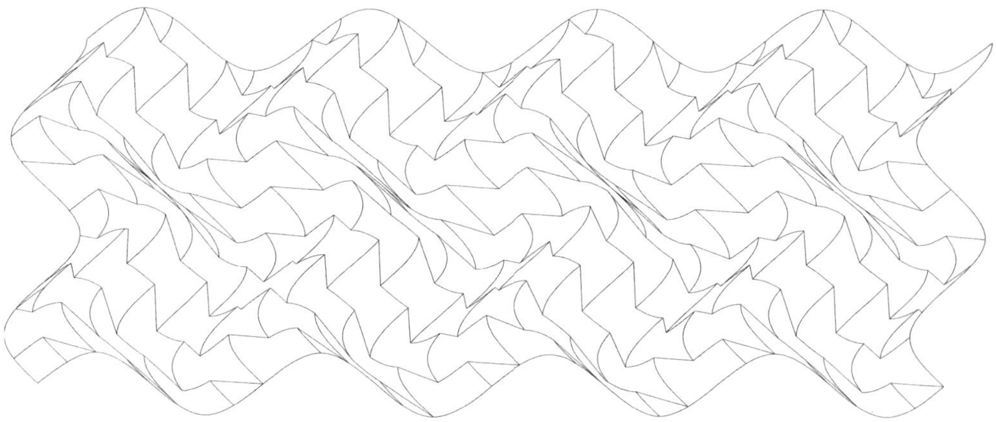

Isa Kirchberger
Tutor: Peter G. Auer

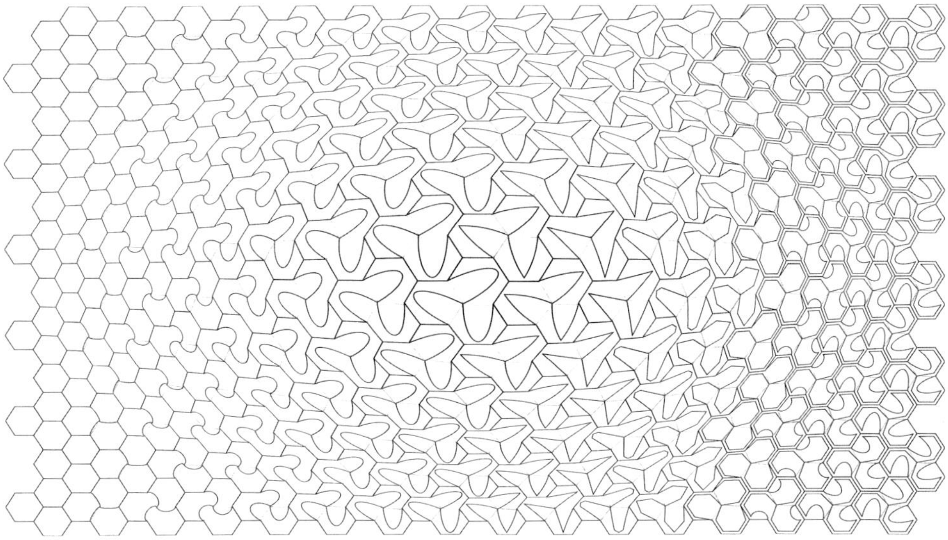

Sacha De Simony
Tutor: Fridolin Welte

Christian Mitschdörfer
Tutor: Judith P. Fischer

Michael Haidinger
Tutor: Christian Kern

Exercise 2
3D Parquets and 3D Parquet Deformation

The study of tiling and parquet deformation was then continued in three-dimensional space. For this purpose, simple polyhedral (e.g., cube, triangular and hexagonal prism, twisted double wedge (gyrobifastigium), truncated octahedron, rhombic dodecahedron) and the spatial lattice structures based on them were assumed. As in Exercise 1, the initial cell was to be transformed first, followed by the entire packing (periodic space filling). This exercise was divided into three steps:

1. Transformation of the Basic Element (Polyhedron)

The shape of the initial cell was changed to create a penetration-free and gapless 3D-tiling of new, congruent (proto)space cells. The reshaping could be of varying complexity (i.e., in one, two, or three directions) and could be brought about by different operations (e.g., bending in or out, dividing, subdividing). Space fillings based on two protocells were also allowed. Enough cells should be generated to occupy the aggregation of the transformed protocell, and the combination possibilities could be investigated.

2. Deformation of the 3D Space-Filling Structure

In the second step, a 3D space-filling structure consisting of the same elements was continuously deformed (at least in one direction, possibly also starting from a center). For this purpose, rules for a continuous transformation had to be established, and consideration had to be given to which surfaces, lines, or points could be "moved" or displaced step by step. Different variants and construction methods were experimented with. A transformation of the constituent spatial grid structure was also possible.

3. Representation/Mode of Construction

Transformed basic elements could be represented, for example, as a sheath unwrapped from cardboard or as a mass model (e.g., XPS/extruded rigid polystyrene foam). However, since a "closed" stacking of solids consisting of massive volumes cannot be viewed, the representation of 3D lattice structures as a rod model was recommended. In addition, alternation of empty space and mass volumes or, in the case of aggregations based on two protocells, representation of only one group of cells should be considered.

Exercise 3
Design Concept

The third exercise step was to develop a form study based on 3D parquet deformation. The design was to be developed from previous studies, a completely new approach was also allowed.

Concept

It was essential that the design was based on a content-related idea, a design concept. It had to be possible to name the concept in the design of the 3D parquet deformation. The concept could be the representation of a movement process, a certain theme or image (e.g., interlocking, growing out of a cell), or an abstract, mathematical-geometric rule or code. A central requirement was that the monotony of a 3D parquetry was broken up. The element of deformation or transformation should also have a visible effect (i.e., not be a minor matter).

Composition

The 3D parquet deformation, which was in principle infinite, had to be limited according to compositional aspects. Depending on the design approach, longitudinally aligned compositions, cubically framed compositions, or compositions organized from a center were conceivable. The elements should be balanced in number and size (not too small, not too large) and above all help to express the conceptual idea. Visually incomprehensible deformations or unintelligible aggregations were to be avoided. In this respect, the construction (representation of edges, surfaces, or volumes) was also an essential component of compositional considerations. The form study was to be conceived as all-view; that is, it was not to be designed for one main viewpoint but had to be attractive from all sides. Different spatial positions and presentation possibilities (e.g., plinths) were to be explored, as they are part of the composition and should be proportioned and designed in relation to the object. The dimensioning of the form study was free, but the dimension 24 × 24 × 24+n cm was considered as an orientation for the composition space.

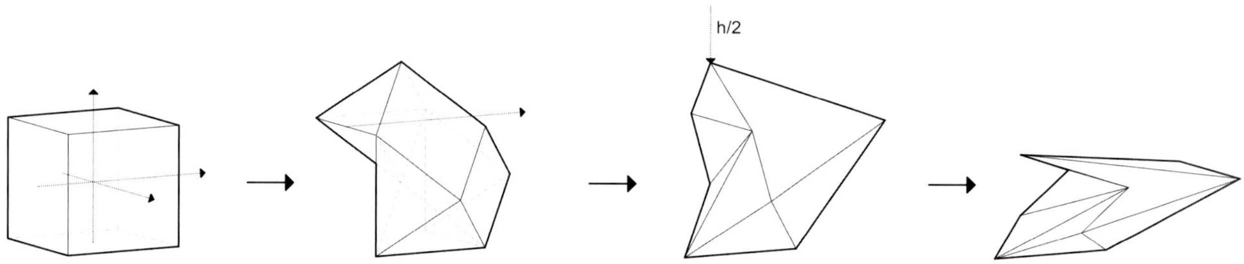

Jennifer Berger
Tutor: Christoph Meier

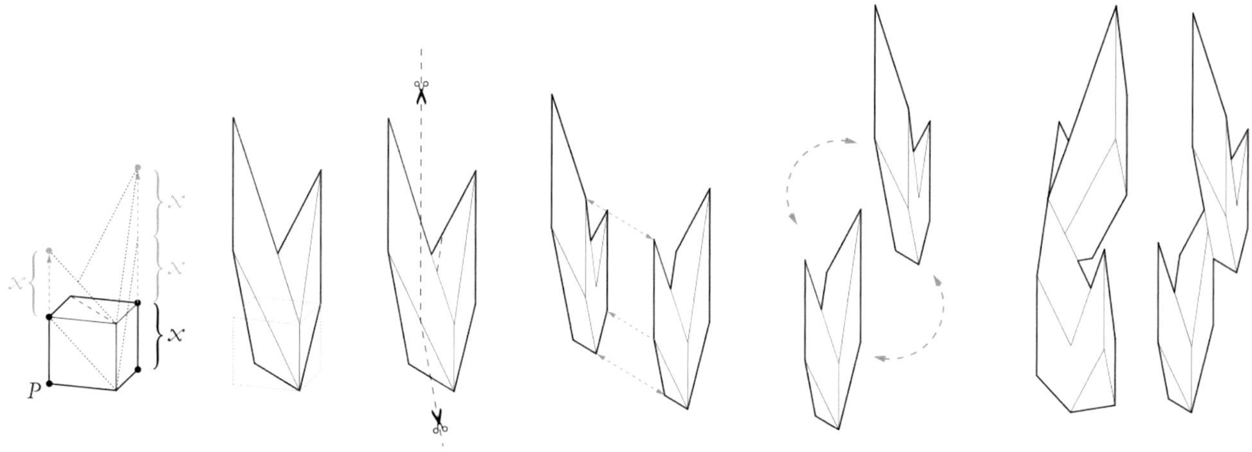

Mahir Kurtalić
Tutor: Christoph Meier

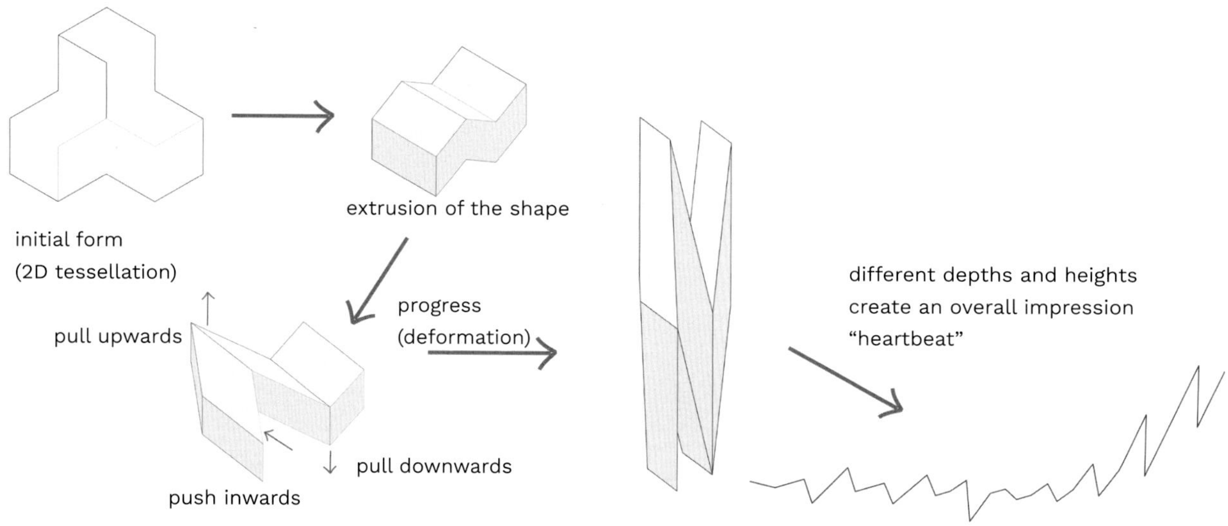

Noura Omar
Tutor: Nora Fröhlich

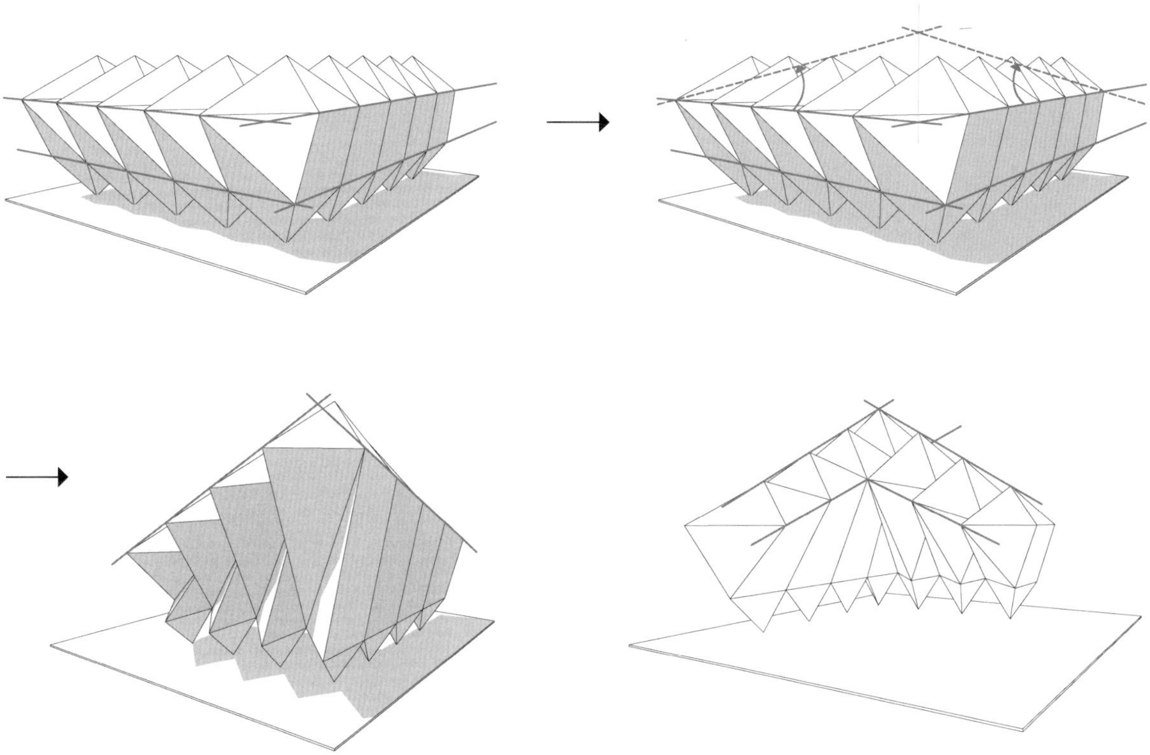

Tobias Speckner
Tutor: Werner Van Hoeydonck

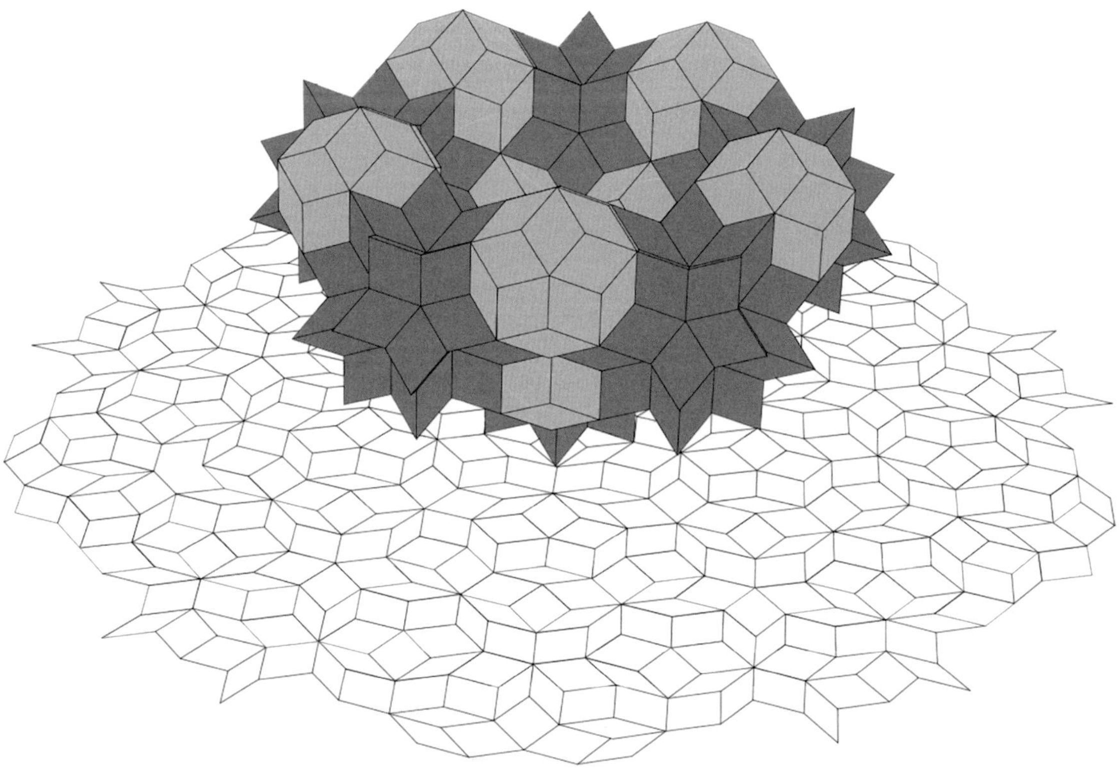

Selma Dervisefendic
Tutor: Werner Van Hoeydonck

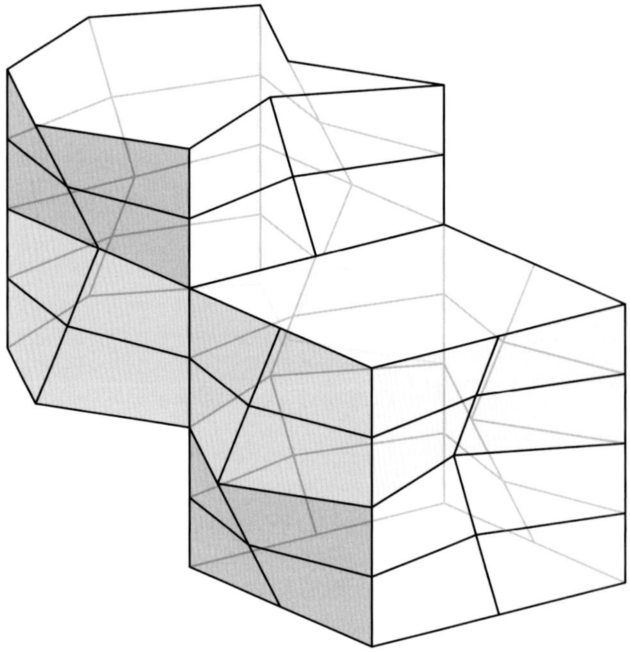

Michael Robert Jimenez
Tutor: Christian Kern

Steliyana Chipeva
Tutor: Manuela Fritz

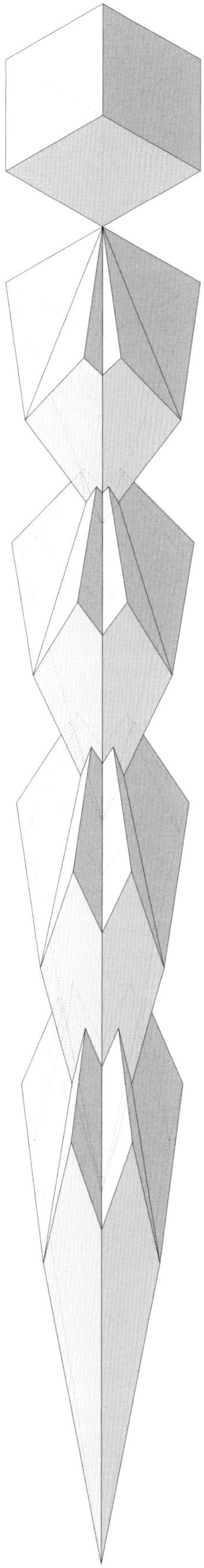

Christoph Paul Hofmann
Tutor: Anita Aigner

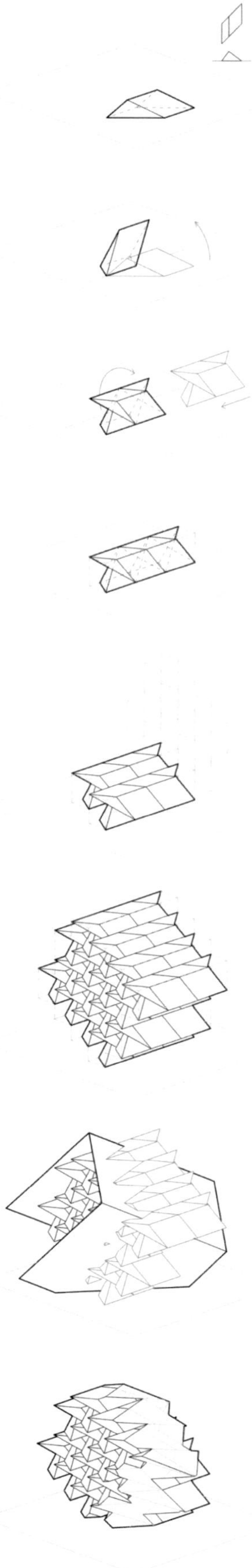

Jakob Kandelsdorfer
Tutor: Christoph Meier

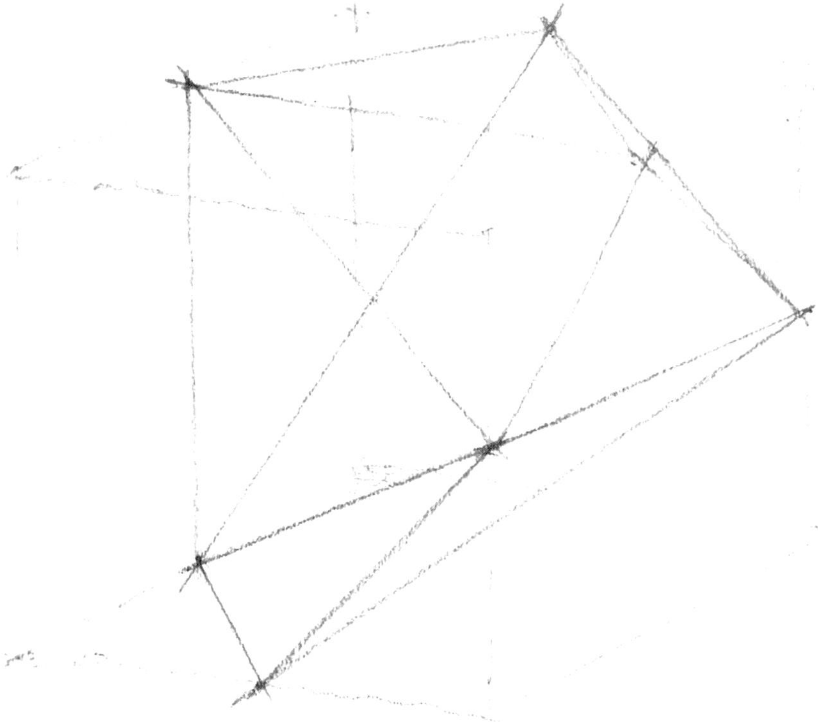

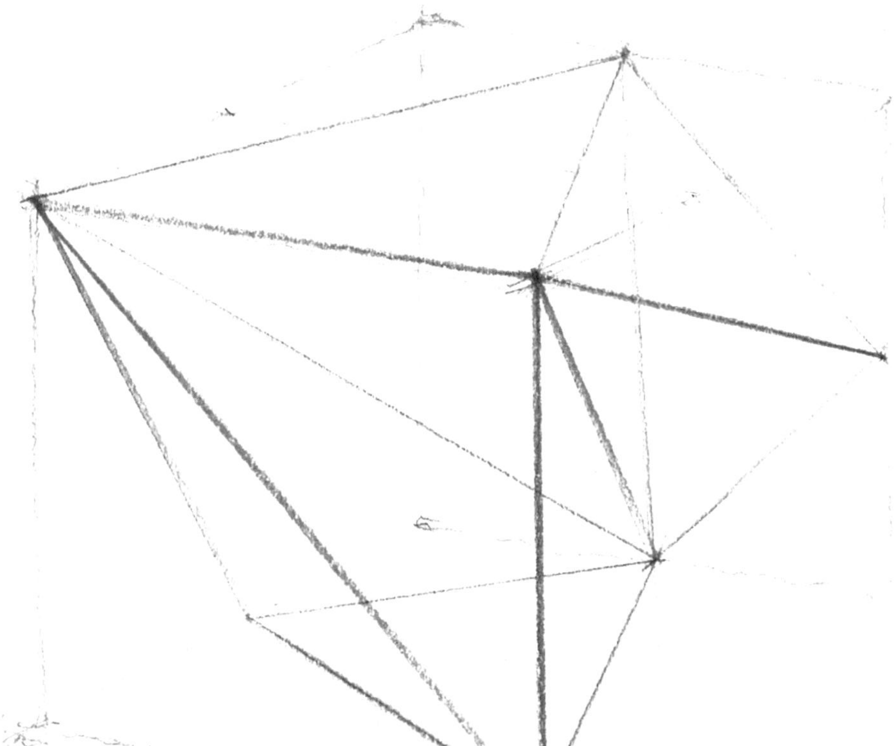

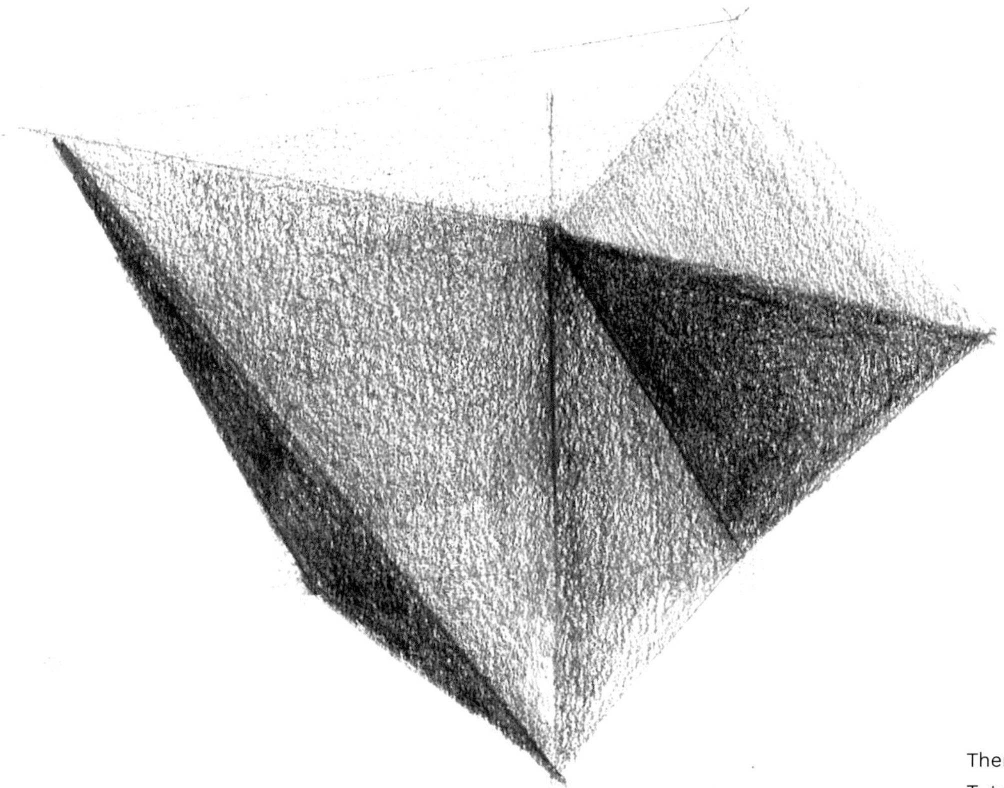

Theresa Steinberger
Tutor: Werner Van Hoeydonck

Exercise 4
Presentation Model

The last step of the exercise was the material realization of the design under the premises of 3D parquet deformation into a sophisticated presentation model.

For the compositional fine-tuning, we first checked whether the essential aspects of the design idea had been concisely conceived. In some cases, the object was optimized with regard to dimensioning, cut-out/boundary, number of cells, and formal expression. The next step was to find the ideal construction method and the ideal material for the form study. With the construction method, students had to make compositional decisions. Depending on whether edges, surfaces, or volumes were represented, the formal expression changed. The decision of whether adjacent cells were represented individually or combined into surfaces also had an effect. With the decision for a certain representation, a design idea could be aesthetically elevated, but also weakened. Therefore, one had to carefully consider which type of construction (rod model, structural model, or shell unwinding or moldable materials for the representation of fully plastic volumes) was best suited for the respective form study. The effect of the form also heavily depended on the spatial position as well as on a reference system (plinth or base plate).

Jennifer Berger
Tutor: Christoph Meier
Pyramids are inserted in a cube and placed on opposite faces in a take-away-and-add process. The resulting solid is deformed along the x-axis. Subsequent and subtle downscaling occurs until half of the initial height generates a series of connectable solids, which is done using threads, allowing the wall-like stacking to move and bend.

Andre Nadtochyi
Tutor: Christoph Bruckner
A wave line is doubled and straightened, divided in three parts with two hinges and three rotation points. A sequence of differently-hinged elements is created and stacked in a step-like manner reminiscent of a fly-through cathedral vault on three levels, defined by the initial wave lines appearing on the outer side.

Kristina Hendker
Tutor: Markus Bauer
A solid 3D interpretation of the so-called Miura folding, named for its inventor, the Japanese astrophysicist Miura. The crease pattern, a combination of straight and zig-zag lines, is used to create a stacking that is able to contract and expand, a true 3D origami.

Barbara Posch
Tutor: Werner Van Hoeydonck
Two opposing vertices of the rhombic dodecahedron are pushed inward, creating a new shape that is subdivided into eight parts and rearranged, respecting the original space-filling aggregation of the rhombic dodecahedron.

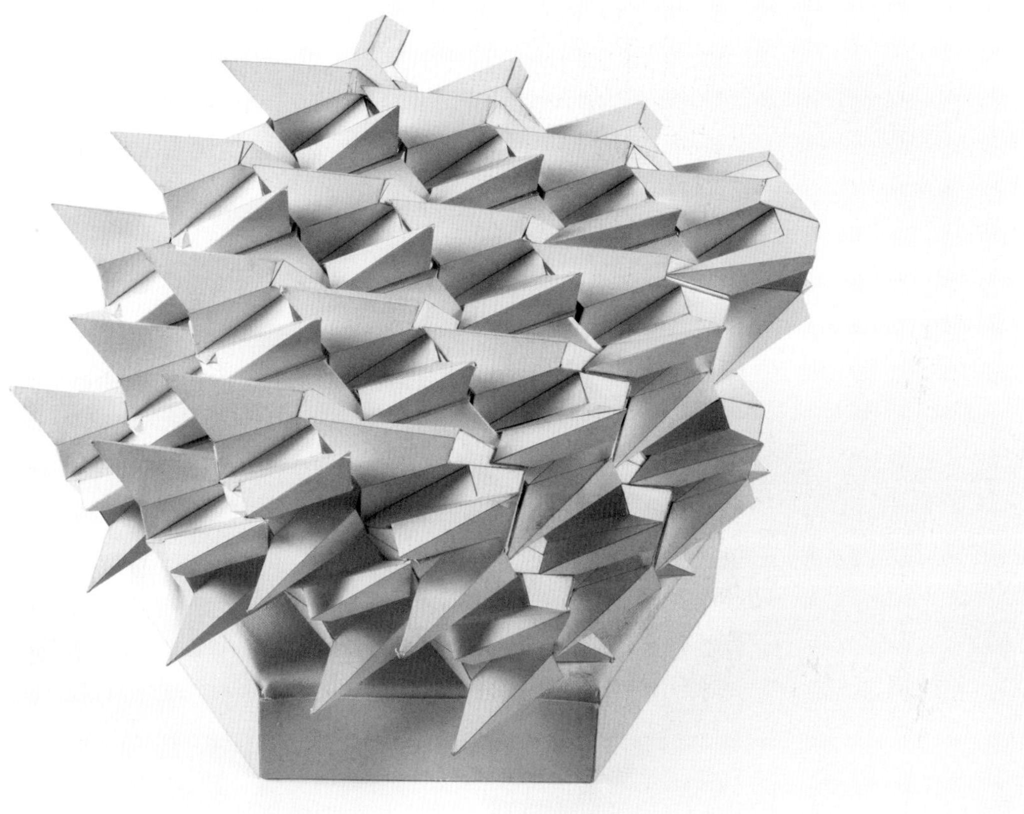

Amer Mahmoud
Tutor: Fridolin Welte
A constellation based on the rhombic dodecahedron that is divided into smaller interlocking cells so that the totality of deformed interlocking cells has the same volume as the original shape, which becomes indiscernible.

Mirkovic Radovan
Tutor: Judith P. Fischer
Inspired by mushrooms, palm trees, or bones, acrylic and plaster cast spheres interact by reflection and rotation operations according to a square grid. Additional elements are introduced in an upward-spiraling arrangement.

Lukas Hansmann
Tutor: Christian Kern
The truncated octahedron is subdivided into four and six identical shapes. Recomposed, they form a rhombic dodecahedron. The void in the middle can be filled with three half-parts of the truncated octahedron.

Selma Dervisefendic
Tutor: Werner Van Hoeydonck
Inspired by a Penrose tiling of golden rhombi, the rhombic hexecontahedron is dissected into 20 acute golden rhombohedra, the rhombic triacontahedron into ten acute and ten obtuse golden rhombohedra, which are recombined into an infinitely extendible crystal-like structure.

Ovcina Hajrudin
Tutor: Werner Van Hoeydonck
The Weaire-Phelan structure consisting of pyritohedra and truncated hexagonal trapezohedra is sliced into half multiple times, replicated, and—through a process of addition and subtraction—recomposed into an arch-like structure.

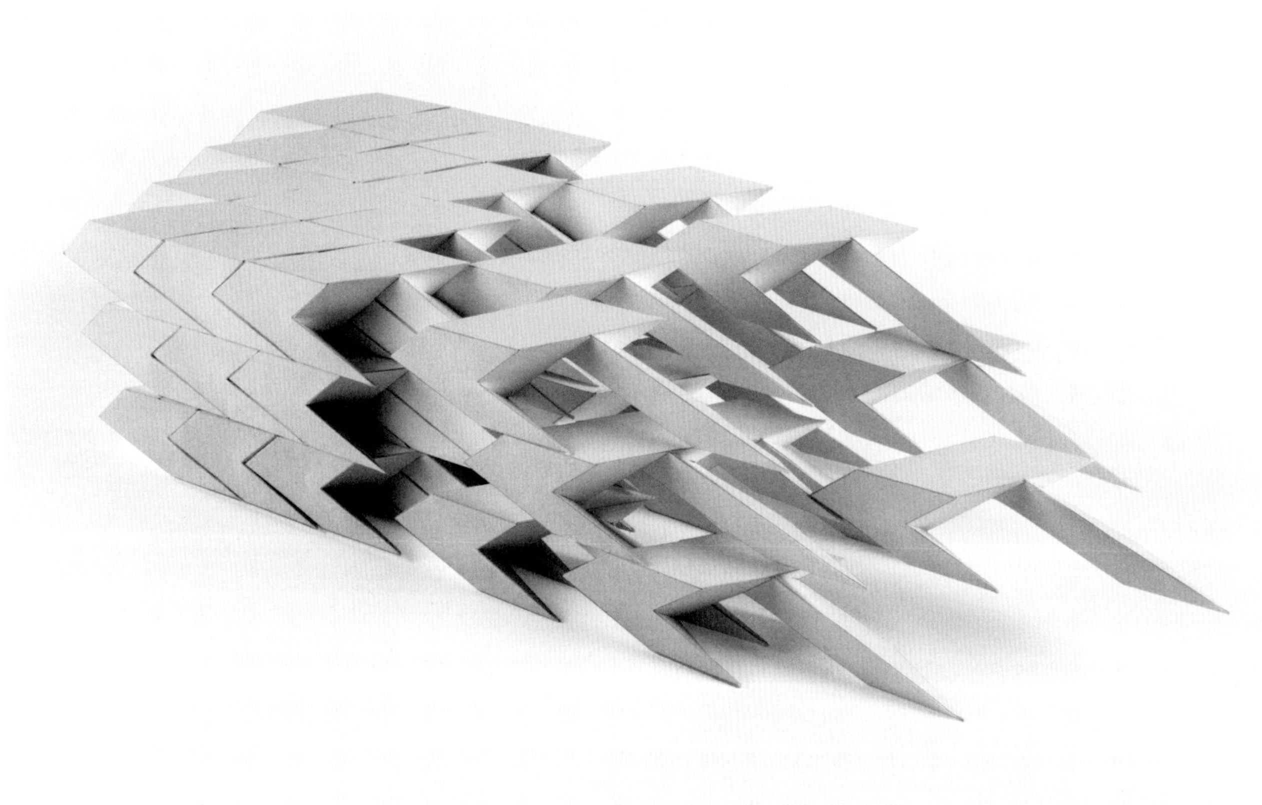

Mahir Kurtalić
Tutor: Christoph Meier
An asymmetrical distortion of the cube is cut in half. Inspired by aerodynamic and aquadynamic shapes such as feathers and shark scales, its subparts are switched in position and rearranged to give a maximum of tension and movement toward dissolution.

Steliyana Chipeva
Tutor: Manuela Fritz
Hexagons and (invisible) squares are connected by concave and convex bends of copper, resulting in a dissolving spatial composition reminiscent of an abstract bouquet of flowers, reflecting its surroundings in different color nuances.

Anja Bezjak
Tutor: Christian Kern
A distorted hexagonal prism is multiplied, mirrored, and recomposed. Inspired by quarries and rice terraces, a dynamic landscape is created in an ever-changing play of light and shadow complemented by gentle surfaces, balancing the work as a whole.

Steffen Alexander Blickle
Tutor: Peter G. Auer
A sequence of three vertex motion operations along the diagonal of the cube generates sharp sides, infiltrating its adjacent cells in a gradual give-and-take process along the diagonals of the cube, made visible by distancing the four aggregations.

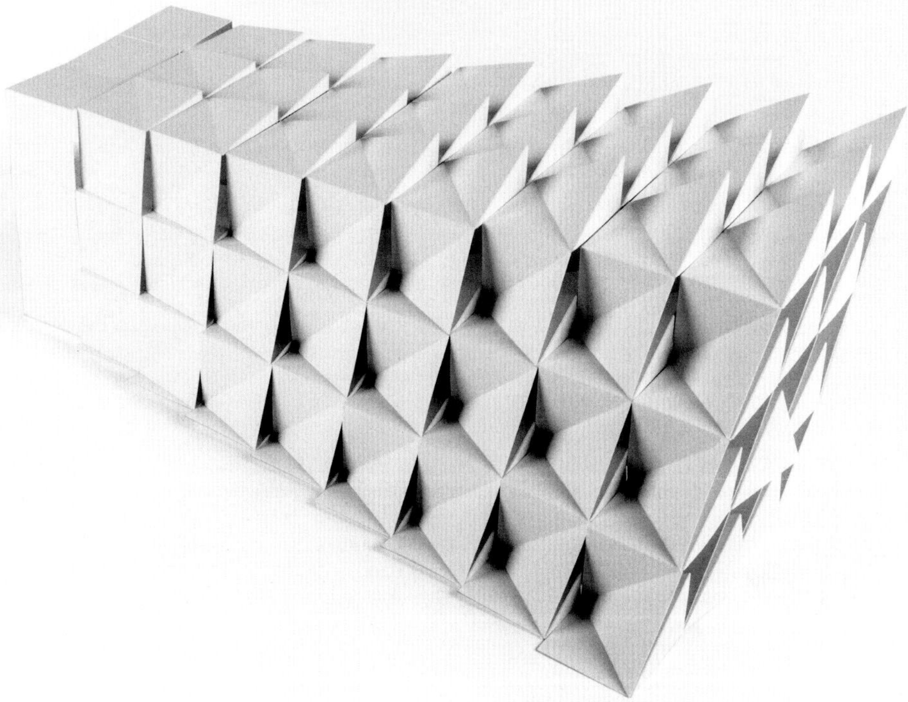

Philip Kaloumenos
Tutor: Anita Aigner
In a 3 × 3 × 9 modular cubic structure, starting with completely closed cubes, a progressive subtle vertex motion operation results in foldings of the cubes' surfaces, generating gradually growing triangular openings in a give-and-take process of lightened-up space.

Berkay Yozgyur
Tutor: Anita Aigner
From rest to movement in six steps: Some of the cube's vertices travel in space in a forward-upward continuous movement, transforming the cube's static faces in a space-filling aggregation of ever-changing spatial triangles, inspired by a sprinter coming into action.

Christoph Paul Hofmann
Tutor: Anita Aigner

Two rows of five cubes undergo a twofold left-and-down deformation. The cube's gradual multidirectional vertex motion is reflected in an equivalent concave deformation of the upper side. The spiky concave drift down instigates its concave counterpart above.

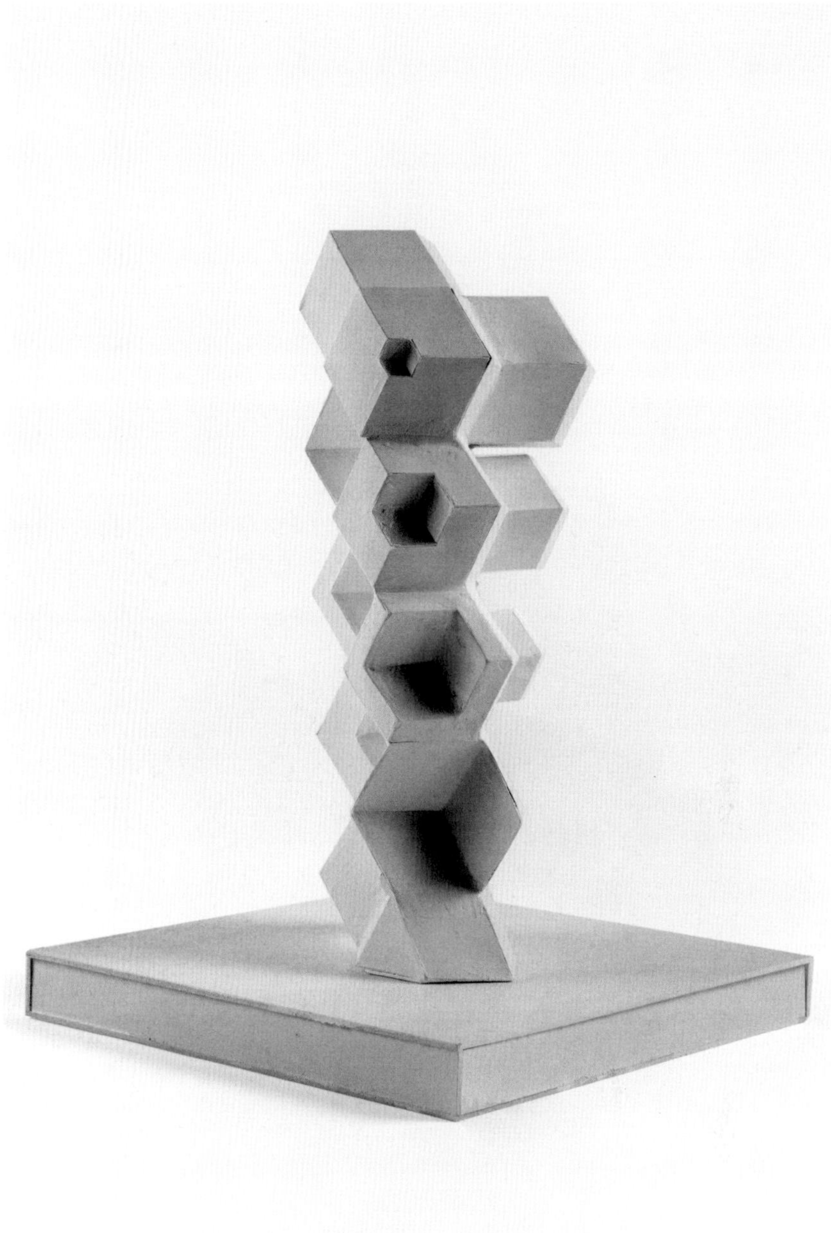

Thomas Ran
Tutor: Werner Van Hoeydonck
A three-step gradual intrusion of the rhombic dodecahedron in opposite vertical directions generates negatives spaces that look like positive spaces. The viewer's eye is challenged to experience a 3D flip-over reminiscent of the figure-ground problem in 2D.

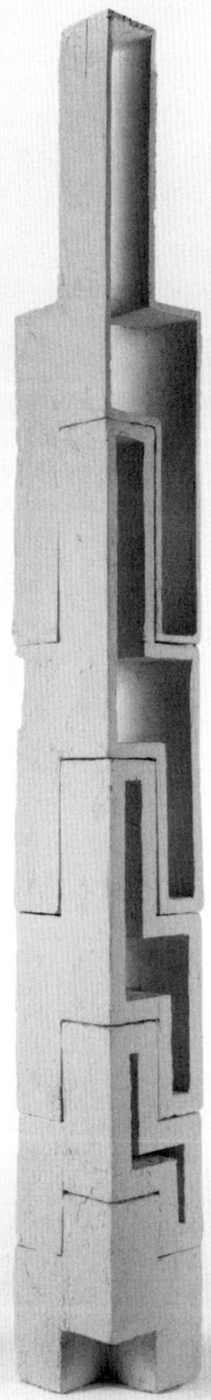

Alexander Keil
Tutor: Anita Aigner
A cube is quartered at its top and bottom, mimicking a checkerboard of positive and negative space. The two diagonally opposite surfaces shift upward and the grid structure elongates: The previously shifted surfaces become progressively extruded. Gradually, the initial cube becomes a loop-like shape.

Theresa Gasteiger
Tutor: Martina Kögl
Eight faces of the twelve-sided rhombic dodecahedron are rotated along their short diagonals, generating five new faces, partly concave, partly convex. The reclined 1 × 3 × 3 module stacking shows the original form at its base and two rows deformed by gradual face rotations.

Tobias Speckner

Tutor: Werner Van Hoeydonck

Extended tetragonal bipyramids combined with (invisible) tetrahedra fill space. A vertex motion operation by half a width on the x-axis on all four corners (in opposite directions) of the bipyramids fuses with a one-unit-high rotation of the composition's two upper horizontal axes.

Markus Biel
Tutor: Anita Aigner
Cubes are distorted by different interrelated vertex motion operations and stacked in a distorted 3 × 3 × 5 modular cubic structure. By omitting cubes in a 3D chessboard-like way, an interplay of light and shadow enhances the spatial exploration of the connected voids.

Noura Omar
Tutor: Nora Fröhlich
Three rhombi are extruded. Deformed cubes and rhombic prisms of different sizes and lengths are created by folding edges up and down, inward and outward, in order to express a dynamic multidirectional 3D heartbeat.

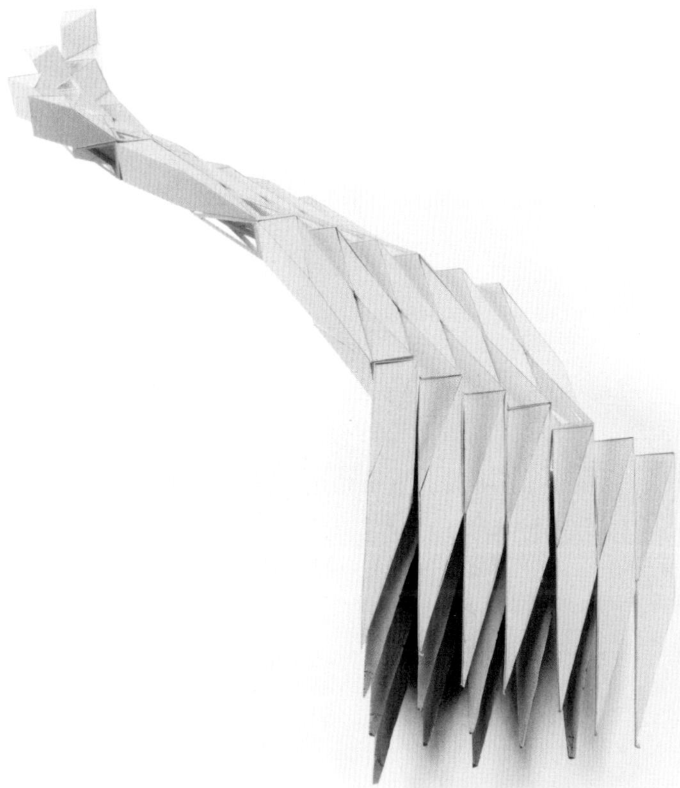

Isa Kirchberger
Tutor: Peter G. Auer
Inspired by animal scales, a cube is gradually reshaped, allowing for multiple and subsequent changes in size, direction, and overlap, permitting a scale structure to open and close and re-orientate according to seemingly effortless, instinctive movements.

Lisa Hirsch
Tutor: Judith P. Fischer
All lines, starting from the outer square, are bent inward; all lines starting from the inner square are bent outward. In this way, the two-dimensional tessellation becomes a three-dimensional sculptural form that can be expanded infinitely.

Jakob Kandelsdorfer
Tutor: Christoph Meier
Sixty-four identical oblique three-sided prisms in massive grained wood are packed in two directions, giving every cell its identity. The regularity is broken through a tilted box which trims away three parts of the stacking, revealing new connections between the cells.

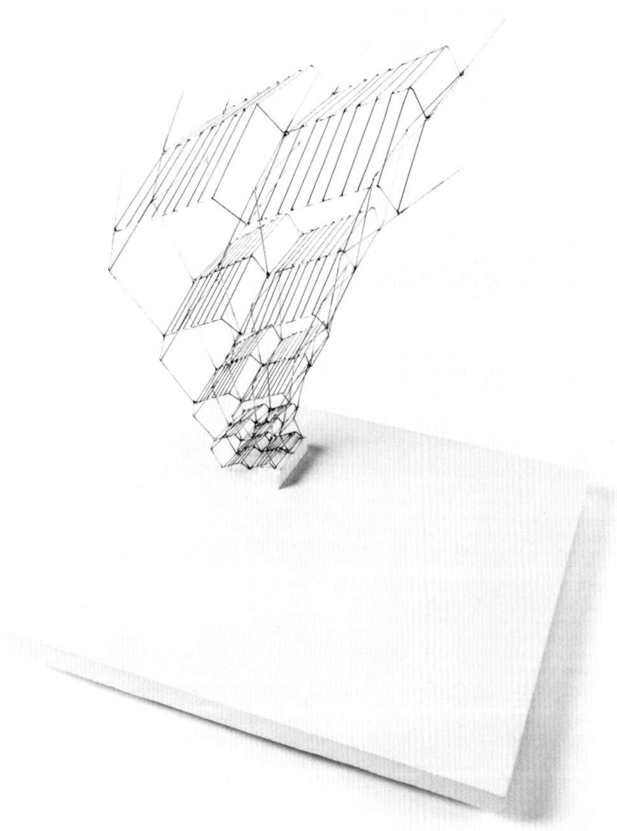

Maximilian Greinwald
Tutor: Martina Kögl
Opposite faces of the cube are respectively bent in and bent out, resulting in a cubic brass rod structure that kinks and bumps through space according to a growth rule. Different levels are made visible by a series of parallel connecting rods. Three predefined positions on its plaster base induce drastic perception shifts.

Christine Bosse-Büchling
Tutor: Fridolin Welte
A subdivision of the cube along diagonals creates five smaller forms that can be recomposed in eight different ways. One of eight possibilities is selected and deformed in several directions, a larger cube, the initial shape of the deformation frames and holds the composition together.

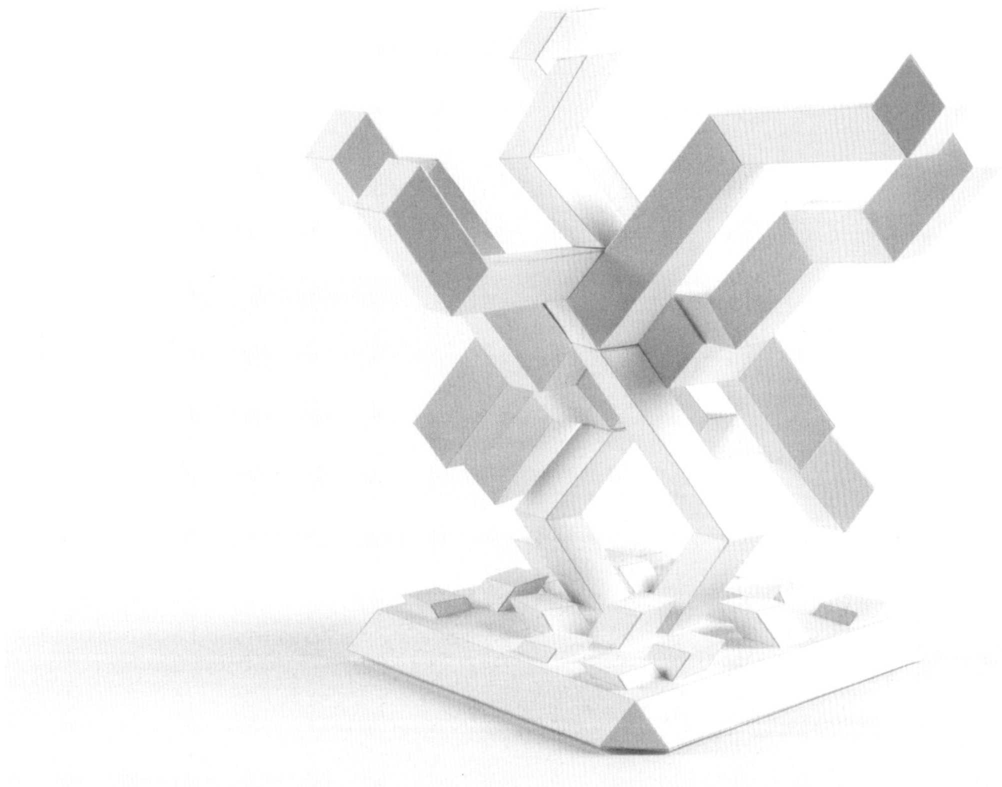

Andreas Frank
Tutor: Werner Van Hoeydonck
The rhombic dodecahedron is divided into four parallelepipeds along all its space diagonals. Extruded parallelepipeds change direction and length in order to make them intertwine. These "threads" soften the strict geometric shapes into a kind of spatial textile.

Michael Robert Jimenez
Tutor: Christian Kern
A 3D tiling is created out of a continuous deformation of three 2D parquets stacked on top of each other, whereby the top and bottom slices are the same form. A “loop” is created by starting at Tile A, going to B and C, and then backward from C to B to A. To interlock, a second 3D tile is created. This time the loop is defined by CBABC.

Cellular Space Sequences

Looking at the densest possible packing of space, the cell (from Latin *cella* = small space) is the epitome of a determining individual element. Its occurrence is manifold in nature and culture. In Western architecture, the term appears early in history (Romans). Ideas of urban densification in the course of the urgent need for housing after the First World War more intensively examined the notion of the cell. This investigation ranges from beginnings in the interwar period (Bauhaus) to high points in the 1950s/1960s with structuralist approaches (Herzberger, Tange, Candilis) and the radical Raumstadt concepts (Constant, Friedman, Schultze-Fielitz, etc.). At present, the desire for urban densification, mixing of functions and population pressure seem to be creating space again for approaches regarding the notion of the cell.

In architecture, the connection of spaces does not only serve functional purposes. The quality of the connections with a choreographed sequence of homogeneous or heterogeneous spaces plays a weighty role, as can be seen in many architectural path concepts (e.g., Egyptian temple complexes, Baroque enfilade, Le Corbusier's Promenade Architecturale, J. Frank, R. Koolhaas). In the winter semester 2018/19, we devoted ourselves to designing and creating interesting spatial sequences within a specific matrix. This matrix is fundamentally cellular in structure and determined by a gapless, three-dimensional tiling of space with the help of convex polyhedra. We worked in a defined systematics and, in order to get size variance for the space-filling polyhedra, methodically made use of the principle of three-dimensional parquet deformation and subdivision, such as the self-similarity of fractals.

The semester-long exercise was an elementary three-dimensional design task on the above topic, freed from functional constraints. This exercise included, among other things, the creation of spatial hierarchies in the sense of a scenographic sequence as well as the conception of large and small spaces and objects in a given systematic structure (cellular matrix).

The exercise started two-dimensionally with clear rules in order to gradually arrive at more individual design strategies, rules, and formal solutions. At the end of the assignment, real three-dimensional, allround attractive form studies with a sculptural effect were produced. The exercise was divided into four individual exercises, the results of which are presented in the following pages.

Exercise 1
Figure Ground

The first exercise started with the choice of one of the following simple polygons: square, rhombus, equilateral triangle, regular hexagon, or cairo tiling. The chosen polygon served as a protocell for a tiling of the plane. Following a comprehensible concept, an inner space with an opening to the outside on only one side of the polygon was drawn in the chosen protocell. The shape of the internal space and the opening could be freely chosen, but both referred to the inherent structure of the initial cell. Attention was paid to the quality of this inner space in relation to the protocell in terms of proportion, tension, and figure/ground relationships.

The protocell complemented with an internal space was to be used in a planar tiling, large enough (not less than 20 elements) so that the figure/ground relationships as well as the visual effects of this surface filling could be understood and assessed. When the choice of a certain protocell allowed it, the possibilities of different congruence mappings (sliding, rotating, mirroring, glide-mirroring) were used. Even if the tiling was theoretically possible to infinity, only a limited section with a simple, clear outer contour was to be used. This section could correspond to the contour of the protocell (e.g., square for squares). The result was a hand drawing in which the contour lines of the protocell should be clearly legible and the “wall” areas should not be blackened, but highlighted with pencil as hatching.

The result of such tiling with only one lateral opening resulted in inaccessible interior spaces. In order to generate spatial sequences in the tiling, individual cells (maximum four to six) were first regularly shifted outwards from the bond to create gaps. This process created new spatial possibilities in the outer area that broke up the strict outer contour. In a final step, simple interventions were implemented to connect the remaining interior spaces that were not yet connected to create an interesting spatial sequence. This spatial sequence became visible by drawing a dotted line (trajectory). The spectrum of such interventions ranged from conceptually well-conceived to completely arbitrary. The latter was to be avoided in order to get an interesting result.

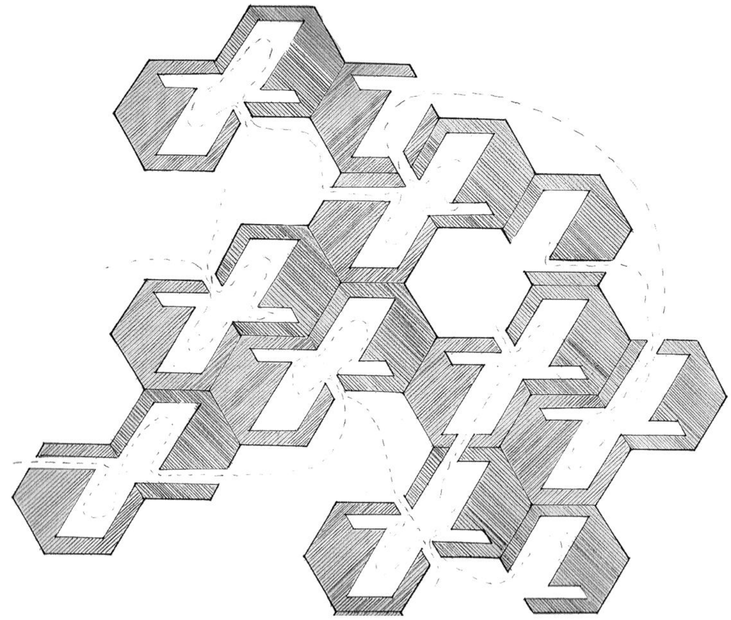

Cristina Cazacu
Tutor: Werner Van Hoeydonck

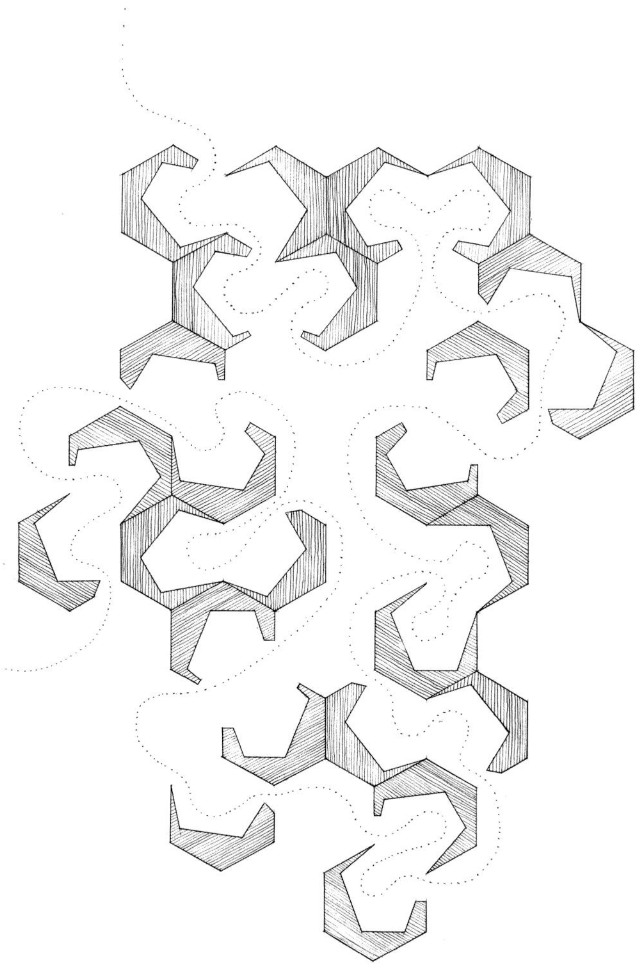

Antonia Maisch
Tutor: Werner Van Hoeydonck

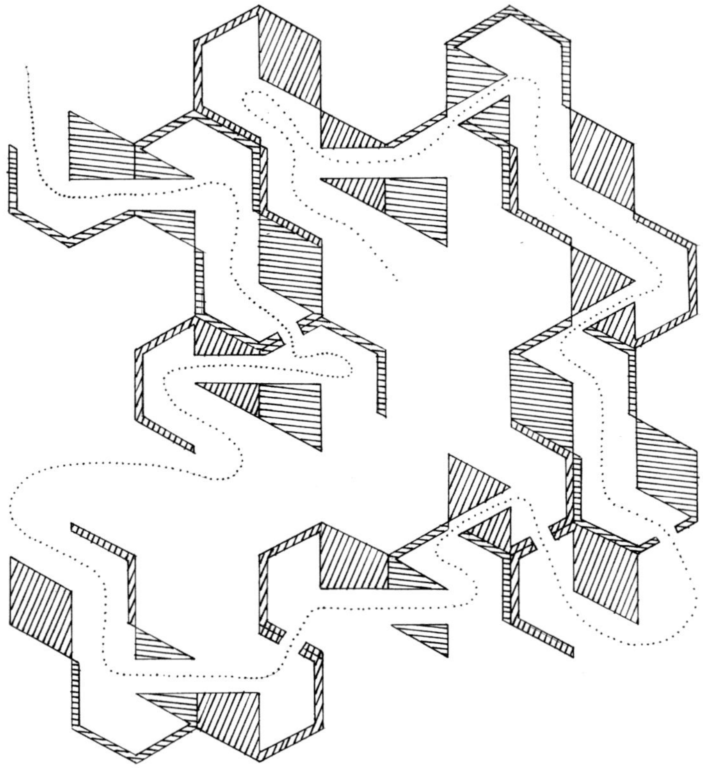

Maria Oikonomou
Tutor: Fridolin Welte

Gabriel Esposito
Tutor: Judith P. Fischer

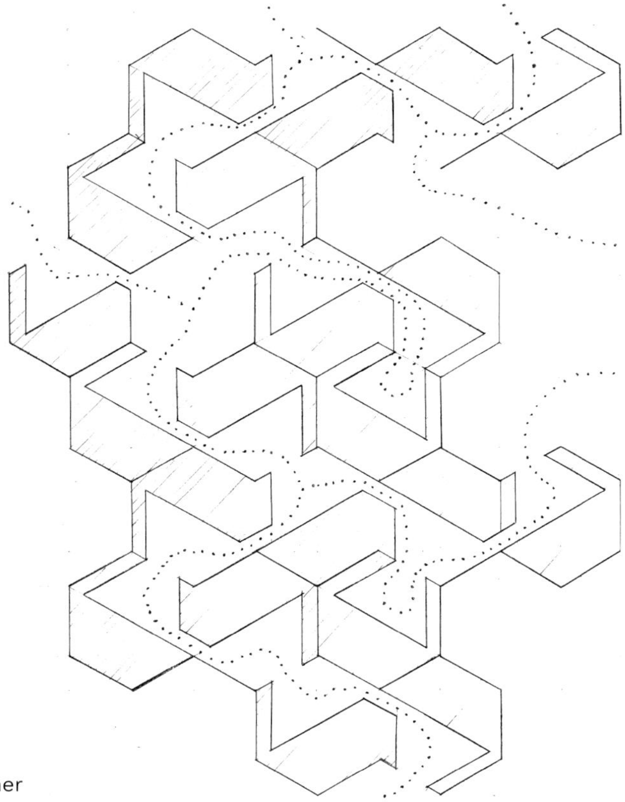

Nikola Stevanovic
Tutor: Judith P. Fischer

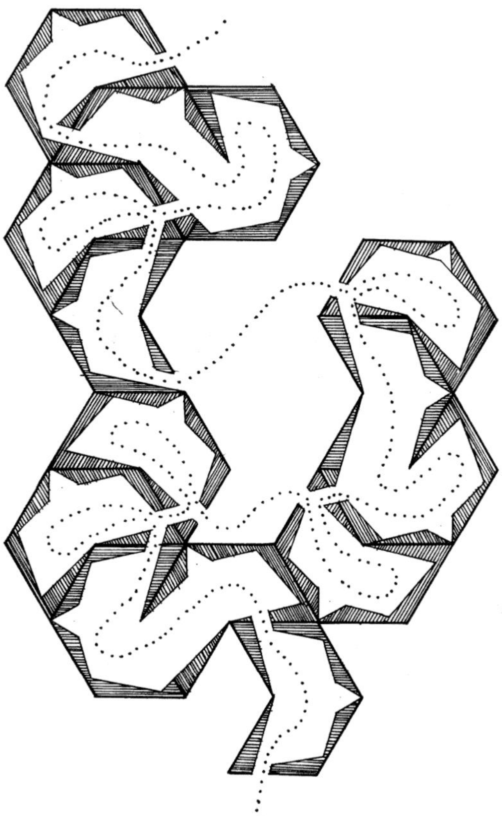

Elena Thöni
Tutor: Nora Fröhlich

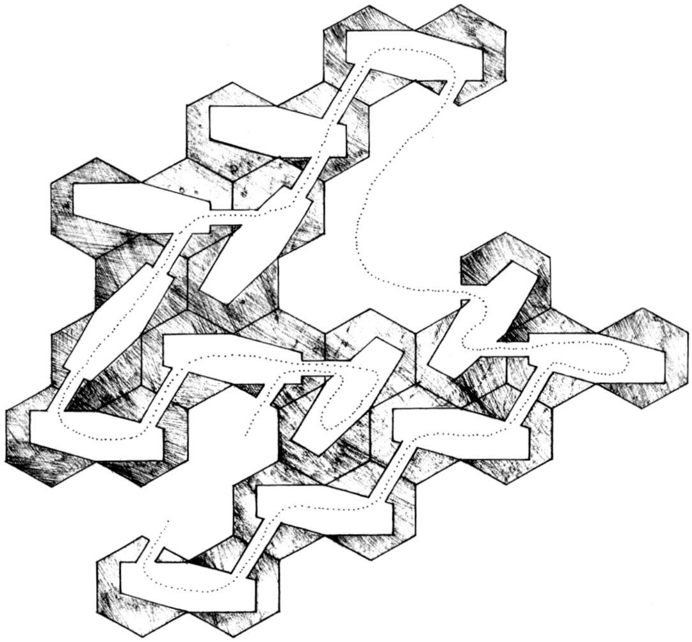

Zsofia Arnhoffer
Tutor: Anita Aigner

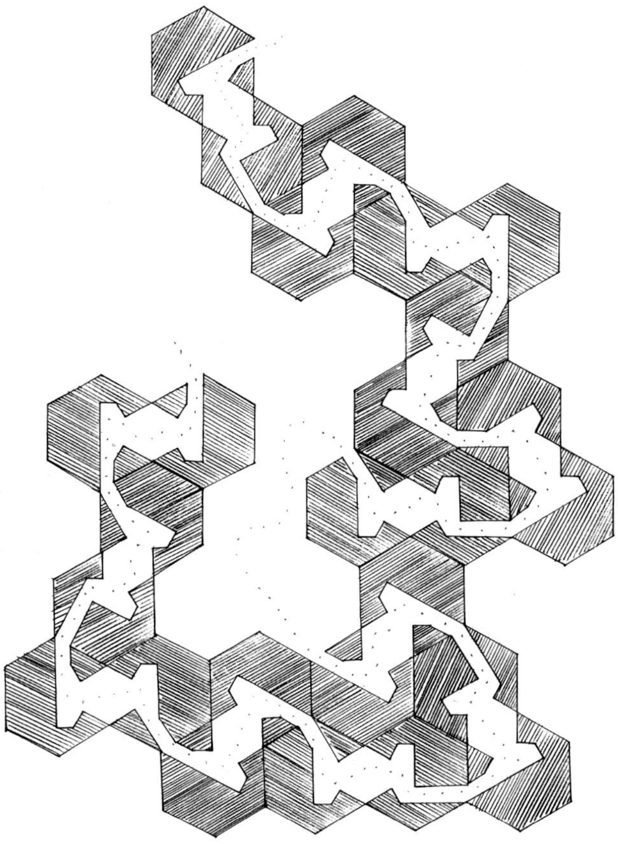

Charlotte Hemmen
Tutor: Manuela Fritz

Svetoslava Svetoslavova
Tutor: Anita Aigner

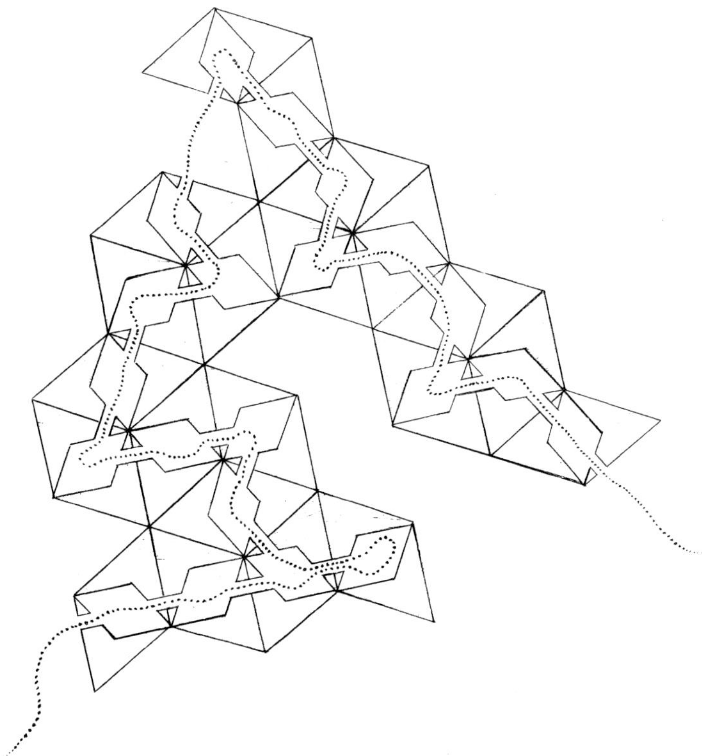

Johanna Grabner
Tutor: Markus Bauer

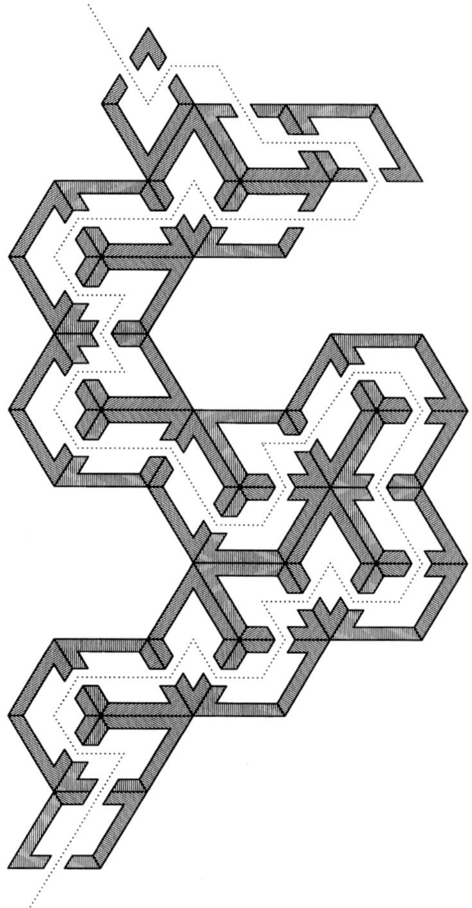

Karin Riedl
Tutor: Anita Aigner

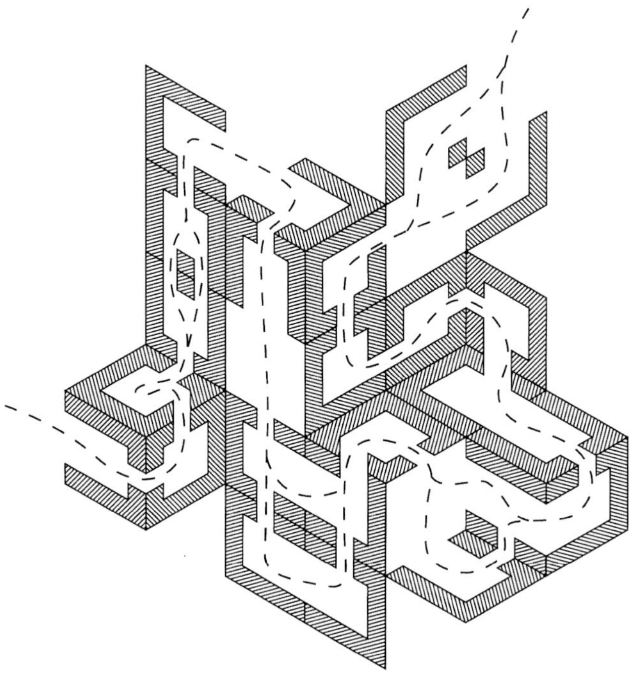

Stefan Binder
Tutor: Judith P. Fischer

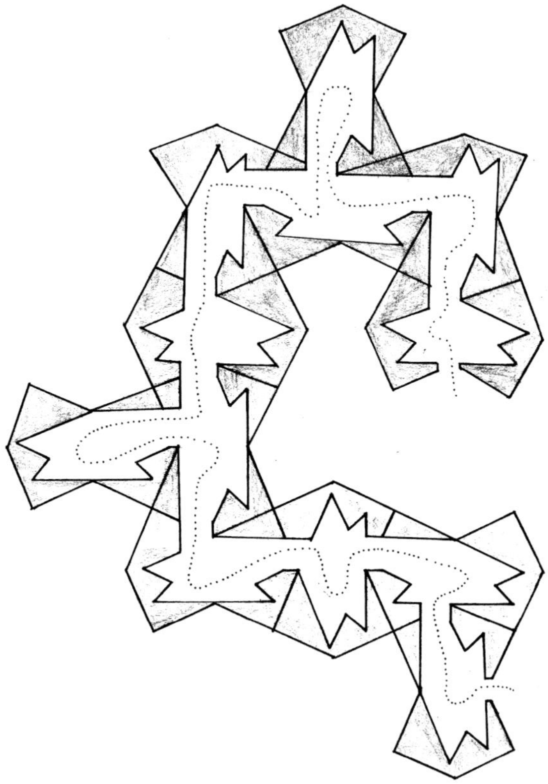

Tanja Punz
Tutor: Anita Aigner

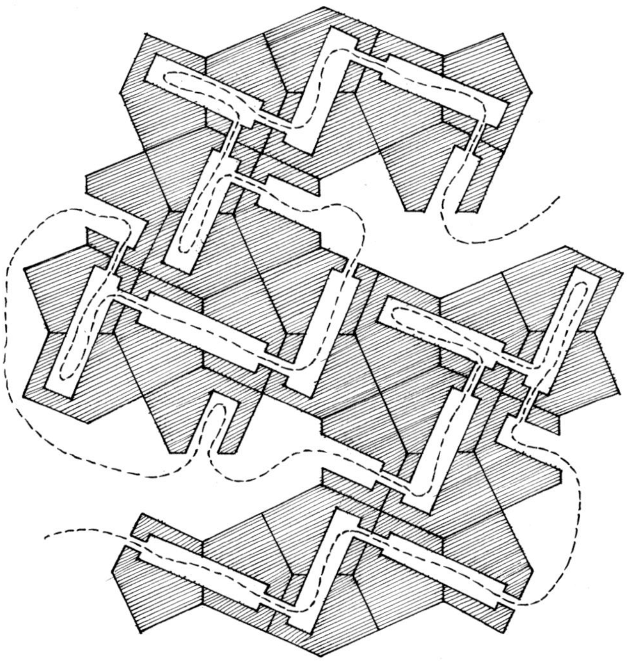

Jana Riernössl
Tutor: Peter G. Auer

Exercise 2
Solid and Void

From the following convex polyhedra, which allow a gapless and overlap-free tiling of the three-dimensional space, one was chosen for further processing: cube (hexahedron), twisted double wedge (gyrobifastigium), or rhombic dodecahedron. The dual form was realized by connecting the centers of adjacent polyhedron faces of the initial solid. These straight connecting lines form the edges of the dual solid.

Two separate working models were created, a rod model of the initial polyhedron (size approximately to fit in a sphere Ø15 cm) and a solid model of its dual. The spatial and plastic qualities of the connection between the two solids and their spatial positions were then examined with sketches. In the next step, the dual solid was subtracted from the initial polyhedron. The result was a shell solid with an interior without openings. From this solid, a working model divided by a deliberate cut was built as a shell model, which we called the "avocado" model.

The dual solid was only one of many conceptual possibilities in the search of an interesting interior space. To explore their own ideas, the students selected another polyhedron from the group outlined above. For this polyhedron, interiors were developed experimentally and following individual rules. It was possible to fall back on approaches from Exercise 1 or to experiment with the dual solid. The shape of the interior could be freely determined. The aim was to create an exciting and conceptually well-conceived interior space that corresponded to the individual formal inclinations in relation to the form of the original solid. Experiments were conducted not only on the conceptual level (e.g., drawings, sketches), but also on the level of different materials and construction methods.

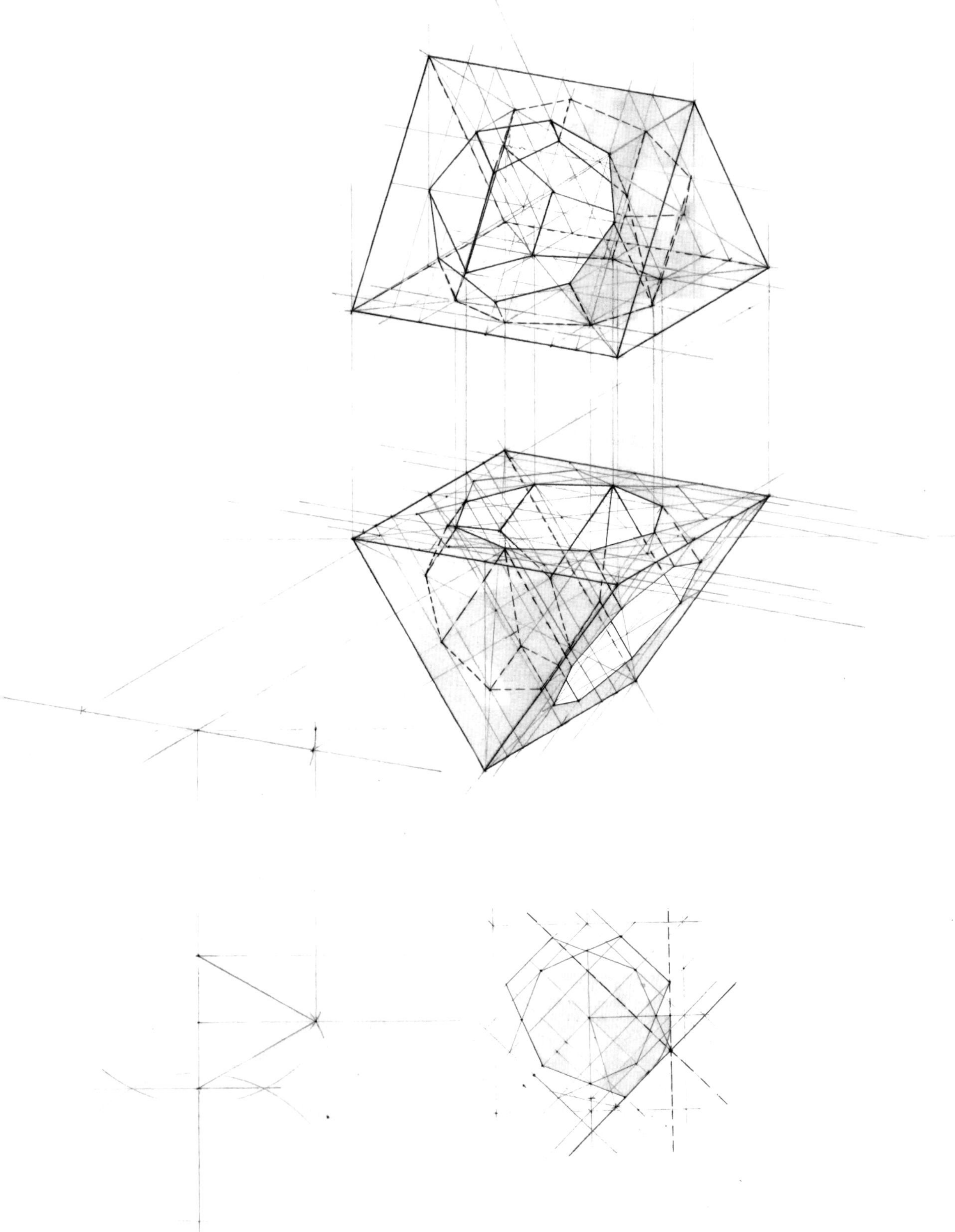

Thomas Emil Rasmus
Tutor: Fridolin Welte

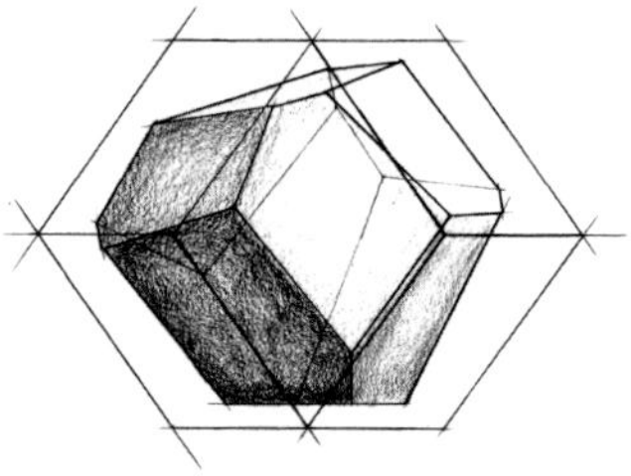
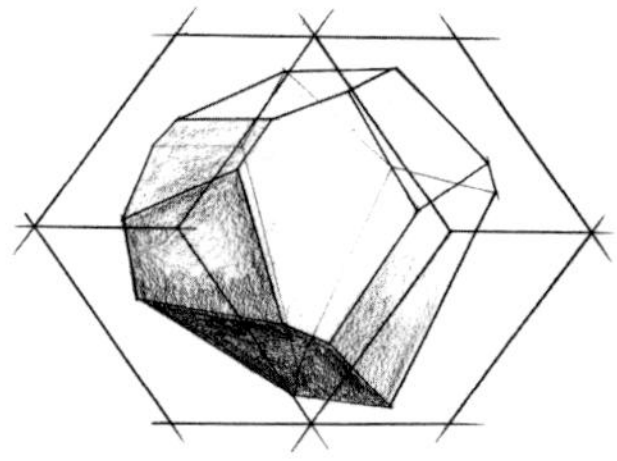
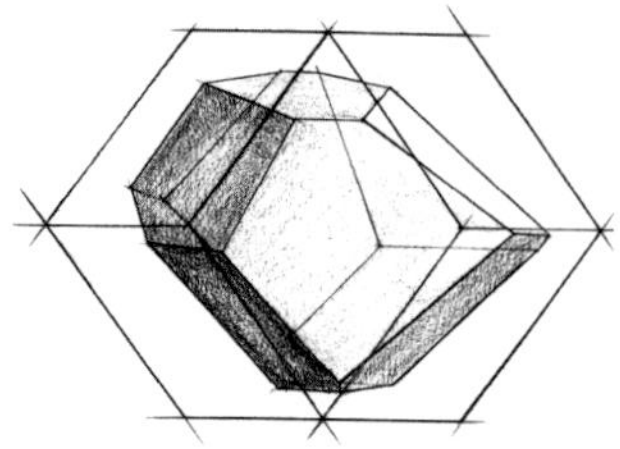
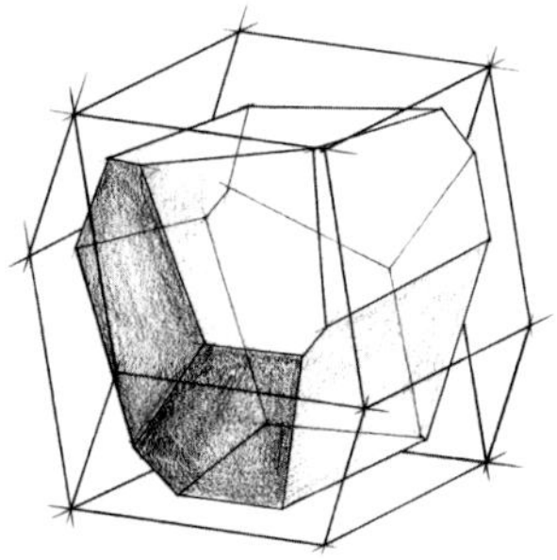
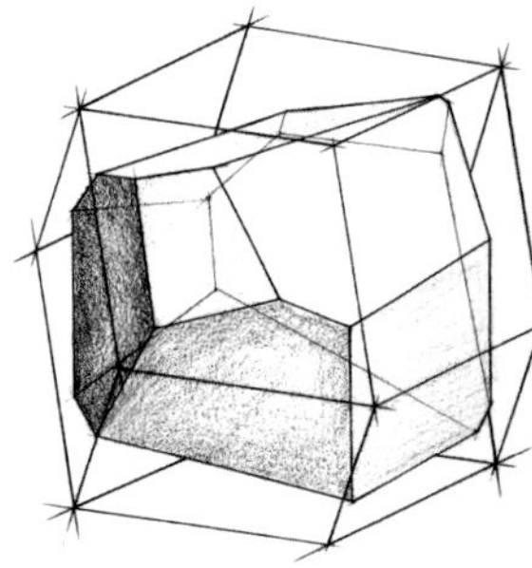
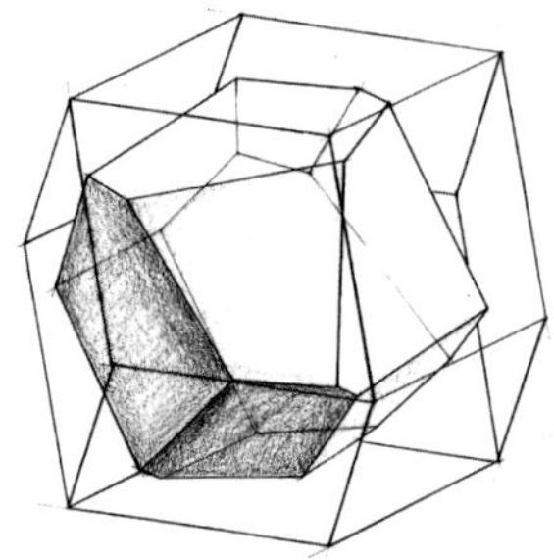
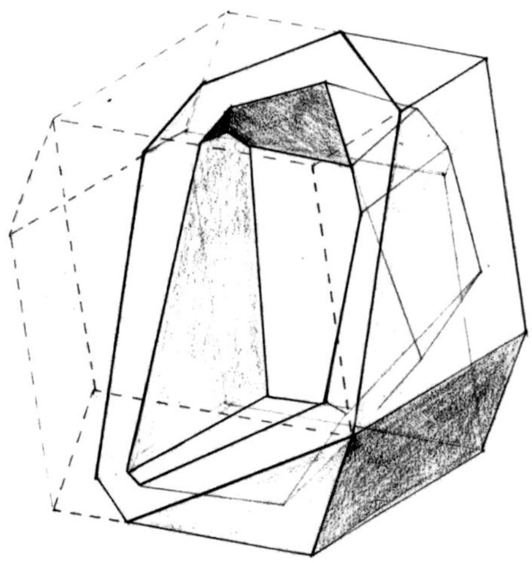
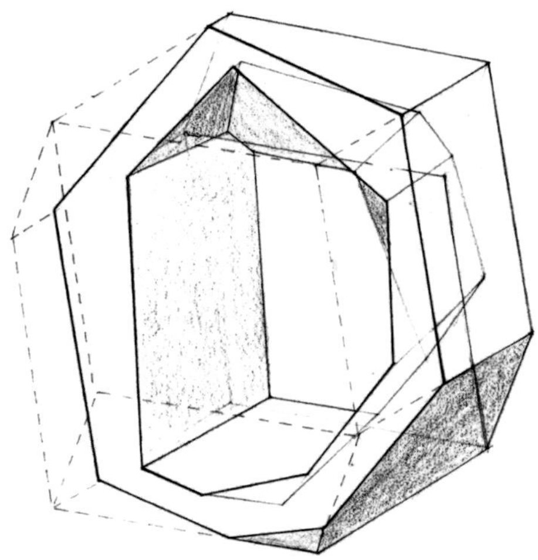
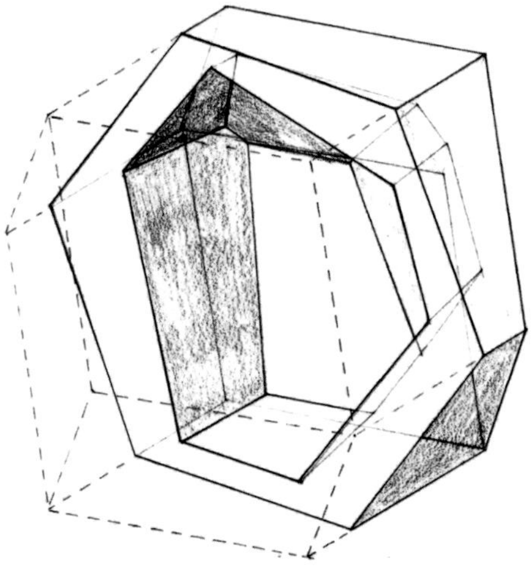
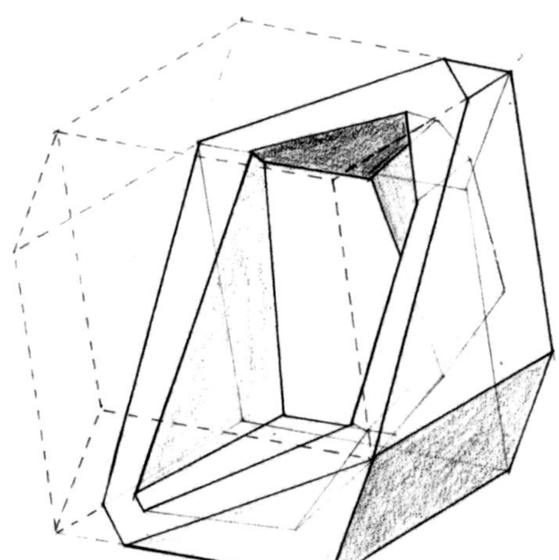

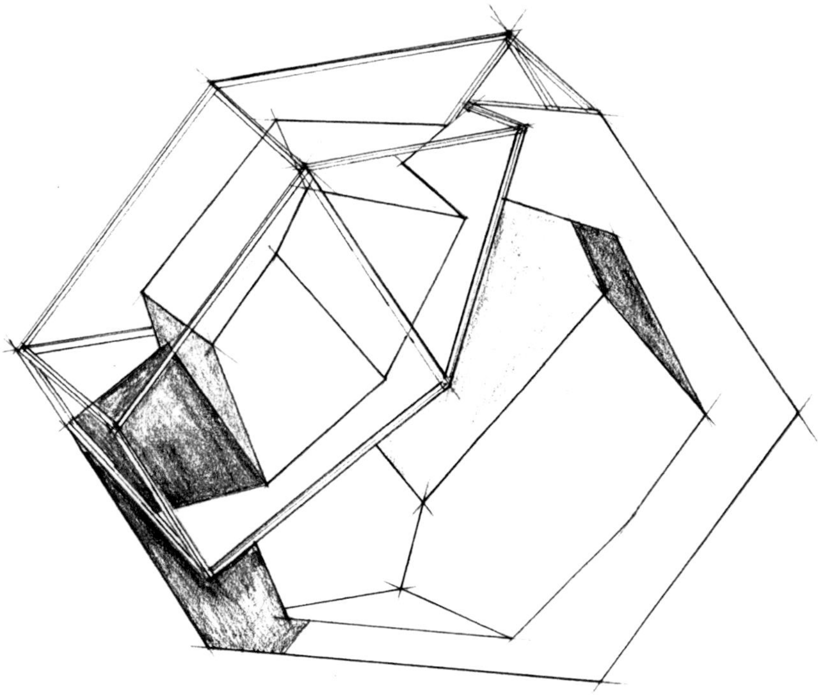

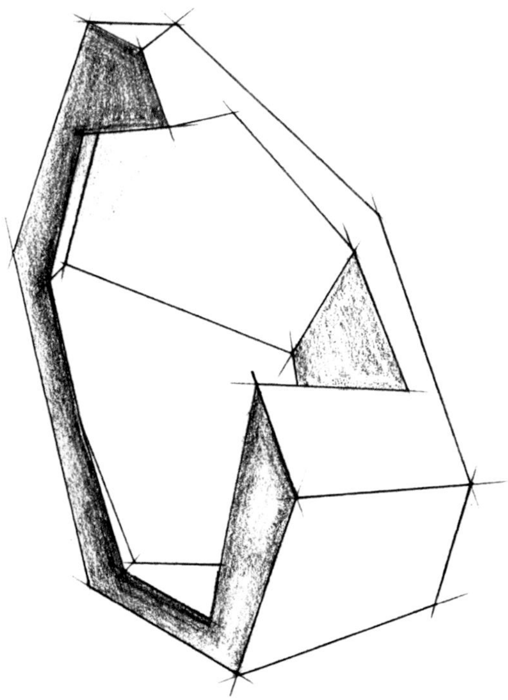

Antonia Maisch
Tutor: Werner Van Hoeydonck

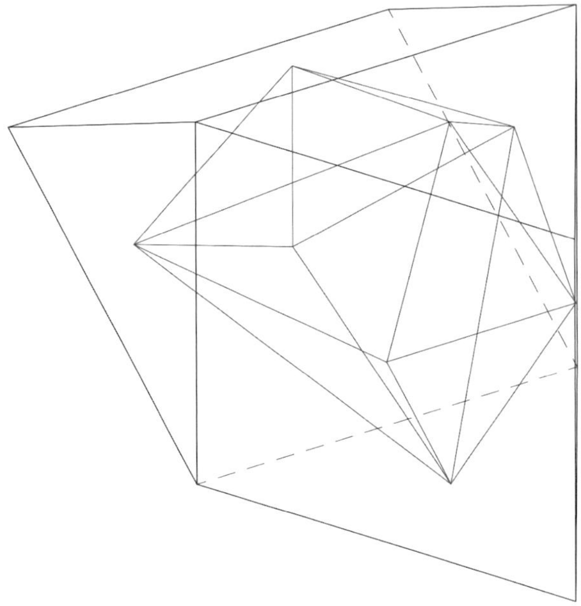

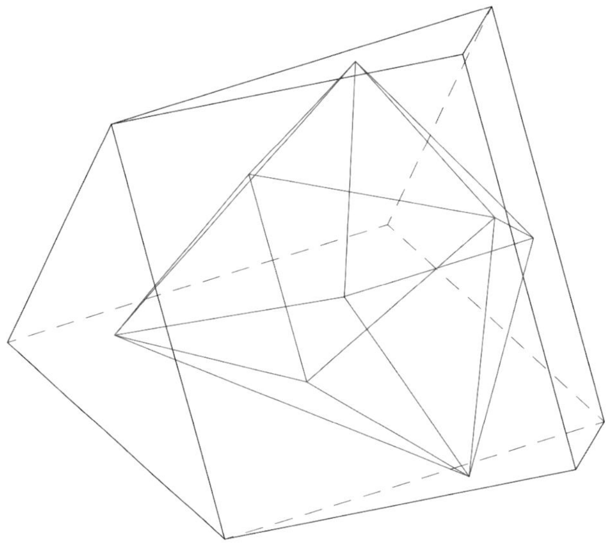

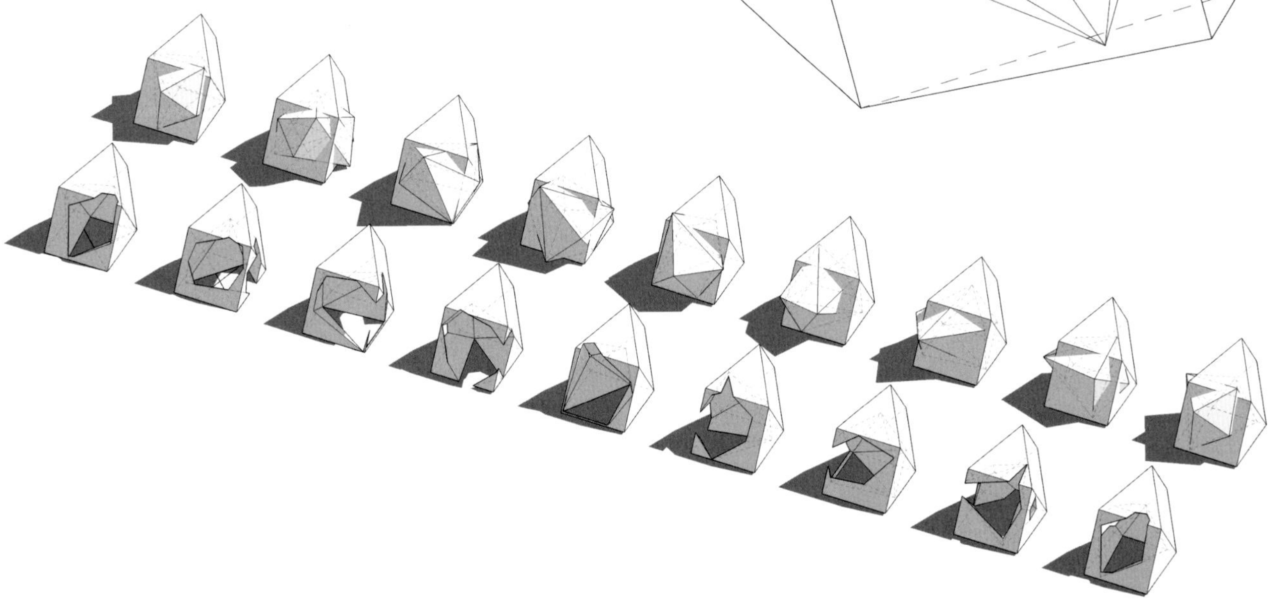

Patrick Neuwirth
Tutor: Nora Fröhlich

1.

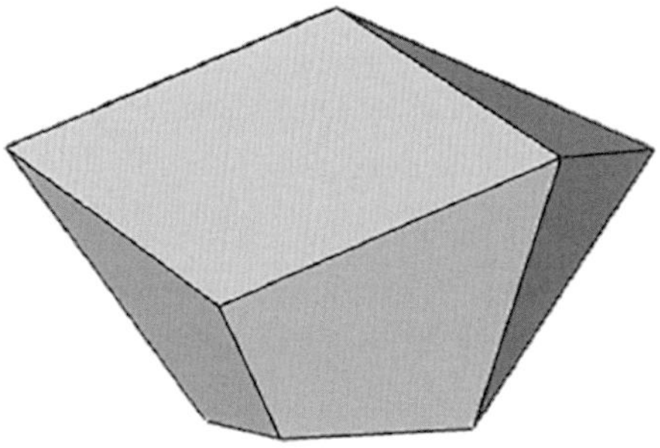

2.

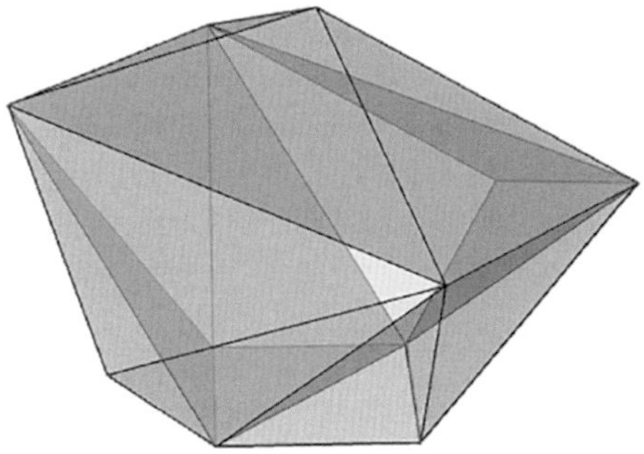

3.

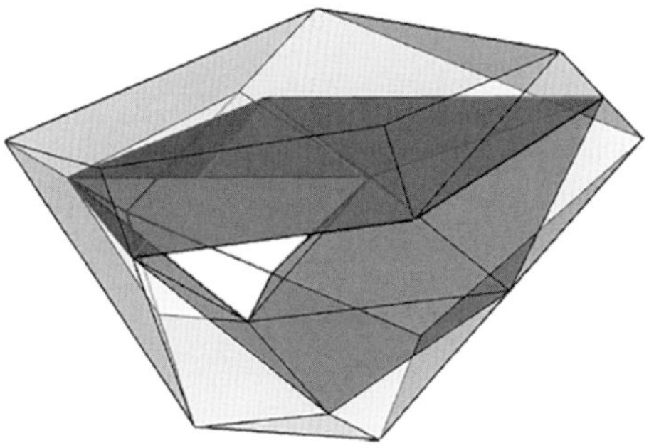

4.

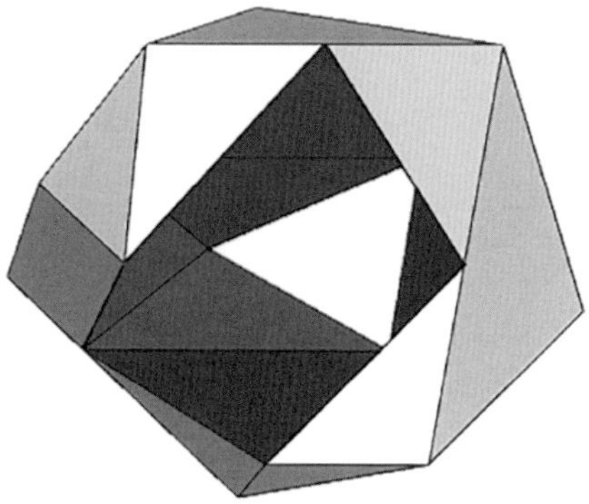

5.

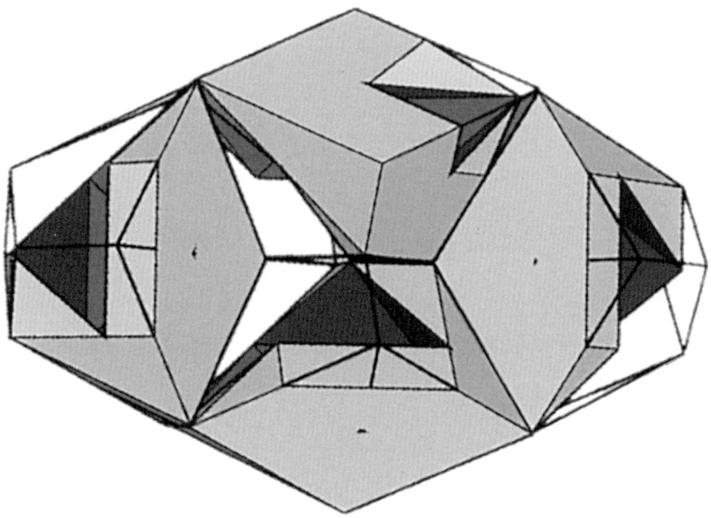

Aia Metnan
Tutor: Werner Van Hoeydonck

Exercise 3
Composition and Design

In exercise 2, different interior spaces were investigated and developed for a chosen initial polyhedron. These polyhedra were multiplied to create a space filling with an appropriate number of cells in all three spatial directions. On the one hand, the result could be a dense packing, cell to cell. On the other hand, by omitting certain cells, loosened conglomerations could be formed without the disintegration of the structure.

For the compositional development of the form study in space, it was necessary to develop and define a basic idea or design concept. For this purpose, a virtual compositional space of 24 cm × 24 cm ×(24+n) cm was proposed as a basic contextual guide (cube or cuboid). Based on the conditions of gravity, a multitude of possible spatial positions arose. Some possible cases were investigated with the help of sketches and on the basis of working models.

In order to produce well-designed sequences of spaces, the interior spaces had to be deliberately opened up and connected. Based on the idea of being able to “fly” through these spaces, the spatial properties of the interior spaces were examined by means of perspective sketches. Essential parameters influencing the quality of the spatial sequences, such as the size and shape of the spaces (scaling), could be controlled, among other methods, by three-dimensional parquet deformation or by fractal subdivision. The form study was to be designed all-view. An important problem was the representation of these spatial sequences for an outside observer. By what creative means could the glances and staged sequences of glances allow for conveying an understanding of the choreographed deep nesting of the interior spaces?

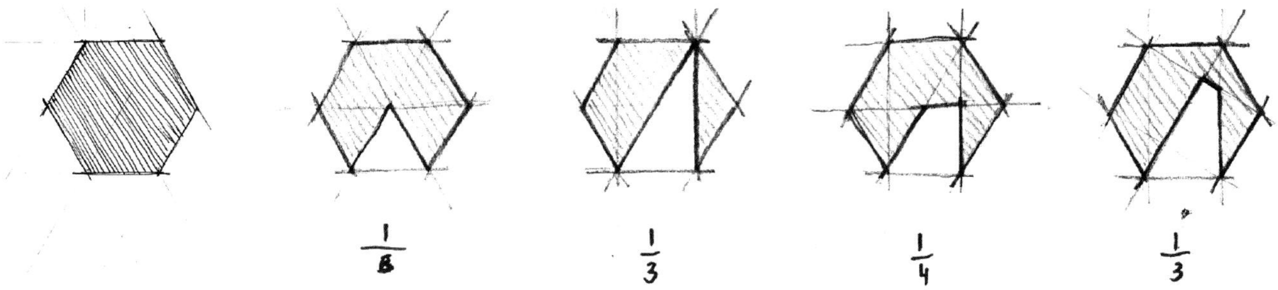

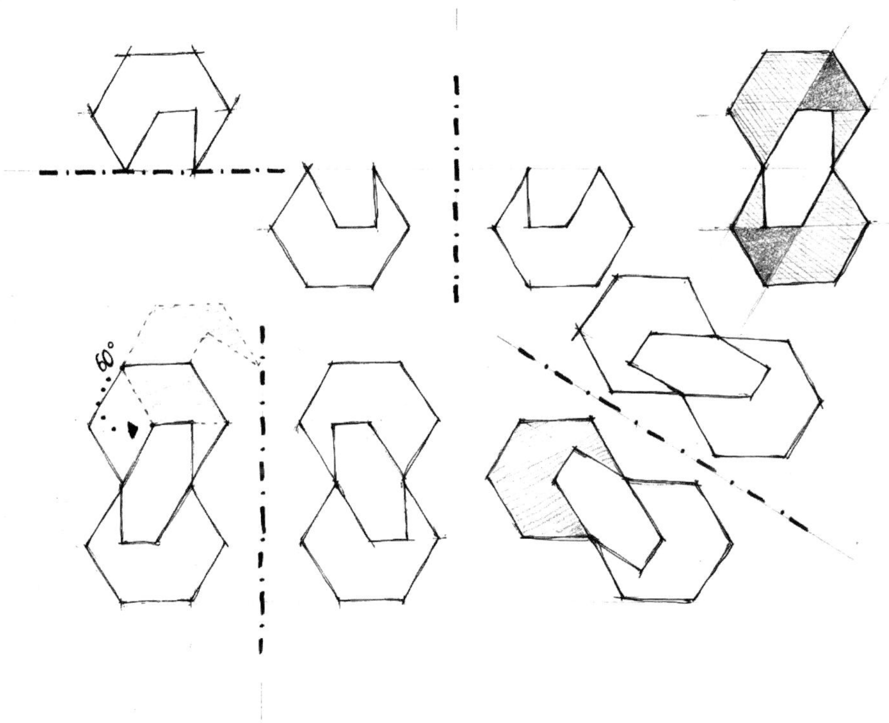

Gisela Eder
Tutor: Peter G. Auer

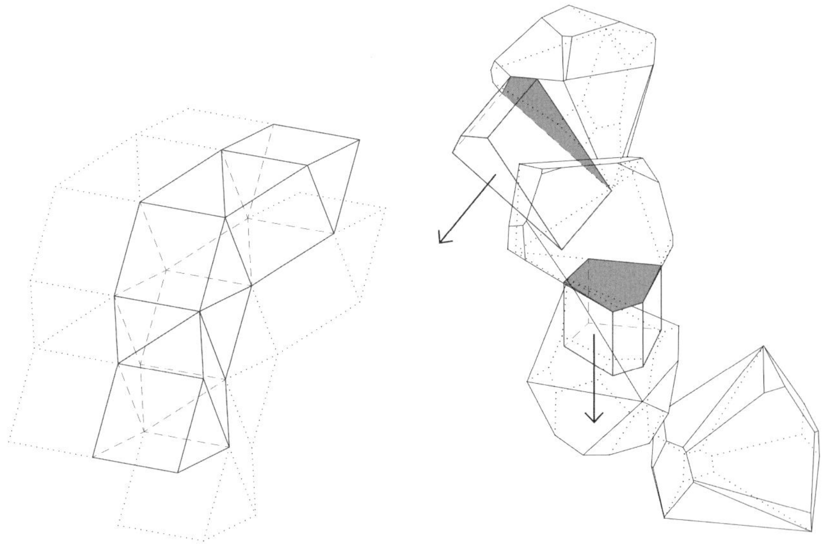

Patrick Neuwirth
Tutor: Nora Fröhlich

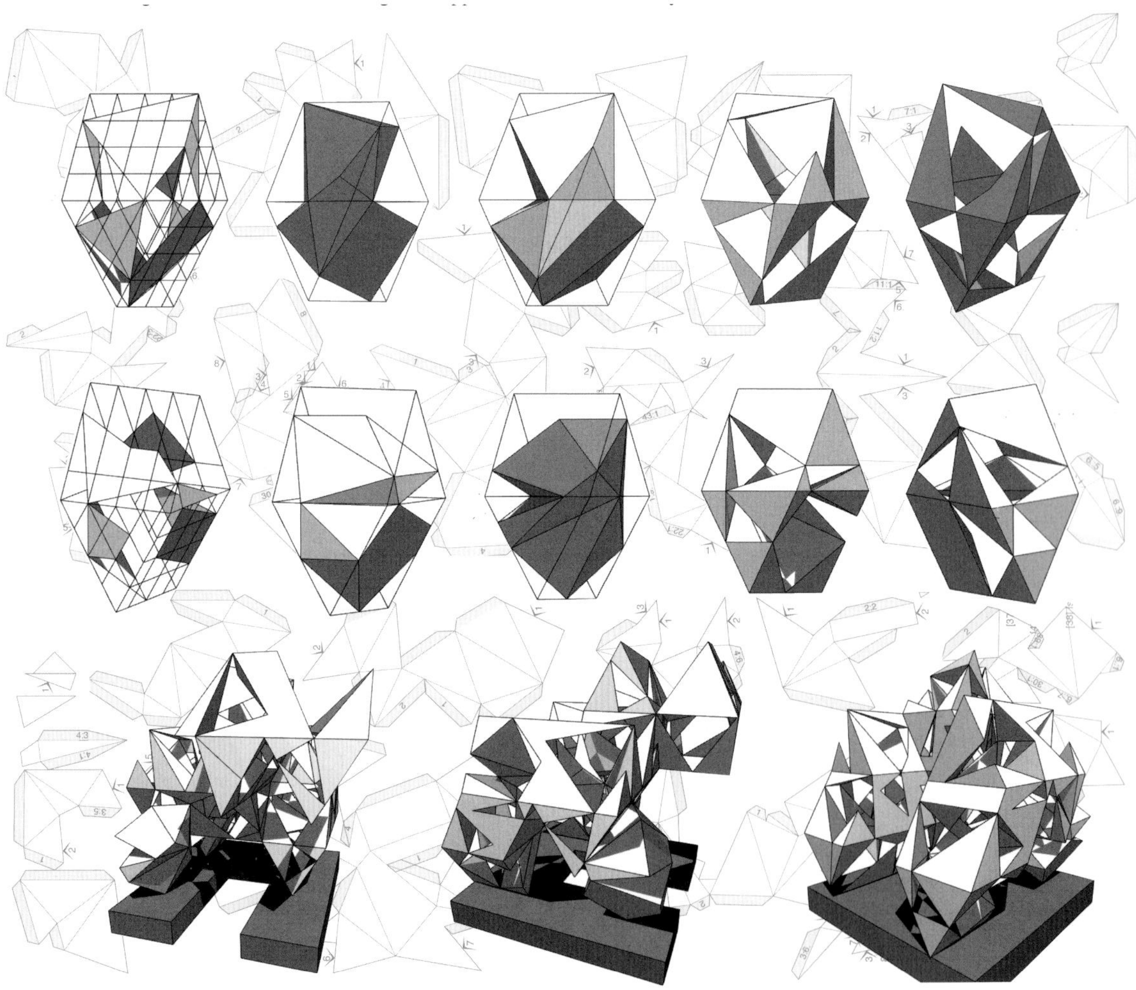

Alea Sokya
Tutor: Werner Van Hoeydonck

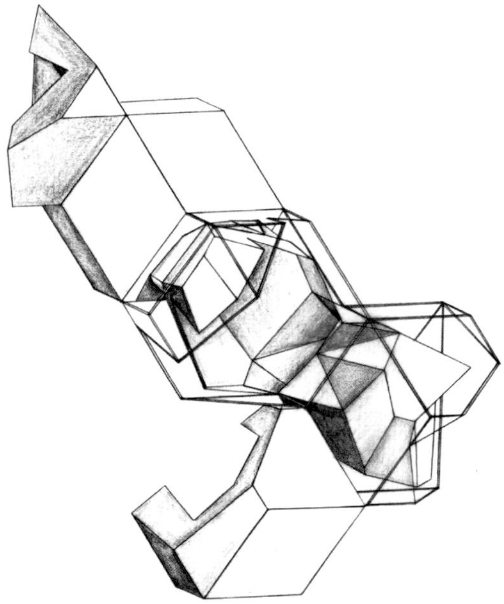

Antonia Maisch
Tutor: Werner Van Hoeydonck

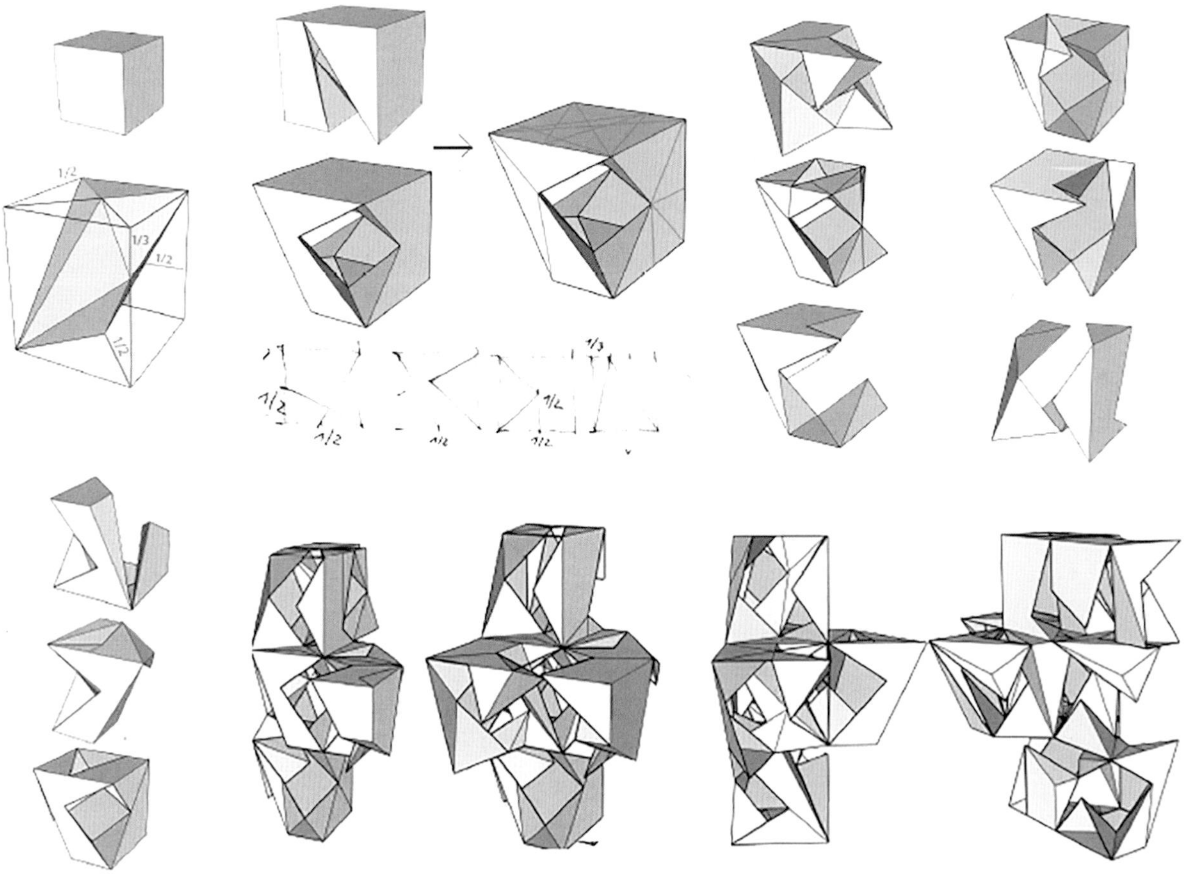

Cristina Cazacu
Tutor: Werner Van Hoeydonck

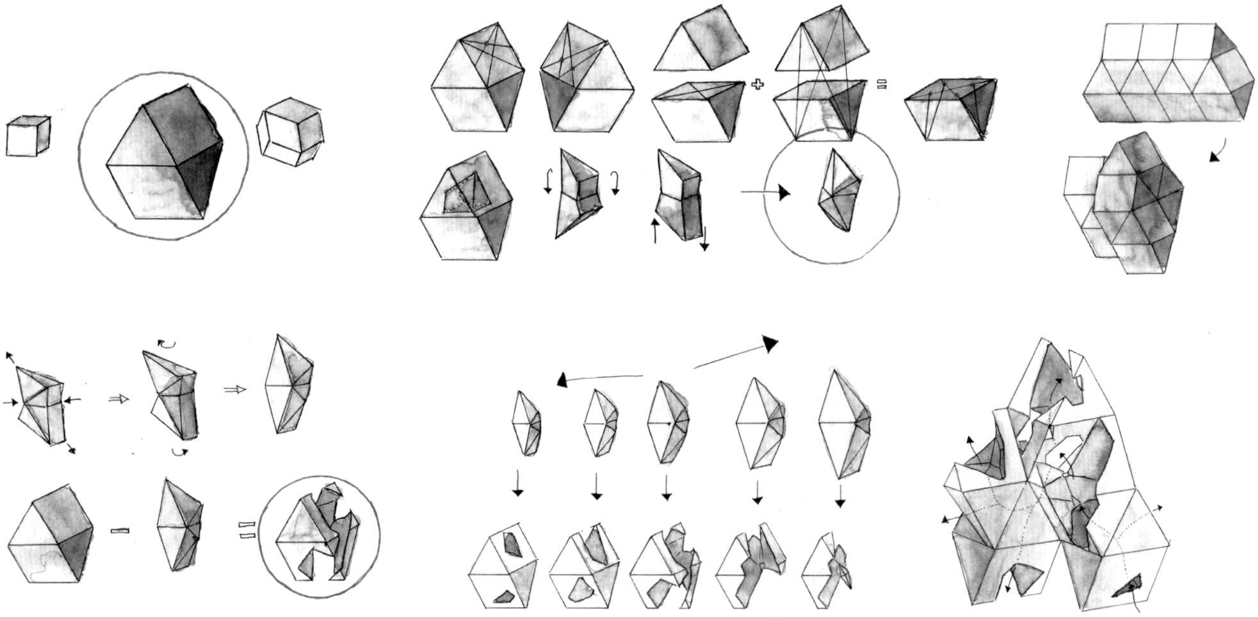

Franziska Veith
Tutor: Nora Fröhlich

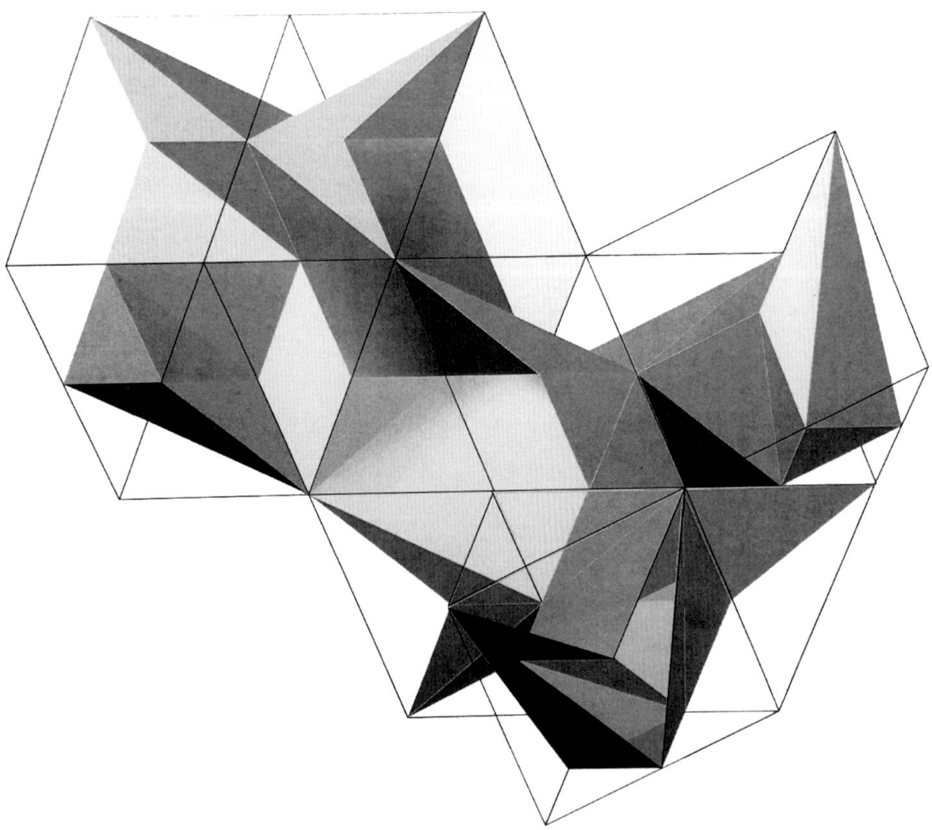

Joline Imwolde
Tutor: Christoph Bruckner

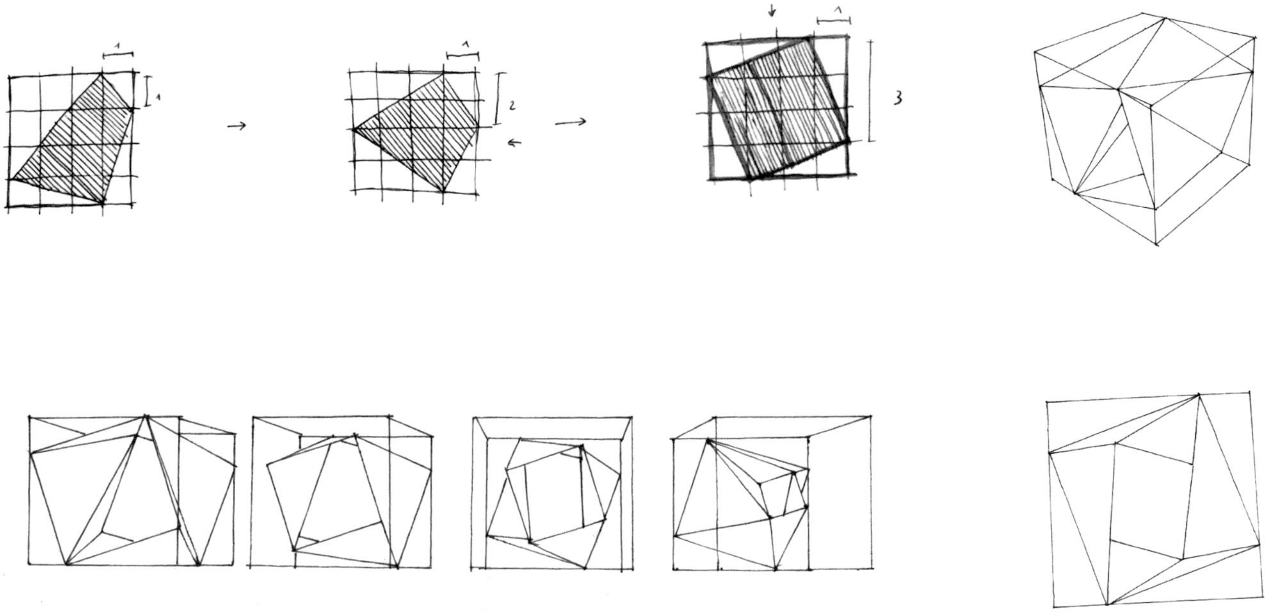

Kim Gubbini
Tutor: Anita Aigner

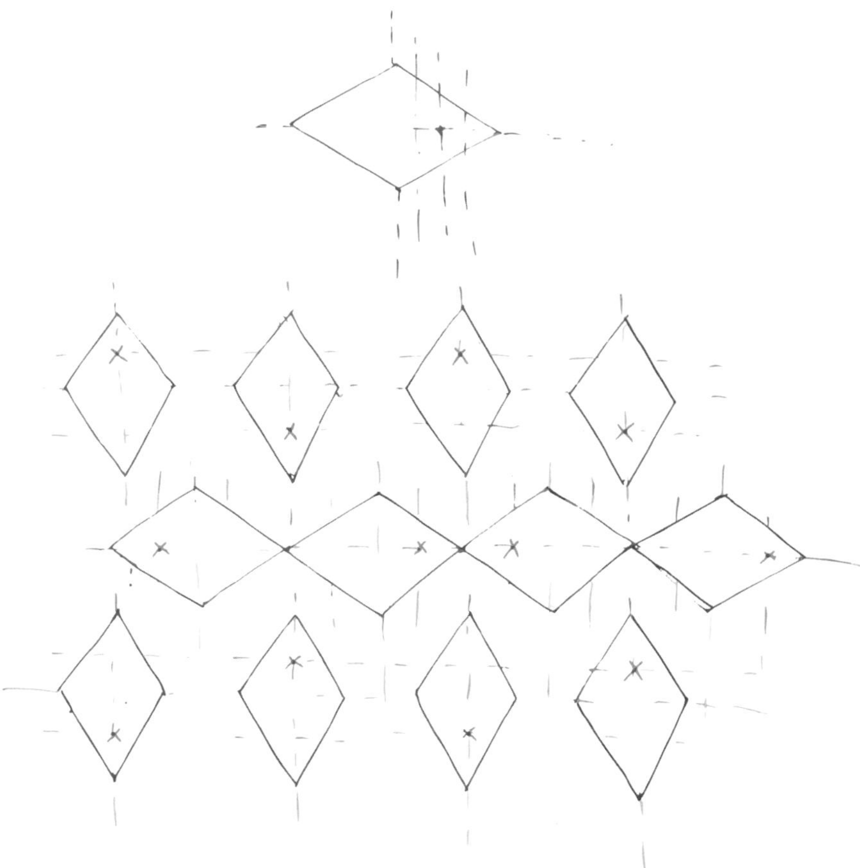

Elisabeth Anna Prantner
Tutor: Christoph Meier

Exercise 4
Presentation Model

In the last step of the exercise, the cellular space sequence was to be converted into a sophisticated and aesthetically convincing presentation model. The task was to check whether the essential aspects of the design idea had been concisely elaborated on. Was the object already optimized in terms of spatial position, cut-out/boundary, number of cells, and expression of form? Could an outside observer see and understand the quality of the spatial sequences? The compositional fine-tuning had to be related to the chosen construction method. Which type of construction was most suitable for the particular form study: rod/structure model, or representation of fully plastic volumes through shell unwinding or malleable materials? The effect of a form also heavily depends on the spatial position/positioning and a reference system, such as a plinth or base plate.

The aesthetic value of the form study was largely determined by the appropriate treatment of the material chosen in each case. This included precise craftsmanship in the execution, degree of abstraction, and also the surface features determined by light and shadow (e.g., structure and texture, edges, contours, convexities and concavities, roughness, gloss). A homogeneous appearance was desired, preferably in white. Supporting and auxiliary constructions foreign to the object were to be avoided so that the presentation model could convince in its compositional development in space, in relation to form and content and speak for itself.

Antonia Maisch

Tutor: Werner Van Hoeydonck

Starting from a concrete base, the rhombic dodecahedron is arranged to maximize view axes. Brass rods define the borders and allow insight into the carefully designed crystalline inner spaces. Every inner space and every connection is designed individually to optimize the potential of multiple spatial sequences.

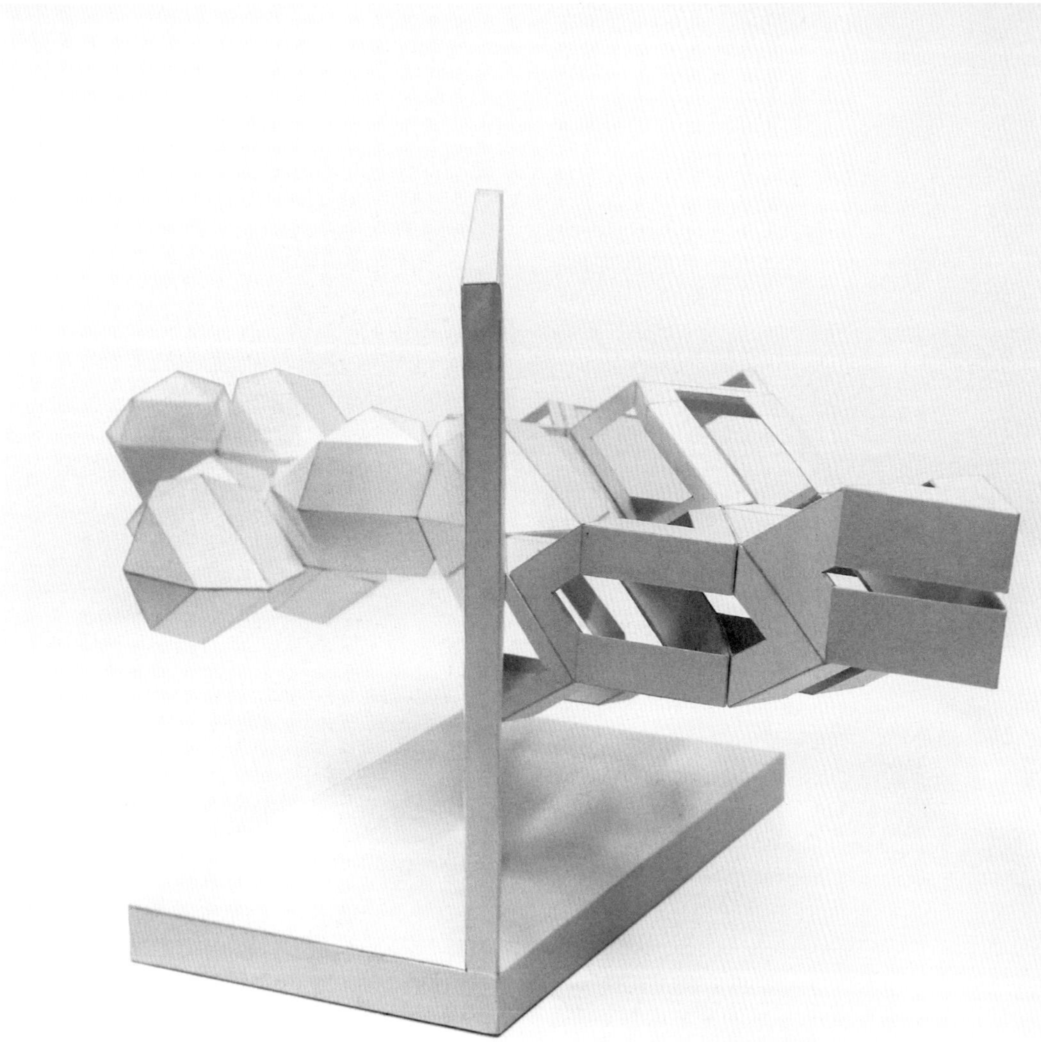

Thomas Emil Rasmus
Tutor: Fridolin Welte
An octagonal bipyramid is subtracted from a gyrobifastigium, creating an interior space with four linear openings. Increasing dimensions results in wider connecting openings. An interrupting "wall" acts as a borderline where bipyramids take over control in their contrasting solidity.

Gisela Eder
Tutor: Peter G. Auer
Two overlapping and deformed square bipyramids carve out a multidirectional complex space into the gyrobifastigium. Triangular "over the edge" openings bring in light, fly-troughs, and see-troughs. By twisting and displacing this concept, a constantly varying dynamic spatial sequence is created.

Cristina Cazacu
Tutor: Werner Van Hoeydonck
By connecting midpoints, thirds, and fourths of edges and diagonals, the cube becomes almost indiscernible. Created by a similar procedure, every interior space has its unique play of light and shadow. In aggregation, a complexity of perspectives, meant to be navigated by close-up visual analysis, displays a multiplicity of insights.

Donart Gallapeni
Tutor: Peter G. Auer
In order to direct visual connections, the outer surfaces are deliberately left closed or open up. Spatial sequences branch into different directions. Crystalline and convex carvings subdivide the cube; spaces and spatial sequences emerge in contrast to massive leftovers.

Patrick Neuwirth
Tutor: Nora Fröhlich
The rotation and translation of the dual solid of the gyrobifastigium around its square faces is explored, the initial shells are broken up, and a set of 18 different interior spaces appears, four of which are chosen and put in aggregation by turning them 90°. Extrusions of polygonal faces of their interiors allow complex, unique connections.

Lena Roth

Tutor: Peter G. Auer

The cube is decomposed into 15 polygonal parts by a Voronoi operation. Seven parts are removed to create an interior space that can be further deformed by taking away more parts. Asymmetric repetitions and mirroring operations build an arch-like portal intended to draw the viewer in.

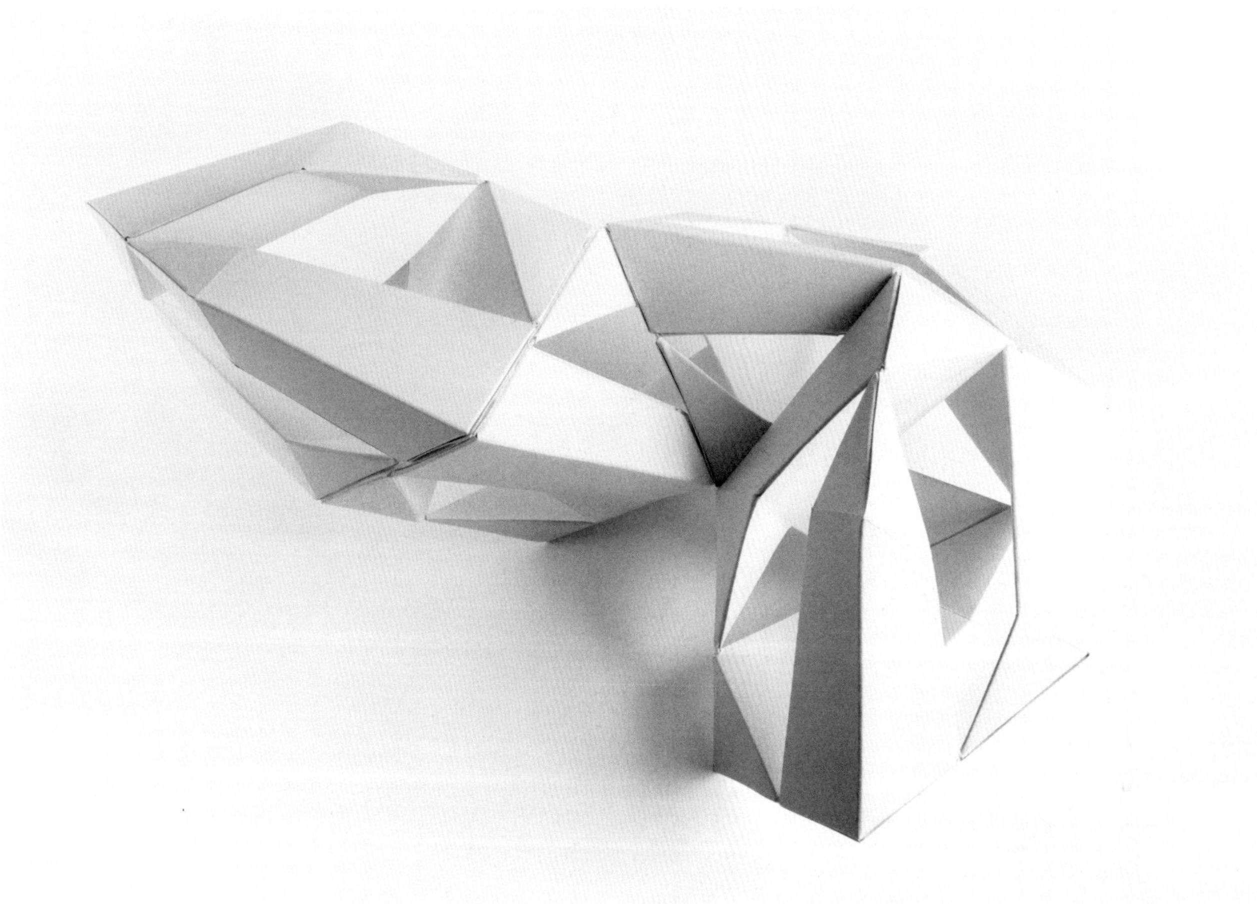

Jakob Fitz
Tutor: Christoph Bruckner
Two identical double wedges that are rotated by 90 degrees intersect, resulting in two identical cutting patterns on opposite faces. Aggregated four times, this creates a nested, complex route inside and negative spaces between the individual modules and the stand area.

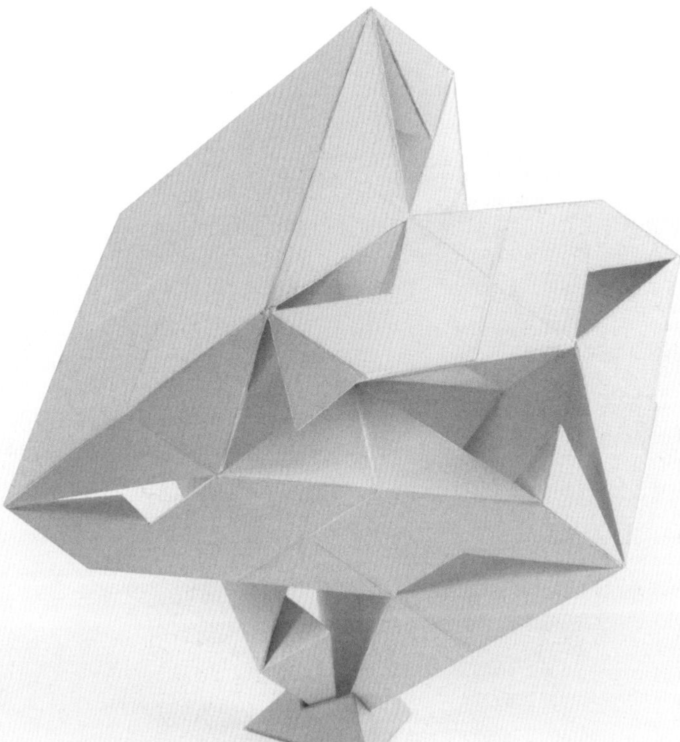

Orsolya Nyulas
Tutor: Peter G. Auer
A crystal-shaped space is extracted from the cube, creating multiple openings on the sides. The cut cube is first mirrored along the x-y axis, then multiplied by rotations of 90°, 180°, and 270° degrees, resulting in a larger cube with a twisted continuous interior space.

Theresa Steinberger
Tutor: Werner Van Hoeydonck
Center points of the cubes' edges are connected to form different triangles, creating two interior spaces with dissimilar triangular surfaces, individually connected in a 3 × 3 × 3 modular graduated arrangement. To allow insights, certain elements of the volume are omitted.

Baraa Hachicho
Tutor: Werner Van Hoeydonck
Named by Michael Goldberg after a playing card, the "ten-of-diamonds" decahedron consists of eight triangles and two rhombi. By connecting vertices with one-third of their opposite edges, an interior space is created in complete geometrical concordance with its initial shape, interacting in a mysterious mathematical balance.

Elisabeth Anna Prantner
Tutor: Christoph Meier
Intersections of important connecting lines within a stacking of rhombic dodecahedra defined by fine brass rods create a multitude of fascinating small crystal-like brass solids, not to be entered, but to be experienced from the outside in an ever-changing play of light, shadow, and reflections.

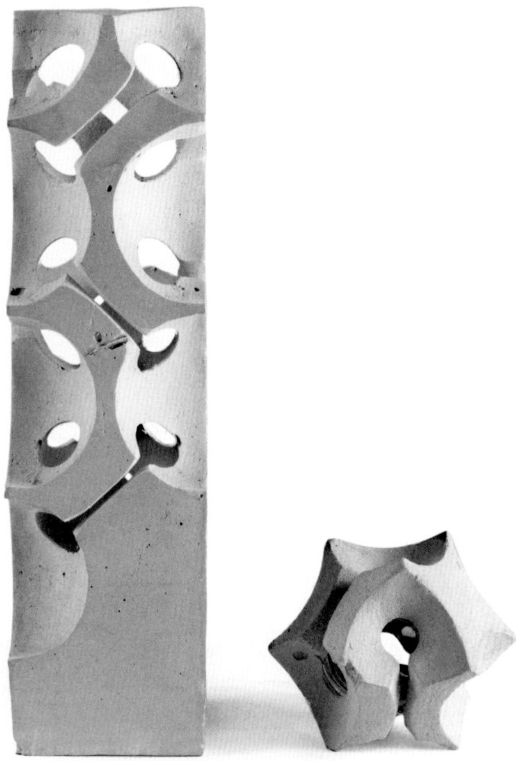

Bernarda Ehrenhöfer
Tutor: Martina Kögl
A sphere on the cube's midpoint—with increasing radius from bottom to top—intersects with eight spheres placed with their midpoints on the vertices of the cube, thereby creating circular insights. In a stack of three such cubes, diagonal connections generate a concatenation of spatial sequences to be explored.

Franziska Veith
Tutor: Nora Fröhlich
The dual of the gyrobifastigium is deformed by mirror, rotation, and vertex motion operations, then scaled up, penetrating its initial form. Small openings lead to large inner spaces and large openings into a void. Cold concrete meets warm gold, static massiveness meets decay, and smooth meets uneven in a union of opposites.

Esraa Metnan

Tutor: Werner Van Hoeydonck

On three locations, center points of surfaces and edges of the truncated octahedron are connected with vertices, resulting in three openings. The tetrakis hexahedron, the dual of the truncated octahedron, is joined with these openings to create an inner space that allows for a great variety of spatial sequences.

Mathias Winder
Tutor: Peter G. Auer
The cube—inert, static, without any notion of movement—is opened up on all six surfaces, two vertices are removed, and a series of geometric operations leads to space-defining polygonal convex solids of various sizes. Mirrored in all possible directions, the crystal-like protocells are aggregated to convey an upward motion of spatial sequences.

Emma Katarina Kaufmann-LaDuc
Tutor: Anita Aigner
Triangles are extruded into prisms within the cube, the apex of each triangle a quarter notch away from the cube's face. What is left of the cube remains solid; the prisms define the openings. Inspired by the philodendron, meaning "tree-loving", the base assumes the role of the tree, allowing the units to (visually) descend again.

Regina Bednar
Tutor: Markus Bauer
A symmetrical connection of vertices and midpoints of the edges of the cube results in points of intersection on the cube's faces. Joining them results in an inner space that is blown up four times in in a stack of a 3 x 3 x 3 modular structure of cubes until inner spaces become outer space.

Kim Gubbini
Tutor: Anita Aigner
Twelve cubes stacked in a 3 x 4 modular structure provide the basic structure. Five of six faces of each cube are removed. A rotated square is connected by plane surfaces with different smaller square openings on the opposite corner side of the cube to create a variety of torsions, negative space, and insights.

Gabriel Esposito
Tutor: Judith P. Fischer
Midpoints of four of the cube's vertical faces are connected with vertices and with the midpoint of the cube's horizontal faces, resulting in eight solids with four triangular sides and four apexes. Connected only with their apexes, a spatial sequence of 128 of these solids creates a symmetrical fragile-looking space.

Denise Redl
Tutor: Manuela Fritz
A spatial sequence of twisted double-wedges is opened up on its square faces to allow a free view on icosahedral inner spaces that are continuously deformed by dropping one or more of its triangular faces and then connected to allow a fly-through path.

Milena Vogl
Tutor: Martina Kögl
The twisted double-wedge consists of both triangular and square faces. The squares are rotated, size-wise, around a corner of the triangular face and reduced as they go more inward. If one of these twisted double wedges is lined up with another, other spaces are created that lead from the small to the large and back to the small again, or vice versa.

Aia Metnan
Tutor: Werner Van Hoeydonck
The hendecahedron, a space-filling polyhedron with eleven faces, has three rectangles in its interior. These are connected through the introduction of new connecting lines from certain midpoints. Components are taken away to create openings. The space sequence shows a 3D Cairo tiling, from which selected solids are removed.

Maria Oikonomou
Tutor: Fridolin Welte
Points on each of the gyrobifastigium's surfaces are connected to form an inner shape. Distorting the inner shape so that it breaks out of the fastigium creates openings on some of its surfaces and results in a new unit. This protocell serves as a building block for a 3D space-filling, which is cut in the middle to expose its inner chaos.

Epilogue

Christian Kern
Werner Van Hoeydonck

In *Research Perspectives*, the first part of the book, we have tried to explore the historical context and possible futures of 2D parquet deformations.
In *Teaching Perspectives*, the second part of our book, we have selected inspiring works that we judged to be a valuable answer to our research question: to express the idea of a subtly developing tile into a subtly developing 3D-tiling.

William Huff pointed out that a parquet deformation forces a more spatiotemporal perception instead of an immediate overviewing understanding. If we had defined too strict rules without allowing interpretations, the results could maybe have been more systematic and consistent, coming closer to what a parquet deformation in 3D should look like. Since it was our first experiment in this domain, our primary goal was to experiment, to give freedom in strategies on how this spatiotemporal idea could be provoked. In our second experiment "Space Sequences", the idea of perception was transferred into a more physical, architectural experience, as if we were able to "fly" through these forms. This second assignment made students more aware of figure-ground relationships, in between spaces, what can be done with the interior of polygons and polyhedra and how to connect them to design a complex choreographed space sequence. In both experiments we tried to encourage the students to refrain from (without forbidding it) the use of CAD in order to enable a more lasting hands-on experience and thus generate a greater understanding of strategy and form.

Student feedback indicated they were very content with the learning effect generated and the positive impact of the fusion of geometrical constraints (the grids, lattices and space-filling structures) and personal creativity. Great benefits to both assignments were reaped by the students: not only the new insight gained concerning 2D-tilings and space-filling structures but also how to subtly transform, perceive and connect them.

William Huff's legacy is so important because it forces students to explore parametrical design without the aid of computers. In the last century, mathematicians contributed immensely to 2D and 3D topology and geometry. Although many architects today do use (mostly computer-generated) patterns in their designs, basic concepts of topology and tessellations are still underrepresented in architectural and artistic education. We truly hope that our book will help to fill this gap and inspire students, architects, artists and designers all around the world.

Acknowledgments

Christian Kern

The observation and analysis in the work shown here is very inspiring and enriching for me as a designer and architect in relation to my own work and research in the field. The text contributions enable me to gain a deeper understanding of the subject in mathematical, artistic, and philosophical terms. I hope that the readers feel my same joy about the experiments, results, and reflections shown here. It has always been important to us to share these results with designers, mathematicians, artists, and all other interested parties.

I would particularly like to thank Werner Van Hoeydonck, who archived and structured the results with great personal commitment and thus made the realization of the book possible. His expertise in geometrical patterns results from many years of creative and theoretical research in this area. A large portion of the texts and important contributions about the concept of the book came from Werner. In publications and at congresses, Werner also established a connection between our discussions and the contemporary research environment. In doing so, contacts were established or deepened with researchers and artists who later offered contributions to this book.

My thanks also go to Eva Sommeregger, who—though originally not involved—took on the task of co-editing the present book with great enthusiasm and competence. I am also grateful to Anita Aigner and Peter Auer, who developed the tasks in coordination with me; the tutors of the exercises, who, especially if they had an artistic background, suffered from the rigid geometrical rules; and especially the students, who study in a world in which ECTS points count more than the content and who generated passion and attention for this exercise. Last but not least, content has to be shared. I am delighted that we have been able to win over the artist and graphic designer Marie Reichel.

Imprint

Editors Werner Van Hoeydonck, Christian Kern, Eva Sommeregger

Acquisitions Editor David Marold, Birkhäuser Verlag, A-Vienna

Content & Production Editor Bettina R. Algieri, Birkhäuser Verlag, A-Vienna

Proofreading Ada St. Laurent

Layout and cover design Marie Reichel

Cover illustration Steffen Alexander Blickle

Image editing Mona Torsan, Augustin Fischer

Texts p. 183, 196, 206, 214–215, 222 based on the assignment sheets by Anita Aigner.
Texts p. 253, 254, 262, 268, 274 based on the assignment sheets by Peter G. Auer.
Texts p. 223–251, p. 275–298 by Werner Van Hoeydonck

Printing Holzhausen, die Buchmarke der Gerin Druck GmbH, A-Wolkersdorf

Paper Condat matt Périgord 135 g

Typeface Work Sans

Library of Congress Control Number 2021948985

Bibliographic information published by the German National Library
The German National Library lists this publication in the Deutsche Nationalbibliografie; detailed bibliographic data are available on the Internet at http://dnb.dnb.de.

ISBN 978-3-0356-2517-2
e-ISBN (PDF) 978-3-0356-2518-9

P.O. Box 44, 4009 Basel, Switzerland
Part of Walter de Gruyter GmbH, Berlin/Boston

9 8 7 6 5 4 3 2 1 www.birkhauser.com

Many thanks for the financial support:

Three Dimensional Design
and Modelmaking
E264/2
Institute for Art and Design
University of Technology Vienna